MUSICAL COMPOSITION IN THE TWENTIETH CENTURY

Musical Composition in
the Twentieth Century,

ARNOLD WHITTALL , A.

OXFORD
UNIVERSITY PRESS

OXFORD
UNIVERSITY PRESS

Great Clarendon Street, Oxford OX 6DP

Oxford University Press is a department of the University of Oxford.
It furthers the University s objective of excellence in research, scholarship,
and education by publishing worldwide in

Oxford New York

Athens Auckland Bangkok Bogotá Buenos Aires Calcutta
Cape Town Chennai Dar es Salaam Delhi Florence Hong Kong Istanbul
Karachi Kuala Lumpur Madrid Melbourne Mexico City Mumbai
Nairobi Paris São Paulo Singapore Taipei Tokyo Toronto Warsaw

with associated companies in Berlin Ibadan

Oxford is a registered trade mark of Oxford University Press
in the UK and in certain other countries

Published in the United States
by Oxford University Press Inc., New York

British Library Cataloguing in Publication Data

Data available

Library of Congress Cataloging in Publication Data
Whittall, Arnold.
  Musical composition in the twentieth century / Arnold Whittall.
    p. cm.
  Rev. ed. of: Music since the First World War.
  Includes bibliographical references (p.   ) and index.
  1. Music—20th century—History and criticism   1. Whitall, Arnold. Music since the
First World War. II. Title.
ML197.W55 1999   780'.9'04—dc21   99-049858
ISBN 0-19-816684-2 (hbk.)
ISBN 0-19-816683-4 (pbk.)

1 3 5 7 9 10 8 6 4

Typeset in Utopia
by Best-set Typesetter Ltd., Hong Kong
Printed in Great Britain
on acid-free paper by
TJ International Ltd, Padstow, Cornwall

Contents

1 MILLENNIAL PRELUDE

In 1989, Alexander Goehr described a fundamental feature of twentieth-century music with exemplary concision:

a great deal of music written in the last seventy years or so cannot be regarded as a straightforward continuation of Classical and Romantic music, either in the way it is conceived or in the way it is meant to be listened to. Background–foreground perception is inapplicable here because, in reality, insufficient background is implied. Continuity is fragmented or constructed of events unrelated to each other, pitch succession too complex to be memorable, and constructional procedures too difficult to be perceived as aural logic.[1]

Goehr associated this situation with an avant-garde attitude on the part of composers:

where earlier composers intended to communicate a particular aesthetic impression, and to do so aimed at clarity, subjugation of detail to broadly moving melody and rhythm, and a carefully graded relationship of certainties and ambiguities, avant gardists prefer saturation and prolixity of musical phenomena, aiming so to kick over their traces and thereby create what might be described as a magical effect. This music is to be instantaneously perceived either in a state of shock created by rapid alterations, or in dreamy states brought about by an apparently endless extension of constantly repeating and more or less identical patterns.[2]

Here Goehr introduces an opposition, often defined as that between 'complexity' and 'minimalism', which is a well-established phenomenon on the contemporary scene, and the tone of his writing indicates his own preference for a less radical, more classical approach than either. Not only does he argue that 'total and continuous fragmentation of texture and continuity rapidly leads to incomprehensibility',[3] but he claims that the modernist project itself is ultimately self-destructive: 'creating new conventions is the inevitable fate of all modernisms, but it also marks the end of them'.[4] Here Goehr seems to join forces with the aesthetician Roger Scruton, who argues forcefully that 'avant-gardism can never be the key to aesthetic renewal'.[5]

To the extent that any 'new conventions' enshrine the essence of modernism, their establishment need not mark the end of modernism so much as its

[1] Alexander Goehr, 'Music as Communication', in *Finding the Key: Selected Writings of Alexander Goehr*, ed. D. Puffett (London, 1998), 231.
[2] Ibid. 233.   [3] Ibid. 295.   [4] Ibid. 94.
[5] Roger Scruton, *The Aesthetics of Music* (Oxford, 1997), 470.

stabilization. In twentieth-century compositional practice, radical modernism or avant-garde extremism has coexisted with a no less resourceful concern to explore possible accommodations between modernism's tendency to proliferate and classicism's impulse to integrate. The traffic between these two apparent alternatives has occurred so pervasively because of the very factor singled out by Goehr—the concern of composers to preserve something memorable, something akin to 'aural logic', in music that does not rely on all the functional relationships and form-embracing hierarchies of traditional tonality. For most of the twentieth century, progressive composers seeking some fundamental continuity with the past have attempted to ensure that sound is perceptible as tone[6] by relying on the repetition and development of motivic material and textural patterns to make the shape of structures perceptible, and the absorbing evolution of such shapes and moods can convey a distinctive musical coherence, even in the absence of traditional harmonic strategies. This does not mean that vertical pitch relations are no longer relevant to or detectable in such 'post-tonal' music, but it underlines that the music can still convey or represent meaning as character, atmosphere, or mood, not least through allusions to particular 'topics'—potent musical shapes which, even in radical twentieth-century styles, can still evoke certain fundamental genres, often to do with varieties of song (like the lament) or dance.

As the drift of the previous paragraph indicates, not even a study focusing on twentieth-century technical preoccupations and procedures can ignore the wise musicological dictum that 'even as we define problems and relationships in apparent autonomy, we are reflecting complex interactions with society of which we are largely unconscious'.[7] Another musicological voice adds the no-less-significant truth that

it is a formalist prejudice that an artwork receives aesthetic value commensurate to the degree that it can be analyzed as an autonomous entity. But no musical piece is born in a vacuum. Every composition exists along a plurality of continuums: the composer's own artistic development, the historical unfolding of a given genre or style, evolving social and aesthetic forces, and so on.[8]

Even if much of my own text may appear to subscribe to the outmoded heresy of autonomy, treating its chosen compositions in isolation from any contexts other than the particular technical features selected by the author, some hint of the world outside the work will break in from time to time. It is the composition as music which dominates, even so, for there is always a sense in which the work of art, with the inevitable element of consolation in face of an alarming world

---

[6] See Scruton, *Aesthetics*, 16–18, for a definition of the distinction between 'sound' and 'tone'.

[7] Rose Rosengard Subotnik, *Developing Variations: Style and Ideology in Western Music* (Minneapolis, 1991), 147.

[8] Thomas Christensen, review article in *Music Theory Spectrum*, 15 (1993), 110.

which it brings with it,[9] represents a triumph over the world and not a mere reflection of it. It is a product of the world that transcends its context. When Scruton writes that 'music inspires and consoles us partly because it is unencumbered by the debris that drifts through the world of life'[10] this is not just a pious poetic fantasy.

It will, I hope, be obvious that a text conceived in the way I have described cannot be regarded as a history of twentieth-century music. Opinions about what could constitute such a history are bound to vary, but I feel sure that there would be a very large consensus in favour of a far fuller account of musical institutions and social factors bearing on the lives of composers and other musicians than is offered here. A proper historical account would give no special priority to the composers and works included in my text. It would be as much about popular or commercial activities as so-called art music, and (in all likelihood) devote more space to the social, political, and cultural forces impinging on, and inevitably affecting, musicians of all kinds than to the description and interpretation of whatever 'serious' composers happened to write down. Where my book may be judged to have become historical (and/or ideological) is in the linkage it accepts between the nature of compositional procedures and the result of those procedures interpreted not purely technically but as manifestations of more general aesthetic attitudes: above all, as demonstrating some relation either to modernism—the embrace of discontinuity as something more than a means of diversifying a unity—or to modern classicism, as the resistance to this strategy.

Such an emphasis can be legitimized on grounds of its association with the kind of attitudes that historians of twentieth-century ideas identify as (in part) the legacy of Nietzsche—'what is needed above all is an absolute scepticism towards all inherited concepts'[11]—and inscribed in the writings of such crucial figures as T. E. Hulme, who declared before 1914 that 'I am a pluralist. . . . There is no Unity, no Truth, but forces which have different aims, and whose whole reality consists in those differences.'[12] One particularly cogent late twentieth-century view of 'politics and culture at the close of the modern age' refers in comparable terms to 'a condition of plural and provisional perspectives, lacking any rational or transcendental ground or unifying world-view',[13] on the way to the suggestion that 'the political forms which may arise in truly post-enlightenment cultures will be those that shelter and express diversity—that enable different cultures, some but by no means all or even most of which are dominated by

[9] See Raymond Geuss, 'Berg and Adorno', in *The Cambridge Companion to Berg*, ed. A. Pople (Cambridge, 1997), 43.
[10] Scruton, *Aesthetics*, 122.
[11] Cited in Christopher Butler, *Early Modernism: Literature, Music and Painting in Europe, 1990–1916* (Oxford, 1994), 2.
[12] Ibid. 209.
[13] John Gray, *Enlightenment's Wake: Politics and Culture at the Close of the Modern Age* (London, 1997), 153.

liberal forms of life, different world-views and ways of life, to coexist in peace and harmony'.[14] Such a development would not of itself imply that the forms of artistic expression that have evolved since the Renaissance and have survived, so far, since the Enlightenment, would cease to have any relevance. But it suggests that the rampant diversity within 'liberal practice' of twentieth-century art music would be likely to yield to different understandings of 'art'—especially those understandings less beholden to what John Gray terms 'the power of calculative thought'.[15] Gray is enough of a pessimist to refer to the inherent 'nihilism' of contemporary Western culture, and a similar attitude can be deduced in Roger Scruton's analysis of a late twentieth-century situation in which 'democratic man is essentially "culture-less", without the aspirations that require him to exalt his image in literature and art'.[16] 'New conditions' exist in which 'it is not only art and music that have undergone a fatal metamorphosis. . . . The human psyche itself has been thrown out of orbit', and Scruton looks to a reaffirmation of tonality as the most likely way to engage with that 'new bourgeois audience' that 'is emerging—one which does not feel the force of modernism's bleak imperatives'. His conclusion is that 'a musical equivalent of *Four Quartets* is needed—a rediscovery of the tonal language, which will also redeem the time. Many of our contemporaries have aimed at this—Nicholas Maw, John Adams, Robin Holloway, and Alfred Schnittke. But none, I think, has yet succeeded.'[17]

Much of the discussion in this study, written well before Scruton's assessment appeared, can be read as an attempt to argue that modernism and tonality are not incompatible: if, that is, we allow for tonality to be enriched by the evolutionary strategies, deriving from such composers as Debussy, Stravinsky and Bartók, whose roots reach down deeply into the music of the nineteenth century. In fact, Scruton himself, while arguing in general that tonality is essentially the full functional system, not dependent for its existence on the Schenkerian concept of a deep structure but never floating free of functional identities, reveals a degree of equivocation when he allows that tonal harmony can be viewed as either 'tending towards' the tonic 'or away from it'.[18] A modernism that works with the opposition of stable (often symmetrical) and unstable elements may tend to reflect the fractured time as much as 'redeem' it. But I firmly believe that such modernism can be authentically affirmative, enabling the music-lover to accept its modernity and be inspirited by it as a positive attribute, appropriate for its time and place: indeed, it can be so without any 'tonality' at all, as Scruton acknowledges when he refers to Elliott Carter's Concerto for Orchestra as 'a work which succeeds in turning an uncompromising modernism to the service of joy'.[19]

The possible connections between what the composer writes down and the

---

[14] Gray, *Enlightenment's Wake*, 155.
[15] Ibid. 184.   [16] Scruton, *Aesthetics*, 505.   [17] Ibid. 507–8.
[18] Ibid. 240.   [19] Ibid. 494.

contingent world within which that writing takes place will tend to reinforce a view of many of the compositions discussed here as both revolutionary and rear-guard action, attempting to preserve the composer's special position in society (an inheritance of the nineteenth century) by transforming some or most of the ways in which that position was represented in the notated work. Twentieth-century composers have, on occasion, sought to present themselves as the hapless victims of circumstance in which irresistible historical forces have driven them to adopt the role of arrogant and self-indulgent outsider, in a kind of exag-gerated parody of romanticism's reverence for the quasi-divine otherness of the creative genius. In an essay dating from his early years in America, Schoenberg declared that 'Music is only understood when one goes away singing it and is only loved when one falls asleep with it in one's head and finds it is still there on waking up the next morning.'[20] Three years later he returned to the topic, declar-ing that

I always insisted that the new music was merely a logical development of [existing] musical resources. But of what use can theoretical explanations be in comparison with the effect the subject itself makes on the listener? What good does it do to *tell* a listener, 'This music is beautiful,' if he does not feel it? How could I win friends with this kind of music?[21]

Schoenberg's outbursts may have been uttered in rare moments of self-pitying disillusionment; on another occasion he acknowledged a more sober possibility, that 'the laws of art work in a way that contradicts the way the popular mind works'.[22] Yet these comments serve to reinforce the argument that, in many varieties of twentieth-century music, certain kinds of 'logical development'—above all, perhaps, of linking tonal and atonal composition by way of motivic processes, or adapting tonal consonance to octatonic modality[23]—make it im-possible for many to sense any 'beauty' in the result. So, while the initially for-midable challenges of Beethoven's late string quartets and Wagner's *Tristan und Isolde* ceased to prevent audiences from recognizing their stature well before the end of the nineteenth century, Schoenberg's own early challenges, like the *Five Orchestral Pieces* and *Erwartung*, and those of other twentieth-century pioneers from Ives to Webern, have not managed a comparable degree of acceptance, still less elevation to the summit of the canon.

For Schoenberg enthusiasts, and devotees of progressiveness in general, this is a price worth paying, an acknowledgement that what is most distinctive about twentieth-century music reinforces its relevance to 'the laws of art', rather than to the imperatives of commerce or other even less worthy factors: after all, Schoenberg's works have not disappeared, and the century's shift of emphasis

---

[20] Arnold Schoenberg, 'Why No Great American Music?', in *Style and Idea*, ed. L. Stein (London, 1975), 180.

[21] Schoenberg, 'How one Becomes Lonely', in *Style and Idea*, 50.

[22] Schoenberg, 'About Ornaments, Primitive Rhythms, etc., and Bird Song', in *Style and Idea*, 299.

[23] An octatonic (eight-note) scale consists of alternating semitones and tones, or tones and semitones.

from live to recorded performance has helped to preserve their presence, and to validate the special qualities of 'serious' musical art.

In 1960 Elliott Carter defined these qualities as follows:

serious music appeals to a longer span of attention and to a more highly developed auditory memory than do the more popular kinds of music. In making this appeal, it uses many contrasts, coherences, and contexts that give it a wide scope of expression, great emotional power and variety, direction, uniqueness, and a fascination of design with many shadings and qualities far beyond the range of popular or folk music.[24]

Carter could not honestly claim that the post-tonal composer had more immediate access to these desirable qualities that his tonal contemporaries or predecessors, but (as the discussion of his work below will try to demonstrate) he could develop certain kinds of interaction between stable and unstable factors which reflect the new tonal thinking that emerged early in the century. Such interactions tend naturally to make for a certain degree of complexity. The sheer diversity of twentieth-century serious styles, intensifying as it has during the century's final decades, has meant that it has become possible for music to be both extremely serious and extremely simple, with a wider appeal for composers like Górecki and Pärt than was conceivable in the more polarized climate prevalent before 1980. Yet the differences between their work and that of 'popular' musicians remain great. It is scarcely surprising that 'simple' music should be more immediately accessible than 'complex' music. But it is a characteristic of the time that the boundaries of even these apparently distinct categories soon become blurred, as part of composers' inherent scepticism, and of that commitment to multiplicity which is twentieth-century culture's principal inheritance from Nietzsche.

This present attempt to tell this story has its own quite intricate history. When I began *Music Since the First World War* in 1975, the century was already three-quarters past, and yet it seemed (not least because the book was to be loosely aligned with others dealing with early twentieth-century developments and with more genuinely contemporary perspectives[25]) that concentration on those composers then perceived as the century's most important in the years between 1918 and 1970 would be most useful. It still seemed useful, in 1988, to provide a reprint with a minimum of correction and updating, avoiding any radical overhaul. At the century's end, however, the possibility of offering a wider overview was too tempting to resist, and what has emerged is a structure in which the core chapters of *Music Since the First World War* are retained, revised, and in some cases radically rewritten, within the frame of new surveys of composers

[24]   Elliott Carter, 'Shop Talk by an American Composer', in *Elliott Carter: Collected Essays and Lectures, 1937–95*, ed. J. W. Bernard (Rochester, NY, 1997), 217.

[25]   Jim Samson, *Music in Transition: A Study of Tonal Expansion and Atonality, 1900–1920* (London, 1977); Paul Griffiths, *Modern Music: The Avant Garde since 1945* (London, 1981).

and their work before 1918 and since 1975. The result offers a very clear contrast between the detailed technical narratives, emphasizing certain incontrovertibly significant composers from Strauss to Shostakovich, and the much shorter, at times impressionistic sketches of many other composers. With greater (though still very selective) comprehensiveness comes even less detailed discussion than was the case in the earlier versions. But this is not accidental, reinforcing my primary objective of providing an introduction, a way into an immensely elaborate, immensely rewarding subject. The character of the new chapters, especially those which end the book, is inevitably much influenced by my own experiences during the years since 1975, as listener, performer (in private!), teacher, writer, and reviewer; indeed, I make no apology for the fact that certain turns of phrase have migrated from reviews in *Gramophone, Music and Letters*, and other journals, where I feel their role as registering immediate and strong impressions of certain compositions has retained its value. Such immediacy may well tend to encourage that quality of 'built-in obsolescence' which is the fate of all interpretative writing, but especially of that with recent or contemporary subject-matter, and pious platitudes about an art most notable for its unsparing reflection of the particular tragedies and turmoils of its time can only contribute to the impression that such surveys are undertaken more out of a sense of duty than of pleasure. I remain defiant in claiming to enjoy twentieth-century music. Yet the upbeat assertions with which I ended my 1977 Preface—'there can be little doubt that society is changing in such a way as to make it more likely that the most radical and experimental aspects of present-day musical life will ultimately achieve wider acceptance than those aspects which seek to conserve the actual linguistic formulae of the past'—can certainly not be blithely reasserted now, despite that carefully inserted 'ultimately'. So this time I will simply affirm my long-standing conviction that there is more than enough to stir the spirit and fascinate the mind in the kind of twentieth-century music considered in these pages to prompt the conclusion that its future disappearance would be a tragic loss to any civilized society.

2   TAKING STEPS: 1900–1918

The Meanings of Modernism

John Cage's statement that 'today's music is characterised by a multiplicity of ways to do things'[1] might seem no more and no less than any composer could have said down the ages. It is difficult to imagine any composer, even one devoted to technical and aesthetic ideals of unity and consistency, supporting the proposition that the creative process always involves doing precisely the same thing in exactly the same way. Similarly, the claims of musicologist Robert P. Morgan that 'the rootless and fragmented nature of current music is ultimately inseparable from the rootlessness and fragmentation of contemporary life',[2] and that 'the pluralism of contemporary music mirrors the lack of consensus in the political, social and religious attitudes that govern how we live, act and interact'[3] could equally well be applied to some if not all earlier eras, each of which would have had its own standards for the governing concepts of 'rootlessness and frag-mentation', as well as 'pluralism' and 'lack of consensus'. Such considerations should inspire a salutary caution in historians—those who attempt to write coherent accounts of particular classes of event or activity—with respect to the criteria they apply to their material, and the terminologies by which they attempt to categorize and clarify. A single-author text can hardly adopt a wholeheartedly plural style, but it can aim to acknowledge, and exploit, the paradox of telling a profoundly heterodox story in an unavoidably consistent manner, as far as matters of topic and chronology are concerned. Selectivity and bias are inevitable, even if the subject-matter is to be presented simply as a sequence of lists, dates, titles, names with attenuated comment of a neutrally 'factual' kind. In this present account, selectivity is evident not only in the way that particular composers and their compositions, as exemplifications of certain technical and aesthetic factors, are isolated from 'the political, social and religious attitudes that govern how we live' in the twentieth century. It is also selective in that the music concerned is, in the main, 'art' or 'serious' music, composed in Europe, Scandinavia, and the United States.

Divorcing compositions from their cultural context and social function means that this study aspires more to the status of an analytical investigation than to

---

[1] Andrew Ford, *Composer to Composer: Conversations about Contemporary Music* (London, 1993), 173.
[2] Robert P. Morgan (ed.), *Man and Music: Modern Times* (London, 1993), 30.
[3] Ibid. 32.

'history' as the term is currently understood. Even so, many problems of terminology remain: for example, concerning the nature of modernity and modernism. Although Pierre Boulez robustly declared that 'You are not modern—you are merely expressing yourself according to the coordinates of your time, and that's not being modern, that's being what you are',[4] the intellectual capital expended during the twentieth century in defining 'modernism' has yielded insights and provocations too powerful in their technical implications to be set aside. In particular, they lead to the striking circumstance in which twentieth-century modernism emerges, not as wholly new, but as a continuation of profound changes in aesthetic and technical orientation which became apparent in the early nineteenth century—the kind of situation to which T. W. Adorno was alluding when he declared in 1958 that 'Berlioz was the prime phenomenon of modernity in music'.[5]

If we accept the proposition that twentieth-century music is more fundamentally and consistently concerned with interactions between continuation and innovation than with undiluted manifestations of the latter, we might as a consequence seek to reduce the radical implications of such concepts as 'atonality', 'neoclassicism', 'minimalism', and all those other labels for twentieth-century music which seems to have very little in common with Berlioz, Chopin, Brahms, or Wagner. Yet it is fundamental to this narrative that the arguments and ambiguities to which such labels give rise reflect the richness and multivalence of the music itself. So there is no real point in seeking to determine whether or not music can be genuinely 'impressionistic' or 'expressionistic'; far better to consider to what extent, if at all, such terms can usefully impinge on an art-form which it would be futile to confine within the boundaries of a single verbal concept. After all, even 'twentieth-century' can be made into a problematic ascription if the issue of works which are claimed to be chronologically 'in' but not aesthetically or technically 'of' that century is brought into the argument.

My starting-point is the insight, most memorably articulated by Adorno, that 'modern society is characterized by transience, by change, fragmentation and alienation':[6] as a consequence, 'the particular problem for the musical work of the modernist period' is 'to construct a unity which does not conceal the fragmented and chaotic state of the handed-down musical material, and yet which does not simply mirror fragmentation through identification with it, but which is able to embody, negate and transcend it'.[7] As Adorno put it in a late essay from 1966: 'the formal problem for composers today: is disintegration possible through integration?' Adorno seemed to have a vision of a music in which 'integration and disintegration are entwined',[8] and in context this is clearly meant as something distinct from the unity-diversified-by-contrast found in Baroque,

[4] Ford, *Composer to Composer*, 24.
[5] Cited in Max Paddison, *Adorno's Aesthetics of Music* (Cambridge, 1993), 242.
[6] Ibid. 54.   [7] Ibid. 158.   [8] Ibid.

Classical and Romantic music composed under the laws of the tonal system. When Adorno spoke of Bartók 'using the folk material as a critique of the "dead forms" of Western art music', thereby throwing 'alienation into relief, while at the same time also forging a new and integrated musical language which does not in the process hide the fractured character of its elements',[9] he was responding to what he perceived to be the differences between a distinctively twentieth-century composer and composers of the pre-twentieth-century past—differences that did not eliminate all possible similarities.

Such strongly sculpted arguments provided Adorno with powerful criteria for defining the different characteristics of twentieth-century composers in surprisingly concrete and absolute terms: for example, Mahler accepted 'the fragmented character of the musical material' and thereby confronted 'the modernist dilemma',[10] whereas Debussy's music, despite being 'radically modernist in its implications' has an immaculate surface that 'leaves no "fractures"', and is therefore 'set apart from society'.[11] Musicology is less inclined to consider relations between music and society quite so dogmatically, and although, as already explained, the following narrative tends to leave the topic of possible social function to one side, there is no gainsaying the eminently social fact that the material discussed has chosen itself through its persistent prominence in the repertory, through live performances, broadcasts, recordings, and publication. For example, even if it seemed to be 'set apart from society' when it was new, Debussy's music is a strong presence in present-day culture, and it is difficult to feel that this is to be regretted rather than accepted as one facet of a rich and self-renewing pluralism.

Any account, even an analytical one, of music in the twentieth century must acknowledge the radical changes in modes of dissemination and reception which have taken place since 1900—radio transmission and sound and film recording emerging, prospering, and to some extent replacing traditional types of public and domestic music-making. It must also acknowledge that music composed since 1900 has not achieved predominance over that of earlier centuries; indeed, music composed since 1900 has had to fight for a platform within the increasing heterogeneity of modern musical culture. There is a sense in which the story of music in the twentieth century is not only that of music composed since 1900, but also the story of how the music of earlier centuries has been explored, revived, and generally welcomed as preferable to most contemporary products. The survival of the old has provided a strong counterweight to the exploration of the new, and while such a phenomenon may not be unique to the twentieth century, the directness and intensity with which the confrontation has been experienced since 1900 is vividly reflected in the multifarious discussions of the issue—by philosophers, composers, critics,

---

[9] Cited in Max Paddison, *Adorno's Aesthetics of Music*, 41.   [10] Ibid. 259.   [11] Ibid. 257.

musicologists—that analysts of twentieth-century composition have at their disposal.

Even those writers primarily concerned with analytical investigation of scores cannot always avoid some reference to the delicate interaction of autonomous and heteronomous factors which inevitably impinge on the works in question. To say that Schoenberg's opera *Erwartung* (1909) is as much the product of the composer's response to contemporary, expressionistic culture in late Imperial Vienna as of the kind of purely musical impulses that forced tonal structuring into oblivion and brought forward elements of intense motivic processing to compensate is—at least when expressed so baldly—little more than a truistic slogan aimed at a painless contextualization within what is presumed to be a seamlessly coherent historical process of evolution and transformation. Yet the claim that fragmentation was a logical development of cultural as well as musical forces is a central, irreducible irony of reading twentieth-century modernism as constructive and necessary, and not as arbitrary and dangerous. More crucial still to the character and evolution of twentieth-century music is the simultaneous functioning of modernist fragmentation and such traditional syntheses as are revealed by the survival of tonality and well-established genres: the circumstance in which symphonies by Elgar or Sibelius which are exactly contemporary with *Erwartung* are regarded as no less valid for their time, and no less valuable in the longer term of the whole century to which they belong. As already suggested, of its very nature, an essentially technical study will tend to find stability even in persistent instability, and writers on twentieth-century music can point with increasing plausibility to the presence of a consistent 'mainstream' in which the consequences of a confrontation between tendencies to fragmentation and tendencies to synthesis are explored through different approaches to the interaction between symmetrical (often octatonic) and hierarchic factors in a huge and imposing range of composers from Debussy and Stravinsky to Peter Maxwell Davies and Magnus Lindberg. The discussion which follows also acknowledges that the technical story of twentieth-century music can be usefully constructed in terms of dialogues between traditional and radical, a process in which the analyst's stabilizing routines are under constant challenge and constraint.

Fauré

Two composers born in the 1850s—Edward Elgar (1857–1934) and Giacomo Puccini (1858–1924)—did their finest work after 1900. Gabriel Fauré (1845–1926) was born even earlier, and although he continued to compose until his final years, he might not be thought to have surpassed the *Requiem* (1887–99) or *La Bonne Chanson* (1892–4) in the music he wrote during the new century. There were significant changes, nevertheless: the expert view is that 'the end of the century was, for Fauré, a time when dissonance was liberated',[12] and the years from 1906 to 1924 were 'a period of radical self-renewal, involving a lightening of instrumental textures, a stiffening of melodic lines and a still greater harmonic audacity resulting from a more consistent emphasis on counterpoint'.[13] Fauré's late style is 'more abrupt, eschewing prettiness and cascades of ornaments, as well as harmonic voluptuousness'.[14] At the same time, however, these years saw the composition of his most ambitious and extended work, the opera *Pénélope* (1907–12).

Pénélope is a distinctive rather than radical score, in which 'Wagnerian influence is more evident in pages of quiet intensity than at climaxes, when the lean, cutting texture is quite unWagnerian'.[15] For Fauré in more progressive vein there is the song collection *La Chanson d'Eve* (1906–10), whose concentrated intensity leads the music 'to the borders of atonality',[16] and the Nocturne No. 12 (1915), with its 'sombre, tumultuous mood'.[17] Significantly, however, Fauré's radicalism was less a matter of sustained atonal exploration than of the clear-cut alternation between progressive and conservative features, and in a substantial work like the Piano Quintet No. 2 (1919–21) his ability to 'blend these disparate elements into a convincing whole'[18] is unambiguous evidence of his resistance to the fragmenting strategies of modernism. The developments that can be traced in Fauré's work after 1900 are therefore emblematic of the twentieth-century experience for a great many later composers.

Puccini

'To think about twelve-note technique at the same time as remembering that childhood experience of *Madama Butterfly* on the gramophone—that is the task facing every serious attempt to understand music today.'[19] Adorno's point, in 1929, was doubtless to highlight the problems facing the intelligent music-lover when confronted with that special twentieth-century tension between Schoenberg's direct engagement with modernity and Puccini's apparent indifference to it—between being truly 'of' the century and being merely 'in' it. In 1929, such a construction might have been comprehensible. At the end of the century, however, it cannot seriously be claimed that Puccini's music (which is probably even more popular than it was in 1904, or 1929) is any less genuinely 'of' the century than Schoenberg's. The persistence of a kind of music which counts, technically at least, as traditional—that is, in essence, tonal—has proved to be

---

[12] Jean-Michel Nectoux, *Gabriel Fauré: A Musical Life*, trans. R. Nichols (Cambridge, 1991), 380.
[13] Ibid. 294–5.   [14] Ibid. 312.
[15] Ronald Crichton, 'Pénélope', *The New Grove Dictionary of Opera*, ed. S. Sadie (London, 1992), iii. 943.
[16] Nectoux, *Fauré*, 368.   [17] Ibid. 390.   [18] Ibid. 415.
[19] T. W. Adorno, *Quasi una fantasia: Essays on Modern Music*, trans. R. Livingstone (London, 1992), 20.

as significant and prominent a part of twentieth-century culture as the critique of that traditionalism mounted by Schoenberg and others. More than that, tonality itself has adapted in various ways as the century has progressed, so that, while much of the music written between Debussy and John Adams will be called 'tonal', its tonality is quite different from that of the 'common practice' era. Indeed, Adorno's comment on Bartók, quoted above, acknowledges as much.

Writers on twentieth-century composition who wish to find a place for Italian music before Dallapiccola in their narratives are likely to choose Puccini as their point of focus. Not only is it possible to emphasize those respects in which his later masterpieces, *La fanciulla del West* (1910), and *Turandot* (unfinished, 1924) display greater progressiveness—more textural discontinuity, stronger emancipation of the dissonance—than their predecessors, *Tosca* (1900) or *Madama Butterfly* (1904): it can also be claimed that it is the capacity to encompass a positive element of progressiveness that distinguishes Puccini from other early twentieth-century Italian late romantics like Pietro Mascagni (1863–1945), Umberto Giordano (1867–1948), and Ottorino Respighi (1879–1936).[20] Puccini's progressiveness might have been prompted by a fascination with the kind of exotic, sadistic subject-matter that can also be found in other, more explicitly radical contemporaries, from Debussy to Richard Strauss, and which tends to be associated with fin-de-siècle decadence. Yet its expression in Puccini reveals an energy and an eloquence that is much more than merely decadent. The focus on farewell as renewal or rebirth, so poignantly apparent at the end of *La fanciulla del West*, can be paralleled in other contemporary works as different (and as forward-looking) as Mahler's *Das Lied von der Erde* (1908–9) and Stravinsky's *The Rite of Spring* (1911–13), and while such comparisons are the stuff of history-with-a-broad-brush, they do little to validate Puccini's engagement with modernism. Rather, they indicate that such 'common' themes can be convincingly treated even when the composer disdains transcendent overtones, by way of a musical imagination that affects the solar plexus as much if not more than the mind. As Carl Dahlhaus observed, 'the great duet at the end of Act 1' of *Butterfly*—possessing a 'melodic urgency and sophistication Puccini was never to surpass'—helped the composer to persuade audiences that this 'trivial if durable plot' is actually 'a story of love and happiness betrayed'.[21] Similarly, the blissful duet at the end of *La fanciulla* does not pale in comparison with its possible model, the rapturous farewell of the doomed lovers at the end of Verdi's *Aida*. Since Minnie and Dick are about to start a new life, the effect is not that of a numinous *Liebestod* but of a comforting affirmation of human values. Love wins through, in a poignantly worldly way, and the stability of the final E major is reinforced by the prominent chromatic inflections (Ex. 2.1).

[20] See Chapter 4 below, pp. 72–3.
[21] Carl Dahlhaus, *Nineteenth-Century Music*, trans. J. B. Robinson (Berkeley and Los Angeles, 1989), 353.

Ex. 2.1. Puccini, *La fanciulla del West*, Act 3, ending

Elgar and Delius

The ability to effect such transformations is an artistic gift that does not need to ally itself with technical progressiveness. Clear-cut stylistic individuality is more to the point, and when such individuality is projected with the assurance of genius the result usually proves durable. An alchemy comparable to Puccini's can be found in Elgar's transmutation of the ceremonial military march into concert works (*Pomp and Circumstance* Marches 1–4, 1901–7) which, as the century has progressed, have come to be seen as eloquent salutes to an imperial grandeur the more ambivalent for its ephemerality. Such an interpretation

Ex. 2.1. (*cont.*)

Ex. 2.2. Elgar, Symphony No. 2, 4th movt., ending

is all the easier because of the clear links of tone and style between the marches and Elgar's greatest orchestral works, from the 'Enigma' Variations (1899) to the Symphony No. 1 (1907–8)—closure as heroic apotheosis—the Symphony No. 2 (1909–11)—closure as profound regretfulness—and on to the still more overt expressions of nostalgia and lamentation in *Falstaff* (1913) and the Cello Concerto (1919). In the final cadence of the second symphony (Ex. 2.2) the securely established Eb major chord is enhanced rather than threatened by the dissonant harmonies that follow the last reference to the finale's main theme, and the crescendo and diminuendo, with timpani roll, as well as the emphasis on the mediant scale degree at the top of the final chords, serve to underline the character of an ending which is both decisive in its affirmation of tonal closure and also imbued with a sense of impermanence, of imminent loss.

The revealing obituary tribute to Elgar as someone who 'prolonged the standing tradition, maintaining it against the hammerings of Strauss, the insidiousness of Debussy, and the provocations of Stravinsky; and he did so not by an appeal to our conservative instincts but by showing what new adventure and discovery lay in the old ways',[22] seems to miss the obvious point that conservatism in art is actually more about finding novelty and adventure within 'the old ways' than about the most literal retention of those ways. But the fractures and ambiguities characteristic of modernity are even less likely to be found in Elgar than they are in other tonal symphonists of the time, such as Sibelius, or, in particu-

---

[22] *Musical Times*, 75 (1934), 306.

lar, Mahler. In his sense of being spiritually, socially at odds with his own age—despite his great public and social success—Elgar reinforces the relevance of romantic perspectives to the twentieth-century cultural landscape.[23]

Something similar can be said of several other British-born late romantics, among whom Frederick Delius (1862–1934) is the most interesting.[24] In many ways the opposite of Elgar, living for most of his life in France and cultivating a far more oblique attitude to inherited musical genres and traditional formal and harmonic techniques, the impassioned evocation of nostalgia and regret which dominates his musical expression is found in a wide range of works, of which the opera *A Village Romeo and Juliet* (1900–1), the Whitman setting *Sea Drift* (baritone, chorus, and orchestra, 1903–4) and the tone poems *In a Summer Garden* (1908), *On hearing the first cuckoo in spring* (1912), and *Eventyr* (1919) are particularly prized by his admirers. What to those admirers is an elliptical, imaginatively personal feeling for chromatic harmony and an admirable refusal to follow predictably regular rhythmic patterns seems to more sceptical ears like a textural diffuseness and lack of focus, compared, for example, to the cool clarity and precise yet understated progressiveness of Debussy, the contemporary composer whose world seems closest to that of Delius. If, as appears plausible, Delius could have subscribed as enthusiastically to the declaration that begins the next section of this chapter as Debussy himself did, then the least the judicious commentator can say is that these two composers drew quite different technical conclusions from it.

Debussy

'I wanted from music a freedom which it possesses perhaps to a greater degree than any other art, not being tied to a more or less exact reproduction of Nature but to the mysterious correspondences between Nature and Imagination.'[25] This declaration, by Claude Debussy (1862–1918), was made in April 1902 at the time of the première of his opera *Pelléas et Mélisande*. It is not a manifesto in favour of unmitigated radicalism, but its focus on 'freedom' fits the prevailing image of a composer who is celebrated not because he puritanically turned his back on late romantic 'decadence', of the kind found in Richard Strauss or Mahler, but because he promoted a music of understatement, of delicacy rather than blatancy, allusiveness rather than explicitness. From at least the time of the *Prélude à l'après midi d'un faune* (1894), Debussy's questioning of tradition, especially Germanic tradition, and his advocacy of spontaneity in preference to calculation, help to define the distinctive atmosphere and techniques of his most important works, and to explain a quality which has had a particular appeal

---

[23] The standard biography is Jerrold Northrop Moore, *Edward Elgar: A Creative Life* (Oxford, 1984).
[24] See Lionel Carley, *Delius: A Life in Letters*, 2 vols. (London, 1983 and 1988).
[25] Cited by Roger Nichols, 'Debussy', *The New Grove*, ed. S. Sadie (London, 1980), v. 307.

for more recent composers, not least the members of the post-1945 avant-garde. For example, Pierre Boulez has stated that 'what interested me in Debussy was not his vocabulary itself but its flexibility, a certain immediacy of invention, and precisely the local indiscipline in relation to the overall discipline'.[26] That 'flexibility' was the result of Debussy's openness to a wide range of influences: his visits to Russia and to Bayreuth in the 1880s alerted him to forms of progressiveness that he would find ways of making his own, and the Javanese gamelan, which he heard at the Paris Exhibition of 1889, opened up a world of non-Western possibilities that proved even more crucial for Debussy's successors (Messiaen, Boulez) than for Debussy himself.

As Roger Nichols has noted, it was *Pelléas et Mélisande* which 'suddenly made Debussy an "important" composer'[27] when it was first performed in 1902, and it is the work which most completely supports the associated judgement that Debussy 'achieved a new psychological penetration through understatement'.[28] *Pelléas* had a long, difficult period of gestation, and its often quiet tone of voice is the more remarkable, given the degree to which the influence of such dynamic precursors as Wagner and Musorgsky (Debussy had got to know the music of *Boris Godunov* in the mid-1890s) had been brought into the orbit of Debussy's own more fluid rhythms and supple syntax. Freedom, for Debussy, did not involve an unrealistic attempt to reject all aspects of tradition, and just as *Pelléas* successfully attempts a distinctively new look at a well-established musical genre, so his other major works, from the orchestral *Nocturnes* (1897–9) to the *Études* for piano (1915) and the late chamber pieces, involve original perspectives on the familiar forms of tone poem, study, and sonata. The music is often energetic, but there is little late romantic intensity of the Germanic kind, and still less of expressionistic disruptiveness. As a result, more recent, more radical musicians have tended to pay tribute to parts of the Debussian inheritance, rather than to the whole.

Given that Debussy's 'vocabulary' was, in essence, that of traditional, tonal harmony and counterpoint, it is not surprising that Pierre Boulez focused his attention on the way that language was used rather than the language as such. Debussy chose to inflect accepted principles of voice-leading and formal organization, preserving the distinction between consonance and dissonance and the presence of keys or modes. Some sense of the way in which Debussy's flexible attitude to a traditional language can promote a radical attitude to established forms and textures is found in a comment by Richard Parks: 'he subordinates the customary role of continuity as a means of grouping like events into coherent entities to that of discontinuity, as a means of separating disparate events: discontinuity defines formal units from without, by determining their boundaries'.[29]

[26] Pierre Boulez, *Conversations with Célestin Deliège* (London, 1976), 96.
[27] Nichols, 'Debussy', 309. See also Roger Nichols, *The Life of Debussy* (Cambridge, 1998).
[28] Ibid. 293.
[29] Richard S. Parks, *The Music of Claude Debussy* (New Haven, 1989), 204.

In this way Debussy's credentials as a modernist may be promulgated, yet it will be clear that subordinating continuity to discontinuity is less drastic than it might be, for as long as the musical vocabulary itself retains some if not all of tonality's structural properties. Such a blend of features makes possible what Simon Trezise describes as 'an ambivalent rapprochement with the nineteenth-century symphony'[30] in *La Mer* (1903–5). Debussy's dialogue with the past did not involve rejection of the past. Nor did his questioning of tradition yield such explicitly radical results as those achieved by his contemporaries—Schoenberg, Ives—whose vocabularies and formal designs were less beholden to the idea of 'rapprochement'. Yet it is precisely the delicate balance between old and new in his finest works that marks him as a central figure who remains a seminal example of progressive thought a century later. A short but representative work of Debussy's will be discussed a little later, after consideration of two of his most important contemporaries.

Satie

If Erik Satie (1886–1925) was not 'central' in the same way as Debussy, it is because he was more radical. As Robert Orledge has observed, not only did he entirely reject 'the nineteenth-century concepts of romantic expressiveness and thematic development': he was 'the first to reject Wagner's influence on French music', and he also 'by-passed impressionism and the beguiling orchestral sonorities of Debussy and Ravel'.[31] Whereas Debussy was a hero to Boulez, Satie was a figure of reverence for John Cage, because he 'despised art'.[32] Satie's view of art 'derived more from painters (especially the Cubists) than from any composer, alive or dead. But his attitude in pursuing his chosen path towards ultimate simplicity, brevity and clarity of expression should be seen both as essentially French and as a positive achievement, however much rejection it entailed *en route*.'[33]

Satie's compositions of the 1880s, like the *Sarabandes* and *Gymnopédies* for piano, have unresolved dissonances which suggest technical analogies to the world of Liszt's late piano music, while offering a very different musical atmosphere. Satie's early works are ritualistic and detached, reflecting his involvement in the Rose-Croix religious cult, and although he soon turned his back on this he never lost interest in the possibilities of a music that was not just understated, like Debussy's, but also utterly purged of allusions to romantic rhetoric. The 'Symphonic drama' *Socrate* (1918) was the fulfilment of an aesthetic attitude that aspired to a vision of archaic purity, even at the risk of what some critics,

---

[30] Simon Trezise, *Debussy: La Mer* (Cambridge, 1994), 47.
[31] Robert Orledge, *Satie the Composer* (Cambridge, 1990), 1.
[32] John Cage, *Silence* (Cambridge, Mass., 1967), 78.
[33] Orledge, *Satie*, 1.

including Stravinsky, felt to be an excess of rhythmic uniformity.[34] The other side of Satie was the musical jester, given to providing his short piano pieces with nonsensically whimsical titles—*Peccadilles importunes* (1913), *Sonatine bureau-cratique* (1917)—and surreal running commentaries. The first of the three short pieces called *Croquis et agaceries d'un gros bonhomme en bois* (Sketches and provocations of a stout wooden puppet) of 1913 arranges its artless yodelling song as a poker-faced slow waltz with just enough added dissonance to make its basic C major diatonicism seem part of the joke. Also part of the joke is the absence of bar-lines, since the music is nothing if not metrical (Ex. 2.3). Such gently sardonic impulses came to fruition after Satie had spent time at the Schola Cantorum (1905–8, studying with Vincent d'Indy and Albert Roussel) with the aim of improving his compositional technique. Fortunately, this exercise failed to cure Satie of his instinct for giving conventional harmonic formulae new meanings through unexpected juxtapositions and unpredictable contexts. This instinct helps to explain why Satie eventually became the darling of Jean Cocteau and the anti-romantic avant-garde that grew up around the Russian Ballet in Paris after 1909. In particular, the ballet *Parade* (1917), with its vivid, anarchic aura of the music hall, won Satie the admiration of Stravinsky as well as of Poulenc and Milhaud.

As Orledge sees it, Satie's career was scarcely lacking in logic or coherence of the kind that, in principle at least, Cage might have found questionable. It formed 'a single span whose unconventional direction was determined by his continual rethinking of the whole aim and aesthetic of music as a reaction to nineteenth-century practice and excesses. A natural tendency towards simplification, succinctness and economy underlies all his work.' And yet, not least because Satie 'rejected all concepts of music as bourgeois entertainment, and in later life he set out deliberately to shock and scandalize his audiences',[35] his music bears consistent witness to the kind of modernism that is not a development of nineteenth-century techniques for the exploration of discontinuity. Rather—and here it anticipates the experimental, minimalist aesthetic that emerged after 1960—it seeks to challenge unity by exaggerating it, rejecting ideas of progress and 'exploring the effects of monotony and boredom'. Even when Satie constructed a form from the 'cellular jigsaw of abrupt contrasts', therefore, 'an overriding melodic logic'[36] can be detected. 'Satie was not concerned with through-composition, and the normal perception of music "getting somewhere" through functional forms and harmonies':[37] logically, therefore, his dislike of creative ambition and what he saw as artistic pretension prevented him from pursuing the fuller possibilities of his own radical agenda. For Cage, of course, that was precisely the point. Not only did Satie despise art, but 'he was going nowhere'.[38] Rightly or wrongly, most of the composers discussed in the following

---

[34] See Igor Stravinsky and Robert Craft, *Conversations with Igor Stravinsky* (London, 1979), 68.

[35] Orledge, *Satie*, 7.   [36] Ibid. 79.   [37] Ibid. 142.   [38] Cage, *Silence*, 78–9.

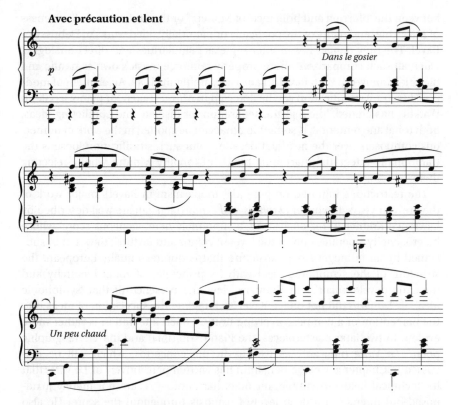

Ex. 2.3. Satie, *Croquis et agaceries d'un gros bonhomme en bois*, No. 1, 'Tyrolienne turque', beginning

pages adopted a less self-denying attitude. Even the concept of music as 'bourgeois entertainment' was not rejected out of hand by most avant-garde composers, whose belief in the rightness of their radicalism was based on the conviction that sooner or later the value of their music would be publicly, culturally accepted, and that such acceptance meant performance in conventional concert environments.

Ravel

Maurice Ravel (1875–1937) was an altogether less progressive figure than Satie, yet the technical and aesthetic cross-currents to be found in his music indicate an achievement of well-nigh Debussian sophistication. Such cross-currents have often been explained in terms of connections with other arts—impressionist painting or symbolist poetry—and there is no law against making associations between the 'blurring and brilliance' of Monet,[39] or the understated allusiveness of Mallarmé, and many of the poetically or pictorially titled works of Debussy or Ravel. The only danger lies in inferring exact similarities and direct analogies, when all such comparisons more properly reinforce music's own semantic and pictorial ambiguity. With Ravel, in any case, ambiguity is all. An element of modernist textural stratification can be detected in *Miroirs* (1905) for piano: as Glenn Watkins has argued, 'the registral separation for discrete and conflicting ideas, both tonal and temporal, is something that can be spotted in the work of numerous composers over the next half decade'.[40] But such stratification loosens the traditionally integrating harmonic bonds of tonality without wholly rejecting them.

The restrictions imposed on potential modernism in Ravel's major work of the pre-war years, the ballet *Daphnis and Chloé* (1909–12), are well described by Lawrence Kramer in his analysis of 'a supremely heterogeneous score' whose heterogeneity 'operates only at the level of colour and texture': that is, it is 'subsumed by an homogeneity of structure that is quintessentially European, the structure of the symphonic ideal with its principles of tonal hierarchy and thematic development'.[41] In Kramer's view, the presence of that 'symphonic ideal' in *Daphnis* did not oblige Ravel 'to integrate the succession of ideas into the perception of a complex, evolving unity'.[42] Such integration is rather more evident in two later masterpieces, the Piano Trio (1914) and the 'choreographic poem' *La Valse* (1919–20)—as well as in the concertos, which will be discussed in Chapter 3. George Benjamin has written perceptively of *La Valse* that its 'technical fields—rhythmic, melodic, harmonic— . . . are not merely juxtaposed but interact at a deep level of osmosis throughout the score'. He also observes that the work's 'teleological conception' is unique in Ravel's output, and concludes that 'with the formidably strong organisational principles behind the expressive sensitivity of his music, he has given some of the earliest and most interesting answers to the twentieth-century's anguished yet exhilarating quest for musical coherence and expression in an age without a functioning vernacular'.[43]

Debussy Analysis: '. . . des pas sur la neige . . .'

Equally early and perhaps even more interesting 'answers' are to be found in Debussy himself, and his subtly progressive mode of musical expression can be demonstrated through an outline analysis of a short but representative work, the

[39] Adrian Stokes, *The Image in Form: Selected Writings* (Harmondsworth, 1972), 257.

[40] Glenn Watkins, *Pyramids at the Louvre: Music, Culture, and Collage from Stravinsky to the Postmodernists* (Cambridge, Mass., 1994), 226.

[41] Lawrence Kramer, *Classical Music and Postmodern Knowledge* (Berkeley and Los Angeles, 1995), 213.

[42] Ibid. 218.   [43] George Benjamin, 'Last Dance', *Musical Times*, 135 (1994), 432–5.

sixth of the second book of *Préludes* for piano (composed in 1910) which has, at the end, the title '. . . des pas sur la neige . . .' (Ex. 2.4). With hindsight, it can be seen that, by 1910, Debussy's career had already begun that decline which, as the result of various factors—illness, financial problems, difficulties connected with his second marriage, musical fashion in Paris increasingly beholden to Diaghilev and Stravinsky—would gradually intensify until his death in 1918. Even so, some of his finest and most ambitious works were still to come—the completion of the orchestral *Images* in 1912, and the ballet *Jeux* of the same year—and many of the smaller compositions also confirm that techniques introduced and developed in the earlier works (particularly *Pelléas*) remained viable and adaptable in new contexts. Writing of *Pelléas*, Richard Langham Smith has described a musical language which ranges 'into modal, whole-tone, diatonic "white-note", even octatonic areas, creating—by the range of possibilities for the presentation of any one motif—a language of extended flexibility with which to respond to Maeterlinck's interplay of themes and symbols'.[44] That 'extended flexibility' was Debussy's most valuable gift to posterity, and '. . . des pas sur la neige . . .' explores it in an imaginative and concentrated way. As the composer declared in 1913, with characteristically barbed irony, 'the century of aeroplanes has a right to a music of its own!'[45]

No specific poetic or pictorial reference has been traced for the prelude's title, but this absence serves to enhance the resonance of the imagery that emerges when the music's techniques are interpreted in terms of their pictorial and poetic associations. The music alludes to motion, to tentatively persistent progress (or attempted progress) across snow-covered ground. It also embodies emotion, feelings determined primarily by the 'sorrowfully expressive' melody which Debussy sets in counterpoint with the slow, regular steps.

This is music in which fixity (the trudging figure) and change (the contexts in which the figure is placed) interact, and it is the essential unity of the musical language—its tonality—which ensures that they do not conflict. Even if the image which Debussy creates of virtual immobility in a changing context has its origin in some of Wagner's orchestral transitions (especially those in *Parsifal*, where the landscape seems to change around the characters, without the characters actually moving through it) this music's quality of intense, visionary restraint is as personal as it is memorable.

The unity of '. . . des pas sur la neige . . .' coexists with many tensions and ambiguities. It is tempting to characterize tonality, even in its later nineteenth-century manifestations, with diatonicism increasingly infiltrated and destabilized by chromaticism, as a 'submerged cathedral' for Debussy, a noble edifice, no longer actively present, whose resonances can nevertheless be heard behind all novelty and innovation. As a 'Prelude in D minor' Debussy's piece is as

---

[44] See Roger Nichols and Richard Langham Smith (eds.), *Debussy: Pelléas et Mélisande* (Cambridge, 1989), 85.

[45] See François Lesure and Richard Langham Smith (eds.), *Debussy on Music* (London, 1977), 297.

Ex. 2.4. Debussy, *Préludes*, Vol. 1, No. 6, '. . . des pas sur la neige . . .'

Ex. 2.4. (cont.)

different in form from preludes by Bach or Chopin as it is in style. But other principles—of dialogue between stability and instability—hint at subtle connections with these much earlier models.

The treatment of tonal harmony is the most progressive aspect of Debussy's prelude. Although triads are plentiful, and there is a final, plagal cadence, the composer consistently bends the basic D minor towards remote regions (D♭ major, G♭ major). He also marks the piece's formal midpoint (bar 15) by arrival on a whole-tone chord whose bass note, C, has the potential for referring to the dominant chord of D minor's relative major (F), but here proclaims its distance from such a functional attribution. Treading on thin ice, the lamenting traveller seems on the edge of an abyss, having progressed into a new, wholly unstable predicament, uncentred symmetry replacing rooted hierarchy.

The analysis might continue in terms of such a personalized narrative, arguing that the prelude's second half (starting when the traveller, turning away from the abyss, steps out again in bar 16) represents a more determined traversal of what the first half opens up, and seems to indicate that what is being lamented is a tender, sad, regretful memory (bars 29–31). The music distinguishes past (G♭ major) from present (D minor), but projects both as coexistent presences. It is nevertheless the final representation of the present that opens out spatially, as if to indicate the distance the traveller has covered, and the gulf that exists at the end between the traveller and the observer, the listener. The lament sinks out of hearing as the steps disappear into the distance.

In technical terms the ending of the prelude might represent the attaining of firm ground. Yet there is little sense of consolation or catharsis, of the satisfying completion of a rite of passage. Debussy's avoidance of any suggestion that some kind of spiritual fulfilment is being celebrated sets him apart from most of his significant contemporaries. Restrained lament is not his only tone of voice, as major works like *La Mer*, *L'Isle joyeuse*, and *Jeux* testify: his characteristic flexibility of formal construction can serve moods of exuberant celebration as well as the questings of gloom and doom. But Debussy's celebratory exuberance is more physical than metaphysical, and the sense of mystery that his more radical technical procedures can evoke, as in the whole-tone ending of the piano pieces 'Mouvement' (from *Images*, 1905), and the prelude 'Voiles' (from Book 2, 1912–13), invariably keeps its distance from more fervent late romantic moods. Recalling Adorno's comment, cited earlier, we might wish to offer this prelude in disproof of the argument that Debussy's music 'leaves no "fractures"', and is therefore 'set apart from society'.[46] There may be no disruptions as spectacular as those found in Mahler or the expressionists, and yet '. . . des pas sur la neige . . .' is far from anti-radical in its use of destabilizing progressions to call formal continuity into question, and it has powerful psychological associations which help to place it at the heart of twentieth-century cultural practice. It can therefore serve to

[46] See p. 10 above.

confirm the truth of Adorno's other insight, that Debussy's music is indeed 'radically modernist in its implications', not least because his compositions often resist purely technical radicalism with such scrupulous independence of mind.

Mahler

Seeking out significant affinities between the winter journey of Debussy's prelude and a distant precedent like the first song of Schubert's *Winterreise* may be regarded as the acme of musicological futility. Even if a common tonality and not-too-dissimilar motivic elements are accepted, and even if a comparable tone of restrained lamentation is observed, the differences of style and form are likely to seem ever more striking as the comparison proceeds. The opening of the early tone poem for string sextet, *Verklärte Nacht* (1899) by Arnold Schoenberg (1874–1951) could be proposed as a closer, more conscious derivation from the Schubertian model: the trudging pace of Schoenberg's travellers is slower but the tonality is the same and, as in the Debussy, motivic resemblances in the shape of poignant descending figures can be found. Schoenberg evokes the Schubertian atmosphere of brooding despair, as well as the structural device of an initial harmonic stability that will soon become subject to challenge and decay. But differences are no less fundamental. Not only is the Schoenberg an unambiguously symphonic work, in the tradition of Liszt's single-movement symphonic poems, but, conforming to the content of the poem by Richard Dehmel which lies behind it, it has a happy ending, moving from sorrow to serenity, from D minor to D major, its many tensions and instabilities ultimately resolved into the purest diatonicism. For the late romantic composer, such resolutions were not the sole prerogative of happy endings; four years after *Verklärte Nacht*, Schoenberg completed a tone poem for full orchestra, *Pelleas und Melisande* (1902–3), whose large-scale single-movement design (in obedience to its source text, the play by Maeterlinck) moves to an unsparingly tragic conclusion, in an unambiguous D minor. In such works, the romantic idea of ending as some kind of apotheosis, of fulfilment or farewell, is powerfully preserved, as in the symphonic music of Schoenberg's near-contemporary Gustav Mahler (1860–1911), which he greatly admired.

Adorno's comment, cited earlier, about Mahler's acceptance of the 'fragmented character' of the musical material,[47] arises from the fact that all Mahler's symphonies contain extreme contrasts. But the potential these contrasts possess for exploding traditionally unified structures from the inside is challenged by acknowledgement of tonality's continuing capacity for synthesis and integration. As Peter Franklin, in his useful commentary on Adorno's Mahler study, notes: 'If the good bourgeois German symphony were defined by its rationalized order

---

[47] See p. 10 above.

and the sanitized relationship between its tasteful material and structural norms, then Mahler's symphonies were conspicuous for their fractured "brokenness," for their refusal to domesticate or prettify the natural sounds, the childlike melodies, the musical waifs and strays they find a home for.'[48] The predominant quality is that of a dialogue between the opposing forces of separation and connection which resists any higher synthesis. This is a modernity which had been evident in music since the immensely diverse structures of late Beethoven and Berlioz, but it becomes typically Mahlerian in the confrontations he sets up between song-like, even 'popular' melodic material and the disciplines of symphonic design.[49] As a result, as for example in the Symphony No. 6 (1903–4, revised 1906), closure is 'as problematic as it is inevitable'.[50]

The potency and originality of Mahlerian oppositions are nowhere more apparent than in the differences between the Symphony No. 7 (1904–5), where the forms are at their most diverse and the musical language at its most progressive, and the Symphony No. 8 (1906), whose choral apotheosis strives (in its setting of the final scene of Goethe's *Faust*) to encompass the unambiguous attainment of transcendental integration. Adorno believed that the power of Mahler's music lay in its failure to fulfil such impossible ambitions: 'joy remains unattainable, and no transcendence is left but that of yearning'.[51] As Franklin shows, in Mahler's late works, as Adorno interprets them, 'the childhood memory of utopia is retained in the knowledge that it is not only lost, but that happiness itself can perhaps only ever be recognized as lost happiness'.[52] And yet the 'scrupulous avoidance' in these late works 'of any easy indulgence in "hope" is precisely what is hopeful about them',[53] since they seem to promise a future for a music that is fully equal to the powerful paradoxes and fractures of modern society.

The Rondo-Finale of the Symphony No. 7, containing as it does an exuberantly unholy confrontation between militarism and religion, march and chorale, could well have been intended to subvert the structures and moods which precede it in that work, and Mahler's yearning, aspiringly transcendent chorale music, an even more prominent, persistent presence in the Symphony No. 8, is imbued in the Seventh with a defiantly secular hedonism, an insistence which has as much of hysteria as of joy about it. As a Rondo whose contrasts seem to be inserted for maximum dislocatory effect, the finale of the Seventh has aroused considerable doubts, even among some of Mahler's most fervent admirers, and although the Eighth has also been criticized for spreading its ideas rather too thinly, at least

---

[48] See Stephen Hefling (ed.), *Mahler Studies* (Cambridge, 1997), 281–2. See also Peter Franklin, *The Life of Mahler* (Cambridge, 1997).

[49] See the discussion of these issues by Carolyn Abbate *in Unsung Voices: Opera and Musical Narrative in the Nineteenth Century* (Princeton, 1991), 119–55, and by John Williamson in *Mahler Studies*, 248–70.

[50] Robert Samuels, *Mahler's Sixth Symphony: A Study in Musical Semiotics* (Cambridge, 1995), 163.

[51] T. W. Adorno, *Mahler: A Musical Physiognomy*, trans. E. Jephcott (Chicago, 1992), 57.

[52] Franklin in *Mahler Studies*, 291.   [53] Ibid. 292.

in the early stages of the second part, it cannot be denied that its symphonism of thematic connection and transformation at the service of harmonic consistency and logic is carried consistently through to a conclusion which somehow seems no less resplendent even if it is heard as demonstrating that joy remains unattainable.

Mahler's next pair of symphonic works, *Das Lied von der Erde* and the Symphony No. 9 (both 1908–9), conclude in a more restrained, even resigned spirit. Both involve confronting still more intensely modernism's tendency (as in Schoenberg's music by 1909) to disrupt the precarious coherencies of progressive romanticism and to abandon the closural eloquence of diatonic consonance. In 'Der Abschied', the last movement of *Das Lied von der Erde*, what might have become an implacable opposition between mundane and transcendent materials, the military-style march and the traveller's metaphysical speculations, is set in question as Mahler strives to balance integration and dissolution. The ending may be technically precarious in the literal sense that resolution to a pure tonic triad is withheld, but the feeling of fulfilment as the rooted triad of C major gently asserts itself against persistent dissonances is unambiguous, even if the feeling itself is nothing if not multivalent, compounded of both joy and sorrow, nostalgia and sublime indifference to mortality (Ex. 2.5). Such multiplicity is carried over into the Ninth Symphony,

Ex. 2.5. Mahler, *Das Lied von der Erde*, No. 6, 'Der Abschied', ending

where there is 'a straining for closure that is essentially Romantic', but also 'an exploration of alternative, plural strategies that is essentially modern'.[54] For Hayden White, 'the difference between this [Mahlerian] uncertainty and the chest-thumping "certainty" of Romanticist heroism is the difference between Modernism and Romanticism in general',[55] and given that essential modernity, it is the more fitting that Schoenberg should have paid musical tribute to Mahler, not in a grandiose choral commemoration, but in the last of his *Six Short Piano Pieces*, Op. 19 (1911), in which the new world of atonality reveals its ability to coexist with the old world of binary—or ternary—form.

Sibelius

There could scarcely be a greater contrast between the sense of an uncompleted project created by Mahler's early death (the so-nearly completed Symphony No. 10 could, after all, have marked the transition to a new phase in his work) and the three decades of virtual silence that separated Sibelius's last symphony from his death. Jean Sibelius (1865–1957) did not, as far as is known, intend his Symphony No. 4 (1910–11) as a tribute to Mahler, and most historians are happy to characterize him as dedicated to many of the things that Mahler sought to set aside. There is ample documentary evidence of Sibelius's unease at the way in which music was developing as the late romantic ideals on which he had built— stemming from Liszt, Tchaikovsky, and the young Richard Strauss—gave way to the more iconoclastic tendencies of Debussy, Stravinsky, and Schoenberg. The controlled yet deeply felt atmosphere of the Symphony No. 4 is indicative both of a sense of alienation from such progressiveness, and of a determination to offer an alternative path to the music of the future. This was how the Fourth, with its 'synthesis of classicism, romanticism and modernism',[56] was seen at the time of its first performances, and such an assessment continues to resonate in recent discussions about what seems best described as Sibelius's 'modern classicism'.[57]

It is in the third movement of the Symphony No. 4 that Sibelius came closest to a personal confrontation with modernism, presenting an 'alternation of self-contained blocks of music with no apparent linking material'. Nevertheless, each block is 'in some respects, a development of its predecessor':[58] there is a sense of moving to a climax of tonal clarification, and there is an even stronger feeling of reinforcing such clarification in the austere purity of the symphony's closing cadences (Ex. 2.6). Such 'classical' thinking is a no less decisive factor in

---

[54] Julian Johnson, 'The Status of the Subject in Mahler's Ninth Symphony', *19th Century Music*, 18 (1994), 120.

[55] Hayden White in Steven P. Scher (ed.), *Music and Text: Critical Enquiries* (Cambridge, 1992), 296.

[56] James Hepokoski, *Sibelius: Symphony No. 5* (Cambridge, 1993), 14.

[57] See ibid. 21, and also Tim Howell, 'Sibelius Studies and Notions of Expertise', *Music Analysis*, 14 (1995), 315–40.

[58] Howell, 'Sibelius Studies', 328.

Ex. 2.6. Sibelius, Symphony No. 4, 4th movt., ending

the Symphony No. 5 (begun 1915, final version 1919). James Hepokoski interprets this as Sibelius's response to a situation in which 'what had been perceived as aggressively modern' had turned 'into something faded and *passé*'.[59] Yet however pessimistic the composer's mood, the symphony moves, in its finale, to a hard-won yet entirely positive affirmation of traditional values, consonant closure winning out over dissonant strivings.

Much musicological attention has been focused on Sibelius's decision to fuse the originally separate first movement and scherzo, so that the latter's function is enriched: it is part of the first movement, yet also a consequence of that movement. Nevertheless, the Fifth Symphony is still some way from the ambiguously formed yet powerfully unified design that would govern the Seventh a decade later. There is a middle movement, 'Andante mosso, quasi allegretto', which, even if 'its larger purpose is to generate the leading rhythms, metres, timbres, motives and themes of the finale to come',[60] stands back in character and tonality from the strenuous dynamism of the outer movements. After this the finale soon establishes a renewed sense of urgency, a need for positive fulfilment that is magnificently realized in the way the great 'Swan Hymn' theme

[59] Hepokoski, *Sibelius*, 8.   [60] Ibid. 71.

gains profundity and, ultimately, resolution in the superb concluding section. Hepokoski underlines the finale's formal multiplicity, while no less correctly emphasizing the imaginative traditionalism of its 'larger aims', as 'the end of the symphony triumphantly gathers up, and then resolves, its beginning'.[61] There is no role for Adorno's Mahlerian fractures in Sibelius, as the discussion of his later works in Chapter 3 will confirm, yet his modern classicism does not preclude a special richness and a memorable ambiguity.

Richard Strauss

James Hepokoski's valuable work on Sibelius is complemented by his no less thought-provoking writings on Richard Strauss (1864–1949), which clarify the modernizing potential of his formal procedures in the early tone poems. Hepokoski reads *Don Juan* (1888–9) as 'no single form; rather, it is a structural process in dialogue with several generic traditions',[62] and he defines 'the ambiguity of *Don Juan*'s form' as 'a provocative set of possibilities rather than a trim, solvable narrative'.[63] Hepokoski also builds on the foundations of earlier writers persuaded by 'the newness of *Don Juan*' through 'the *compounded* aspect of its many-layered "modern" form, which arises out of fragments'.[64] Against such a background, Strauss's progression from tone poem to expressionistic music drama, diverse in structure and extreme in expression, seems logical. Moreover, there has long been general agreement that the superior quality of the music helps to ensure that the extravagant, often sadistic 'decadence' of *Salome* (1903–5) and *Elektra* (1906–8) is experienced as something more than merely sordid or trivial in the theatre. The inexorably evolving symphonic forms and the coherent, hugely imaginative thematic processes are resourcefully built on Wagnerian foundations, even though the subject-matter may be even more extravagant, or decadent, than anything in Wagner.

Such musical treatment of such subject-matter promotes the kind of ambiguities that confirm Strauss's position as a founder of twentieth-century modernism. In particular, the music for the troubled, troubling character of Klytemnestra in *Elektra* begins to approach the expressionistically febrile mood of Schoenberg's deranged protagonist in his atonal monodrama *Erwartung*, written at much the same time, although it never completely loses touch with the poignantly inflected consonances of its more nostalgic moments (Ex. 2.7), a dimension absent from Schoenberg's nightmare vision. Given his temperament, it is not surprising that Strauss should soon have turned to topics in which a strong human sympathy could attach itself to more appealing characters, like

[61] Hepokoski, *Sibelius*, 84.
[62] In Bryan Gilliam (ed.), *Richard Strauss: New Perspectives on the Composer and his Work* (Durham, NC, 1992), 152.
[63] Ibid. 166.   [64] Ibid. 142.

Ex. 2.7. Strauss, *Elektra*, from two bars before Fig. 145

the Marschallin sunk in regret for her lost youth and lost love at the end of Act 1 of *Der Rosenkavalier* (1909–10). *Die Frau ohne Schatten* (1914–18) was Strauss's most ambitious attempt to combine vulnerable, sympathetic characters with heroic subject-matter. Here symphonic mastery and a drama rich in humanity come together, in what Carl Dahlhaus claimed as the most important 'turnabout' in Strauss's long career.[65] It may also be regarded as the highest point of that career—even by those who admire the later operas, to be discussed in Chapter 4.

Ives

Charles Ives (1874–1954) is another important composer, active in the first decade of the twentieth century, to whom talk of 'discontinuous stylistic citations and allusions' being 'used to form . . . a fragmented organism' can usefully be applied.[66] For example, in *The Unanswered Question* (1906) for (off-stage) strings, four flutes, and trumpet, a troubled human 'traveller' discordantly confronts the impassively serene indifference of 'cosmic' consonance, not merely through the consistent juxtaposition of strongly contrasted textural strata, but through their superimposition: while the strings sustain serene consonances in chorale style, the trumpet repeatedly asks its question, and the flutes offer increasingly insecure responses. *The Unanswered Question* is wholly representative of a style in which tonal and atonal tendencies are brought into a steady state of confrontation from which no resolving synthesis can emerge, and although it is not exactly typical of Ives in containing no literal quotations from hymns or other 'found' material, the chorale style of the string parts is a clear allusion to such material, and the work is cast in a form which acknowledges the abiding force of traditionally evolutionary musical structures even as it attempts to turn its back on the whole idea of progress to closure and resolution.

The special tensions found in Ives's work have inevitably encouraged diverse interpretations of his aesthetic and techniques. Whereas the early response to the *Concord Sonata* (1910–15) was that 'it sways as freely as a tree top in the wind. Indeed, there is no unity of idea in the sense that one part grows out of another',[67] recent theory-based studies argue that, in keeping with Ives's belief that great music 'is both profoundly expressive and skilfully organized',[68] his own compositions aspire to reflect his vision of the universe as 'inherently orderly and logical'.[69] Even so, this undoubtedly sincere aspiration can simply serve to strengthen the sense of confrontation between system and what Philip Lambert

[65] Dahlhaus, *Nineteenth-Century Music*, 372.

[66] Leon Botstein in Bryan Gilliam (ed.), *Richard Strauss and his World* (Princeton, 1992), 19.

[67] Henry Bellamann (1921), cited in J. Peter Burkholder (ed.), *Charles Ives and his World* (Princeton, 1996), 282.

[68] Philip Lambert, *The Music of Charles Ives* (New Haven, 1997), 2.

[69] Ibid. 205.

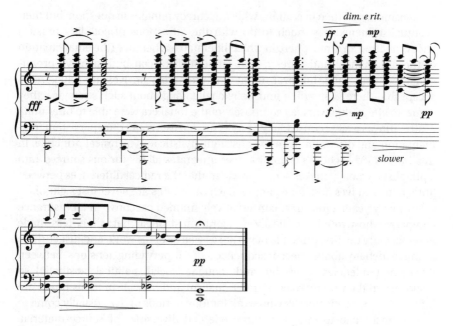

Ex. 2.8. Ives, *Concord Sonata*, 'The Alcotts', ending

expressively describes as 'scramblings' in the music itself,[70] reinforcing the basic truth of Lawrence Kramer's statement that 'Ives made heterogeneity the first principle of his music'.[71]

The fundamental technical point, for Ives, was a simple one: 'Why tonality as such should be thrown out for good I can't see. Why it should be always present, I can't see.'[72] This 'simple' view nevertheless creates complex technical challenges for a composer, and no less complex in Ives's case were his relations with European tradition, some elements of which he despised, other aspects of which he revered. For example, his impatience with Debussy—whose 'content would have been worthier . . . if he'd hoed corn or sold newspapers for a living'[73]—is more than offset by his devotion to the heroic strivings of Beethoven, so idiosyncratically recalled at various places in the *Concord Sonata*, for example, the end of 'The Alcotts' (Ex. 2.8), where the initial ideas of both the Symphony No. 5 and the *Hammerklavier* Sonata can be heard.

Most of Ives's scores, including such essays in controlled (that is, fully notated) chaos as *Putnam's Camp* (1912), were not heard for many years after their

---

[70] Philip Lambert, *The Music of Charles Ives*, 94.
[71] Lawrence Kramer, *Classical Music and Postmodern Knowledge* (Berkeley and Los Angeles, 1995), 174.
[72] Charles Ives, *Essays before a Sonata and Other Writings* (London, 1969), 117.
[73] Ibid. 82.

composition, and then in editions whose accuracy remains in question: but their eventual influence has much to do with the attractions of colliding musical styles, creating an atmosphere in which liberated exuberance (the emancipation of the dissonance) and unrestrained emotionalism can both achieve prominence. As with Satie, however, many commentators on Ives are reluctant to accept that there is anything unusually challenging about such strategies; they argue, in effect, that whereas composers of the tonal era were able to offer unity of structure as well as consistency of style, modernists could offer persistent fragmentation and discontinuity as a consistent stylistic and technical principle. In this way, David Nicholls's claim that Ives integrates all his various sources 'into a pluralistic whole'[74] makes sense, provided that the radical differences between 'integration' in Ives and, for example, Bach or Brahms are never lost sight of.

For many years a full-time, conservatively minded executive in an insurance company who wrote his radically nonconformist music part-time, Ives made heterogeneity the first principle of his life as well as of his work, and just as there is much debate about the consequences of all-pervading tensions between divergent tendencies in his life and thought (social, political, aesthetic) so responses to the varying roles of traditionalism and radicalism in his music are bound to vary. Musicologists who work for long periods on Ives usually come to view him as able to integrate unprecedented diversities of source-material, anxious as they are to counter any suggestion (despite or because of its appeal to the likes of John Cage) that he was nothing more than a musical anarchist. Such judgements tend to assume that to carry the collage or montage principle to its logical conclusion is actually a bad thing. But the degree of integration, or consistency, in any Ives work needs very careful analysis. Does Ives ultimately achieve an all-embracing synthesis, at least on the relatively small scale of a composition like *The Unanswered Question*, or does he demonstrate—and positively enhance—confrontation, strength through incompatibility, the healthy coexistence of independent, yet fully realized characters? Whether or not one's answer to this question supports the relatively conservative or the relatively radical option, all are likely to agree that, in the years before 1914, Ives was more explicitly radical than most contemporary composers, and not least because (unlike Satie) he made his distance from, yet fascination with, 'traditions' of various kinds so clear.

Rakhmaninov

It is all too easy, in the late twentieth century, to plot lines of connection from Tchaikovsky and Musorgsky to Shostakovich and Schnittke, while not forgetting to do justice to other, international lines of influence—from Musorgsky to

---

[74] David Nicholls, *American Experimental Music, 1890–1940* (Cambridge, 1990), 6.

Debussy, Tchaikovsky to Sibelius, and even from the early Stravinsky to his later selves. It could even be argued that the collapse of Soviet Communism during the 1980s was just another manifestation of the cultural dynamics that have made responses to romantic libertarianism the primary force behind twentieth-century Russian music. That focus will certainly seem right to those who believe that the twentieth century's greatest Russian-born composer is Sergei Rakhmaninov (1873–1943). The popular indestructibility of, in particular, the Piano Concerto No. 2 (1900–1), the *Rhapsody on a Theme of Paganini* (1934), and various shorter piano pieces may have more to do with the short-term memorability of tuneful melody than anything else, but such factors are complemented by the structural strengths as well as the emotional power found in the Symphony No. 2 (1906–7), the Piano Concerto No. 3 (1909) and the Symphonic Dances (1940). That Rakhmaninov's range extended beyond the narrowly romantic—taking in allusions to Russian chant and to the more modern tendencies of Prokofiev—cannot dilute the obvious point that his music has little of purely twentieth-century progressiveness about it. Yet, like Puccini's, or Elgar's, it is both utterly personal and also entirely persuasive in its revitalization of traditional essences—an achievement that makes the failure of so many other attempts to repeat the trick the more obvious.

Skryabin

There has never been any question that the earlier years of the twentieth century produced other romantically inclined Russian composers besides Rakhmaninov, other progressives besides Skryabin and Stravinsky. No less clearly, it is the latter pair who have been the most vivid presences within the century itself, Skryabin never completely eclipsed in either concert programmes or historical surveys by the towering achievement and influence of the great Stravinsky.

Alexander Skryabin (1872–1915) has found particular favour with musicologists studying the transition from late romantic tonality to expressionistic atonality because his output is relatively compact, and focused as much if not more on short piano pieces as on larger scale structures. There is nevertheless a clear division of opinion as to whether or not that transition is fully represented in Skryabin's own music. For James M. Baker, and those who think like him, Skryabin moved from an early period, up to 1907, in which he relied on traditional tonal structures, even if certain details are innovatory, to a period of transition (1903–10) which leads to the explicitly atonal language of his later years.[75] For Richard Taruskin, on the other hand, the later music is not atonal at all, but concerned with forms of octatonic structuring which, Taruskin contends, Skryabin 'conceived of . . . as a novel form of tonality'.[76]

---

[75] James M. Baker, *The Music of Alexander Scriabin* (New Haven, 1986).
[76] Richard Taruskin, *Stravinsky and the Russian Traditions: A Biography of the Works through Mavra*

The conflict between these readings may be more apparent than real, coming down to the simple matter of 'it depends what you mean by atonality', or by 'a novel form of tonality'. Moreover, if it is the case that 'Skryabin's most significant contribution to the creation of new forms and procedures' was to enable 'traditional tonal language . . . and symmetrical non-tonal pitch-elements, like the whole-tone scale, to operate in an integrated manner to create a unified composition',[77] this reinforces the anti-modernist aspect of Skryabin's progressiveness. James Baker has argued that 'this type of structure corresponds strikingly to the Theosophical teaching concerning interpenetrating planes of existence', yet Baker continues to talk of 'differentiation' between background tonal bass progressions ('the material plane of existence') and an atonal surface ('the spiritual plane') in his study of *Prometheus*.[78] At the very least, then, the idea that 'the material simply evaporates into the Unifying principle, in this case the triumphant F sharp major chord which concludes the piece'[79] makes it possible to acknowledge that Skryabin's unifying ambitions could produce some very blatant, even banal musical effects. Whether his music achieves integration or reinforces incompatibility, it often seems uneasily adrift between two worlds.

Skyrabin's reluctance to jettison the essentials of late romantic tradition is surely beyond dispute: there was more of post-Lisztian boldness in his style than of true expressionism. Skryabin's rhythms remain too regular, his textures too refined in a late romantic manner, for any more radical tone to make itself felt. Where Skyrabin did admit a radical element to enter was in his acceptance, again following Liszt, of the emancipation of the dissonance. From the time of the *Feuillet d'Album* Op. 58, and the *Prelude* Op. 59 No. 2, both composed in 1910, he felt able to abandon traditional cadential endings, with their tonality-confirming consonances (Ex. 2.9). The often mystical strivings of his final works seem nevertheless to be reaching back to earlier Romantic ideals as much as forward to a Brave New post-war World, and his early death inevitably promotes the judgement that true progressiveness with a Russian accent is to be found elsewhere.

Stravinsky

Richard Taruskin's pioneering and illuminating work on Stravinsky's debt to Skyrabin, as part of an exploration of the former's debts to 'Russian traditions', in the broadest and deepest sense, is an example of how perceptions about a

(Berkeley and Los Angeles, 1996), 809. Taruskin's view is reinforced by Cheong Wai-Ling's analysis of the sixth piano sonata as a work in which 'tonal centricity . . . assumes important form-giving roles. . . . By abandoning tonality while retaining centricity in his exploration of the octatonic at its purest, Scriabin recreates the sonata form.' Cheong Wai-Ling, 'Scriabin's Octatonic Sonata', *Journal of the Royal Musical Association*, 121/2 (1996), 228.

[77] James M. Baker, 'Scriabin's Music: Structure as Prism for Mystical Philosophy', in James M. Baker *et al.* (eds.), *Music Theory in Concept and Practice* (Rochester, NY, 1997), 77.
[78] Ibid. 88.   [79] Ibid. 96.

Ex. 2.9. Skryabin: (i) 'Feuillet d'Album', Op. 58, ending; (ii) Prelude, Op. 59 No. 2, ending

particular composer's position within history may be made to change, even when his actual compositions do not suddenly become more popular or alter their status as objects of musicological enquiry. Taruskin's brilliant detective work is unlikely to alter the long-established judgement that Stravinsky's rapid rise to fame with his first ballet *The Firebird* (1909–10) and its immediate successors, *Petrushka* (1910–11) and *The Rite of Spring* (1911–13), launched a career of the greatest importance for the history of twentieth-century music. It was with *Petrushka* that 'Stravinsky at last became Stravinsky',[80] in what was the first, 'momentous' coincidence of folklorism and modernism in Stravinsky's music.[81] Stravinsky was nevertheless already that 'rightist of the left',[82] as Taruskin characterizes him, in that he sought ways of countering the 'uncouth and unmediated'[83] with new stabilizing factors. He does this, in the 'Chez Petrushka'

[80] Taruskin, *Stravinsky*, 662.   [81] Ibid. 713.   [82] Ibid. 770.   [83] Ibid. 720.

Ex. 2.10. Stravinsky, *Petrushka*, ending

episode, by taking 'the interpenetration of the octatonic and the diatonic to a new structural level unprecedented both within the ballet and within the traditions that fed it'.[84] Even so, the work's extraordinary ending—'Stravinsky's idea entirely'[85]—in which the confrontation between Petrushka's ghost and the 'real world' is shown in stark juxtaposition (Ex. 2.10), has a modernistic purity from which Stravinsky could only retreat. As Taruskin puts it, 'One can easily separate the "folk-derived" from the "original" elements in *Petrushka*. This is no longer possible in *The Rite*,'[86] and although to speak, Adorno-style, of its 'continuity-by-means-of-discontinuity'[87] makes plain that the essential innovations of *Petrushka* have by no means been abandoned, it is clear that the continuing dialogue between classicism and modernism that fuelled Stravinsky's creative drive for the next half-century stemmed directly from the extraordinary originality manifested in *The Rite*.

It was . . . because *The Rite* was so profoundly *traditional* both as to cultural outlook and as to musical technique, that Stravinsky was able to find through it a voice that would serve him through the next difficult phase of his career. Precisely because *The Rite* was neither rupture nor upheaval but a magnificent extension, it revealed to Stravinsky a path that would sustain him through a decade of unimaginable ruptures and upheavals brought on by events far beyond his control.[88]

The modernism of *The Rite* may indeed seem much more wholehearted than that of almost all other contemporary works, the harmony more dissonant, the rhythms more irregular, the textures more stratified. Yet there are persistent tonal

---

[84] Taruskin, *Stravinsky*, 757.   [85] Ibid. 686.
[86] Ibid. 949.   [87] Ibid. 965.   [88] Ibid. 847.

features as well as a convergence between elements deriving from folk music and art music. The very ending, the climax of the 'Sacrificial Dance', can be regarded simply as a grimly riveting portrait of a single death that, according to the ritual, is necessary to guarantee collective survival. Yet the insistent repetitions of brief musical units, and their ultimate relation—even if they do not express this directly—to a tonality of D, seem to suggest that this survival, this renewal, is indeed inherent in the musical fabric itself as well as in the ballet's scenario. Even though the work as a whole displays those techniques of opposition, juxtaposition, and superimposition to which Taruskin refers under the useful heading of 'active . . . polarity',[89] the sense of convergence, and of integration, while inevitably far less stable and secure than 'tradition' decreed, is no less palpable. The much later comment attributed to the composer in *Poetics of Music* that 'the tone of a work like *The Rite of Spring* may have appeared arrogant, the language that it spoke may have seemed harsh in its newness, but that in no way implies that it is revolutionary in the most subversive sense of the word'[90] is far from a feeble attempt retrospectively to bring the composition within the respectable orbit of neo-classicism. It belongs with the composer's surely genuine and sincere belief that

a real tradition is not the relic of a past irretrievably gone; it is a living force that animates and informs the present . . . Far from implying the repetition of what has been, tradition presupposes the reality of what endures. . . . Tradition ensures the continuity of creation . . . A *renewal* is fruitful only when it goes hand in hand with *tradition*.[91]

As this book aims to makes clear, such sentiments resonate far more widely than their direct and exclusive application to Stravinsky's own music, or that of other 'neo-classicists', might suggest.

Schoenberg

It is a topic of endless fascination to the musicologist that such a different, but no less original composer as Arnold Schoenberg should have reached full creative maturity at the same time as Stravinsky. Moreover, there is another historically resonant conjunction in the fact that Schoenberg was born just over two months before another Austrian composer who embodied radically different musical values. Franz Schmidt (1874–1939) retained tonality, a late romantic style, and expansive structures which, at his best, as in the Symphony No. 4 (1932–3), and *Das Buch mit sieben Siegeln* (1935–7), he used to considerable effect. Yet, although traces of composers more progressive than Bruckner and Reger can

[89] Ibid. 756.
[90] Igor Stravinsky, *Poetics of Music*, trans. A. Knodel and I. Dahl (New York, 1947), 12.
[91] Ibid. 58–9.

occasionally be found in Schmidt's music, he completely lacked the 'radical' gene that turned Schoenberg—almost against his will—into an icon of nonconformity and visionary, discomfiting innovation.

There was no 'rapid rise to fame' in Schoenberg's case, of course; eight years Stravinsky's senior, he had 'progressed' much further by 1910, from the late romantic opulence of his early works, initiated by the remarkably confident *Verklärte Nacht*, to the atonal expressionism that first emerged in 1908-9, in the song collection *Das Buch der hängenden Gärten*, Op. 15, and the *Three Piano Pieces*, Op. 11.

The connotations of expressionism in music are no less problematic than those of impressionism, or symbolism. Recent commentaries range from the dismissive—'Schoenberg's aesthetic precepts were never overtly "expressionistic" but motivated . . . by a quest for functional integrity and a moral crusade against extraneous ornament'[92]—to the cautiously accepting:

if it is to have any specific significance, musical Expressionism means *espressivo* in music without manifest underpinnings in traditional compositional means, whether syntactical, formal or tonal . . . In that sense it cannot describe a repeatable or repeated style, still less a school of composition or an epoch in music history, but at best a point of crisis, in this instance the brief period of radical atonality . . . during which Schoenberg composed his works opus 11 to opus 22 and whose pinnacle is undoubtedly *Erwartung*.[93]

Such careful placement of the issues is at the opposite extreme from a kind of criticism which cheerfully asserts that, in the case of the painter Oskar Kokoschka, 'his development and transition from Jugendstil to Expressionism closely parallel Schoenberg's'.[94] It might indeed be argued that, at least from the time of Edvard Munch's painting *The Scream* (1893) and the plays of August Strindberg, especially *A Dream Play* (1903), which has a 'disconnected but apparently logical form' in which characters 'split, double, multiply; they evaporate, condense, scatter and converge',[95] a kind of expression existed in painting and literature which demonstrated a 'point of crisis' with regard to the relation between progressive and conservative that music could hardly fail to match, if not outdo, in the sense that the contrast between tonality and atonality was greater than anything literary language could provide and was only paralleled in painting with the appearance of Kandinsky's earliest abstracts in 1910-11. The friendship between Schoenberg and Kandinsky encourages this particular comparison, while also reinforcing the obvious and fundamental differences between technique and expression in painting and musical composition. The ambiguity of the concept of musical expressionism (something which has gained

[92] Christopher Hailey, in S. Behr *et al.* (eds.), *Expressionism Reassessed* (Manchester, 1993), 108.

[93] Ibid. 126.

[94] Jelena Hahl-Koch, *Arnold Schoenberg and Wassily Kandinsky: Letters, Pictures and Documents*, trans. J. Crawford (London, 1984), 177.

[95] Christopher Butler, *Early Modernism: Literature, Music and Painting in Europe, 1900-1916* (Oxford, 1994), 92.

new force in the 'neo-expressionism' of some important composers since the 1950s—Kurtág, Schnittke, and Maxwell Davies, for example) can be gauged when it is observed that the abandonment of tonal structuring itself was not a prerequisite for a kind of unprecedentedly forceful emotional expression which, as the later stages of Strauss's *Salome* indicate, can be achieved without abandoning tonality, but rather by subjecting tonal harmony to extreme stress. By contrast, many works displaying 'radical atonality', like Schoenberg's Op. 19, or Webern's Op. 7 and Op. 11, seem almost self-consciously understated, and the evident novelty of their textures does not prevent them from being strictly disciplined in their rejection of 'superfluous ornament'.

Such matters leave the usefulness of expressionism as a label appropriately open-ended, a matter of individual instinct and preference. By contrast, the technical facts of musical evolution may appear less open to question. Whereas in March 1908 Schoenberg was still ending his compositions—like the third and fifth songs of his George collection *Das Buch der hängenden Gärten*—with enriched versions of traditional cadences and consonant progressions (Ex. 2.11(i), (ii)), by February 1909, in the first of the Op. 11 piano pieces, the final 'cadence' has moved away from such clear associations with the past, achieving its 'functional integrity' most explicitly in the motivic sphere, in the sense that both the descending second in the bass and the three-note chord above can be related to the piece's predominant thematic material (Ex. 2.11(iii)).

In retrospect, Schoenberg claimed that 'the transition from composition which still emphasized key (while always containing many dissonances) to one where there is no longer any key, any consonances, happened gradually, in accordance not with any wish or will, but with a *vision*, an *inspiration*; it happened perhaps instinctively'.[96] Yet this gradual, instinctive process was scarcely a slow one. With extraordinary rapidity and creative imagination, in the Chamber Symphony No. 1 (1906), String Quartet No. 2 (1907–8), the *Five Orchestral Pieces* (1909), and *Erwartung* (1909), Schoenberg found a way of integrating an uncompromisingly modern approach to traditional genres with his newly forged, all-motivic (if also 'athematic') musical language. In doing so, however, he created an enormous challenge to musicologists, which still survives at the end of the century in arguments about the merits of interpreting such music in the abstract, atonal terms of set theory, as well as or instead of the more traditional concepts of developing, motivic variation.[97]

Schoenberg soon sought to counter the acute psychological penetration of the short opera for a single character, *Erwartung*, as well as the more detached yet still disturbingly decadent emotional world of *Pierrot lunaire* (1912), with an approach that aspired to renew associations with transcendence. In another brief but complex dramatic work, *Die glückliche Hand* (1910–13), and also in the

---

[96] See Willi Reich, *Schoenberg, a Critical Biography*, trans. L. Black (London, 1971), 241.

[97] For a recent consideration of the debate, see Ethan Haimo, 'Atonality, Analysis, and the Intentional Fallacy', *Music Theory Spectrum*, 18/2 (1996), 167–99.

Ex. 2.11. Schoenberg: (i) *Das Buch der hängenden Gärten*, No. 5, ending (March 1908); (ii) *Das Buch der hängenden Gärten*, No. 3, ending (March 1908); (iii) *Three Piano Pieces*, Op. 11 No. 1, ending (February 1909)

proposed symphony with choral movements (begun in 1914) and the unfinished oratorio *Die Jakobsleiter*, begun in 1915, Schoenberg pursued his quest for a workable modern alternative to ultra-expressionistic lawlessness, and sought for techniques as well as subjects to fit his belief that art was of the highest spiritual

as well as cultural significance. It is only appropriate, therefore, that the fragments of the symphony, and the substantial drafts for *Die Jakobsleiter*, should
show Schoenberg's earliest experiments with what was to become the twelve-
note technique.[98]

Bartók

Just as the cultural life of early twentieth-century Vienna helped Schoenberg
to define his own creative ambitions, and test his technical resources, so that
of Budapest did something similar for Béla Bartók (1881–1945). Even those who
resist the extravagant but not wholly untenable argument that Bartók's very best
works belong to these early years—with the opera *Bluebeard's Castle* (1911)
arguably the finest of all—must surely acknowledge the special significance of
his early compositions in the context of the interplay between progressive works
of art and contemporary social, political developments. Leon Botstein has
claimed that 'the integration of politics and aesthetics—the sense of urgency
within a generation to define a new Hungarian nation through modernist art—
lent Bartók's compositional output, from *Kossuth* [1903] on, its coherence',[99] and
Botstein further contends that Bartók 'demonstrated how a truly novel, formal,
modernist aesthetic strategy could be developed from the Hungarian folk
sources whose use had become commonplace in the arts during the first years
of the century'.[100] The possibility of viewing modernism as capable of embodying nationalist attributes is important for the century's music as a whole, and
extends well beyond the association of folk sources with other cultural elements.
In Botstein's view, 'Bartók's lifelong project was to represent, through music, a
Hungarian identity at odds with the nineteenth-century construct, and adequate
to modernity'.[101] The possible working out of that 'project' after 1914 will be the
concern of Chapter 5, but it was clear well before that date that such conjunctions between the composer's sense of identity and his commitment to modernity might fuel many different initiatives, not least in times of social and political
crisis. Hence, perhaps, the predominance of moods of foreboding and even
despair in works, ranging from the small-scale piano *Bagatelles*, Op. 6 (1908) to
Bluebeard's Castle itself, whose expressionistic aura might reflect the composer's
doubts about his social role and his personal identity in a world where the place
of high art was having to be renegotiated within new political systems, some
aspiring to democracy and some resisting it.

---

[98] See Ethan Haimo, *Schoenberg's Serial Odyssey: The Evolution of his Twelve-Tone Method* (Oxford,
1990).
[99] See Peter Laki (ed.), *Bartók and his World* (Princeton, 1995), 24.
[100] Ibid. 36–7.   [101] Ibid. 50.

Berg and Webern

Of the composers who subjected tonality to the most rigorous critique in the years before 1918 none were more significant, in view of their later achievements, than two of Schoenberg's pupils, Alban Berg (1885–1935) and Anton Webern (1883–1945). The complex, often fraught relations between master and pupils offer critical biographers one of twentieth-century music's most fascinating subjects, and even the general historian cannot evade some engagement with the thorny topic of 'who influenced whom'? With some justification, not least on grounds of the extent to which he maintained links with tonality throughout his career, as well as a style that never lost its debt to Mahler, Berg may be seen as a relatively conservative figure. He was also something of a late developer, who, despite the excellent qualities of his works between the Piano Sonata Op. 1 (1907–8) and the Three Pieces for Orchestra Op. 6 (1913–14), achieved complete maturity and greatness only with the opera *Wozzeck* (1914–22), to be discussed in Chapter 9. Techniques which 'maintain links with tonality' and styles which retain a Mahlerian dimension promote a fundamental consistency of approach which, a leading authority has argued, 'transcends surface distinctions of "tonal", "atonal", and "twelve-tone" periods',[102] and the knowledge that they have become a fruitful source of inspiration for many later composers invests comments about Berg's 'late' development and 'relatively conservative' profile with a certain degree of irony.

Webern came closer than Berg to the most radical aspects of Schoenberg himself in the years 1908–9. In December 1908, after he had already been studying with Schoenberg for four years, Webern heard Debussy's *Pelléas et Mélisande* for the first time in Vienna—'very fine, very strange, in places wonderfully beautiful'[103]—and it is tempting to interpret this enthusiasm as proof of Webern's own preference for intimate, understated expression, for shunning the emphatic intensity of Strauss, Mahler, or even of Schoenberg himself, as revealed in those imposing symphonic works of the years between 1899 and 1906, *Verklärte Nacht*, *Pelleas und Melisande*, String Quartet No. 1, Chamber Symphony No. 1. That Schoenberg himself was capable of more restrained, allusive music becomes clear in his settings of Stefan George, and Webern also turned to this poet for two sets of songs which mark a break with the tonal syntax of his earlier works (up to Op. 2) if anything even more decisive than Schoenberg's. Caution is needed in making such claims, not least because the songs we know as Op. 3 and Op. 4, although composed in 1908 and 1909, were not published until 1921, and, like other early works, evidently underwent revision during that twelve-year period. One authoritative view is that 'works written on the basis of Webern's earlier, "expressionistic" aesthetic were adapted, in the process of revision, to his later

[102] Dave Headlam, *The Music of Alban Berg* (New Haven, 1996), 11.

[103] See Hans and Rosaleen Moldenhauer, *Anton von Webern: A Chronicle of his Life and Work* (London, 1978), 104. See also Kathryn Bailey, *The Life of Webern* (Cambridge, 1998).

ideal of comprehensibility . . . the philosophy that also led to Webern's adoption, in 1924, of the twelve-note technique',[104] and which involved clarifying and rein-forcing motivic connectedness in compensation for the lost, unifying power of tonality. Without pursuing the topic in depth here, it seems clear that Webern also sought to enhance the music's escape even from the kind of delicate allu-sions to tonal centrality that the final bass D of the original version of Op. 4 No. 5 provided.

Webern Analysis: No. 2 of *Five Movements* for String Quartet

Back in 1909, Webern was able to demonstrate not only his versatility, as instru-mental as well as vocal composer, but also his ability to employ up-to-date tech-nical procedures to serve a vividly characterized expression. The second of the *Five Movements* for String Quartet Op. 5 (1909) (Ex. 2.12) returns us to the world of '. . . des pas sur la neige . . .' to the extent that the form encompasses the 'journey' of a melodic line and its dialogue with accompanying material. The mood is bleak, the lament-like melody redolent of fragments of Wagner and Mahler. The occasional chords contain perceptible elements of triadic conso-nance (especially the opening and closing major sixths in the cello) and the ending takes the music as close as it can decently come to tonality in the brave new era of emancipated dissonance.

The music's radical intent is no less explicit at the outset in the way the first melodic phrase uses pitches not present in the supporting chords: and yet, although there appears to be a clear-cut opposition between the whole-tone character of the viola phrase and the semitone, A♭/A♮ clash embedded in the accompanying chord, the tendency for the music to float between opposition and convergence is indicated by the way the sonority ending the phrase in bar 2 can be derived from a symmetrical pitch-class construction—C♯, D, F, A♭, A. This symmetry foreshadows a similar entity at the end of the piece, whose outline—A, B♭, C, D♭, E♭, E—is that of a segment of an octatonic scale.

Without pursuing such microscopic analysis further, it should be clear that a full account of this composition can proceed by way of a divergence/conver-gence dialectic, as part of a more broadly based dialogue between older and newer factors: even such a detail as the brief but expressively prominent octave doubling between the violins in bar 5 comes across as an acknowledgement of 'tradition' that a more consistent radicalism, such as Webern himself soon adopted, would tend to reject. Indeed, the rapt sense of gloom inherent in this music might be as much the result of regret at what is being lost as of appre-hension in face of the unknown.

Whether or not the melancholy mood of Op. 5 No. 2 is sufficiently intense to

---

[104] Felix Meyer and Anne C. Shreffler, 'Webern's Revisions: Some Analytical Implications', *Music Analysis*, 12 (1993), 376.

Ex. 2.12. Webern, *Five Movements for String Quartet*, No. 2

merit labelling as 'expressionist', the explosive concentration of the first movement not only earns that label unambiguously, but, in the present context,
signals Webern's lack of the kind of balletic exuberance that Debussy could
evoke. Op. 5 No. 1 is of especial interest as an early example of the 'atonal sonata-
form', predicated on the attempted synthesis of forward-looking technique and
backward-looking formal model. While not seeking a modernism of stratified
textures—the reliance on imitative patterns is well-nigh 'neo-classical'—the
piece embodies strong signs of an element which such modernism would make

Ex. 2.12. (*cont.*)

its own: the fascination with mirror symmetry, a 'centre-out' strategy (such as is noted above in Op. 5 No. 2), in stark opposition to traditional 'bottom up' harmonic thinking. The throwaway final chord of this first movement (Ex. 2.13) is not only a wry allusion to conventional cadential closure, but a model of symmetrical stability. A rationale for the chord's notes can certainly be found, yet it is the structure of the sonority that matters most. Even the most expressionistic modernism is unlikely to reject all balance, all coherence.

Busoni

Of all the composers considered in this chapter, Ferruccio Busoni (1866–1924) is the least likely to be granted the accolade of 'first-rate' by a wide cross-section of music-lovers and commentators. He nevertheless provides a useful focus for

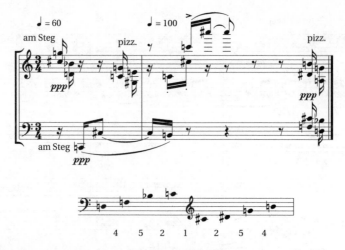

Ex. 2.13. Webern, *Five Movements for String Quartet*, No. 1, ending

the general sense of transition from old to new that was such a fundamental factor in music between 1900 and 1918. Busoni was active in many different musical worlds—as performer and writer (his *Sketch of a New Aesthetic of Music* was published in 1907) as well as composer, although, as Chapter 4 will argue, his finest composition came after 1918, in the unfinished opera *Doktor Faust*. His earlier work is perhaps most interesting for the ambivalence of its progressiveness, for demonstrating a sense of unease about the need to strike out on new paths which has remained a persistent twentieth-century trait. While the *Elegies* for piano (1907) indicate a modernistic tendency to exploit the juxtaposition of strongly contrasted materials, and to resist the stabilizing qualities of a fully orthodox tonality, they show little relish for expressionism. Busoni was less concerned to 'deconstruct' late romanticism through intensification than to counter it with a new anti-programmatic classicism rooted in Bach's tonal counterpoint and Mozart's melodic writing, something very different from the more confrontational and abrasive kind of neo-classicism that Stravinsky and his followers would exploit.[105]

As a young, radical pupil, Edgard Varèse was

surprised to find his [Busoni's] musical tastes and his own music so orthodox. . . . He could never understand how most of the works of such a master as Mozart, his favourite composer, could bore me. . . . But it was also Busoni who wrote: 'The function of the creative artist consists in making laws, not in following those already made'.[106]

[105] See Jim Samson, *Music in Transition: A Study of Tonal Expansion and Atonality, 1900–1920* (London, 1977; repr. Oxford 1993), 19–31.

[106] Louise Varèse, *Varèse: A Looking-Glass Diary* (London, 1975), 49.

Busoni's creative path was nevertheless far from predictable: his great classicizing initiative, the *Fantasia contrappuntistica* for piano (1910, rev. 1912) preceded the more radical harmonic explorations of the Sonatina No. 2 and the *Nocturne symphonique* (both 1912). It might even appear that his floating of experimental ideas in his book—about the possibility of using microtones, for example—was a way of underlining their speculative rather than practicable status. That such developments have become an accepted part of later twentieth-century compositional vocabularies serves to underline the fact that all radical technical innovations create anxiety as well as excitement. The story of twentieth-century music concerns the consequences of both states of mind.

The main part of this chapter looks in detail at three composers, born between 1865 and 1872, who wrote symphonies after 1918. Carl Nielsen (1865–1931), Jean Sibelius (1865–1957) and Ralph Vaughan Williams (1872–1958) were, in various productive respects, independent of the German late romantic symphonic mainstream, culminating in Mahler. Of the three, Sibelius may well prove to have had the most far-reaching impact, if only because more recent symphonists, from Vagn Holmboe to Peter Maxwell Davies, have revealed specific debts to him, but the fact that the symphonic principle itself (usually, if not invariably, in connection with some kind of tonality) has been reaffirmed and reinvigorated in the century's later years lends new significance to the achievements of all three composers considered here.

Nielsen

The relationship of Nielsen and Sibelius to the German symphonic tradition has been well described by Robert Simpson, whose own symphonic compositions, discussed in Chapter 16, owe much to both of them.

Nielsen, with his origins in Beethoven and Brahms, and Sibelius, with his in Beethoven and the Russian symphonists (with increasing awareness of Beethoven as he developed), together form an antithesis to the southern German-Bohemian, post-Schubertian-Wagnerian, completely romantic world of Mahler and Strauss. . . . What they shared was a common ideal, a desire for discipline and forceful economy achieved without sacrificing warmth of expression.[1]

In Sibelius this ideal found its most radical outlet in the Symphony No. 4 (1911),[2] which prefigured the special concentration and intensity of the last three symphonies and *Tapiola*. Nielsen's progress was less assured, his achievement more uneven in quality, but his Symphony No. 5 (1921–2) is one of the century's undoubted masterpieces.

This symphony was the first since No. 1 (1890–2) to which the composer did not give a general descriptive title, but it had its origins in preoccupations which were far from abstract. Its predecessor, the Symphony No. 4, *The Inextinguish-*

---

[1] Robert Simpson, *Sibelius and Nielsen, a Centenary Essay* (London, 1965), 4, 6.
[2] See Ch. 2, p. 30.

able (1916), ends in a mood of triumphant optimism. Six years later, Nielsen was 'a man torn between his need for peaceful security and a real-life situation which seemed to offer anything but that',[3] with problems in his personal life as well as the feeling that 'the whole world is in dissolution' in the aftermath of the war.[4] The two-movement form of the Fifth Symphony was the outcome of Nielsen's increasing scepticism about the viability of the traditional four-movement design, a scheme which offered the clearest sense of fundamental contrast between poles:

if the first movement was passivity, here [in the second] it is action (or activity) which is conveyed. So it's something very primitive I wanted to express; the division of dark and light, the battle between evil and good. A title like 'Dreams and Deeds' could maybe sum up the inner picture I had in front of my eyes when composing.[5]

However 'primitive' the musical expression, in Nielsen's terms, the Symphony No. 5 is a work of considerable originality and sophistication. Because neither movement can be neatly aligned with classical formal precedents like sonata or rondo, analysts tend to refer to their sectional divisions, with the first movement having eight (tempo giusto) and four (adagio) sections, and the second movement four (allegro, presto fugue, andante fugue, recapitulation of the allegro).[6] This sense of form as sectional succession, with no single, all-embracing structural span—even in the second movement, the two fugues which separate 'exposition' and ' recapitulation' are far more independent in character and content than a traditional 'development' section—is naturally reflected in tonal organization. While it is true that 'every stage in [the symphony's] unfolding drama is absorbed into the hierarchic language of tonal harmony',[7] it is no less true that every stage of that drama has its own hierarchy, its own distinctive tonal orientation. The hierarchies themselves are connected, of course, but this is not a symphony whose movements compose out single background structures, after the classical model, and to this extent the judgement of Per Nørgård 'identifying a confrontation between the principles of organic growth and absolute contrast'[8] goes to the heart of the matter.

As with many twentieth-century tonal masterworks, ambiguity plays a crucial role on every level, from the large-scale structural exploitation of balance between wide-ranging changes of musical character and the continuous development of basic motives, to the small-scale but equally basic employment of chromaticism as a normative element, the appearance of pure diatonicism having a distinctly 'unreal' quality as a result. Traditional thematic procedures— the return of initially stated ideas, not just their constant transformation— are most apparent in the second movement: the elements of traditionally functional harmony are pervasive, but Nielsen exploits the creation, frustration, or

[3] David Fanning, *Nielsen: Symphony No. 5* (Cambridge, 1997), 14.
[4] Ibid., citing a letter of 27 Oct. 1914.
[5] Ibid. 13.   [6] Ibid. 16.   [7] Ibid. 43.   [8] Ibid. 44.

fulfilment of expectations with undeniable genius. Since the main thematic elements are of the simplest kind, their changes of character tend to be easily perceptible, and even without that sense of perfect pitch which would enable a listener to identify the precise nature of the progressive tonal processes involved, it is impossible not to respond to the drama of the way in which such changes of tonal area are paralleled by strongly defined stages in the thematic process.

In the broadest terms, the 'programme' of the symphony involves a progression from uncertainty to security, from apprehensiveness to joyful exuberance, which is attempted, and frustrated, in the first movement; then asserted, challenged, and ultimately reinforced in the second. Every listener is likely to interpret the different stages of this process, and to identify the points at which changes begin or end, in different ways. In the context of the present discussion, it is less important to attempt to provide an accurate, detailed, emotional map of the work than to establish that its essential emotional progression is achieved by the consistent use of a particular musical language: indeed, the success of the work lies in the adaptability, as well as the coherence of that language. A comparison of the beginning and ending of the symphony is fruitful here. Initially, there seems to be total contrast, not merely of mood and tonality but of language itself. At the start (Ex. 3.1) there is no key signature, Nielsen having 'toyed with, but then suppressed, a one-flat key-signature',[9] and for several bars the key in use could be C major, A minor, D minor, or F major. By contrast, the tonality at the end (Ex. 3.2) is an unmistakable E♭ major, affirmed not simply by the key signature and the final five-bar tonic chord, but also prepared by a thrilling dominant pedal.

The ambiguity at the opening is sustained until bar 13, when the two bassoons begin to give greater emphasis to F and C than to any other notes, thereby making F major the most likely key. Yet even though the F and C, in alliance with the A of the viola accompaniment, complete a tonic triad, the language is emphatically more chromatic than diatonic, more ambiguous than explicit, especially with reference to that all-important cadential definer of diatonicism, the leading note. Nielsen, like both Sibelius and Vaughan Williams, showed supreme skill in using the avoidance of the conventional leading note as a means of achieving the most productive tension between a chromatic foreground and a diatonic background. Only rarely does such a technique enable one to describe the music as modal, at least as far as the sole involvement of the old church modes like the Dorian or Phrygian are concerned; conventional hierarchical relationships may no longer obtain, either, but there is still an overall tonic or tonal centre to which all but the most uncompromisingly chromatic episodes refer. The specific point about the altered leading note is so important because, whereas at the very start of the symphony it leads to the most gripping kind of ambiguity—is the C in the violas the altered leading note of D minor?—at the

[9] Fanning, *Nielsen*, 19.

Ex. 3.1. Nielsen, Symphony No. 5, 1st movt., bars 1–16

end it contributes to the affirmation of E♭ major. From Fig. 114 to within five bars of the end, the cadential harmony involves D♭ not D♮; the crucial chromatic feature of the entire symphony is therefore not eliminated but absorbed, a positive effect of colour rather than, as at the beginning, a force ensuring tonal ambiguity (Ex. 3.2).

This is Nielsen's most powerful technique: the harnessing and directing of forces which at first create ambiguity, until they become agents of resolution. It would be possible to undertake a rewarding but gigantic analysis of this symphony and consider the way in which every degree of ambiguity pertaining to every single note was incorporated into a coherent overall scheme—how a note may be a tonic of one key or the dominant or subdominant of another, culminating in its potential chromatic function as an altered leading note or in some still more disruptive role. Yet of even greater structural importance is the

Ex. 3.2. Nielsen, Symphony No. 5, 2nd movt., Fig. 114 to the end

way in which the more fundamental background shifts of tonality are organized. 'Shifts' is the crucial word, for there is very little stability in this work: chromaticism within keys and modulation between keys dominate the action and the intensity of the expression ensures an inexorably logical motion. For all the shifts of perspective, this background never totally disappears: yet, as noted above, form on the large scale is a matter of succession, the kind of progression that matches the overall tonal journey to an E♭ major which, as Fanning puts it, 'is pulled out of the hat rather than regained'.[10]

In the the broadest sense, the two main parts of the first movement advance from F major to C major and on to G major, a process involving three similarly related areas:

F   C   G
subdominant ⟶ tonic
                subdominant ⟶ tonic

Such is the 'programme' of the movement, however, that not merely is G the most firmly established of the three, but the mood of its music casts it more as an *opponent* of F and C than as a relative. The comparative stability of G is no more a matter of the avoidance of all chromatic inflection than is that of E♭ major at the end of the second movement, however. Stability is ensured principally by pedals in the bass, and the central conflict of forces is therefore appropriately launched when a dominant pedal in G major with a *stretto* above it (conventionally the means of preparing a final enhanced assertion of the tonic triad) is assailed by disruptive material from earlier in the movement, the very first statement of which (woodwind six bars after Fig. 31) has cancelled G major's F♯ leading note in favour of the more ambiguous F♮. A less subtle composer might have allowed his taste for naive symbolism to lead at this point not only to the rapid erosion of all tonal stability, but to an even more desolate recapitulation of the opening material. Nielsen's purpose is very different, and reinforces the primacy of evolutionary factors in the work's form. After one of the most thrilling battles in all music, in which the dominant pedal is supported for much of the time by a subdominant one as well, a triumphant resolution on to the tonic triad of G major takes place (Fig. 37). As the climax subsides, however, the music begins to display all the signs of exhaustion, of losing the will to survive. It is not just the continued presence of F naturals in the woodwind figure (five bars after Fig. 37), nor the expiring flutters of the aggressive side-drum figure which assist this rapid decline, but also the way the final clarinet cadenza seductively transforms material which, in the violas six bars after Fig. 3, was one of the earliest signs of menace in the first part of the movement.

This coda, for all its gravity, indicates that the issue is unresolved: the serene music cannot itself eliminate all trace of the initial inertia, and it survives attack only to lose its own positive strength and drive. In this respect it may be significant that there has been no further progress along a purely tonal path. One might, for example, expect the second half of the first movement to have moved on from G major to D major, but, while D is indeed the last note of the final clarinet melody, it still functions as the dominant of G major. The chain has been broken, but a particular stage has been reached which is a whole tone above that

---

[10] Fanning, *Nielsen*, 77.

from which the symphony began. The second movement is to end in the tonal area a whole tone *below* that in which the symphony began, and the change of direction is achieved with the elimination of inertia by energy. Yet anticipations of an even more basic tonal scheme than any hitherto discussed, involving such a symmetrical element—

$$\text{1st movement} \quad \downarrow \quad \text{2nd movement}$$
$$G \longleftarrow\! \quad F \quad \longrightarrow E\flat$$

—are frustrated by the simple fact that the finale begins, not in F, but with strong suggestions of the key as far away from F as possible: B major. There is some evidence of the working of a symmetrical element in the first movement, in the long passage between the two main parts (Figs. 24 to 25 + 15 bars), when 'negative' F is finally induced to yield to 'positive' G by the emphasis on A♭ and D, the notes a minor third either side of F itself. This process of exorcism or neutralization cannot be considered purely in terms of symmetrical elements, however, for D obviously has an even more pressing function here as the dominant of G. Nor are the parallels between the two movements of the work symmetrically exact. The first movement begins indecisively in a grey key area, the second decisively in a bright area, its main internal contrasts involving darker keys and both faster and slower tempi (the first movement has only the basic tempo change from 'tempo giusto' to 'adagio non troppo'). The second movement undoubtedly presents the same basic conflict as the first, but the perspective is different, the outcome is different, and so—in a highly significant way—is the tonal scheme. Even though the early stages of the movement rapidly invert the ascending fifths scheme, to move down from B to E then down again to A, the sheer rapidity with which this occurs is a clear indication that a more elaborate process is now being prepared. If the conflict between inertia and energy is to be positively resolved, the fierce confidence of the second movement's opening stages must be challenged and tested, and the diatonic clarity, with its almost mocking reversal of the first movement's hard-won progress, must be blurred by that more expressive and characteristic chromaticism which was Nielsen's most potent linguistic device (it will be noted that the A♯ leading note of B major yields to A♮ when the movement is only eleven bars old and that there has been a three-sharp key signature from the beginning). Nielsen dramatizes the challenge and the conflict by undermining both the movement's dynamic momentum and its tonal confidence. After an exciting, unsuccessful attempt to recapture the initial B major (Fig. 60 ff.), the key feeling blurs and darkens, and the recall of the eerie alternations between D and A♭ which had separated the two parts of the first movement similarly serve here (Fig. 67) not to press the claims of either key but to force a decisive change of mood as the only escape from the inertia of rhythmic stasis and tonal confusion.

In the first movement, the A♭ and D neutralized the already negative F, and the D was carried over into the next stage as dominant of G major. But A♭ and D also enclose B♮, and it is this crucial tonal plateau which is neutralized at Fig. 67 in the second movement. Now it is the A♭ (not the D) which achieves functional status with the establishment of F minor as the new key, and of a mood, as different as possible from the serene calm of the first movement's G major, which turns out to be energetic in the wrong way. The Presto fugue (Fig. 71), for all its hectic contrapuntal ingenuity, is too panic-stricken to achieve a genuine resolution: its climaxes lead only to disintegration, a new decline into exhaustion in which F minor is clouded but still not completely relinquished. It is now evident that a positive change of key—and, perhaps, insurance against the potential return of first-movement characteristics—can only be achieved with an extreme change, not of form but of mood. So a second fugue (Andante un poco tranquillo, Fig. 92), less self-confident than the G major counterpoint of the first movement but for that very reason more fully integrated into the entire expressive fabric of the work, begins what proves to be the final climb out of conflict. This fugue also shows that F is no longer merely a negative hindrance to the work's eventual fulfilment, but an element which must be transfigured rather than eliminated. Even when the B-centred opening music of the finale returns (Fig. 99) to initiate a compressed recapitulation, it is soon diverted from its original path through the sharp keys, so that a final scheme of descending perfect fifths can function, starting with the F of the fugues, then moving to B♭ as dominant of the concluding E♭. This is indeed the tritonal 'answer' to the finale's initial B–E–A, the resolution of the first movement's inconclusive F–C–G: the tonal scheme of the finale is a triumphant rethinking of the principles that governed the 'unsuccessful' first movement.

Nielsen's genius lies in shedding new light on, and extracting new dramatic purpose from, the simple idea of a difference between subdominant relatives and dominant relatives. The descending fifths of the second movement—each tonic also a dominant of the next tonic—succeed where the ascending fifths— the subdominant relatives—of the first movement fail. In these admittedly basic terms, the supreme, strategic moment of unification and transformation comes at Fig. 110, where the alternations of woodwind and strings over the E♭ major dominant pedal recall the similar moment of crisis in the first movement (Fig. 33). There a resolution was achieved only to turn to ashes: now there can be no question of frustrating the victorious assertions of E♭. It is not merely the last lap of a long journey, but a totally convincing conclusion to the arguments which that journey has created.

Sibelius

Although Nielsen composed several significant works after the Fifth Symphony—in particular, the strongly dramatic Clarinet Concerto (1928)—he did not surpass the symphony's superbly sustained balance between expressive intensity and expansive form. With Sibelius, likewise, an element of retreat from the epic concerns of his Fifth Symphony[11] can be detected in all his subsequent works. Such concerns are not completely absent, but they are explored with even greater concentration of form and through material the more eloquent for its extreme economy. After the prolonged struggles with the Fifth there came a five-year period of virtual silence, and the Sixth Symphony (1923) is still sometimes characterized as a gentle, unassuming piece, a reaction against the grandeur and drama of its mighty predecessor. Regression of a kind might be inferred from the reversion to a four-movement pattern, and the use in the first three movements of flexibly adapted sonata-form schemes. Yet the dramatic tensions which justify the use of such schemes arise from a supremely skilful deployment of a harmonic language of the greatest refinement and sophistication, in which chromaticism functions with a dramatic force as great as that found in the broader paragraphs of Nielsen's Fifth. The texture is a marvellously fluent blend of contrapuntal and harmonic events, but the nature of those events, and of the way they evolve, is governed by Sibelius's sovereign feeling for purposeful ambiguity.

The most fertile tension in the Symphony No. 6 is between the diatonic tonality of D minor and the Dorian mode on D. Yet this is just the first stage in a whole network of relationships which expands to embrace F major, C major, G minor and B♭ minor, with their capacity for degrees of diatonic or modal interdependence. This is, in fact, the symphony *par excellence* about tonality, but it never becomes merely an intellectual exercise; indeed, the third movement is one of the wittiest in the entire symphonic repertoire, with canons which seem to mock the contrapuntal earnestness of other parts of the work. Expressive impulse and technical process go hand in hand. For example, the first movement begins with gently interacting polyphonic lines using only 'white-note' material: these gradually achieve greater homophonic solidity and chromatic ambiguity, culminating in a chord which might be expected to resolve into D or G, but which is startlingly underpinned by a C♮, and so is directed towards C major: when first heard in bars 17 and 18 of the movement, this chord had resolved smoothly on to a triad of D minor, and so this new event is both structurally significant and expressively potent. Another telling effect occurs at the climax of the finale, where a treble *forte* assertion of B minor is diverted with superfine dexterity on to the tonic second inversion of D minor (Ex. 3.3).

Such instances could be multiplied, especially those involving a rapid return to the principal tonal area from some remote point, and they indicate a further facet of the interaction between freedom and constraint which Veijo Murtomäki connects to 'the surprising paradox about Sibelius's late works'[12]—the fact that 'he achieved an organic way of developing material and an apparently fantasia-like form' while at the same time approaching 'a new kind of classicism, a

[11] See Ch. 2, pp. 31–2.
[12] Veijo Murtomäki, *Symphonic Unity: The Development of Formal Thinking in the Symphonies of Sibelius* (Helsinki, 1993), 241.

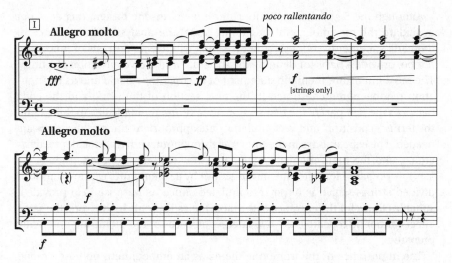

Ex. 3.3. Sibelius, Symphony No. 6, 4th movt., eight bars from letter I

compressed and an abstracted musical thinking'. The sense in which the 'greatness' of the Symphony No. 6 is 'more covert and enigmatic'[13] than that of its
predecessors derives in part from its consistently subtle interplay between diatonicism and modality, and from the circumstance in which, despite 'the
relatively free applications of traditional forms . . . the movements are linked
with one another in a remarkably coherent way'.[14] This enigmatic greatness was
even more richly explored in the single-movement Symphony No. 7 in C major,
completed in 1924.

The prevailing consensus among the many commentators on Sibelius's last
symphony, which at one stage was called 'Fantasia sinfonica', is that 'it is not a
gigantic movement in sonata form nor several movements put together into a
single movement in the manner of Liszt's B minor Sonata. It is something new
and revolutionary in the history of symphony.'[15] For that very reason, opinions
about how its 'new and revolutionary' form is best described vary greatly,
depending on the extent to which the commentator in question seeks to underline unity or variety, organic connectedness or fantasia-like contingency,
thematic flexibility or harmonic stability. Wisely seeking to acknowledge the role
of all these factors, Murtomäki concludes that because the structure includes
only a few 'strong cadences'[16] it is highly unified: and yet that unity serves a form
that is 'equivocal',[17] in the sense that it positively invites different interpretations
and resists (in what we might interpret as the symphony's only concession to a
modernist ethos) the strait-jacket of a single, 'correct' identity.

---

[13] Murtomäki, *Symphonic Unity*, 193.   [14] Ibid. 241, 240.
[15] Ibid. 243.   [16] Ibid. 278.   [17] Ibid. 280.

Although the Seventh is not a four-movements-in-one design, this does not invalidate the terminology of traditional structural analysis. The presence of thematic statements and restatements, along with clear contrasts of mood and tempo, provide a basis for defining the structure as the diversification of a unity. The most important thematic statement of the opening Adagio and its continuation reappears reorchestrated in the final section of the work, and the coda balances the first part of the first section, tonally and thematically. To this extent, the terms 'exposition' and 'recapitulation' are appropriate, but qualifications are needed. The exposition is in the tonic key throughout, with only incidental deviations, and the main thematic statement (the awesome trombone theme, Ex. 3.4(i)) is prepared for (after the introduction) by a solemn procession mainly for divided strings which is never recapitulated. Since its purpose is to provide a suitable climax for the entrance of the most majestic theme in the work, the same effect cannot be repeated: the two later recurrences of the theme are differently prepared.

The importance of the trombone theme as an embodiment both of a mood and of a tonality is reinforced by its appearance at the centre of the symphony, still in the trombone but in the tonic minor and with a less obviously heroic character (Ex. 3.4 (ii)). If this is felt to constitute *development* of the theme, then the central segment of the overall sonata scheme can be added, and we can view the work as comprising a single sonata-form design with other elements separating and linking the three basic sections. Sibelius may very well have had some such intention at one stage, but his 'exposition', 'development' and 'recapitulation' are

Ex. 3.4. Sibelius, Symphony No. 7: (i) first appearance of the trombone theme, bars 59–69; (ii) second appearance of trombone theme, bars 221–36

not sufficiently conventional to suggest that they have done more than provide a background principle to be greatly modified in practice. On grounds of tonality alone, the very strong emphasis on a single key suggests rondo rather than sonata, and may indeed be a relic of Sibelius's intention to compose a 'Hellenic' rondo as the finale of a three-movement scheme. So rather than over-categorize, it is surely sufficient to note the unifying function of the first and third statements of the trombone theme, while recognizing that the second statement confirms the thematic unity and also reflects an important stage in the emotional progress of the symphony.

Development can most obviously be found after the first statement of the trombone theme has run its course, and discussion of the ascending scale and other motives from the introduction gradually evolves towards a less explicit reliance on C and a much faster tempo. No sooner is this scherzo-like liberation achieved, however (Vivacissimo), than Sibelius begins to prepare the return both of C (though minor) and of the trombone theme. This passage is a particularly subtle example of Sibelius's mixing of formal functions. The Vivacissimo has the potential to become an independent scherzo section, its material derived from that of the earlier exposition but its tonality distinct (G♯ minor perhaps). Yet no sooner is it launched than its more urgent function is revealed: not to reinforce a new mood, but marking, as it begins, the most distant remove reached from basic mood, key and material so far, to prepare for the early return of more fundamental elements. The return will not be 'complete'—of course: it is too soon for that—and at the very end of the C minor statement of the trombone theme, the music throws out an emphatic reminiscence of the Vivacissimo idea, bending the harmony briefly towards a surprising E major.

So far the work has revealed two basic levels, the 'slow' (introduction and trombone theme; central recurrence of trombone theme; recapitulation of trombone theme and coda) and the 'fast' (the abortive 'scherzo', which is paralleled by the Vivace section heard immediately before the build-up to the final return of the trombone theme). With transitions mediating between these extremes we seem to have a near-symmetrical arch form.[18] Yet one section of the work remains unaccounted for: the extended Allegro molto moderato, which follows on from the C minor trombone statement, and which is itself ternary with an introduction! Many commentators have shown how the material of this section derives from previously stated motives. But what is its structural and tonal function? An obvious effect is to prevent the form from falling into 'predictable' symmetry. Yet at the same time the music seems to mediate between the extremes of tempo and mood which the 'arch-form' elements propose. If mediation is one factor, postponement is another, for the interpolation performs a function not dissimilar to that of the non-recurring central part of the

[18] Murtomäki, *Symphonic Unity*, 279–80, and Tim Howell, 'Sibelius Studies and Notions of Expertise', *Music Analysis*, 14 (1995), 331–6.

'exposition' in ensuring that a statement (the last in this case) of the main theme of the whole work is placed in the most telling and satisfying position.

Tonally, the function of the Allegro molto moderato is equally essential to the dramatic yet organic unpredictability of the structure. It restores a pristine C major to counter the *Sturm und Drang* of the central, minor-mode trombone statement and its hectic but transitional aftermath. Yet its own middle section recalls that aftermath, and the tonality darkens, so that the main material returns in a diatonic E♭ major. Thus the 'episode' does not merely postpone the clinching return of the main theme, but prepares the ground for the most dramatic tonal event of the entire symphony: the recovery of C after its displacement by E♭, a situation prefigured but not fully realized by the first 'scherzo' and central trombone statement. This new function ensures that the second scherzo is no carbon copy of the first, but a still more urgent search for the stability necessary to end the symphony.

Tapiola (1925), a tone poem inspired by the landscape and legends of the far north, was Sibelius's last important work. We have no evidence that he intended it as a disguised Eighth Symphony, yet it is difficult not to see it as the final stage in a process of symphonic compression. In the Seventh Symphony, strong contrast had a positive role to play: *Tapiola* tends to concentrate on different aspects of a single idea. Hence the feeling that there is no genuine symphonic progress through argument to resolution but, instead, the exploration of a landscape seen in a single frozen moment: a painting. *Tapiola* raises the paradox of time and timelessness far more acutely than many more radical works which contrast measured and unmeasured material. But whether or not the differences between it and the Seventh Symphony are definable as the differences between non-symphony and symphony, the sheer severity of its design makes it easy to accept as a last word.

Sibelius's long silence after *Tapiola*—an Eighth Symphony and other scores were, apparently, destroyed—was a tragedy, both for the composer himself and for modern tonal music. Yet the originality and refinement of his progression from the Symphony No. 1 to *Tapiola* is such that it is difficult to imagine how their creator could have continued along a path of further concentration and exploration. Perhaps if the late works had been less successful he would have written more: in which case, it was not self-criticism but self-awareness which led to thirty years of silence.

Vaughan Williams

Ralph Vaughan Williams made a much slower start than Sibelius. If he had stopped composing at the age of 60 in 1932 his very finest works would not exist, and it was only after 1915 that he began the series of seven symphonies (Nos. 3–9) which, while less innovatory in purely structural terms than the later Nielsen and

Sibelius, have roots in a language in which a modality and thematic character closely related to folk music were brought into fruitful confrontation with the much more disruptive resources of modern tonal chromaticism. Vaughan Williams's four best symphonies—Nos. 3–6—seem to invite discussion as two pairs, Nos. 3 and 5 being essentially pastoral and reflective, Nos. 4 and 6 tougher and more active. Yet this parallel soon breaks down when matters of technique are considered. For example, No. 3 ends by moving away from the principal tonal centre of the work, while No. 5—in many ways just as subtle an example of the propulsive ambiguity of diatonic and modal interactions—affirms the purest tonic harmony in its final bars. No. 4 ends vehemently with a chromatically spiced but uncompromising cadence in the principal key of F minor: the conclusion of No. 6 could not be more different—unless it were demonstrably atonal—since the passive, eerie alternations of E♭ major and E minor triads, both in second inversion, serve less to establish the ultimate primacy of E minor as tonic for the whole work than to confirm that the symphony has been fundamentally and persistently concerned with the undermining of keys by those a semitone or a tritone distant. Since all four symphonies are in four movements it is certainly instructive to compare them purely at the structural level; but useful though it may be to discover what, for example, the relative proportions allotted to development sections or second subject-groups may be, there is still greater value in attempting to identify the workings of the musical language which brings the forms to life.

As far as the Symphony No. 3 (the *Pastoral*, completed in 1921) is concerned, the relationship between reflectiveness of mood and ambiguity of language is strikingly close. What might have been a symphony in G major—or in G minor, or even in the Mixolydian or transposed Dorian modes—becomes a symphony about what happens to G as a tonic when a wide variety of pressures—diatonic, chromatic, modal—are applied to it. The use of flowing rhythms, lyric thematic ideas, and the major or minor triad as principal harmonic unit ensures that the tensions which this language generates rarely become overt. Indeed, a better sense of focus is found in later symphonies, where there is a more effective balance between drama and lyricism, and a genuine opposition is suggested between cycle-of-fifths hierarchies and other forces.

The Symphony No. 4 (1934) is a fine example of economically organized form, vividly unified thematic process and tautly controlled chromatic harmony. The Symphony No. 5 (1943) is again more lyrical, but this does not invalidate a truly dramatic tonal scheme in which the modally oriented ambiguities of the first movement are recalled and diatonically dissolved in the serene coda of the finale.[19] Yet it is the Symphony No. 6 (1947) which, of all the nine, deserves the closest study: it is the nearest Vaughan Williams came to Sibelian concentration,

[19] See Arnold Whittall, ' "Symphony in D major": Models and Mutations', in Alain Frogley (ed.), *Vaughan Williams Studies* (Cambridge, 1996), 187–212.

for although only the most basic sustained notes link the four movements—Allegro, Moderato, Scherzo (Allegro vivace) and Epilogue (Moderato)—there is an undeniable sense of continued consideration of the same essential issue throughout. Since that issue, in its simplest form, is the clashing semitone, the Sixth Symphony might even be regarded as a further essay on the subject-matter of the Fourth: after all, such a subject is of inexhaustible interest to a modern composer committed to tonality but acutely conscious of the factors which most insidiously call it into question.

The purely thematic unity of the work is prominent, and an important contributory factor to the general sense of concentrated processes at work. Even when contrast of mood is almost total, as with the cantabile second subject of the first movement, there are motivic connections with first-subject material. Yet the greater the underlying thematic connections, the more important a purely tonal conflict between opposites and alternatives becomes. In the first movement this involves not only E major and E minor, but F minor and E minor, C minor and B minor, Bb minor and B minor. What might potentially be a straightforward, traditional scheme of E minor–B minor–E major is complicated by the tendency of tonic and dominant to be shadowed by keys a semitone away. Moreover, when the mediant achieves prominence at an early stage (Fig. 4), it is not as G major but minor, whose own mediant, Bb, is to play a crucial role later in the work.

No sooner has the first movement countered its brief, confident assertion of E major with E minor, than the triad as such vanishes and a single E is left to die away against the Bb with which trumpets launch the second movement (Ex. 3.5). The tritonal opposition is expressed through a theme which constantly pits major and minor seconds against the Bb, and although the F minor–E minor argument is referred to during the course of the movement, the Bb, reiterated relentlessly in the later stages, provokes despairing assent from the rest of the orchestra in one of Vaughan Williams's most hard-hitting climaxes. The price of assent seems to be the avoidance of a root position triad of Bb minor, however; instead, first inversions of G minor and Gb major bring the semitonal opposition into the foreground of the argument again. At the end of the movement this has shifted to the even more basic level of Bb/Cb [B], and it is one of the roles of the Scherzo to carry the harmonic/tonal argument into an entirely new area. Its contrapuntal texture involves entries of the tritone-generated theme a perfect fifth apart, thus increasing the structural significance of the conflict between semitones at a critical stage. The underlying tonal argument is thereby sustained and intensified, especially when C minor, a potential bridge to the 'real' dominant, B, achieves prominence in the 'trio' (Fig. 16). With the return of the Scherzo, however, any progress towards a resolution is halted by the welter of imitative entries of a theme which contains so much contradiction within itself that even triadic harmony is scarcely possible in such a context. The return of the trio theme as a barbaric march (Fig. 39) halts the atonal drift by focusing on a

Ex. 3.5. Vaughan Williams, Symphony No. 6, end of 1st movt., beginning of 2nd movt.

persistent if unstable A♭, but in a chilly transition the tritonal material returns again, to be finally summarized by a bass-clarinet line descending over two octaves from F to E.

The knowledge that Vaughan Williams connected the finale of the Sixth Symphony with the speech from *The Tempest* ending 'We are such stuff as dreams are made on; and our little life is rounded with a sleep,'[20] is still no preparation for the extreme, anti-romantic bleakness of this Epilogue. It is not so much an image of death as of life laid waste. The analogies with post-nuclear landscapes are as apt here as with Varèse's slightly later *Déserts*. Yet even if the music is a suppressed *cri de cœur*, its organization is strictly disciplined. The threads are gathered together, as the semitones and tritones of the opening idea demonstrate. When the tonic E is at all firmly emphasized, however, it is in a stifled Phrygian cadence and on an icy minor ninth chord. Only at the very end does the return of pure triads crystallize around the G♮ of the first violins. Clashes have become oscillations, and although there is still enough 'function' left in the D♯ of the penultimate chord for us to sense a resolution from something subordinate on to something basic, the absence of root position and more decisive rhythmic treatment ensures little sense of true finality. We are at the opposite pole from

---

[20] Michael Kennedy, *The Works of Ralph Vaughan Williams* (Oxford, 1971), 302.

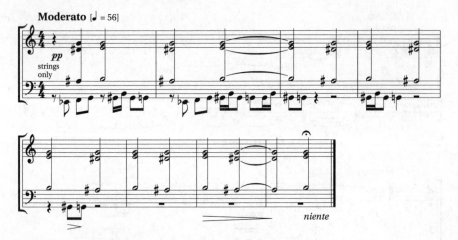

Ex. 3.6. Vaughan Williams, Symphony No. 6, 4th movt., ending

where we began: the cataclysm which launched the argument has been exhausted. The argument itself is unresolved (Ex. 3.6).

The Sixth Symphony marked the end of an important phase in Vaughan Williams's creative life, a phase which produced his finest and most appealing music. To some extent, it was a phase of unresolved alternatives, so that it is possible to argue that the Fifth and Sixth Symphonies belong to quite different, even mutually exclusive worlds of feeling, which were only integrated in the last three symphonies.[21] These are an old man's music and are likely to grip the listener less forcefully than their predecessors. They are by no means negligible, but they seem at times to be repeating well-tried effects. However, there can be no doubt that Vaughan Williams was a symphonist of exceptional individuality and skill, matched by none of his British contemporaries. The most productive symphonists among them, Havergal Brian (1876–1972), Arnold Bax (1883–1953), and Edmund Rubbra (1901–86), all have their passionate partisans, but even when they have received their due from posterity it seems unlikely that Vaughan Williams will suffer in comparison. Moreover, the healthy state in which he left the genre is indicated by the strength and variety of his British symphonist successors, who include Malcolm Arnold, Michael Tippett, Robert Simpson, and Peter Maxwell Davies.

Vaughan Williams's greatest British near-contemporary was Gustav Holst

---

[21] See Hugh Ottaway, *Vaughan Williams Symphonies* (London, 1972), 59. For further discussion of aspects of allusion and interdependence in these works, see Oliver Neighbour, 'The Place of the Eighth among Vaughan Williams's Symphonies', in A. Frogley (ed.), *Vaughan Williams Studies* (Cambridge, 1996), 213–33.

(1874–1934), who would probably be ranked much higher if he had found accepted forms more attractive and relatively radical harmonic devices less appealing. Even so, the superb tone poem *Egdon Heath* (1928) is by no means unsymphonic in form and method, and it is tragic that Holst did not live to finish the symphony for which a Scherzo was completed in 1933. Vaughan Williams's debt to Holst was deep. Even the Ninth Symphony originally had a programmatic idea centring to some extent on the world of Thomas Hardy which *Egdon Heath* so memorably portrays.[22] In his old age, one of the finest of all twentieth-century symphonists was still finding inspiration in the landscape of the country whose most personal and primitive forms of musical expression he had done more than anyone to integrate into the mainstream of modern musical development.

Roussel, Ravel

In France there was no symphonist of the stature of Nielsen, Sibelius or Vaughan Williams, and the concern of Albert Roussel (1869–1937) for continuing the symphonic tradition can be used as evidence that even his best work displays 'more sense than sensibility, more integrity than imagination'.[23] Roussel's best works are the songs and ballets (notably *Bacchus et Ariane*, Op. 43, 1930) and the short descriptive pieces and choral compositions, like Psalm 80, Op. 37 (1928). The three symphonies which he composed between 1919 and 1934 still merit study, however, if only to demonstrate the kind of problems facing a composer who was no structural innovator, and who did not want to compose wholeheartedly neo-classical (or anti-romantic) symphonic works. In the Symphony No. 2 in Bb (1919–21), the last of the three movements is the least conventional in form, but at the same time it unifies the work by developing first-movement material. The Third Symphony in G minor followed in 1929–30, but structural problems here are if anything more pronounced than in the earlier work. In particular, the design of the opening Allegro vivo is flawed by a second subject which does not balance the main tonality clearly enough and at the same time seems too detached from the mainstream of the movement as a whole. Such dangerous diversity of material also weakens the finale.

One diagnosis of Roussel's difficulties sees him as attempting to extricate himself from the influence of Prokofiev's style—especially his ballets *Chout* and *Le Pas d'acier*—and David Drew, whose convincing thesis this is, examines the Fourth Symphony in A major, Op. 59 (1934), as the crucial work in which 'Roussel attempted to come to terms with his problems'.[24] The first movement (Allegro)

---

[22] See Alain Frogley, 'Vaughan Williams and Thomas Hardy', *Music and Letters*, 68 (1987), 42–59.

[23] David Drew, 'Modern French Music', in H. Hartog (ed.), *European Music in the Twentieth Century* (Harmondsworth, 1961), 258.

[24] Ibid. 259.

has similar flaws to that of No. 3, yet the rondo-like finale is far better than its predecessor and the central movements—a Lento molto and a Scherzo—have impressive moments, notably the climax of the Lento.

Of Roussel's French contemporaries, only Maurice Ravel belongs to the present chapter, by virtue of his two piano concertos, composed so close to one another, yet so strikingly different in certain basic respects. The Concerto for Left Hand in one movement and the Concerto in G in three movements were both completed in 1931, and while the former is an imaginative reconstitution of the world of Lisztian romanticism, the latter unites—and transmutes—a wide variety of less grandiose sources: Scarlatti, Mozart, Saint-Saëns and Gershwin among them. Both works also have an admixture of that Spanish flavouring which Ravel found so difficult to resist, and indeed the G major was initially planned as a Basque Rhapsody for piano and orchestra. The fashion-conscious aspect of the two-hand work is obvious, but inoffensive when the result is so light and elegant. Gershwin's *Rhapsody in Blue* (1924), which enjoyed a great vogue in Europe during the late 1920s, has left distinct echoes behind, but there is more parody than imitation in Ravel's work and more good humour than a composer seriously jealous of popular trendsetters would be likely to display. Sonata and rondo-type movements frame the elegant Adagio whose main melody, apparently inspired by Mozart's Clarinet Quintet, captures for some the spirit of a Fauré song. The dissonant climax before the return of the melody (piano accompanying cor anglais) is evidence that Ravel could still contrive a dramatic effect of appropriate proportions. This charming work is never merely superficial.

Greater concentration is to be expected from the single-movement Left-Hand Concerto, which relates to the sombre grandeur of *Gaspard de la Nuit* (1908), as the G major does to the delicate fantasy of *Le Tombeau de Couperin* (piano version 1914–17, orchestration 1919). The dark, doom-laden orchestral opening and the rhetorical piano entry certainly conjure up visions of heroic confronta-tions, of impossible odds challenged, with the obvious technical limitations of a single hand appealing to Ravel's delight in ingenuity. The form may not be ideally balanced, since the slow Sarabande which precedes the main fast music does not unfold with totally convincing momentum, and the cadenza which its return provokes near the end seems overlong, but the sardonic dance elements of the main Allegro have ample verve and bite. In spite of increasing illness, Ravel in his later years was far from effete and self-indulgent, or able only to convince in languid episodes like the Adagio of the G major concerto. It can indeed be argued that 'in certain respects, the most consistent and the most innovatory of Ravel's late works is that much maligned piece, *Bolero*',[25] but the 'calculated mating of the sophisticated and the barbaric', which determines the quality and character of *Bolero* (1928), is more attractively harnessed to symphonic aims in the Left-

---

[25] Drew 'Modern French Music', 256.

Hand Concerto. Both *Bolero* and the concerto are easily vulgarized in performance, but, like the *Don Quichotte* songs (1932–3), Ravel's last composition, the concerto has an aura of romantic bitterness which is disturbing and hauntingly memorable.

The Background

Attempts to argue that opera in the modern age is an anachronism have never carried much conviction, and even composers who, in youth, dismissed the genre with contempt have found themselves drawn to the challenge of developing a personal response to its opportunities for large-scale structuring. Many of these efforts will be chronicled in later chapters. This one concentrates on composers who remained committed to tonality, and whose careers flourished, or were well-launched, before 1950.

The later twentieth century has been as much concerned with rediscoveries and rehabilitations of earlier twentieth-century composers as with sustained support for its chosen, canonical masters. As far as opera is concerned, this has had its greatest effect in the German-speaking countries, and the picture, sustainable during the century's middle years, of Richard Strauss as the sole exponent of a dying tradition, resisting the atonal threats of Berg (*Wozzeck*) and Schoenberg (*Moses und Aron*), has been significantly revised. Where Italian opera is concerned, Puccini has retained that solitary role. His career reached a triumphant conclusion with *Turandot* (1920–6) which, despite its somewhat perfunctory completion by Franco Alfano, is equal, if not superior, to any of his earlier works.[1] *Turandot* has total conviction of style, firmly established form, and although the exotic sadism of the plot may seem crude for its time—more like an old-fashioned melodrama than a psychological case-study—economy of means, the briskness of pace, and concentrated intensity of expression counter the dangers of overemphasis. No contemporary Italian composer came near the Puccinian flair and panache after 1914; his most significant rival, Ottorino Respighi (1879–1936), is best known for colourful orchestral works like *Fontane di Roma* (1914–16) and *Trittico botticelliano* (1927), though his opera *La bella dormente nel bosco* (original, marionette version, 1916–21) has been described as 'unassuming yet wholly captivating'.[2] Pietro Mascagni (1863–1945) and Umberto Giordano (1867–1948) composed their most successful operas before 1900, and, though far from insignificant, neither Ermanno Wolf-Ferrari (1876–1948) nor

---

[1] See William Ashbrook and Harold Powers, *Puccini's* Turandot, *the End of a Great Tradition* (Princeton, 1991).

[2] John C. G. Waterhouse, 'Respighi', *The New Grove Dictionary of Music and Musicians*, ed. S. Sadie (London, 1980), xv. 758.

Riccardo Zandonai (1883–1944) have achieved anything approaching Puccini's prominence on the international scene. Of later, more radical Italian composers, before Luciano Berio, to be discussed in Chapter 14, only Luigi Dallapiccola (1904–75) showed how to preserve Puccini's dramatic devices, even down to the element of sadism, in the very different style of his serial one-acter, *Il Prigioniero* (1944–7), discussed in Chapter 11.[3]

The pre-eminence of Richard Strauss in the field of German opera seems, with hindsight, to have become unassailable well before 1914, with *Salome*, *Elektra*, and *Der Rosenkavalier*.[4] Nevertheless, although Strauss continued to compose regularly for the theatre until his final masterpiece, *Capriccio* (1940–1), he was by no means the only prominent figure, and was far from winning universal approval.[5] In an operatic field embracing radical initiatives as different as Berg's *Wozzeck* and Weill's *Die Dreigroschenoper*, the demand for new yet more conventional work remained strong during the inter-war years. Hans Pfitzner (1869–1949), Siegfried Wagner (1869–1930), Alexander von Zemlinsky (1871–1942), Franz Schreker (1878–1934) and Erich Wolfgang Korngold (1897–1957) were all well-known at the time, and their work has gained new audiences in more recent decades, thanks to the makers of CDs, and to the more adventurous opera companies.

With its lovingly worked symphonic texture and compelling, if in places rather diffuse, melodic writing, Pfitzner's *Palestrina* (1912–15) is an outstandingly original response to Wagnerian principles and practices, shunning the flamboyance and decadence associated with both expressionism and realism in opera.[6] Korngold's *Die tote Stadt* (1920) and *Das Wunder der Heliane* (1927) are altogether more melodramatic and eclectic—bold, ripe confections building resourcefully on elements from Mahler, Strauss, and Puccini and stopping short of large-scale atonal expressionism. Even more potent displays of progressive late romantic eclecticism can be heard in Zemlinsky's *Eine florentinische Tragödie* (1915–16) and *Der Zwerg* (1920–1) as well as in the earlier operas of Franz Schreker. The up-to-the-minute mixture of exoticism and the high-flown in *Der ferne Klang* (1912) and *Die Gezeichneten* (1918) ensured their success when new. But Schreker's attempt to develop a more restrained style (in, for example, *Die Schatzgräber*, 1920) rendered his music increasingly vulnerable to politically motivated accusations of irrelevance and undesirable internationalism, in comparison, at first, to the exuberant radicalism of Hindemith and Krenek, and later to what were perceived as the more purely German qualities of Richard Strauss.[7] Even so, around 1920, it was Schreker, not Strauss, who was 'Germany's foremost opera composer', with

[3] See below, pp. 231–4.
[4] See above, Ch. 2, pp. 32–4.
[5] For an attack on *Die Frau ohne Schatten* at the time of its first performance, see Christopher Hailey, *Franz Schreker (1878–1934): A Cultural Biography* (Cambridge, 1993), 112–13.
[6] See John Williamson, *The Music of Hans Pfitzner* (Oxford, 1992), 126–205, and also Owen Toller, *Pfitzner's Palestrina: The 'Musical Legend' and its Background* (London, 1997).
[7] Hailey, *Schreker*, 173.

his first three operas receiving 'some 32 productions and over 250 performances between 1917 and 1921'.[8]

Richard Strauss

The partial rehabilitation of Schreker, Zemlinsky, and Korngold since 1970 was part of a wider enthusiasm for the kind of uninhibited late romanticism that could be regarded as representing heroic resistance to the grim astringencies of progressive expressionism, rather than a timid failure to transcend them. Yet admiration for *Der ferne Klang*, *Das Wunder der Heliane*, and *Palestrina* has not seriously undermined the pre-eminence of Richard Strauss, whose own later operas also gained in stature during the century's later decades as new productions and recordings have appeared. In particular, *Die Frau ohne Schatten* (1914–18) has been hailed by some as even greater than the first work in which Strauss retreated from the front line of harmonic advance, *Der Rosenkavalier*. He retained the ability, well displayed in both *Rosenkavalier* and *Die Frau ohne Schatten*, to transcend kitsch in the creation of climactic, ecstatic apotheoses—heard also at the end of *Ariadne auf Naxos* (1911–12, revision 1916) and *Daphne* (1936–7) and also, in gentler but still potently eloquent vein, in *Capriccio*. It is the fully rounded humanity of Strauss's characterization that helps to make his operas so effective in the theatre, and *Die Frau ohne Schatten* includes one of the finest, Barak—the nearest Strauss ever came to a Sachs. The strongest characters in the later operas tend to share a degree of Barak's down-to-earth solidity, though Christine Storch in *Intermezzo* (1924), Mandryka in *Arabella* (1933), and La Roche in *Capriccio* (1941) are all more impulsive, more conscious of being on stage and needing to entertain an audience. Barak's simple, resigned nobility, as expressed at the end of Act 1 of *Die Frau ohne Schatten*, is never matched again, though the only slightly tongue-in-cheek final stages of La Roche's great monologue in the ninth scene of *Capriccio* run it close.

Analysis: *Capriccio*

For all its self-conscious elegance, there is nothing superficial about *Capriccio*. The fact that it is, ultimately, an opera about opera does not preclude the expression of very real human emotions, and the passions of the composer Flamand and the poet Olivier for the Countess are more important than their devotion to their respective arts. A relatively serious tone for the expression of those passions is not ruled out either, though once they have been expressed—and the same is

---

[8] Hailey, *Schreker*, 109.

true for La Roche's hymn of devotion to *his* art—the mood must be quickly lightened, and the passion safely defused, by the high-flown lyricism of the Countess's response.

In general, the conversational episodes and ensembles which occur regularly in the earlier parts of the opera, none of which lacks musical interest, serve to contrast with the more serious monologues and solo sections which increase in number as the work proceeds. This gradual, cumulative heightening over an unbroken span of two and a half hours is superbly managed by librettist and composer, and the greatest dramatic stroke of all is the postponement of the Countess's most passionate outburst until the final scene, when she learns that she must soon confront her two suitors simultaneously and choose between them. This final scene is nevertheless not about how she arrives at a decision, but about how she regains the equilibrium which makes either a decision, or no decision, possible. The Countess recovers that serene poise which is also the principal musical quality of the entire work, and which Strauss projects as memorably as he does the very different moods of tragedy and despair that dominate the purely instrumental *Metamorphosen* (1945).

As a tonal composer, Strauss was quite capable of exploiting tensions within and between keys when these were dramatically appropriate. A good example in *Capriccio* is the dual tonal tendency of La Roche's monologue: C (major or minor) and E♭. In less forthright passages, inevitably, chromaticism becomes more purely a matter of colour, enriching the harmony without creating any lasting doubts about the eventual tonal outcome. A chromatic chord or progression need not positively undermine a tonality in order to enhance expression.

The closing stages of the opera (from ten bars after Fig. 281) provide an example. The overall tonality of D♭ major is by now well established and its stability is unlikely to be seriously questioned. As Examples 4.1 and 4.2 make clear, what matters is not so much a low level of chromaticism as a low level of dissonance, with unessential melody notes and passing chromatic chords alike tending to poke slight gaps in the prevailing concordant chromaticism. Yet there is fine craftsmanship in the way the entry of the voice—'Du Spiegelbild' (Ex. 4.1)—is prepared.

At the beginning of Ex. 4.1 the music has moved into the supertonic (E♭ minor) but before it makes the easy step back to the second inversion tonic chord of D♭, Strauss inserts a gliding gloss over the simple chromatic bass line E♭, F, G♭, G♮, A♭ to give the return of D♭ just the right sense of resolution. The real point of the slight delay is, however, to enhance the much longer postponement of *root position* tonic harmony. During the next nine bars we may not experience disruption, but we do feel suspense, as the harmony floats freely around its tantalizingly tangible goal; and then the voice enters, two bars before the resolution is complete.

Ex. 4.1. Strauss, *Capriccio*, closing scene (Scene 12), from four bars before Fig. 283

The principal chromatic deviations in the remainder of the scene are all side-steps on to full triads like E major, A major, and D major, a semitone away from diatonic chords (Ex. 4.2). These may reach the discerning ear as substitutes for the 'real' harmony, and even as an aural equivalent of the difference between reflection and reality as the Countess looks into the mirror and asks for an answer 'which is not trivial' to the question, whom—or what resolution—shall she choose? The operatic situation itself may indeed seem trivial, judged by the standards of epic, myth, or psychological naturalism, but the music ensures its memorability.

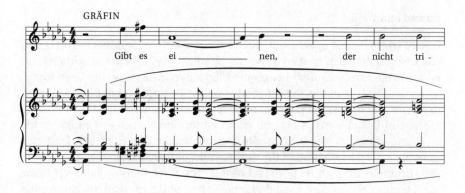

Ex. 4.2. Strauss, *Capriccio*, closing scene, from eight bars after Fig. 284

Busoni and Weill

Busoni wrote several operas, but *Doktor Faust*, which he began in 1916 and was still working on when he died in 1924, is by some way the most important. The performable completion by his pupil Philipp Jarnach has usually been found 'less than ideal',[9] and it is the version by Antony Beaumont that has done most to ensure that the work has begun to be taken as seriously as it deserves.

Many of Busoni's works may be criticized for nondescript—or simply inappropriate—material, but *Doktor Faust*, if not totally free from this fault (for example in its presentation of the only significant female character, the Countess), triumphs through its portrayal of the central relationship between Faust and Mephistopheles. The force and imagination of the musical invention connected with these characters override the potentially dangerous gulf in the musical language between functional and non-functional elements. The opera is less a synthesis of styles than a compendium, where modal counterpoint, impressionistic progressions, and almost Straussian late romanticism contribute in turn to a dramatic impact which may be blurred in focus but is all the more intriguing for its very unpredictability. Busoni pulled no punches in *Doktor Faust*. His treatment of the subject is not tinged with any inhibiting reverence for this most resonant of German myths. There is even something ironically Wotan-like about the way Faust cheats the devil at the end to the extent of ensuring survival through his miraculously resurrected child, and there is a cool, conspiratorial side to Mephisto himself which suggests affinities with Wagner's Loge. The importance of purely orchestral music is considerable, but the vocal ensembles and set-pieces show confidence in the adaptation of conventional designs. *Doktor Faust* is a highpoint of non-Straussian German opera, and its special character is seen in still clearer focus if it is compared with the work of the younger generation, not least Busoni's own pupils, during the same period.

Near the end of his life Kurt Weill (1900–50) wrote that

my teacher Busoni . . . hammered into me one basic truth which he had arrived at after fifty years of pure aestheticism: the fear of triviality is the greatest handicap of the modern artist. . . . Instead of worrying about the material of music, the theory behind it, the opinions of other musicians, my main concern is to find the purest expression in music for what I want to say, with enough trust in my instinct, my taste and my talent to always write 'good' music, regardless of the style I am writing in.[10]

While 'triviality', however 'pure', was not necessarily the prime factor in Busoni's idea of new classicality, his attitude, and not least the way he resisted the hyper-

[9] Antony Beaumont, *Busoni the Composer* (London, 1985), 350. Beaumont's version of the opera was first performed, under his own baton, in Bologna in 1985.
[10] See Kim H. Kolwalke (ed.), *A New Orpheus: Essays on Kurt Weill* (New Haven, 1986), 301.

romantiç tendencies in Weill's remarkable Symphony No. 1 (1921), had consider-able influence and helped to lay the foundations for the abrasive modernism of Weill's mature musical language.

This had begun to emerge even before the celebrated collaboration with Bertolt Brecht, since, despite its musical mixture of intense, well-nigh atonal late romanticism, and Stravinskian neo-classicism, Weill's early opera *Der Protago-nist* (1925) anticipated those principles of 'Epic Theatre' with which their col-laborations are particularly associated, at least to the extent that it aimed at 'moving the audience without enlisting its sympathy'.[11]

Weill's association with Brecht began with the *Mahagonny Songspiel* (1927), closely followed by *Die Dreigroschenoper* (1928), and the intention of providing a musical entertainment of immediate and wide appeal, thereby emulating its source, John Gay's *Beggar's Opera*. Weill had already begun to mix references to jazz idioms into his style, for example in his second opera *Royal Palace* (1925–6), and the fashion for such a blend of popular musical characteristics and topical subject-matter had also been exploited by Krenek (*Jonny spielt auf*, 1925–6) and Hindemith (*Neues vom Tage*, 1929).[12] Yet *Die Dreigroschenoper* has proved to be the most enduring of all such works. As a portrayal of a decadent society it could hardly be more different from Berg's *Wozzeck*, first performed in 1925 and seen by an admiring Weill as the ultimate manifestation of traditional, Wagnerian music drama. Weill and Brecht were not concerned with charting the extent to which individual personalities and human relationships are governed by emo-tional and social forces. They were not interested in psychological motivation but in political action, hence the need for an unpretentious theatrical style, which would make people sit up, take note, and act: hence, musically, the impor-tance of popular idioms.

Die Dreigroschenoper exemplifies Brecht's idea of Epic Theatre, the very reverse of the Wagnerian *Gesamtkunstwerk* which the term so easily conjures up. Brecht stressed that Epic Theatre, emphasizing the independence of text, music, and stage presentation, was the opposite of traditional opera, which aimed to engage the sympathy of audiences directly through an integrated expression involving words, music, and staging. Since the whole point of Epic Theatre is that 'musical and dramatic effects are not calculated to constitute an overall unified structure',[13] the result, as in *Die Dreigroschenoper*, has distinctly modernist attributes. As Stephen Hinton acknowledges, 'with its juxtaposition of narrative text, spoken dialogue and musical numbers' the work is 'a montage, not an organic construction'.[14] It employs 'a style of wilful and relentless equivocation on absolutely every level, which stamps the work as "modern" in a quintessen-tially twentieth-century sense. Any message the work might contain at once

---

[11] See Kolwalke, *A New Orpheus*, 154.
[12] See Ch. 7, p. 136.
[13] Stephen Hinton, *Kurt Weill: The Threepenny Opera* (Cambridge, 1990), 5.
[14] Ibid. 6.

undermines itself',[15] its 'pervasive ambiguity at every level seems positively to encourage contrary readings',[16] and Weill's music in general is as far as possible from blandly consistent 'easy listening', attacking 'the *idées reçues* of modernity as fiercely as it does those of commercial music manufacturers'.[17] Without such unsettling ambiguities, it is difficult to believe that *Die Dreigroschenoper* would have survived the time for which it was conceived. After all, what could be more appropriate for a theatre piece aiming to provoke political and social action on the basis of moral judgements than music which is harshly critical of decadent conventions?

There is no doubt that Weill shared Brecht's convictions about what Epic Theatre should aim to achieve. But the poet was wary of music which verged on the lyric or romantic, and difficulties therefore arose with their most extended operatic venture, *Aufstieg und Fall der Stadt Mahagonny* (1929), which was partly derived from the earlier *Mahagonny Songspiel*. As part of the revisions asked for by the publisher, Weill added the beautiful 'Crane' duet (Ex. 4.3), whose 'astonishingly delicate lyricism is dangerous from the Brechtian point of view, for it compels the onlooker to identify himself with the feelings of the protagonists. It provides him with sensations instead of "forcing him to take decisions" ',[18] as Epic Theatre should do, and for this reason David Drew can claim with conviction that 'the truthfulness of *Mahagonny* may well be greatest' when the 'Crane' duet is omitted.[19]

Ultimately, therefore, Weill's achievement—which ensured an early break with Brecht—was to find a new tension between simplicity and concentration, just as the late romantic Mahler had explored a new tension between simplicity and elaboration. The opera *Die Bürgschaft* (1932), the play with music *Der Silbersee*, and the play with songs *Die Sieben Todsünden* (both 1933) exemplify Weill's desire 'to cultivate a style less superficially contemporary'.[20] As Ian Kemp has put it, with reference to *Der Silbersee*, Weill 'accepts the tragic and will not accept it. He accepts the banality of life and resists it. In these contradictions lie the peculiar tensions of his musical language'[21]—and also, we might add, its inherent, essential modernity. Whatever one's response to the theatrical works that Weill composed during his enforced exile in America, like the 'musical play' *Lady in the Dark* (1940) or the 'American opera' *Street Scene* (1947), it is difficult to argue convincingly that they sustain, or aspire to sustain, such a 'less superficial' modern quality.

---

[15] Hinton, *The Threepenny Opera*, 189.   [16] Ibid. 192.

[17] David Drew, 'Topicality and the Universal: The Strange Case of Weill's *Die Bürgschaft*', *Music and Letters*, 39 (1958), 243.

[18] David Drew, 'Brecht versus Opera', *Score*, 23 (July 1958), 8.

[19] David Drew, *Kurt Weill: A Handbook* (London, 1987), 185.

[20] Stephen Hinton, 'Kurt Weill', *The New Grove Dictionary of Opera*, ed. S. Sadie (London, 1992), iv. 1126.

[21] Kowalke, *New Orpheus*, 146.

Ex. 4.3. Weill, *Aufstieg und Fall der Stadt Mahagonny*, Act 2, No. 14, from four bars before Fig. 390

Janáček

Leoš Janáček (1854–1928) wrote only one work before 1914 which is widely known today, the opera *Jenůfa*, and it is in the field of opera that the greater and finer part of his remarkably rich later output belongs. Janáček's style is instantly recognizable, its personal accents making it easy to regard him as a nationalist *par excellence*: and, though the extent to which the rhythms and colours of Czech speech determine his musical processes can easily be exaggerated, it is undeniable that the character of the music is significantly related to that of the language.[22]

Jenůfa (1903, revised version by 1908) did not achieve any real success until 1916. *The Excursions of Mr Brouček* also has a long history, from 1908 to 1917, but the last four operas were composed with considerable rapidity, and reflect this in their concentration and brevity.

The three acts of *Kát'a Kabanová* (1921) last less than two hours.[23] Based on Ostrovsky's play *The Storm*, it tells how a woman, living in the repressive atmosphere of a small country town, is unfaithful to her husband and driven to suicide when her lover is forced to leave. In basic outline, it may seem little different from the plot of a Puccinian tear-jerker, yet Janáček's powers of musical characterization, of both individuals and their environment, achieve a dramatic conviction in which stylization has no part. There is a simple intensity which can rise to heights of the greatest eloquence even though the expansive lyricism conventionally associated with such an atmosphere in romantic music is normally absent. In purely musical terms, as with the handling of tonality and thematic development, this simplicity may be actual or deceptive. Of all the composers discussed in this book, moreover, Janáček is the least amenable to generalization, so no summary discussion of his procedures can do more than provide isolated instances of techniques which are protean in their variety. For example, he may make the simplest use of dominant preparation when moving from one tonal area to another, as in the extended scene for the lovers in Act II (Ex. 4.4). Alternatively, a dominant preparation may lead into surprisingly remote regions, as at the magical moment of Kát'a's first appearance in Act I (Ex. 4.5). This example also shows how such an effect can be enhanced by the use of simple thematic variation.

Nowhere is Janáček's musical personality more tangible than in the simple, basically diatonic phrases whose chromatic inflections seem to express a whole world of hope or despair. Nor is there anything more moving in the entire repertory of modern tonal music than those passages in Kát'a's final scene where the harmony seems to be striving for the security of an uninflected G♭ or C♭ major, but is ultimately defeated, like Kát'a herself. The climax of this scene, when Kát'a decides to kill herself, is also a useful example of Janáček's utterly uncomplicated musico-dramatic technique. The entire passage is only fifteen bars long, and harmonically it moves from A♭ major to G♭ minor. The thematic motive is in the orchestra, and consists of a short descending figure stated no fewer than seventeen times in only slightly varied forms. Such simplicity of means inevitably enhances the cumulative effect of the harmonic motion: and even the relatively

[22] On Janáček, see John Tyrrell, *Janáček's Operas: A Documentary Account* (London, 1992), and Tyrrell's article in *The New Grove Dictionary of Opera* (London, 1992), ii. 872–80. See also *Intimate Letters: Leoš Janáček to Kamila Stösslová*, ed. and trans. J. Tyrrell (London, 1994) and *Janáček's Works: A Catalogue of the Music and Writings of Leoš Janáček*, ed. N. Simeone *et al.* (Oxford, 1997).

[23] See Nicholas John (ed.), *Jenůfa/Kát'a Kabanová* (ENO Opera Guide No. 33; London, 1985).

Ex. 4.4. Janáček, *Káťa Kabanová*, Act 2, Scene 2, from eight bars after Fig. 20

Ex. 4.5. Janáček, *Káťa Kabanová*, Act 1, Scene 1, from one bar after Fig. 30

slight degree of thematic variation throws the progress of the harmony into greater relief. A similar technique used on a larger scale can be studied in the crucial scene between Kát'a and Boris in Act II. The scene as a whole is a marvellous portrait of the vulnerability and essential innocence of the central characters, framed as it is with the folksong-like music for the second pair of lovers, Varvara and Kudriash. Each section is built around the frequent repetition of simple thematic phrases in the orchestra, which the voices occasionally match but which are most important as background to vocal phrases whose every detail—register, rhythm, relationship of repetition to variation—serves to create the greatest romantic intensity.

Janáček's next opera, *The Cunning Little Vixen* (1922–3), is as sharply focused with regard to fantasy as *Kát'a Kabanová* is to naturalistic tragedy. Even before the serene beauty of the Forester's concluding monologue, however, the work contains moments of an almost Straussian opulence which contrast so extremely with the more parlando passages as to create a feeling of aimlessness (at least with regard to harmonic direction) in the latter. Whether or not Janáček himself was aware of the disruptive potentiality of a style with two such different constituents, it is a fact that neither of the last two operas, *The Makropoulos Case* (1923–5) and *From the House of the Dead* (1927–8), contains nearly as much pure lyricism. Their language may be more obviously unified, but the loss of lyric contrast ensures a new, much less instantly appealing austerity, for which the grim subject-matter of *From the House of the Dead* is especially appropriate. It may be possible to criticize the way in which Janáček adapted Dostoevsky's tale of prison-camp life, but the overall effect is of an intensity as implacable and grim as anything in *Wozzeck*, and the music, while unfailingly powerful, never strains after exaggerated effects.

The emphasis on narration (each act contains an extended monologue for a different character) demands particularly clear structural organization, and Janáček achieves unity without sacrificing inner momentum. Šiškov's narration in Act III may be overlong—its content is almost a Janáček plot in itself—but it accumulates a truly horrific tension, which is released without dilution in the concentrated actions of the opera's ending. *From the House of the Dead* is one of the great radical twentieth-century operas in the way it achieves total dramatic conviction through the most uncompromising exploitation of a remarkably individual musical idiom. Janáček's native tongue may have made it that much easier for him to achieve this originality: but it was his musical inventiveness which enabled him to breathe dramatic life into what might so easily have become large tracts of arid recitative. As (very differently) with Weill, the secret lies in the tension of simple 'units' of harmony and rhythm, which need not behave according to traditional 'rules'. Janáček perfected a language of total coherence and clarity. The blazing diatonic perorations of all his late works may not have ensured the indefinite survival of the tonal system itself, but they summarized the immediate emotional response and the deep humanity of a genius who achieved the aim of all true creative minds: to communicate widely and yet to preserve complete individuality.

Ravel, Szymanowski

One of the most satisfying things about *The Cunning Little Vixen* is the unmawk-ish way in which Janáček characterized the animals. Ravel's *L'Enfant et les sortilèges* (1920–5) is another opera from the same decade presenting a fantasy in which animals (and in Ravel's case normally inanimate objects like armchairs and teapots) make use of human speech. The brevity of Ravel's work (it lasts barely fifty minutes) and the use of dance idioms—foxtrot, slow valse, 'valse américaine'—help to ensure an engagingly frivolous tone, while the touching delicacy of the child's E♭ major song supports the judgement that the lyrical sec-tions of the opera are among the best things in Ravel's later work. The closing chorus, with the penitent child's cries for his mother, is perhaps a little too saccharine for comfort, but even here the lyric diatonicism spiced with gentle dissonance makes an attractive conclusion to one of Ravel's most spontaneously imaginative pieces.

At the furthest extreme both from Ravel's delicate fantasy and the social con-cerns of Weill and late Janáček is *King Roger* (1918–24) by the Polish composer Karol Szymanowski (1882–1937). In several respects it is comparable with, though hardly similar to, Busoni's *Doktor Faust*: both are fine works by uneven com-posers, late romantic, and therefore, in some sense, 'old-fashioned' in style, though Szymanowski's roots are in Debussy and Skryabin rather than Wagner and Strauss, and both involve a powerful recreation of a literary archetype: in *King Roger*, the *Bacchae* of Euripides.

Roger was a twelfth-century king of Sicily, and the opera tells of his con-frontation with two rival forces, representing repression (the medieval Christian church) and liberation (a young, pagan shepherd, the god Dionysos). Given its epic subject-matter, the opera may seem surprisingly short—three acts, each less than an hour long—and the emphasis is less on an elaborately explicit plot than on a brief sequence of crucial events in which much remains implicit. In spite of this oblique approach, however, it is clear that at the end Roger has succeeded in rising above both the stultified traditions of the Church and the dangerously impulsive indulgences of the Shepherd—though these have been the agency of his enlightenment. The last act confirms that the opera is principally concerned with the conflicts within Roger himself, and their resolution is the means of giving full realization to his own personality: the outcome as far as concerns his position as king of a specific country with specific problems is not shown, nor could it be without contradicting the entire dramatic character of the piece. In giving such emphasis to inner rather than outer action, Szymanowski was cer-tainly unfashionable, and even if his approach was in large part simply the result of inexperience (he had composed only one earlier opera, *Hagith*, between 1911 and 1914), *King Roger* still achieves an immensely convincing climax.

That it does so is because Szymanowski's musical style is equal to the demands of the subject. The drama is projected through an epic lyricism, into which simpler song elements are well integrated, just as the late romantic harmonic framework can encompass more conventional triadic moments without incongruity. There may be no all-pervading use of functional tonality, but the work relies on the kind of tensions and resolutions which only a language accepting the ultimate primacy of the triad can enforce. Not the least surprising thing about *King Roger* is its ending—in contrast to Wagnerian and Straussian precedents—with a triumphant monologue for a *male* singer. Szymanowski never equalled this achievement in his later works, which display a more Bartókian concern to use folk-music-like material in the service of art-music forms. This change of style, which took place when Poland gained political independence after the 1914–18 war, apparently hindered the completion of *King Roger* itself, and although the later music is by no means negligible—the ballet *Harnasie* (1923–31), in particular—it is *King Roger*, along with other compositions of the period from 1915 to 1920, like the Violin Concerto No. 1 (1916) and the Symphony No. 3 (1914–16), which represent Szymanowski's best work.[24]

Prokofiev

Prokofiev's greatest achievements in the field of instrumental music—principally the symphony—date from after his return to Russia. The blend of lyric and dramatic impulses in the Fifth and Sixth Symphonies produces an epic breadth which does not demand the total elimination of those more sardonic characteristics of the pre-Soviet period. Such a richness of range—equally evident in the full-length ballet *Romeo and Juliet* (1936)—might have been expected to find the same, if not a superior, fulfilment in opera; and Prokofiev's trials and tribulations here could be conclusive evidence that an essentially bitter, tragic core lies at the heart of his often apparently easy-going, good-humoured style—a core which could only find full expression in dramatic subjects likely to be regarded as subversive by Soviet dogmatists. The abundant flair, versatility, and originality of the two operas Prokofiev wrote between 1918 and 1927 were construed by his principal Soviet biographer as evidence of nihilism, involving a 'rejection of the principles of classical operatic form'.[25] Certainly, neither *The Love of Three Oranges* (1919) nor *The Fiery Angel* (1919–23, revisions 1926–7) is a flawless masterpiece, yet the structural problems which remained unsolved were created by the composer's sensible and scarcely unprecedented attempt to devise a dramatic form appropriate to the subject-matter.

[24] See Jim Samson, *The Music of Szymanowski* (London, 1980).
[25] Israel Nestyev, *Prokofiev* (London, 1960), 445.

As a fantastic farce, *The Love of Three Oranges* is probably more effective in its adaptation of the anti-romantic accents theatrically in vogue at the time, than *The Fiery Angel* is in its attempt to trump the expressionist music drama. If the first is economically discontinuous, the second seems too protracted, its flamboyant rhetoric becoming tedious and self-parodic. What both works share, with each other and with much that is good in many other early twentieth-century operas, is the convincing realization of an exotic setting, while the importance of diabolic possession in *The Fiery Angel* creates links with the entire German romantic tradition, reaching back to Weber's *Der Freischütz*. If the composer's third version of the work had been completed (it would have reshaped the five acts as three, and included two new scenes), the impact might well have been much more powerful and better controlled.[26] As it is, it is difficult not to feel that the Symphony No. 3 (1928), derived from the opera, presents a more satisfying statement of the dramatic musical essence.

Prokofiev began his third version of the work after the Metropolitan Opera in New York had indicated in 1930 an interest in staging it (in fact, it was eventually staged in Venice in 1955, two years after Prokofiev's death). Presumably the revision was abandoned at the time that the composer decided, in 1933, to return to Russia. He can have had few illusions about the prevailing Soviet attitude to his earlier music, particularly the operas, and it was not until 1939, with the double success of the ballet, *Romeo and Juliet*, and the cantata, *Alexander Nevsky*, behind him, that he approached the genre with which Shostakovich, with *Lady Macbeth of Mtsensk* (first performed in 1934), had provoked a major political attack.

The omens must have been good. *Romeo and Juliet* was later praised with the words that 'few composers have achieved in music alone, without the aid of a sung or spoken libretto, so concrete and realistic an embodiment of life,'[27] and although at one stage it had been intended to revive Juliet in time for a happy ending, even the stark tragedy of Shakespeare's own conclusion was not interpreted as a symbolic criticism of the capacity of the Soviet state to survive.

'Realism' is also the key term in the Russian eulogies of *Alexander Nevsky*. The inference was clear: Prokofiev was eminently suited to compose a realistic opera rooted in the events of the time—an opera of the kind of which Shostakovich was apparently incapable. With hindsight, it seems regrettable that Prokofiev did not follow up the other possibility in acceptable dramatic themes: Shakespearian tragedy. He actually composed some incidental music for a production of *Hamlet* in 1937–8, but the operatic project which he began the following year was *Semyon Kotko*, a story of peasant life during the civil war that followed the 1917 revolution. It was first performed in Moscow on 20 September 1940, and failed.

[26] Richard Taruskin, 'The Fiery Angel', in *The New Grove Dictionary of Opera*, ed. S. Sadie (London, 1992), ii. 190.
[27] Nestyev, *Prokofiev*, 270.

Nestyev's diagnosis is predictable: the techniques of the earlier operas, which involved 'the rejection of traditional operatic forms . . . were not at all suitable for the writing of a contemporary folk drama'. He was nevertheless prepared to concede that Prokofiev had 'found new, flexible expressive means in the work',[28] and Western authorities have found much to admire in it.[29]

In deciding to use Tolstoy's *War and Peace* as the basis of his next opera, Prokofiev retained the essential nationalist appeal of a 'local' subject while ensuring a more universal interest as well. The task of transforming the huge Tolstoyian novel into a workable opera was, not surprisingly, a protracted and complex one, which occupied the composer on and off for the last twelve years of his life, and the various results never satisfied the Soviet authorities. The first version was completed in 1942, and Prokofiev was soon under pressure from the Committee on the Arts to revise it. In all, *War and Peace* went through five versions, and although the constant tinkering and patching which such revision involved might seem a recipe for disaster, the authoritative conclusion is that the opera has a 'perfection of form', resulting in large part from the fact that the composer was able to give its two halves 'a hidden, mutually, reinforcing correspondence'.[30] Though one may indeed regret the demoralizing effect of uncomprehending criticism on the composer as he struggled to achieve an accommodation between his own creative aims and the demands of officialdom, the opera is a compelling rendering of Tolstoy's epic, and among Prokofiev's finest achievements. The essentially traditional character of the harmony is especially effective in the characterization of the Russian folk hero Marshal Kutuzov, whose music is appropriately hymn-like and inspirational in nature (Ex. 4.6(i)) yet darkens in moments of self-doubt (Ex. 4.6(ii)).

Prokofiev wrote two other operas in the 1940s. *The Duenna* (1940), an adaptation of Sheridan's play, found local favour by virtue of its clear, number-opera design and avoidance of caricature in favour of a lyricism recalling that of *Romeo and Juliet*. *The Story of a Real Man* (1947–8) was written at a time when Stalinist repression was at its height. It is a last attempt to dramatize the life of a Soviet hero, a fighter pilot, and in spite of the composer's rather pathetic statement of intent—'I intend to introduce trios, duets and contrapuntally developed choruses, for which I will make use of some interesting northern Russian folk-songs. Lucid melody, and as far as possible a simple harmonic language, are the elements which I intend to use in my opera'[31]—it was immediately suppressed, and only achieved public performance in 1960 in a version that inflicts many alterations on Prokofiev's original.

[28] Nestyev, *Prokofiev*, 313, 318.

[29] See Richard Taruskin, 'Semyon Kotko', *The New Grove Dictionary of Opera*, ed. S. Sadie (London, 1992), iv. 312–13.

[30] Richard Taruskin, 'War and Peace', *The New Grove Dictionary of Opera*, ed. S. Sadie (London, 1992), iv. 1105.

[31] Richard Taruskin, 'The Story of a Real Man', *The New Grove Dictionary of Opera*, ed. S. Sadie (London, 1992), iv. 556.

Ex. 4.6. Prokofiev, *War and Peace*, Scene 10: (i) from Fig. 383; (ii) from Fig. 388

Britten

Prokofiev's statement of intent with regard to *The Story of a Real Man* could equally well have been made by Benjamin Britten (1913–76) when writing his first opera, *Peter Grimes*.[32] First performed in 1945—an earlier operetta, *Paul Bunyan*, had been discarded, though it was eventually revived—it was his most substantial composition of any kind at that date, and established him as a composer capable of giving musical life to serious subjects and major issues. Not that the earlier works lack individuality, and the choral variations *A Boy was Born* (1932–3), the Variations on a Theme of Frank Bridge for strings (1937) and the Violin Concerto of 1939 (particularly its final pages) provide the clearest indication of an expressive certainty remarkable for a composer still in his twenties. This aspect of Britten's style owed much to kinship with late romanticism, notably Mahler, and while the early works also display an abundant technical

---

[32] The most substantial study of Britten's work is Peter Evans, *The Music of Benjamin Britten*, rev. edn. (Oxford, 1996). For the life see Humphrey Carpenter, *Benjamin Britten: A Biography* (London, 1992).

facility and a dazzling sardonic wit deriving from the neo-classical masters, there is at times a simpler lyricism whose origin is, perhaps, more local. Britten was helped to bring these various elements together into a fully mature, personal idiom by his principal teacher, Frank Bridge (1879–1941), and the first works in which maturity as well as mastery are unmistakably present are all vocal: the Rimbaud cycle *Les Illuminations* for high voice and strings (1939), the *Seven Sonnets of Michelangelo* for tenor and piano (1940), and the Serenade for tenor, horn, and strings (1943). All display Britten's abundant capacity for drama as well as lyricism: it was inevitable that he should turn to opera.

Peter Grimes is about an anti-hero, a misfit who longs to conform to social conventions ('society' being represented by the inhabitants of a Suffolk fishing village) but whose instincts and impulses make such conformity impossible. The essentially romantic nature of this theme needs no labouring, though Grimes as a character has few of the attractive, noble qualities of the true romantic outcast: he is not portrayed as a superior being, but as a 'sad case', intriguing and pathetic enough to attract well-meaning sympathy, but too eccentric and, in all probability, too perverse to deserve more than token toleration by a society which can only survive if all its members accept its conventions.[33] Needless to say, society itself is not depicted in the opera as a wholly good and worthy thing. Without approaching the degree of disgust in face of establishment figures which *Wozzeck* displays, Britten and his librettist Montagu Slater provide shrewd and unvarnished portraits of a variety of local worthies, most of whom are motivated by delight in power, on however small a scale, and who turn naturally to persecution of any whose faces fail to fit. The subject, and the opera, succeed principally because these universal issues are given the most convincing natural setting. Britten's genius as a musical illustrator provides a framework of sun, sea, and storm which could so easily have become a naive accompaniment to the events enacted. Yet the strong sense of locality—of a particular Suffolk landscape and climate—which the opera possesses does not seem to have hindered its appreciation in many other countries. Britten may have been in some respects a latterday nationalist, but his music has a wider appeal than that of any other twentieth-century British composer.

Peter Grimes is a motivically unified psychological drama retaining strong links with the traditional number opera, while being more romantic than neoclassical in style. The tonal harmony is typical of the period, balancing functional and non-functional progressions and retaining that clear distinction between discord and concord which remained Britten's principal expressive and structural device. While it may seem predictable that the chromatic semitone and tritone should be given great emphasis both thematically and harmonically,

---

[33] See Philip Brett (ed.), *Benjamin Britten:* Peter Grimes (Cambridge, 1983), which contains the first sustained attempt to explore the musical implications of Britten's sexuality.

naive parallels between musical and dramatic symbolism are avoided. Grimes himself is not represented by one key to which all others are opposed, but the work as a whole persistently probes the stability of diatonic harmony and hierarchical relationships. The structural use of clashes between opposing tonal centres is to be expected at more overtly dramatic moments, as in the Prologue to Act I or the Round in the final scene of Act I where Grimes disrupts the stable E♭ major and moves the tonality into E major before the chorus regains the initiative. Conflicts also permeate the more lyrical passages, however—even the most beautiful of them all, the short quartet for female voices which ends the first scene of Act II.

The quartet ('From the gutter') is in three parts, the second and third being variations of the first, and the first itself having an A–A₁–B structure in which each segment is preceded by an orchestral cadential phrase. The character of the music is determined by two types of tonal ambiguity, simultaneous and successive. The simultaneous type is less explicit, concerning the tendency of accompaniment and vocal lines in the A or A₁ segments to pull in different directions. In the first A segment, for example, the accompaniment has triads of C minor, the voices of B♭ major, and it is a personal matter whether these are felt to belong together diatonically or to clash (Ex. 4.7).

The successive ambiguity is much more explicit, however. The first A section shifts from C minor to D♭ major, and this epitomizes the movement within the quartet as a whole. Sometimes the shifts within phrases are of a semitone, at other times of a whole tone, as at the end where the final D♭ major is arrived at by progression from E♭ minor. But the uneasy oscillations of the harmony here are perfectly attuned to the troubled lyricism of the music. Britten's personal voice is perhaps at its clearest in such contexts, where economy of means is the dominant factor, rather than in moments of high drama and elaborate ensemble. Similar passages can be found in the later operas—the male narrator's superb description of the camp at night in *The Rape of Lucretia* and the ballad in the third scene of Act II in *Billy Budd*. But their effect, and the effect of the contrast between them and overtly dynamic episodes like Tarquinius' ride to Rome and the potential mutiny when Budd is executed, is never more powerful than in *Grimes*. The work is an assertion of a specially fertile association between dramatic subject and musical language which always remained valid for Britten. The vulnerable protagonist is a failure as much on account of greater sensitivity and awareness as because of inability to fulfil the expectations of society, and the vulnerable tonal system is threatened, undermined by the sheer weight of chromatic tensions. Yet tonality itself is not destroyed: it survives because Britten's deepest impulse was to dramatize the conflict between its diatonic and chromatic extremes, rather than portray an issue of that conflict. Hence the lack of totally unambiguous resolution in works as sensitively constructed as *Billy Budd* or the *War Requiem*. Normally the tonal outcome is perfectly explicit,

Ex. 4.7. Britten, *Peter Grimes*, Act 2, Scene 1, from two bars after Fig. 39

though such explicitness can be given disturbing resonance, as at the end of the Hardy cycle, *Winter Words* (1953), where a bright D major supports an anguished cry for release from the burden of feeling.

It nevertheless seems unlikely that Britten consciously sought to renew the diatonic–chromatic conflict in every work, or deliberately employ only such subjects and texts as showed some concern with social outcasts. The strength of his music lies in the way his chosen language is used, and a symbolic association between sound and subject, however close, will not satisfy unless the sounds themselves are memorable. If it were not for this directly musical appeal, the deep pessimism which often rises to the surface would probably disturb and even disgust many more people than seems to be the case. For all its frequent allusions to Christian imagery, there is little positive hope in Britten's world: there is considerable beauty, and often the music involved in expressing fascination with corruption and loss of innocence—especially the operas *The Turn of the Screw* (1954) and *Death in Venice* (1973) and the song cycles *Winter Words* and *Who are these Children?* (1969)—is itself positively beautiful.

As a conservative committed principally to vocal music, Britten was more skilful at adapting existing genres than in developing new ones: to this extent, the promise of the early choral variations was not fulfilled. He produced two major works, the Spring Symphony (1949) and the *War Requiem* (1961), which are in a kind of expanded cantata form, but the latter is surely more genuinely symphonic in its use of a unifying, evolving musical argument, and not even the purely instrumental Cello Symphony (1963) has a more satisfying overall design. In the field of the song cycle for solo voice and orchestra or piano, Britten favoured related themes or a varied selection from a single poet, rather than attempting to tell a story. English is the favoured language (though he set French, Italian, Russian, and German), images of night, corruption, and death the obsessively recurring elements. Britten achieved great intensity when linking the separate songs of a cycle together, as in the *Nocturne* (1958) and the *Songs and Proverbs of William Blake* (1965), and also by employing recurring thematic ideas, but the relative loss of continuity in those cycles where the songs are completely separate hardly produces any loss of coherence or expressive power, even when there is apparently no 'logical' scheme of tonal relationships within the cycle as a whole.

It is easy, in discussing Britten's operas, to relate their subject-matter to the same central theme as that of the cycles and other vocal works. His main achievement was to demonstrate both the inexhaustibility of the subject and the variety of ways in which it can be convincingly treated. Britten preferred material which had been created in another form by a great writer: Shakespeare, Maupassant, Melville, James, and Mann were among his sources. Yet whether the source was a great writer or merely an efficient librettist, he demonstrated the versatility of music drama in an age when lavish productions in large theatres became less and less practicable. The majority of Britten's works for the theatre qualify as 'chamber operas' (in terms of the forces employed). This concern with economy was initially the result of attempting to launch performances of several operas by a new company in the early post-war period, but it proved to have an attraction for the composer beyond the immediate practical necessity of the late 1940s. The first two such chamber operas—*The Rape of Lucretia* (1946) and *Albert Herring* (1947)—were well contrasted, but they employ identical accompanying ensembles: thirteen players in all. Of similar dimensions are the arrangement of John Gay's *The Beggar's Opera* (1948) and the 'entertainment for young people', *The Little Sweep (Let's make an Opera)* of 1949. Specific commissions, for the

Festival of Britain and the coronation of Queen Elizabeth II, led Britten back to the full-size opera house and larger orchestral forces, but here, too, there is a remarkable contrast between the claustrophobic world of *Billy Budd* (1951, revised 1960) and the ceremonial display of *Gloriana* (1953). The next opera, *The Turn of the Screw* (1954), with its accompaniment for chamber orchestra, its two-act structure, and explicitly unified musical design, involving the linking of scenes by interludes which vary a twelve-note theme, represented another obvious reaction, and is the most clearly transitional of all Britten's major compositions, anticipating features of *Owen Wingrave* (1970) and *Death in Venice*. The tensions between natural and supernatural forces, the inability of Good to conquer Evil, which are the essence of James's chilling ghost story, are paralleled by an increased concentration of musical procedures which focus more directly on diatonic/chromatic conflicts. It was nevertheless not until after his necessarily more expansive and relaxed version of *A Midsummer Night's Dream* (1960) that Britten moved consistently towards a musical language in which tonality could still exist without consistent triadic emphasis or clarification.

The three 'parables for church performance'—*Curlew River* (1964), *The Burning Fiery Furnace* (1966), and *The Prodigal Son* (1968)—represent the ultimate in dramatic stylization and musical compression. Though even the longest—the last—is only seventy-two minutes in duration, they are still more than negatively or residually operatic: distinct elements of aria and ensemble are still discernible, and gesture, regulated by principles derived from the Japanese theatre, makes an unusually strong contribution to the dramatic character of the parables. The sheer starkness of the music, framed by and in large part derived from Gregorian Chant, gives dramatic conviction to the unambiguously moral plot-material, yet prevents them from becoming mere sermons. Not surprisingly, the experience of writing these works for a select group of chosen artists, and his involvement in the preparation of their performances, left an indelible mark on Britten's two later operas, even though these revert to more universal dramatic subjects and forsake church for opera house. *Owen Wingrave* was in fact

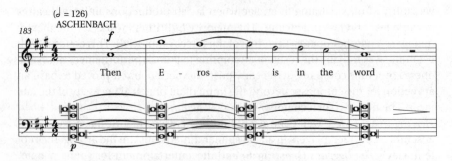

Ex. 4.8. Britten, *Death in Venice*, Act 1, Scene 7, from Fig. 183

originally written for television, though staging in the theatre was always envisaged. The plot explores the paradoxes of a conflict between Owen's open otherness—a pacifism that is often held to stand for homosexuality in Britten's
work—and the repressive belligerence of the Wingrave family and their associates. In *Owen Wingrave* Britten attempted his most ambitious confrontation
between twelve-note and tonal features, ending inevitably in a fading ambiguity rather than a grand, healing synthesis. *Wingrave* is virtually twice the length
of the single-act church parables, and in places the sustained austerity of the
writing weakens both harmonic direction and dramatic plausibility. Possibly it
was awareness of this which led Britten to give less prominence to quasi-serial
elements in *Death in Venice*, though they are still to be found, and as a result a
more satisfying overall design can be sensed, in which the acknowledged homo-
sexual otherness of the central character is explored through another of Britten's
favoured metaphors for difference, the sounds and modal constructs derived
from gamelan music.[34] These provide an appropriately intense focus for some of
the opera's most urgently lyrical declamation, as in Aschenbach's great scene of
self-discovery at the end of Act 1 (Ex. 4.8).

Death in Venice completed a return from the moralities dominated by religious
thought and imagery to a thoroughly secular subject with sexual elements recalling similar undertones in *Grimes* and *The Turn of the Screw*. We should be wary
of suggesting that a circle was completed, however, even though the tonality of
A is central to all three operas. *Death in Venice* shows the extent to which Britten,
for all his conservatism, was able to continue deepening and developing an
idiom of the greatest communicative power—a quality no less evident in other
late works, like the String Quartet No. 3 (1975) and the orchestral suite *A Time
There Was* (1974). Yet what is communicated is, invariably, a deep sense of inse-
curity. Even love leads to destruction, and it seems that tonality is clung to as the
ideal embodiment of something both cherished and vulnerable. With Britten,
one aspect of the contemporary crisis was expressed in remarkably direct form.
The attempt to absorb manipulation of twelve-note thematic shapes into a
tonal scheme neither exorcises the one nor permanently transforms the other.
Twentieth-century music continued to concern itself with interactions between
tonal and anti-tonal phenomena as well as with declarations of exclusive
allegiance to one or the other. It remained at once profoundly heterodox, and in
persistent pursuit of an ideal synthesis.

[34] See Donald Mitchell (ed.), *Benjamin Britten:* Death in Venice (Cambridge, 1987).

1915–1927

Béla Bartók completed his Second String Quartet in October 1917, and Halsey Stevens rightly said that 'the whole direction of Bartók's later writing might be deduced from this one work'.[1] Back in 1911, when he finished his opera *Blue-beard's Castle*,[2] Bartók had still not written a wholly successful instrumental work on a large scale. The First String Quartet (1909) has many remarkable qualities, but it is not a completely coherent conception, and the composer's confidence was hardly increased when *Bluebeard's Castle* was rejected by a Budapest competition jury. Bartók devoted himself to the collection and arrangement of folk music, only returning to 'serious' composition when war broke out and travel became difficult. The Second Quartet, like its contemporary, the ballet *The Wooden Prince* (1914–17), took a significantly long time to complete, but it laid the foundations for the next twenty-five years of creative achievement, not only in the way its musical language explores Bartók's distinctive stylistic conjunction between the materials of folk and art music, but also in the tension between tonal and post-tonal characteristics which his determination to preserve the large-scale sonata-based structures of earlier times made possible. This stylistic character gave Bartók a distinctive angle on the kind of interactions between symmetrical and hierarchic modes of structuring that often focus, with him as with so many others, on the octatonic scale;[3] at the same time, his no-less-distinctive concern to work with substantial, even symphonic forms helped to align him with modernist initiatives involving a far less stable association between the connected and the fractured. In his later years Bartók was most consistently radical, and explicitly post-tonal, in small-scale compositions like the piano piece 'Minor Seconds, Major Sevenths' (*Mikrokosmos*, Book 6, 1933), but his larger works embody the full richness of the subtle interaction between

[1] Halsey Stevens, *The Life and Music of Béla Bartók*, 3rd edn., ed. M. Gillies (Oxford, 1993), 54. This remains the standard 'Life and Works'. For a thorough and fascinating account of aspects of compositional process, see Lázló Somfai, *Béla Bartók: Composition, Concepts, and Autograph Sources* (Berkeley and Los Angeles, 1996).
[2] See Ch. 2, p. 45.
[3] For a detailed account of this topic, see Richard Cohn, 'Bartók's Octatonic Strategies: A Motivic Approach', *Journal of the American Musicological Society*, 44 (1991), 262–300. The most substantial discussion of Bartók in terms of consistently controlling, symmetrical interval cycles is Elliott Antokoletz, *The Music of Béla Bartók: A Study of Tonality and Progression in Twentieth-Century Music* (Berkeley and Los Angeles, 1984).

tradition and innovation on which his lasting reputation rests, and this quality is already present in the String Quartet No. 2 (1915–17).

The principal tonal centre of the quartet is an A which, although it only emerges gradually and is not established or exploited through traditional triadic progressions, functions as a tonic for the first and third movements of the work. (Its close relative, D, is the centre for the Scherzo.) The avoidance of such triads involves a parallel avoidance of emphasis on the interval of the perfect fifth, and it is clear that the tritone and minor third, with their function of dividing the octave symmetrically and thereby of contradicting and conflicting with traditional hierarchical relationships within the octave, are already suggesting not only particular types of folk-orientated thematic material but also a new kind of tonal organization, in which the symmetries of octatonicism promote subtle dialogues between the tendency to reinforce tonality and the no-less-urgent impulse to disrupt it.

The Second Quartet uses forms derived from traditional models, though the slow third movement is freer in this respect than most of Bartók's later finales. There are also motivic relationships between the movements, and the character of the music involves frequent reference to national rhythmic and melodic features: indeed, the Scherzo is one of the most explicitly folk-inspired pieces Bartók ever composed. These, then, are the main characteristics of the Second Quartet, and they were to be continued, developed, and reshaped—but never abandoned—in Bartók's later compositions. The palpable disparity between hierarchic structural backgrounds and those often more explicitly symmetrical concerns which helped to determine harmonic as well as motivic elements is vividly reflected in Adorno's perception, quoted in Chapter 2, that Bartók's use of folk material was 'a critique of the "dead forms" of Western art music', and that he succeeded in forging 'a new and integrated musical language which does not in the process hide the fractured character of its elements'.[4] Inevitably, therefore, commentaries on the composer tend to proceed either from the conviction that 'the integration of materials derived from folk melodies with atonal techniques of composition comprises the cornerstone of Bartók's mature work',[5] or from the belief that such integration is often difficult to hear as a secure and stable foundation. The question of how 'one might reconcile internal, syntactic, atonal hearings' of a composition like the first movement of the *Sonata for Two Pianos and Percussion* 'with the external, semantic tonal hearings that might also be present', makes it difficult to resist 'a more pluralistic stance, regarding tonality and atonality, syntactic and semantic, internal and external readings as capable of coexisting in the same composition, and even in the same passage of music'.[6] (Both writers cited here use 'atonal' to refer to the kind of motivic processes that

---

[4] See Max Paddison, *Adorno's Aesthetics of Music* (Cambridge, 1993), 41.
[5] Mark Nelson, 'Folk Music and the "Free and Equal Treatment of the Twelve Tones": Aspects of Béla Bartók's Synthetic Methods', *College Music Symposium*, 27 (1987), 65.
[6] Cohn, 'Bartók's Octatonic Strategies', 298.

work with transpositions, inversions, and retrogrades of a basic cell, in such a way as to undermine the consistent functioning of hierarchically organized harmony.)

The consequences of such considerations are apparent in several works, discussed below, and many of the factors present in the Second Quartet remain salient. The quartet was first performed in March 1918, by which time the ballet *The Wooden Prince*, first performed in May 1917, had brought Bartók a degree of public success at last, and the long-delayed first performance of *Bluebeard's Castle* followed in May 1918. These events did not provoke an increase in creative activity, however. The publication of folk music still occupied much of Bartók's time, and although he composed another ballet, *The Miraculous Mandarin* (1918–19, orchestrated 1923–4), its controversial subject-matter deterred any theatre from accepting it, and the music remained unperformed until 1926. There is a vehement intensity in the two sonatas for violin and piano (1921–2), and the commitment to tonality itself, however extended, seems in danger of being lost. That 'danger' was soon averted, but the medium of chamber music would remain of the greatest significance for Bartók to the end of his life.

The commitment to traditional structures in the violin sonatas is far from wholehearted, and the apparent reluctance with which the rhapsodic, large-scale first movement of No. 1 discloses a basic adherence to sonata form may be the main reason for the general opinion that it is not a complete success. Bartók himself evidently accepted this verdict, since he was willing to let the work be played without it. The harmonic direction of the second and third movements is certainly more precisely focused, and with the appearance of more specifically Hungarian material the virtually atonal impressionism which Bartók seems to have learned most directly from his Polish contemporary Szymanowski is less apparent. The two-movement Second Sonata is the finer, with clearer form and surer harmonic control. There are nevertheless signs that Bartók's desire to demand a high degree of virtuosity from both players helped to dictate a somewhat disjointed, episodic form in the second movement; and the overall scheme, presenting problems which are not all solved with equal success, may have prompted a further attempt at a single-movement scheme with two basic parts, in the String Quartet No. 3 (1927).

A less aggressive, experimental tone is struck by the Dance Suite (August 1923), which exists in orchestral and solo piano versions. It was the work which, in Bartók's own view, closed the first phase of his career. After three years (1923–6) in which his only works were a handful of folksong transcriptions, a flood of new compositions established him unmistakably as one of the leading modern masters. In them his reactions to the two innovatory giants of the post-war musical world—the neo-classical Stravinsky and the serial Schoenberg—can be clearly observed; in particular, Bartók seemed to share their concern to keep lyricism, and with it any overtly romantic qualities, in a subordinate position. Nevertheless, there was no likelihood of Bartók's becoming a wholehearted disciple of either: his own ideas were now too clear-cut, and his own genius too strong, to permit any decline into stylistic subservience.

Analysis: String Quartet No. 3

Of all Bartók's mature compositions, the Third String Quartet is perhaps the most imaginative in form and the most intense in expression. Both the imagination and the intensity are rooted in compression: the work is in one movement and lasts little more than fifteen minutes. Yet the compression serves to sharpen the contrasts between dramatic and lyric types of material, between contrapuntal and harmonic textures, and it also presents one of Bartók's most rigorously organized arguments between tonal centres; the argument is at once about degrees of relationship (old and new) and about the need to establish a single supreme centre, which may ultimately be diatonically, if not triadically, asserted. The single movement of the quartet is divided into four sections: Part One, Part Two, the Recapitulation of Part One, and Coda. Within such a compressed scheme, one would expect a large degree of unity in every dimension, but it is the most fundamental technical feature—the type of conflict between tonal centres—which is the most basic unifying factor. Thematic interrelationships are less important, less immediately perceptible, pertaining principally to the first and third, and second and fourth sections respectively. The main thematic contrasts are *between* rather than *within* sections, however, and this reinforces a deep-seated duality which is one way in which the fundamental tonal argument is carried through.

The forms of the individual sections are not as easily absorbed into predetermined ternary or sonata schemes as are most of Bartók's later designs. In Parts One and Two the structures serve to prepare and present a particular tonal conflict (C♯ versus C♮)—a conflict which takes very different guises in both but is resolved in neither. To this extent the same essential issue is approached by way of two radically different types of material, and two forms which have an ancestry in ternary and sonata design, but which are adapted to the unique purposes of this particular work.

Part One is slow, Part Two is fast; Part One is lyrical and builds to a melodic statement of gravely simple beauty; Part Two is hectic, dramatic (and distinctly more folk-like); its climax is an essentially harmonic, virtually athematic confrontation of the most aggressive kind, in which the tonal, and therefore the structural, issue is for once completely on the surface. There is still no resolution, however, and the third and fourth sections of the work, with their remarkably free rethinking of the issues presented in the first two parts, ultimately resolve the problem by sheer vital force, though in a way which proves that, as in all hierarchical tonal schemes, rivals are also to a degree associates.

Any brief analysis of so subtle a score risks abject surrender to over-simplification, and different approaches, inevitably, yield different results. Most explicitly reductive is the kind of commentary that follows up Ernö Lendvai's interpretation of tonality in terms of axes of symmetry, rather than cycles of fifths, and which interprets the Third Quartet's polarization of C♯ and C♮ as the opposition of tonic (C♯, E, G, A♯) and subdominant (F♯, A, C, D♯) axes.[7] Such designations, standing as they do for large areas of highly differentiated music, are least attractive to analysts who seek a more linear interpretation of events on the musical surface. For Paul Wilson, the possible existence of different tonal centres in a kind of deep background relationship is less relevant than the large-scale composing out of the work's initial D♯ over C♯.[8] Wilson seeks to distinguish such hierarchic processes from the Schenkerian prolongational model which is not easily adapted to music exemplifying the 'emancipation of the dissonance', but his reading of the Third Quartet's 'large-scale harmonic processes' offers many hostages to fortune in the way its clear-cut neo-Schenkerian notation resists straightforward interpretation in terms of traditional, diatonic contrapuntal function. Given that it is precisely because 'large-scale harmonic processes' are called into question in post-tonal composition, an approach emphasizing the connections between local tonal centres and pervasive motivic materials may still be preferred.

In Part One of the Third Quartet the principal motive (a rising fourth and falling third) emerges in the sixth and seventh bars, and is also of considerable importance between Figs. 3 and 5 (plus two bars), and between Fig. 11 and the end of the part. Although the central segment of this ternary scheme evolves away from the original form of the basic motive, it provides clear indications that C♯ is truly central (for example, four bars before Fig. 9), and that the issue at stake is more its survival than its supremacy. With the return of the basic shape in the final stages of Part One, however, the white-note melodic version is dominant, while C♯ and G♯ are given greatest prominence in the bass, and the clarity with which the contrasting harmonic areas are stratified promotes a degree of stability (Ex. 5.1). This provisional stability is expressed in its most basic form four bars from the end of Part One, with a 'chord' (C♯, G♯, G♮) which confirms that an important element in the conflict involves the orthodox dominants of the tonal centres, and their ambiguous position in Bartók's scheme of things. G♮, as a dominant, may be a powerful agent of C♮ in conventional terms, but as the tritone relative of C♯ and with a position precisely midway between one C♯ and another, it may in the end be given an even stronger function in that connection.

In Part Two of the quartet, the mood changes and the tonal argument modulates with it. Immediately, in the D♮–E♭ trill of the second violin, the shift can be perceived, and the new, scalic, thematic material confirms the location of this

[7] Ernö Lendvai, *Béla Bartók: An Analysis of his Music* (London, 1971), and *The Workshop of Bartók and Kodály* (Budapest, 1983).
[8] Paul Wilson, *The Music of Béla Bartók* (New Haven, 1992), 85–118.

Ex. 5.1. Bartók, String Quartet No. 3, *Prima parte*, from three bars after Fig. 11

new stage in the conflict of semitones. Just as, in Part One, the argument was pursued principally through the opposition between 'white' and 'black' note forms of the main motive, which in development tend to interact, so in Part Two the same essential principle is established in the early stages.

Attempts to define the overall form of Part Two in terms of a single archetype are unsatisfactory, and it may well be that Bartók here achieved a blend of variation and sonata form of the kind attempted later by Webern in the first movement of the String Quartet Op. 28 and the Variations for Orchestra Op. 30.[9] Yet the presence of modulatory features in Bartók's case naturally creates a much greater closeness to the traditional sonata model, and his 'variations' are equally perceptible as stages of development.

The exposition of the second part is certainly over at Fig. 5. By then Bartók has established his two thematic elements: first, the modal-triadic 'white-note' cello idea, which immediately provokes a brief 'black-note' retort, but is allowed some canonic development before a fully worked-out 'black-note' theme is stated. At Fig. 3, this is heard in the first violin (it is not, of course, exclusively 'black-note': the most important thing about it is that it is centred on E♭), and is unfolded in immediate combination with the cello triads, pointing up at once their similar motivic constitution and a tonal polarity which the sharing of F♮ and C♮ does nothing to alleviate (Ex. 5.2).

The first stage of variation/development (Figs. 5–7) inverts the 'black-note' idea, and suggests a transitional function in its double departure: from the

[9] See Ch. 10, p. 212f.

Ex. 5.2. Bartók, String Quartet No. 3, *Seconda parte*, from Fig. 3

confrontation between two versions of a similar basic shape, and from the conflict between D and E♭. This section actually restores the C♯/C opposition for much of its length, and also includes a subsidiary clash between F and E.

The fierce and concentrated logic of the developmental processes between Figs. 7 and 36 are best studied directly in the score, but some general points concerning texture and the direction of the tonal argument can be made in words. Once the fundamental terms of the harmonic argument have been restated, between Figs. 7 and 8, in the reiterated D/E♭/A unit, the composer gradually shifts the emphasis away from tonal conflict as such into a polyphonic development of the main motives, which enables the purely tonal argument to unfold on a larger scale. At one bar before Fig. 12 a long series of canons begins, initially involving only the two violins (tonal centre C, moving to E), then, at Fig. 14, shifting to the viola and cello (centre A), back to the violins at Fig. 15 (centre D), and viola and second violin four bars later (centre G). All this, using the cello version of the main motive as thematic material, is merely a preliminary flexing of muscles, however: the canons so far having involved assent rather than conflict. At Fig. 16, all four instruments are involved for the first time in a double canon by inversion, principally at the tritone with C and F♯ as the most basic 'poles'. Once again, the more fundamental tonal oppositions of Part One are recalled, though in a context where the absence of C♯ itself confirms that the conflict as such has not been renewed: in so pervasively contrapuntal a texture, no clear feeling of tonal centre can emerge at all.

An important new stage begins at Fig. 19 with the restoration of D (supported by both F♮ and A♮) as tonal centre for a passage of concentrated canonic development of the 'black-note' motive. As the music descends sequentially, so the area of C♯/C is touched on: as if to prevent this gaining in importance, the texture solidifies, canon disappears temporarily, and both D and E♭ are added to form a four-note cluster (four bars before Fig. 23).

The rest of the development section can be divided into two main parts. Between Figs. 23 and 31 the 'black-note' version, restored initially to its original E♭ basis, sweeps aside a renewed attempt at canons on the 'white-note' version. Clashes between D/E♭ yield again, as they did at Fig. 5, to C♯/C: there is an unmistakably recapitulatory quality here, but at the climax the prime associate of D/E♭ (A) is fully in control (Fig. 31).

The final variation, or stage of development, then achieves the greatest contrapuntal concentration yet. It begins as a 'double fugato' centred on A, the close relative of C and the most powerful opponent of C♯. After 'orthodox' answers on E, the subject (deriving from the 'black-note' motive) gradually builds up a sequence of stretti which inhibit the emergence of any clear tonal direction. A stasis similar to that at Fig. 23 seems the only possible outcome. But this time the cluster is a whole tone higher: instead of C/C♯/D/E♭ we have D/E♭/E/F. It is the F which, as E♯ in enharmonic disguise, runs on into the recapitulation at Fig. 36 and helps to confirm C♯ rather than D as the principal tonal centre (Ex. 5.3).

It is this substitution, engineered by Bartók with sovereign inevitability, which provokes the virtual collapse of the thematic process in the closing stages of Part Two, and the naked clashes, not between C♯ and D, but between C♯ and C♮, the original *alter ego* for which D has in effect been acting as a substitute throughout Part Two. Of course this has to remain unresolved. At four bars before Fig. 49, C♯ in the cello underpins a full C major triad in the upper instruments. In the rapid collapse which ensues, the two notes parry each other like fencers, and when the cello 'resolves' its last C♯ on to a D, this is the very reverse of a triumphant conclusion but an admission that the whole issue remains in doubt (Ex. 5.4).

After the brutal denouement of Part Two, when the attention has been focused on tonal issues to the exclusion of thematic issues, the third section (Recapitulation of Part One) reasserts the thematic process but suspends the tonal argument almost completely. Bartók's title for the section is only approximate: it is an allusive restudying of the thematic material of Part One, with virtually nothing in the way of exact repetition. Yet its function is both to reassert the thematic process, and to prepare the ground for the final thematic *and* tonal argument of the Coda. It has an oddly hesitant foreboding which creates no sense of anticlimax or of marking time. In fact its psychological necessity and appropriateness are more remarkable than its technical function within the scheme of the work as a whole. The C♯/C♮ conflict is still to be heard (e.g. five bars after Fig. 3), however, and the final bars seem to be moving decisively in favour of C♯, when the Coda suddenly takes over in a mood of barely suppressed hysteria and firmly rooted on a cello C (Ex. 5.5).

The Coda is at once a thrilling reworking of material from Part Two and a final establishment of the fact that C♮ is subordinate to C♯. The last cadence, with its

Ex. 5.3. Bartók, String Quartet No. 3, *Seconda parte*, from four bars before Fig. 36

long 'dominant' preparation in which the bass note G♯ has C♯s and D♯s strongly in evidence above it, indicates that, if this were a simple diatonic ending, then C♮ would *really* be the leading note B♯, and would therefore need to resolve on to its tonic (Ex. 5.6).

Such functions are scarcely relevant here, but the final chords serve both to summarize the conflict which provoked the entire work and also to project a satisfying outcome to that conflict. Yet 'satisfaction' is not to be confused with a sense of resolution and triumphant closure along Beethovenian lines. The constitution of the final chords reinforces the structural importance of major as well as of minor seconds, perfect fifths as well as tritones, to the fabric of the work as a whole. They clarify persistent tensions and indicate how these may be preserved within an appropriate gesture of completion, and suggest a less

Ex. 5.4. Bartók, String Quartet No. 3, *Seconda parte*, from four bars before Fig. 49

wholeheartedly unified effect than that proposed by Mark Nelson. For Nelson 'the climactic octatonic/glissandi passage of the Coda' is 'a distillation of the canonic imitation, sustained chromaticism and paired ascending and descending motion intrinsic to one theme's transformations, and a condensed resumé of the rhythm and Dorian/octatonic alterations characteristic of another', comprising thereby 'an extraordinary synthetic alloying of the work's essential thematic elements'.[10] This reading follows on from Nelson's argument that in the quartet the octatonic scale not only 'manifests a propensity to conciliate disparate forces' but also 'facilitates a fusion of the identifying features of two distinct themes', enabling Bartók to meld 'numerous values and phenomena from two utterly different but ultimately complementary worlds'.[11] Linguistic fusion

[10] Nelson, 'Folk Music', 103–4.   [11] Ibid. 114.

Ex. 5.5. Bartók, String Quartet No. 3, *Recapitulazione della prima parte*, from 2 bars after Fig. 7

and melding are undeniable, but with Bartók, no less than with Stravinsky, as will be seen in Chapter 6, the structural tensions set up by their use within the framework of a formal design derived from classical models are too great to make possible, still less desirable, an outcome in which synthesis and integration is all. Ultimately, the greatness of Bartók's Third Quartet lies in the lucidity and coherence with which music of such passion and power is projected, not to dissolve its modernistic attributes, but to enable them to serve, and be embodied in, that lucidity and coherence, with maximum effectiveness. It was a triumph which the composer never surpassed.

Ex. 5.6. Bartók, String Quartet No. 3, *Coda*, from four bars before Fig. 14 to the end

Bartók after 1927

During the remaining eighteen years of his life, Bartók produced a series of instrumental compositions which refine and reflect the explorations of the period between the Third and Fourth Quartets. It was not a period of major innovations and many of the works display similar methods. Nevertheless, there is nothing in the least monotonous about Bartók's exploitation of his hard-won stylistic maturity, and even in those works where structural symmetry is all-pervading, the material is treated with unfailing inventiveness. The predictability of large amounts of exact repetition is always avoided, even though the conflict between rival tonal centres is normally less hectic and triadic harmonies more frequent than in the Third Quartet. Bartók continued to produce folksong transcriptions, and in 1939 completed the large *Mikrokosmos* sequence of 153 progressive piano pieces, his most important educational legacy. His personal life was severely disrupted by the outbreak of the Second World War. Like many, he sought refuge in America: unlike many, he found absence from his native land almost unbearable, and ill-health and public indifference made his last years miserable and less crowningly productive than might have been hoped. In view of Bartók's long struggle for creative stability and public acceptance in Hungary—which he attained without facile compromise and by intensifying rather than diluting his commitment to what he believed to be the most fundamental cultural features of his own nationality—his early death in exile remains one of the tragedies of twentieth-century culture. More than any other great European composer, he was a victim of political forces: the man who had sought to integrate progressive artistic ideas into the fabric of a nation's life was in large part himself destroyed by the Hitlerian perversion of nationalism.

A study of the major compositions of the period from 1928 to 1945 reveals the establishment of a new equilibrium, wherein the 'poise' of structures in which many basic features are predetermined is projected through material of great appeal and compelling plasticity, often employing further refinements of the symmetric/hierarchic conjunctions identified above. There are three five-movement works: the String Quartets No. 4 (1928) and No. 5 (1934) and the Concerto for Orchestra (1943). Parallels between the quartets are easily demonstrated: the themes and forms of the first and fifth, and the second and fourth movements are related in each case, with the central movement acting as the pivot of the 'bridge' or 'arch'. The greater forcefulness of the Fourth String Quartet (which became a five-movement work at a relatively late stage, when Bartók added what is now the fourth movement) is accounted for largely by the fact that it has only one slow movement (the third): in the Fifth the second and fourth movements are both slow. The other significant difference is that the later work starts with unmistakable tonal emphasis, on B♭, whereas the main centre of the Fourth Quartet (C) emerges far less obviously or immediately. The greater radicalism of the Fourth is also inferable from its tendency to be 'all-thematic', whereas the Fifth, though with no shortage of contrapuntal writing, exploiting inversional symmetry in tightly imitative textures, is not so easily analysed in virtually serial terms. Since there is always the temptation to proceed with the discussion of these two powerful works along mutually exclusive lines, it is important to emphasize the finely shaped melodic writing of the Fourth Quartet's central movement and the discordant expressionism of the Fifth's outer movements. The Fifth probably has the wider expressive range, encompassing the enchanting delicacy of the third movement's trio and the blatantly bitter naivety of the last-minute classical parody (Finale, bar 699), while the Fourth has the more concentrated dramatic impact, its tonal argument reflecting the turbulent subtleties of its near-contemporary, No. 3.

In the much later Concerto for Orchestra, a more expansive score, the intellectual implications of symmetry are not pursued further, or even as far. As with the Fourth Quartet, there is a central slow movement of considerable eloquence—and the material is linked with that of the introduction to the whole work—but the atmosphere of the flanking pairs of fast movements is more relaxed than is the case with the quartets. Bartók's own note on the work speaks not of symmetrical equivalences but of 'a gradual transition from the sternness of the first movement . . . to the life-assertion of the last one'.[12] Technically, apart from its dazzling exploitation of the orchestra, the texture ranges from intricate polyphony to sumptuously harmonized, folk-derived melody, including another brief parody recalling that in the Fifth Quartet, though this time there is a specific victim: the 'Fascist' march theme from Shostakovich's Seventh (*Leningrad*) Symphony. The concerto has disappointed those who prefer Bartók's more adventurous earlier style, and the forms of the individual movements, particularly the second and fourth, are indeed uncomplicated to the point of obviousness. Yet the play with tonality, at times triadically enforced, at times less simply presented, is as vigorous as ever, and as convincing, not least in the context of the kind of tensions that can be identified when the work is seen as 'a lament for man's inhumanity to man' as well as 'a positive vision of a world in a kind of harmony in which chaos and order, the primeval enemies, are held in dynamic equilibrium'.[13]

The three four-movement works from this period are very different: the *Music for Strings, Percussion and Celesta* (1936), the String Quartet No. 6 (1939), and the Sonata for Solo Violin (1944). These are the only major mature works in which Bartók ever employed a four-movement scheme, unless it is argued that the Third String Quartet itself belongs under that heading. It is certainly not inappropriate to consider the structure of the *Music for Strings, Percussion and Celesta* alongside that of the Third Quartet, for although the former is in four distinct movements rather than four linked sections, the sequence of moods

---

[12] See Stevens, *Life and Music*, 280.
[13] David Cooper, *Bartók: Concerto for Orchestra* (Cambridge, 1996), 2.

(neither beginning with a 'symphonic' allegro) can be equated and there are thematic links between all four movements of the *Music*, extending the alternating links of the Third Quartet and prefiguring the 'motto' theme of the Sixth. Most importantly, however, the two works provide perhaps the most impressive examples (apart from the Second Quartet) of that 'transition' of mood to which Bartók referred in his note on the Concerto for Orchestra; true, the Coda of the Third Quartet is perhaps too hectic and concentrated to be described simply as 'life-asserting', but it brings the work to a triumphant as well as intellectually convincing end. The *Music for Strings, Percussion and Celesta*, by contrast, fits Bartók's terminology precisely. It would be oversimplifying to say that the chromatic searchings of the start are dissipated in diatonic radiance at the end: there is never any real doubt about the central function of A, the first note of the work, but there is a world of difference between the lugubrious counterpoint to which it gives rise in the first movement and the exciting thrummed major triads which launch the finale.

The *Music* also makes extensive use of that opposition between tritone and perfect fifth which was fundamental to the Third Quartet, and it is the more explicit here in view of Bartók's willingness to employ simple triadic harmony (in the sonata-form second movement, C, F♯, and G are deployed, and this element is inverted—F, F♯, and C—in the arch-form third movement). The primary tritone is, however, A-E♭, unchallenged in the initial fugue, but in effect forced, or encouraged, to resolve on to A-E (though not to disappear) in the rondo-like finale.

The dialogue between hierarchic and symmetric tendencies inherent in Bartók's musical language has an even more prominent role in the Sixth String Quartet, a work very different from the *Music for Strings, Percussion and Celesta* in its overall character and shape. In a sense, the shape is the reverse of that of *Music*, with the fastest movement coming first and the slowest last—Bartók's first slow finale since the Second Quartet, and one of his simplest yet most eloquent inspirations. As the Second Quartet showed, ending in slow desolation does not necessarily mean ending in tonal ambiguity, but in the Sixth Quartet, for the only time in his mature output, Bartók does not conclude with an absolutely explicit tonal emphasis. Instead, two of the members of the 'tonic axis', D and F, coexist with their respective fifths. In view of the fact that the cadential progression of bars 84 and 85 involves a very clear movement on to D and A from their tritones, and the further fact that the D and A remain sounding after the cello's F major triad has died away, those who wish to allot a single centre to the work will associate this ending with the conclusion of the first movement and choose D. If it is D, however, it is with an unusual degree of ambiguity which is acceptable only because it is implicit in the material and manner of the work's generating idea (Ex. 5.7). This idea is a 'motto' theme (Ex. 5.8), which prefaces each of the first three movements and forms the principal subject of the fourth. It will be noted how clearly the first phrase of the motto outlines the tritone G♯/D, even though

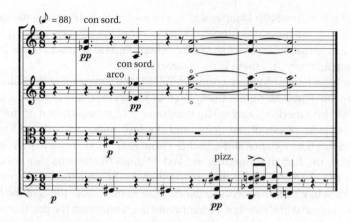

Ex. 5.7. Bartók, String Quartet No. 6, 4th movt., bar 83 to the end

Ex. 5.8. Bartók, String Quartet No. 6, 1st movt., bars 1–13

the context is more chromatic than octatonic. But the motto as a whole presents a move away from such decisiveness, with a positive assertion of ambiguous intent in the prolonged 'D', which acts as a C𝗑 resolving on to D♯ (bar 8).

Tonal explicitness does not seem required of such a melancholy theme, so that although the tonal framework of the piece as a whole remains faithful to a basic symmetry—B is central to the March, A♭ to the March's 'trio', F (ironic major triads) to the Burletta, D to its central Andantino—the finale itself starts from an A minor triad, which could be a 'real' dominant but is powerless to establish any permanent effect because of the chromatic nature of the motto theme, whose harmonization it initiates. Even the return of first-movement material in the central section of the movement does nothing to press any relevant tonal claim. In fact the suspense becomes truly agonizing, the issues so delicately balanced that no decisive outcome is rationally conceivable. For that the motto theme itself would have to change its nature.

At the end of the score Bartók wrote 'Saanen Budapest, 1939, VIII–XI'. A few months later he was in America, and although he returned briefly to Hungary to settle his affairs, the Sixth Quartet was a genuine farewell, an ending the sadness of which is all the more touching for being so economically expressed. It may in a technical sense be 'inconclusive', but when the end is reached the listener knows instinctively that there is no more to be said.

Bartók's last four-movement composition was the Sonata for Solo Violin which he wrote for Yehudi Menuhin. Completed in March 1944, it is in many ways the best of all the American works. The toughness and concentration of the music recall the finest pieces of the 1920s, and the four movements do add up to a sonata rather than a dance suite, so there is no exact, neo-classical parallel with Bach. True, the first movement is marked 'Tempo di ciaccona', but this refers more to the character of the first theme than to the structure of the whole, a sonata form in which the second subject, centred on E♭ after the G of the first, is much more lyrical in character. Development deals only with the first theme, and after a recapitulation which itself involves further development, the relatively restrained coda changes the tonal emphasis from G minor to G major.

Bartók's skill at fugal writing can often be observed, but the second movement of this sonata is the only example of a complete fugue in the late works, apart from the first movement of the *Music for Strings, Percussion and Celesta*. A four-voice fugue for a violin naturally requires the greatest skill if the result is not to seem strained or even ugly. Bartók's fugue is a severe affair, with a terse, aggressive subject and the use of many contrapuntal and violinistic devices, as when a statement of the subject (bowed) is combined with its own inversion (plucked), but it is written from a profound understanding of the potentialities of the instrument. It is demanding, for both player and listener, but never ungrateful or unrewarding.

After such concentration a degree of relaxation is essential, and the third movement, a slow 'Melodia', is broadly lyrical without losing itself in sentimentality, even in its more florid later stages. The Presto finale is a rondo with two episodes, in which G is re-established as tonal centre after the C of the fugue and the B♭ of the Melodia: a relatively strong assertion of traditional, functional relationships.

All Bartók's concertos (excepting the first for violin of 1907–8) are in three movements; so, from the later period, are the Sonata for Two Pianos and Percussion (1937), which the composer also transcribed as a concerto for two pianos and orchestra, and two slighter pieces, *Contrasts* for violin, clarinet, and piano (1938) and the *Divertimento* for string orchestra (1939).

The whole of Bartók's final period—a period in which the tonic triad, not just the tonic note, is restored to a degree of prominence—is framed by the Second and Third Piano Concertos (1931 and 1945 respectively), for the Viola Concerto was left too incomplete to qualify as true Bartók. The two piano concertos present two distinct types of form, both of great importance for the composer. The first type, found in the Second Concerto, relates to arch form, with sharing of material and character (though not, in this case, form) between the outer movements. The second type, that of the Third Concerto, is more traditional, lacking symmetrical parallels and involving outer movements quite distinct in character, the finale lightening rather than reflecting the mood of the first movement. For purposes of analytical comparison, it is worth concentrating on what are probably the two finest representatives of these structural types from the late period, the Sonata for Two Pianos and Percussion and the Second Violin Concerto (1938). The fundamentally asymmetrical form of the Sonata is compensated for by a more obvious exploitation of internal pitch symmetry involving the tritone (note, for example, the progression of the slow introduction from F♯ to C and the replacement of F♯ by G in the third bar of the main Allegro).[14] There is in any case an obvious difference of character between the works, since one would hardly expect the same kind of emphasis on lyrical melody in a work for two pianos and percussion: here there is a more epic tone, at least in the first movement, with much contrapuntal interplay to set off the massive harmonic climaxes, yielding to an expansive *bonhomie* in the finale which can at times seem too self-consciously jolly. Much of the material of the sonata reflects the limitations of percussion instruments in its concentration on simple reiterated motives, but there are more haunting moments: for instance, the second subject of the first movement (bars 84 ff.), and the central episode of the second movement in which the two pianos generate a dialogue of riveting tension.

The sonata is not the most spontaneous of Bartók's works, and the exactness with which the first movement conforms to 'Golden Section' proportions might have something to do with that;[15] the Second Violin Concerto is, however, that rare phenomenon, a modern masterpiece wholly characteristic of its creator which uses traditional textures and structures in a fresh and valid way. The danger with symmetrical interrelationships is always that they may produce mechanically predictable results: here, however, the finale, for all its clear derivation of theme and form from the first movement, has that extra degree of informality which is precisely right for the work.

The concerto's character is immediately established by the way in which the lyric first subject, triadically introduced, though its progressions soon cease to be conventionally diatonic, moves into more energetic transitional material. This might sound perilously close to the reverse of what an effective sonata-form movement should propose, but it works superbly well, since Bartók's melodic ideas have exactly the right air of controlled freedom to warrant the more business-like passage work of the transitions. 'Formality' is well integrated into

[14] Cohn, 'Bartók's Octatonic Strategies', 279–97. Cohn shows how the first movement's octatonic elements require consideration from both 'tonal' and 'atonal' (motivic) perspectives.

[15] Lendvai (see n. 7 above) links Bartók's use of Golden Section proportions, and Fibonacci series, to 'axis' principles. Golden Section is the division of a structure so that the relationship of one segment to the other is as the other to the whole. A Fibonacci sequence of numbers is one in which each term is the sum of its two predecessors: 1, 2, 3, 5, 8, etc.

this first movement by such effects as the inversion of the first theme in the development (bar 194) and of the transitional material in the recapitulation, the 'twelve-note' second subject (stated over a pedal), and the hints of symmetric structuring (the development begins on F major triads). But it is the capacity of aristocratic poise and peasant vigour not merely to coexist but to interact which makes this movement such a fine one.

'Aristocratic poise' may likewise describe the theme of the central movement's set of variations, centred on G with prominent C♯s. Violinistic conventions (e.g. the double stopping at bars 43 ff.) are functionally integrated as in few other modern concertos, and the variety of mood achieved against the background of the charmingly contemplative theme makes one regret that Bartók did not write more sets of variations.

The finale, its sonata structure and material paralleling those of the first movement at every point, is itself a large-scale variation, much faster than the original and in triple time. No work of Bartók's better demonstrates the satisfaction which can accrue from such a tonally centred, thematically unified technique, in which evolution and repetition are held in delicately purposeful balance. The concerto is as 'progressive' a work as one from which thematic unity is completely absent, even though it may rely more on conventional details of figuration and form than the Third or Sixth Quartets.

The high level of achievement in three such different works as the Third and Sixth String Quartets and the Second Violin Concerto shows the exceptional range of which Bartók was capable. Yet these works have a still wider significance. Of all twentieth-century composers who have accepted and preserved the fundamental principle of tonality, Bartók was perhaps the most successful at justifying that preservation through his parallel adaptation of traditional formal elements. Yet, as argued earlier, his resourceful rethinking of such traditions is far from ensuring the unambiguous retention of the 'classical' values of unity and stability. David Cooper is one recent commentator who has argued that the much-hyped Bartókian 'synthesis', designed to claim the composer for 'classicism' rather than 'modernism', 'may well be illusory. Perhaps we should admire Bartók's music as much for its ability to accommodate, as for its tendency to assimilate difference, for its admission of the coexistence of disparate materials, as much as their integration.'[16] Cooper's technical argument, that 'it is the surface disruption of Bartók's music, rather than its deeper level integration, which gives it a living, vital quality',[17] no less than his shrewd observation about tensions between symmetrical scale-forms and asymmetrical structural schemes, is extremely persuasive. His conclusion, that the Concerto for Orchestra, 'a work in which difference is celebrated as much as consensus, fragmentation as much as unity', may risk hyperbole, but his more general view that Bartók's 'is an unstable music with complex and fragmentary boundaries'[18] rings true. In

---

[16] Cooper, *Bartók*, 1–2. [17] Ibid. 76. [18] Ibid. 84.

such a way we can begin to do justice to Adorno's perception, cited earlier, that the use of folk material as a critique of Western traditions forges 'a new and integrated musical language which does not in the process hide the fractured character of its elements'.[19]

[19] See above, p. 10.

New Paths?

'In borrowing a form already established and consecrated, the creative artist is not in the least restricting the manifestations of his personality. On the contrary, it is more detached, and stands out better, when it moves within the limits of a convention.'[1] These comments were included in the *Autobiography* of Stravinsky ghost-written by Walter Nouvel and first published in 1935–6. They can stand as a declaration of that neo-classic aesthetic whose elements may already have been latent within the 'profoundly *traditional*' attitudes to 'cultural outlook' and 'musical technique' of *The Rite of Spring* and the works which preceded it,[2] and such attitudes became even more decisive when explicit reference to actual, 'classical' (earlier) stylistic and structural elements began to emerge. More broadly, it can be argued that, for Stravinsky, the most fundamental of all conventions was not the nexus of stylistic and formal characteristics of European music from Bach to Beethoven but the preference, basic to much nineteenth-century music in Russia and elsewhere, for the consistent colouring of diatonic tonality with chromatic, often octatonic inflections. This preference not only creates links between Stravinsky, Debussy, Bartók, and many other major twentieth-century figures: it also helps to create important associations between the various phases of a career whose recourse to its generative Russian predilections was constantly and resourcefully rethought, but never totally rejected, even in his most unambiguously modernist works of the years after 1918.

From 1913 Stravinsky was cut off from his native Russia by war and revolution, and such a decisive change in personal circumstances might in itself have been sufficient to motivate a change in artistic direction even without any feeling that the large orchestral resources and elaborate theatrical context of *The Rite* represented a *ne plus ultra*. The greatest of the wartime works, *Svadebka*, or *Les Noces* (completed in short score in April 1917, but not achieving its final instrumental form until 1923), employs a language which, in its concentration and vigour, is already remote from the expansive, romantic exoticism of Stravinsky's earliest compositions, but the work retains strong links with the thematic and harmonic characteristics of *The Rite*, as well it might, given its profoundly Russian ritual-

---

[1] Igor Stravinsky, *Autobiography* (New York, 1962), 132.
[2] Richard Taruskin, *Stravinsky and the Russian Traditions: A Biography of the Works through Mavra* (Berkeley and Los Angeles, 1996), 847. See also above, p. 40.

ism. It was these cultural characteristics which the 'ballet with song', *Pulcinella* (1919–20), most decisively set aside. *Pulcinella* 'was my discovery of the past, the epiphany through which the whole of my later work became possible. It was a backward look of course—the first of many love affairs in that direction—but it was a look in the mirror too.'[3] It is possible to argue, as Richard Taruskin has done, that on technical grounds the comic opera *Mavra* (1921–2) represents a more decisive change of direction (involving the reassertion of such traditional procedures as bass-orientated harmony) than *Pulcinella* itself,[4] but aesthetically the earlier work, with its radically different sound (compared to *Svadebka*, *Renard*, or *L'Histoire du soldat*), asserts itself as the initiation of a new stage in the life-long Stravinskian dialogue between 'Russian traditions' and other musical materials—a stage which is as important for its modernist as for its neo-classic initiatives.

The reliance in *Pulcinella* on pre-existent material—by Pergolesi and other eighteenth-century composers—is unusually explicit, with some movements being closer to arrangements than parodies or recompositions. Even here, however, Russian connections can still be heard: Robert Craft has said that 'after our return from the USSR [in 1962] I began to hear Russianisms even in *Pulcinella*—the horn counter-melody at No. 65, for example, and the D minor tenor aria, titled "Troika" in the original ms'.[5] What is involved is not a complete break with an exhausted early Stravinskian idiom, but a radical reorientation, not merely with respect to that idiom, but in relation to the entire history of music. In exploiting the conflicts and conjunctions between his own present, with its emancipated dissonances and sharply juxtaposed textures, and various musical pasts (including his own) in which continuity and unity were much more directly and positively engaged, Stravinsky reinforced the claims made as early as *Petrushka* for a musical modernism of supreme accomplishment whose influence on other composers would be pervasive and profound.

Stravinsky's claim that 'the musicians of my generation and I myself owe the most to Debussy'[6] can be regarded simply as a transparent attempt to conceal his longer standing debt to his Russian precursors and near-contemporaries.[7] Debussy's example, in rejecting essentially Germanic aesthetic and technical constraints, should not be underestimated, however, since it promoted an attitude of mind in which significant tensions between older and newer procedures could become the subject-matter of a composition, involving matters of rhythm as well as harmony, with regular accentuation and tonal functionality alike displaced. The most memorable moments in Stravinsky's neo-classical works often occur when triads fulfil a final, cadential function, and there is still a

[3] Igor Stravinsky and Robert Craft, *Expositions and Developments* (London, 1962), 113.
[4] Taruskin, *Stravinsky*, 1501–1603.
[5] Robert Craft, *Stravinsky: Chronicle of a Friendship, 1948–1971*, rev. edn. (Nashville and London, 1994), 319.
[6] Igor Stravinsky and Robert Craft, *Conversations with Igor Stravinsky* (London, 1959), 48.
[7] Taruskin, *Stravinsky*, 309.

sense of discord resolving on to concord, even without unambiguous reliance on conventional diatonic harmony. This is the practical application of that concept of 'polarity' described in *The Poetics of Music* in terms of 'poles of attraction' which 'are no longer within the closed system which was the diatonic system' and can be brought together 'without being compelled to conform to the exigencies of tonality'.[8] Of its nature, however, such a concept relates significantly to the 'closed system' of tonality; its entire justification is in the way it modifies rather than rejects traditional precepts, often creating a modernist context in which competing poles of attraction are more active in the musical fabric than a process of unambiguous resolution in favour of a single tonal centre.

Stravinsky's continued tendency in his neo-classical years to structure his harmony around the relationships to be found within the octatonic scale served not only to counter diatonicism with chromaticism, but also to create a musical atmosphere in which organic harmonic processes were regularly destabilized and their closural potential thrown into question. As late as 1960 Robert Craft quoted the composer as commenting: 'Let's say that I was a kind of bird, and that the eighteenth century was a kind of bird's nest in which I felt cozy laying my eggs.'[9] Yet the musical results in this fundamentally unstable world were rarely cosy or comforting, ranging from the frothiest wit (the Octet) to stark tragedy (*Oedipus Rex*), from a troubled serenity (*Apollo*) to energetic exuberance (the Violin Concerto). Underpinning the approval of 'classical' principles enshrined in the 'bird's nest' comment is a loathing for the kind of nineteenth-century music (Wagner, but not Weber, the earlier Verdi, or Tchaikovsky) which is 'more improvised than constructed', and for 'the perpetual becoming of a music that never had any reason for starting, any more than it has any reason for ending'.[10] Stravinskian neo-classicism at its most personal seemed to require the opposition between different rationales to be worked through as precisely as possible, not with the object of imposing a resolution, but rather to achieve an understanding of how such differences can coexist productively.[11]

New Techniques

Stravinsky's recourse to traditional genres—Sonata, Concerto, Symphony—is not evidence of any naive desire to produce carbon copies of classical structural models, but demonstrates his belief in the extent to which such models could be

[8] Igor Stravinsky, *Poetics of Music*, trans. A. Knodel and I. Dahl (New York, 1947), 39.

[9] Craft, *Chronicle of Friendship*, 228.

[10] Stravinsky, *Poetics*, 65.

[11] Among the studies of Stravinsky which can be associated with these ideas, see Marianne Kielian-Gilbert, 'Stravinsky's Contrasts: Contradiction and Discontinuity in his Neoclassic Music', *The Journal of Musicology*, 9 (1991), 448–80; Lynne Rogers, 'Stravinsky's Break with Contrapuntal Tradition: A Sketch Study', *The Journal of Musicology*, 13 (1995), 476–507; Anthony Pople, 'Misleading Voices: Contrasts and Continuities in Stravinsky Studies', in C. Ayrey and M. Everist (eds.), *Analytical Strategies and Musical Interpretation* (Cambridge, 1996), 271–87; Chandler Carter, 'Stravinsky's "Special Sense": The Rhetorical Use of Tonality in *The Rake's Progress*', *Music Theory Spectrum*, 19 (1997), 55–80.

reshaped without losing their essential identities. The resulting tension between old and new can also be found in the individual harmonic units which range, as previously noted, from simple triads to complex and, in themselves, atonal aggregates. To study the relationship between borrowed stylistic elements and Stravinskian transformations is a fascinating but difficult process, and the difficulty lies in description and definition.

Pulcinella has already been described as an extreme instance, in its use of relatively untransformed material. Certainly the Larghetto and Gavotte are examples of movements which, from the purely harmonic viewpoint, are virtually arrangements. Stravinsky-isms appear more in matters of spacing and instrumentation. Given the simple nature of the borrowed material, moreover, it is not surprising to find that harmonic modifications principally take the form of introducing a freer use of diatonic dissonance, rather than 'chromaticizing' simple diatonic elements. The Coda is a good example. Here the key of C major is implied both by the short tag which provides the main thematic element and by the C major triads which are the principal harmonic feature of the first seven bars. The other chords in those bars show a thickening-out of the harmonies (unacceptable in the eighteenth century) implied by the top and bottom parts. We could still provide conventional labels for them, but the speed at which they move ensures that they are heard as relatively discordant subordinates to the tonic chord, into which they all resolve. To this extent, we can still sense progression, and this sense is equally strong in the final bars of the work, where 'perfect' cadences articulate the flourishes on the triad of C major. As long as the bass continues to move clearly from dominant to tonic, we can experience the cadential effect, even if the 'dominant' chord is not a simple triad but an eleventh with the third omitted. We can relate what Stravinsky actually writes to a functional cadential progression, and hear one against the background of, or as a replacement for, the other (Ex. 6.1). It is less a question of the independent, superimposed strata of more determinedly modernist music, and more a matter of filling out, and destabilizing, to a degree, a still homogenous tonal fabric.

The *Symphonies of Wind Instruments* (1920) is not neo-classical after the explicit fashion of *Pulcinella*, and its most notable harmonic characteristic is its avoidance of pure triads, even in cadential contexts. As a result, chords which in certain rhythmic and harmonic contexts may seem especially discordant can lose such connotations under different conditions.

The final section of the work (Fig. 65 onwards) can be regarded as an expansion from one basic progression, and again the term progression is appropriate in spite of the absence of pure triads, for some of those elements, which in a C major perfect cadence need resolution, do resolve. One B rises to C, though another remains stationary. The lower D and A♭ resolve by step, the upper D does not. The F falls a step to E. Such a progression can be expressed even more simply as two ninth chords, one minor and one major, but it is a vital aspect of Stravinsky's reappraisal of individual chords that the traditionally fixed root–third–fifth–seventh hierarchy is broken down.

Allegro assai

Ex. 6.1. Stravinsky, *Pulcinella*, finale, Fig. 203 to the end

The final section, summarized in Ex. 6.2, is in two parts. The first is dominated by its initial chord and reflects its internal tension, the clash between A♭ and G which prevents the G major triad at the top of the chord from functioning diatonically. So this first section, for all its repetitiveness, has no clear tonal direction, and we experience less a process of tension and relaxation than a state of suspense. There is still a thematic process: the music is not static, but it does not yet contain the means to resolve its own tension. The decisive stage in this process occurs between Figures 70 and 71. Here, for the first time, the initial chord resolves outwards on to another chord with strong C major qualities and when that chord in turn is abandoned the A♭ has shifted to the upper area of the harmony and can be resolved on to a G.

The second part of the section begins with a chord whose upper segment is identical with that of the initial chord of the first section, but the lower segment is more euphonious, and the whole is diatonic to C major. All that remains is to show that even this chord is inconclusive—too tense—and to resolve it on to a harmony which combines triads of G major and C major (and therefore includes E minor). For the third time the bass moves down from D to C: this time the ambiguous A-B♭ clash is avoided, and the result is the most stable closural gesture of the whole composition (Ex. 6.2).

The *Symphonies of Wind Instruments* is a 'radical' work both in its freely coherent form and in the absence of any traditionally triadic harmonic progressions. At the same time, the degree of convergence on to the tonal centre of C at the end[12] reinforces a characteristic of Stravinskian modernism: the sustained

[12] The classic analytical discussion of this process is in Edward T. Cone, 'Stravinsky: The Progress of a Method', *Perspectives of New Music*, 1 (1962), 18–26. For a discussion of the work's octatonic features, see Pieter van den Toorn, *The Music of Igor Stravinsky* (New Haven, 1983), 337–44.

Ex. 6.2. Stravinsky, *Symphonies of Wind Instruments*, Fig. 69 to the end

opposition between different centres, or poles of attraction, may be dissolved, but the effect of that dissolution is still very different—less stable—than the conclusive resolutions of classical symphonies in C.

The concentrated intensity of the *Symphonies of Wind Instruments* indicates why a pure triadic ending would have been unconvincing. Such endings often work best in Stravinsky when the mood is exuberant and witty, as at the end of the Octet (1923) or the Piano Concerto (1924), or when the intention appears to be almost ironically naive, as in the bald E major harmony without fifth at the end of the Piano Sonata (1924). By contrast, the 'opera-oratorio' *Oedipus Rex* (1927) conveys the stark tragedy of its ending by stressing pitches (G, B♭) which are close relatives in traditional harmony but do not function here in traditional cadential fashion. The spirit of gentle serenity at the end of the ballet *Apollo* (1928) could hardly be more different, and the harmony in the final stages includes perfect fifths above the bass. But a degree of harmonic ambiguity is ensured by the use of sharpened fourth and naturalled seventh, as well as by a sense that the polar contrast between B minor and D major with which the concluding 'Apotheosis' begins is not decisively resolved in favour of the latter.

The *Symphony of Psalms* (1930) has a systematically progressive scheme of basic tonal and harmonic relationships, drawn from particularly clear-cut octatonic sources.[13] Since the first movement begins with an E minor triad and ends with a G major triad, this establishes not merely a precedent for structural motion between tonal areas a minor third apart, but also for defining those areas principally in terms of triads: root, third, and fifth. What makes the rest of the work particularly satisfying is that while the structural motion is continued—the E♭ of the second movement, the C of the third—neither is finally expressed in simple triadic form. The second movement adds supertonic and submediant notes to the major triad, while the finale subtracts the dominant, leaving only the tonic and mediant, the tonic doubled several times over.

Such nice distinctions may seem too nice, and therefore unnecessary. A tonic can still be felt as a tonic, whether we have a single note emphasized or a chordal 'aggregate' of six or seven. Yet it is precisely in his exploitation of the relationships within a tonic chord—and of the listener's responses and expectations in

---

[13] van den Toorn, *Music*, 295–8 and 344–51.

respect of those relationships—that Stravinsky shows such unsurpassed imagination. The hostility of Schoenberg and others to such neo-classicism seems
likely to have contained a strong element of unwilingness to recognize the exciting vitality which Stravinsky could display in spite of his 'failure' to follow the
'inevitable' move into totally chromatic serialism.

Just as Stravinsky's octatonically inflected tonal harmony is flexible enough to
include traditional chord progressions as well as his own personal inventions, so
too it is possible to find modulation as well as juxtaposition of different keys or
tonal areas. The issue of tonal relationships cannot be considered independently
of form, however, and so it is best approached by way of two very different
genres, represented here by the opera-oratorio *Oedipus Rex* and the Symphony
in C.

Analysis: *Oedipus Rex* and the Symphony in C

It might seem heavy-handedly unfunny, in view of its subject-matter, to begin
a discussion of *Oedipus Rex* with the remark that it is about the discovery of
relationships: but in purely musical terms this is apt. Most commentators have
sought parallels between the events of the plot and the sequence of tonal centres,
Eric Walter White describing the work as 'an inspired example of the use of mode
and key to achieve psychological insight in musical terms'.[14] Certainly, whether
or not the sequence of centres which the work presents was contrived as a
precompositional scheme, or whether each new centre was chosen simply as the
most appropriate at any given point, the final result is a musical organism with
specific and definable properties.

The whole work begins on B♭ (minor key in tendency) and ends on G (also
minor key in tendency): so there is an overall progression between relatives a
minor third apart. This progression also functions as the basis for the first of the
two acts, though here the final G is major mode and asserted triadically with
added notes in a context stressing its closeness to C. Of the other principal tonal
centres in Act I, C and E♭ stand out, both with major key associations. The
only unrelated note to be stressed with any persistence is B. We may therefore
summarize the situation in Act I as involving specially strong associations
between two pairs of keys each a minor third apart: G and B♭, C and E♭. If B were
present on equal terms, its associate would be D, the dominant of G.

In the early stages of Act II, D appears as a centre for the first time, approached
initially from G but associated (more orthodoxly, in the context of the work) with
both its upper and lower minor thirds, F and B. The two pairs of relationships
from Act I continue to receive prominence, but at the climax of the drama—
Oedipus's moment of truth, when he realizes that he has murdered his father and

[14] Eric Walter White, *Stravinsky: The Composer and his Works*, 2nd rev. edn. (London, 1979), 334-5. See
also Stephen Walsh, *Stravinsky:* Oedipus Rex (Cambridge, 1993).

married his mother—the F/D pair is stressed until, with the appearance of F♯, the other association, that between D and B, is logically suggested (Ex. 6.3). The final stages of the work give G the supremacy (with some use of its lower minor third, E), and C and E♭ appear as subsidiaries. B♭ does not reappear in its own right, having been as it were cancelled out by the implied Bs already mentioned.

Like any interpretation, this one is clearly both slanted and selective. It does not account for every possibility in the harmonic organization of *Oedipus Rex*, but it does isolate what I believe to be a factor of special importance, Stravinsky's exploitation of tonal identities and polarities in terms of dominant rather than tonic relations, and the inherent ambiguities that result.

Ex. 6.3. Stravinsky, *Oedipus Rex*, Act 2, from one bar after Fig. 167

If G, whether major or minor, is the main tonality of the work, then D, its dominant, has a particularly significant role. In a classic study, Wilfrid Mellers chose to regard the key of D major as central, arguing that the work is dominated by the search for it, and defining it as 'the key of the inner light'.[15] To accept this view we need also to accept that the music to which Oedipus sings the words 'Lux facta est' is in D major (Ex. 6.3). The *chord* of D major has appeared earlier in the work, as has the key of D minor, yet this, it is urged, is the only time that the *key* of D major appears. One counter-argument is to claim that the music is not in D at all, but in B minor, while another response might be that it could be in either key, depending on how one hears the music, and that in any case ambiguity is surely of the essence here. Or, again, is it not rather the case that, as Stephen Walsh suggests, 'there is not so much an ambiguity as an enrichment, an opening out of possibilities'?[16]

If we confine the concept of enrichment to contexts, in *Oedipus Rex* or elsewhere, where a tonality has first been unambiguously established, then that is not the case with either D major or B minor at this point. The general concept of tonality may be being enriched, but what seems to justify the dramatic, ironic use of ambiguity with respect to actual keys is the association between Oedipus's devastating moment of illumination and its consequence, his self-inflicted blindness. The essence is in the irony, and since Stravinsky had already used a fully resolved D major triad in the work for an undoubted moment of truth, at the end of Tiresias's aria, at the words, 'The king is the king's murderer', the composer might have thought in terms of an ironic masking of such certainty, or, at least, an understated quality which is quite the reverse of Tiresias's triumphant outburst, for Oedipus's moment of supreme crisis.

A particular situation has arisen in which the composer is seeking an idea of clarificatory simplicity: all is light, but all will become dark. So he uses his most expressive device, the consonant major third without fifth (or root). In doing so, he highlights a situation in which the strongest tension, or polarity, to use Stravinsky's preferred term, is between major and minor thirds. (One way in which *Oedipus Rex* is a precursor of the *Symphony of Psalms* is now clear.) But that is only the beginning. Other tensions, other polarities, exist between triadic harmonic and non-triadic harmonies; between asserted key-associations and traditional, modulatory means of moving from one to another, and between an approach to form that involves both the raw juxtapositions of extreme contrast and what Walsh has described as 'an elaborate fusion of more or less discrete, more or less transparent musical and textual images'.[17] With respect to harmony, Stravinsky relies very much on our expectation that the 'dominant' will confirm the 'tonic'. By contrast, the major or minor third in isolation is ambiguous: it

[15] Wilfrid Mellers, 'Stravinsky's Oedipus as 20th-Century Hero', in P. H. Lang (ed.), *Stravinsky: A New Appraisal of his Work* (New York, 1963), 34–5. For a very different, octatonic reading, see van den Toorn, *Music*, 298–305.

[16] Walsh, *Stravinsky*, 61.   [17] Ibid. 30.

tends to suggest, not affirm, not least because it can open up the anti-diatonic symmetries of octatonic harmony, and does so with particular clarity in the *Symphony of Psalms*.

In *Oedipus*, D as a possible centre is therefore kept in reserve while G is established by way of B♭ and C. And the moment of ultimate truth, when the 'inner light' receives outward expression, sees the clarity of the 'true' dominant being clouded by the stark reality of its minor third associate. The positive serenity of the end of the *Symphony of Psalms* can be interpreted as C major confirming the original dominant G, even though the dominant note itself is absent from the final chord. The tragedy of Oedipus, by contrast, ends with the complete collapse of 'dominant' certainties. The minor third *ostinato* summarizes the main structural feature of the work, and the entire final passage (Fig. 201 ff.) contains only one D♮. This is still 'tonal' music. But in its bleak austerity it seems the only possible outcome of a drama in which the technical processes have paralleled the events of the plot with perfect precision. The strongest association after that of the minor third is the perfect fourth—the C and G of the central chorus. Here the music seems on the verge of the expansion that would focus on tonic and dominant as mutually dependent entities. Psychologically, their failure to articulate this function is profoundly right: it gives *Oedipus Rex*, not a negative excellence, but a coherence deriving from a positive integration of subject and style which is disturbing and intensely dramatic.

Oedipus Rex was composed against the structural and stylistic background of the 'number opera' from Handel to Verdi, and tradition had established no set of absolute precedents for the handling of tonal relationships within the form, nor whether there should in fact be any overall scheme, relating to one principal key, or not. With the Symphony in C, however, the precedents were more precise, and the tensions between foreground and background are altogether more absorbing. In *Oedipus*, for all its separate 'numbers' (arias, ensembles, choruses), Stravinsky was involved with what was in dramatic terms virtually a new form. The Symphony in C is the closest he ever came to the most common structural scheme of a classical symphony, and the work is one of his most impressive assertions of the artistic need for order: not all-pervading symmetry, but coherent process, in which the mutual interdependence of tonality, harmony and theme is fully and imaginatively worked out, in pursuit of the multivalent possibilities inherent in a truly modern classicism, where a new synthesis is glimpsed, if not already in place. Surprise is sometimes expressed that this often genial and refined symphony could have been written in what Stravinsky himself described as 'the most tragic year of my life'[18]—it was the year in which his first wife died. Yet that is precisely the time when a work like *Oedipus Rex* could not have been written, for without detachment Stravinsky's classic objectivity would surely have crumbled into formlessness. The Symphony in C is an affirmation,

---

[18]   Igor Stravinsky, *Themes and Conclusions* (London, 1972), 47.

though it ends with unassertive restraint. It is not so much the work of a composer triumphing over tragedy as it is of one whose art transforms rather than imitates life.

The title provokes two questions: 'symphony in what sense?' and 'in C in what sense?' As to the first, there are four separate movements—the outer ones thematically related—which preserve much of the essential nature of traditional symphonic structure. The parallels between it and any symphony by Haydn, Beethoven, or Tchaikovsky (Stravinsky admits having had symphonies by those composers to hand) are naturally not exact, but the differences are meaningful to no small degree precisely because they are deviations from something approximating to a norm. Critics of the work will point to what they define as its 'static' or 'balletic' character, so any defender of its symphonism must demonstrate the presence of dynamic processes, and those processes are often most apparent in the motivation for structural 'deviations' from a generally accepted symphonic norm, which modify the concept but do not contradict it, old and new coexisting in a modern equilibrium.

As for the second question ('in C in what sense?') the same kind of answer might suffice: not a classically functioning C major, but an unmistakable emphasis on a tonal and harmonic area associated with C as tonic. Here, too, there are 'deviations', however: and just as Stravinsky will reshape sonata form, so he will modify the relationships within the traditional C major scale to produce elements which are then consistently employed. Not surprisingly, these elements involve the establishment of ambiguities: what is involved, as Peter Evans observes, is the 'simultaneous acknowledgement and denial of classical precedent'.[19]

In *Oedipus Rex*, the whole issue of the relationship between a tonic and its mediant, subdominant and dominant, is fundamental with regard both to chords and key areas. The Symphony in C, too, is concerned with this matter, as the opening illustrates (Ex. 6.4). The main motive of the movement is stated at once, but with greatest emphasis given to its first note, B. In a work which began with clear C major harmonies, its true function as leading note would probably be perceived at once. Here the context is ambiguous. With the rapid movement away from C to G in bar 2, and the presence of F♯ in the harmony of bar 4, the B might rather be the mediant of G—or the dominant of E minor. And what Stravinsky is doing, as the whole of the first movement illustrates, is regarding chords of C major, G major, and E minor as possessing particularly strong resemblances, especially C major and E minor, with their common pitches, E and G. The presentation of the first theme of the sonata exposition (Fig. 5 ff.) shows what is in essence another version of the situation at 'Lux facta est' in *Oedipus*. There we had a major third which could either be one triad without a root or another without a fifth. Here we have an accompanimental minor third, and although

[19] See Martin Cooper (ed.), *Oxford History of Music*, x. *The Modern Age* (Oxford, 1974), 390.

Ex. 6.4. Stravinsky, Symphony in C, 1st movt., beginning

the melodic line supplies the missing root, suggesting first-inversion harmony, the essential quality of the passage lies in the absence of the root from the bass, and therefore of a full triad (it is hard to feel, here, that the Bs in the oboe are completing E minor triads).

This is tonal music in which the tonic note is subordinate: and its authority is not so obvious as to render its presence unnecessary. The entire harmonic character of Stravinsky's style rests on this ambiguous treatment of single notes, the real presence of which is vital if a tonal scheme is to achieve adequate solidity and coherence. The issue has become, yet again, one of thirds. In the first movement we have an exposition which ends in E, and a development which ends in E♭ (in neither case is the dominant note excluded). And a root-position C major triad is only firmly established in the coda (Figs. 71 and 72), before the final chords of the movement assert a destabilizing combination of E minor and C major—with E in the bass—and with persistent clashes between B and B♭ above (Ex. 6.5).

The use of sonata form in this movement is such as to give maximum dramatic focus to the tonal harmonic issues involved. The first subject tends to move 'flatwards' from C to D minor and F, raising the question whether the second subject will be in the (orthodox) dominant. The balance between diatonic and, however briefly, 'atonal' passages (e.g. the first subject restatement and the short transition, pp. 6–8) serves to keep the whole topic of the relationship, and tension, between tonal clarity and structural process alive, and in the second part of the transition passage the harmony clears and settles on to a long dominant preparation, using the dominant seventh of G major.[20] At its climax this provokes contradiction, and the second subject section, which begins at Fig. 19, is in a mainly diatonic F major. (This means that the characteristic minor third oscillation in the bass is between A and C.) The section ends with more tonal and thematic drama; a darkening into B♭ minor provokes a move into the true dominant which is unstable from the start, so that the exposition can only reach a point of adequate finality by moving up to E major.

[20] See Edward T. Cone, 'The Uses of Convention: Stravinsky and his Models', in Lang (ed.), *Stravinsky*, 21–33.

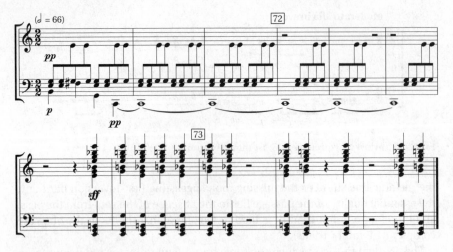

Ex. 6.5. Stravinsky, Symphony in C, 1st movt., last eleven bars

As Cone has emphasized, the recapitulation is notable for the way in which the main second subject restatement (now 'on' C) is moved between the two parts of the transition passage: this means that the long dominant preparation (now on G) comes at a later, more critical point, where its function is no longer to prepare a surprise deviation of tonal area late in the movement, but to balance a coda which gives new developmental emphasis to the movement's main motive (see horns, one bar before Fig. 62). Here, as tension increases, comes the second dominant build-up of the movement, and this time the final clarification can take place, even to the extent of allowing C major its moment of root-position stability. The reshaping of the recapitulation, and the 'redundant development' or first part of the coda, have perfectly fitted the need to dramatize the problems of a tonal centre which cannot, literally, root itself until all the stresses and strains of a chromatically dominated harmonic language have been—if not resolved—then adequately rehearsed. The movement is in modified sonata form, but the modification is organic, not arbitrary, achieving an equilibrium parallel to that between the stable and unstable tendencies of the harmony.

A similar sensitivity informs the three remaining movements. The slow movement adopts the subdominant F as principal tonal centre, the Scherzo the dominant G. Not unexpectedly, the finale returns to C, yet it is not a C purified of the ambiguities so vital to the first movement, and by no means absent in slow movement and Scherzo. The actual presence of first-movement material ensures that the same issues are reviewed, and the calm processional ending, as different in character as possible from the terse cadences which concluded the *Moderato alla breve*, achieves the uneasy finality of a multivalent C major/E minor/G major chord rooted on E (Ex. 6.6). At this late stage, the tonality as such

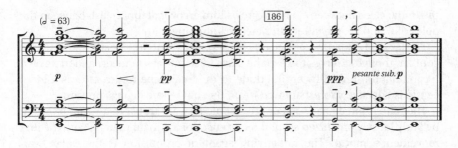

Ex. 6.6. Stravinsky, Symphony in C, 4th movt., last nine bars

cannot be questioned, yet the polarities within it cannot be wholly eradicated, and the ending is the more satisfying for their presence.

Stravinsky in the 1940s

The two major works of Stravinsky's last decade as a tonal composer are the *Symphony in Three Movements* (1945) and the opera, *The Rake's Progress* (1948–51), which are respectively his most ambitious 'abstract' and theatrical projects. Discussion of the symphony must begin with the nature of its symphonism, which is structurally less clear-cut than in the Symphony in C. Even if we regard 'Three Symphonic Movements' or 'Concerto for Orchestra (with concertante piano and harp)' as more appropriate titles, and give due emphasis to the composer's own remarks about the specific stimuli which the work reflects—'a documentary film of scorched earth tactics in China' for the first movement; a scene called 'Apparition of the Virgin' intended for the film *Song of Bernadette* for the second; and 'reaction to the newsreels and documentaries . . . of goose-stepping soldiers' and other wartime connotations for the third[21]— the work must stand or fall on the effectiveness of its overall design. In sonata-form terms, the opening fast movement is finely organized to ensure that considerable internal contrasts do not result in any loss of the tremendous momentum generated by the opening paragraph, with its extreme tension between simple motivic shapes and the chromatic clashes of the harmony. The considerable extent of the central development (Figs. 34–88) prepares a compressed and reshaped recapitulation, whose main function is not simply to re-establish the inexorable dynamic temper of the exposition, but to resolve this out into the uneasy stability of the final bars, where the war between A♭ and G is temporarily settled in favour of the latter as the fifth of a seventh chord on C.[22] That this is not another Symphony in C will only be decided in the finale, where

---

[21] Igor Stravinsky and Robert Craft, *Dialogues* (London, 1982), 50–2.

[22] An octatonic interpretation of the first movement is in van den Toorn, *Music*, 351–66.

the initial clash between G and A♭ grows into an overall tonal clash between the poles of C and D♭, the latter ultimately triumphing.

The languid Andante (centred on D) does not contribute directly to this titanic conflict, though it serves to keep the clash of semitones in focus, and in its own recapitulation (linked by an Interlude to the finale) the return of C as a tonal centre is effectively foreshadowed (from one bar before Fig. 138 onwards).

The March-Finale has such an irresistible forward thrust that it can afford to be fairly loosely organized around recurrences of the main material and the first movement's 'motto'. The underlying agent of propulsion is the polar 'war' between C and D♭ (with its dominant, A♭), but this is less immediately perceptible than the array of orchestral effects, ranging from dazzling tuttis to eccentric moments of chamber music, like the 'fugal' duet for trombone and piano at Figs. 170–2.

Other, less ambitious instrumental works of the 1940s—the Sonata for Two Pianos (1943–4), the Ebony Concerto (1945), and the Concerto for Strings (1946)— demonstrate Stravinsky's continuing willingness to adapt traditional tonal forms: a willingness which persists into the Septet (1952–3) with its ternary first movement: exposition–fugue–recapitulation. This period is nevertheless dominated by a group of stage works, with the relatively lightweight *Danses Concertantes* (1941–2) and *Scènes de Ballet* (1944) preceding the much more substantial ballet *Orpheus* (1947), and the bracingly austere Mass (1948) preceding *The Rake's Progress*.

The climax of *Orpheus* (two bars before Fig. 137) shows a clear link with the Symphony in Three Movements. Yet the elegiac restraint of the First and Third Scenes is more typical of the ballet as a whole. The music for the Furies takes second place to that for Orpheus and Eurydice, and there are no simpler nor more memorable bars in Stravinsky's whole output than the *Pas de deux*, which starts with such tenderness and breaks off near the end in anguish as 'Orpheus tears the bandage from his eyes. Eurydice falls dead.'

This humanizing eloquence is much less evident in the Mass, where personal religious feeling rarely breaks through the veil of liturgical objectivity. There is joy in the Sanctus, earnestness in the Credo, and a kind of self-denying abasement in the Agnus Dei. Stravinsky has surely succeeded here in his aim of writing very cold music. Yet there is majesty in the very economy, and in the use of the ten wind instruments. The Mass is the most important anticipation of the mood of the later, serial 'Requiems'—and this in spite of its frequent reliance on harmonic rather than contrapuntal textures and the way in which its tense progressions still cling to the inherent ambiguities of neo-classical tonality.[23]

The juxtaposition of Mass and opera inevitably evokes the names of Mozart and Verdi, and it is Mozart's influence which pervades the subject and style of

---

[23] See Kofi Agawu, 'Stravinsky's *Mass* and Stravinsky Analysis', *Music Theory Spectrum*, 11 (1989), 139–63.

The Rake's Progress more profoundly than any other.[24] It might have been predicted that Stravinsky would remain as remote as ever from that musico-dramatic through-composition which he vilified so entertainingly in his various writings. It was less inevitable that the result should be no artificial parody of pre-Wagnerian operatic conventions but a work which is entertaining and moving in its own right, with a libretto by W. H. Auden and Chester Kallman whose metrical sharpness and verbal idiosyncrasies were tailor-made for Stravinsky. The secret lies in the utter rightness of the subject. The 'fable' is a morality: the object is not so much to create sympathy for the destroyed pro-tagonist as to learn from his destruction and avoid one's own: hence the over-riding parallel with *Don Giovanni*. Unlike the typical twentieth-century operatic 'victim', Tom Rakewell deserves his fate:[25] but his very weakness of character gave Stravinsky the chance to provide him with appealing and attractive music, direct yet idiosyncratic, and these qualities extend into the opera as a whole.

As his largest work, *The Rake's Progress* offers the most substantial display of Stravinsky's rhythmic resourcefulness and tonal-harmonic imagination, showing, too, his unique skill as a writer of vocal lines in which familiar conventions are given new expressive life. Ex. 6.7, from Act I, Scene 3, is a marvellously lyrical outpouring for Anne Truelove which manages to make its contra-intuitive verbal accentuations seem natural and inevitable,[26] matching this destabilizing technique with dissonant chromatic incursions into the basic B minor. Elsewhere in the opera, Stravinsky moves closer to the explicitly stratified gestures of authentic modernism, as in the Duettino from Act III, Scene 3, in which 'the subtle play and inherent ambiguity between the tonal and the non-tonal' cannot be definitively resolved out in favour of one or the other.[27] As a whole, *The Rake's Progress* offers particularly well-delineated examples of that 'conflict between styles' which is increasingly recognized as revealing what is 'most essential' in Stravinsky.[28]

The Rake's Progress was first performed in Venice on 11 September 1951, a few week's after the composer's sixty-ninth birthday, and less than two months after the death of Arnold Schoenberg. In spite of all that has been written about the opera itself, we have no real idea of how Stravinsky saw his own future at this time. Having composed his most ambitious neo-classical work, did he feel a need not merely for renewal but for change? Was he conscious that the death of Schoenberg gave serialism a 'historical' perspective which made adoption of it just another kind of neo-classicism? Whatever Stravinsky's thoughts may have been, his music shows that the testing and adaptation of serial processes was a

[24] See 'The Composer's View', in Paul Griffiths (ed.), *Igor Stravinsky:* The Rake's Progress (Cambridge, 1982), 2–3.
[25] For an extended discussion responding to this and other views on the opera, see Geoffrey Chew, 'Pastoral and Neoclassicism: A Reinterpretation of Auden's and Stravinsky's *Rake's Progress*', *Cambridge Opera Journal*, 5 (1993) 239–63.
[26] See Taruskin, *Stravinsky*, 1119–236.
[27] Carter, 'Stravinsky's "Special Sense"', 77–8.   [28] Ibid. 58.

Ex. 6.7. Stravinsky, *The Rake's Progress*, Act 1, Scene 3, Anne's aria, from Fig. 183

gradual affair, beginning in 1951–2 with the composition of the *Cantata on Old English Texts* and ending on 21 March 1958 with the completion of *Threni*, his first completely twelve-note work: Stravinsky then continued to employ twelve-note techniques for the rest of his life. The works from the Cantata to the ballet *Agon* (1957; the immediate predecessor of *Threni*) are transitional, both in the way that tonal and serial elements may be juxtaposed or combined in them, and in the way that the serial elements are not necessarily twelve-note. Stravinsky's first twelve-note movement (and the order is not strict even then) is the tenor aria 'Surge, aquilo' from the *Canticum Sacrum* (1955). Ultimately, the significance of *Threni* is not just that it shows Stravinsky accepting the particular virtues of an all-inclusive twelve-note technique, but that such a technique has led to the loss of all *tonal* feeling. In *Threni* Stravinsky became not merely a twelve-note composer, but an atonal composer, and although the later twelve-note works may emphasize certain pitches from time to time, and attach structural significance to such emphasis, the possibility of tonally centred serial music, which the transitional works contemplated, had clearly been rejected. As a serialist, Stravinsky remained committed to a modernist aesthetic in which oppositions between tendencies to stable and unstable contexts were reinforced. The dissociations of pluralism engage with synthesizing strategies, as the account of his later works in Chapter 11 aims to show.

Preliminaries

Chapter 3 dealt principally with composers who, in respect of date of birth, were the seniors of Schoenberg, Bartók, and Stravinsky. This chapter gives its main emphasis to those who were born between 1890 and 1910 and therefore came to creative maturity after the principal issue of early twentieth-century music—to retain or reject tonality—had already been raised. Hindemith, Prokofiev, and Shostakovich all ultimately opted to retain tonality, although (as with Bartók, Stravinsky, Britten, and many others) it was often an intensively chromaticized tonality with properties appropriate to the kind of 'modern classicism' that attached great importance to the preservation of the traditional genres of symphonic music.[1] Particular modal alternatives to diatonicism, like the octatonic scale, were a fruitful source of ambiguity, and the effect of their use was to challenge, if not seriously undermine, the relative stability, and tonal unity, of modern classicism, rather than, more radically, to prevent the establishment of such unity and stability in the first place.

Hindemith, Prokofiev, and Shostakovich all produced a consistent flow of large-scale compositions, both vocal and instrumental, confirming their commitment to traditional genres. Yet there were others, prominent in twentieth-century concert programmes and record catalogues, if only for one or two scores, who retained tonality but whose preferred forms were less symphonic, favouring less abstract modes of expression. The rest of this section considers a few of them.

The Spanish composer Manuel de Falla (1876–1946) can be compared to Bartók in that his aim was to create a synthesis embodying an imaginary folk art, rather than an idiom that exploited tensions between genuine folk material and an international art-music style. Falla's most distinguished stage and concert works—*El amor brujo* (1914–15), the *Fantasia bética* (1919), *El retablo de maese Pedro* (1919–22), and the Harpsichord Concerto (1923–6)—have a distinctive Spanish flavour, and demonstrate fine formal judgement. But he was unable to continue building on the achievements of this relatively short period of creative excellence, and failed to complete his intended *magnum opus*, the 'scenic cantata' *Atlántida*, on which he laboured for so long. For a Spanish voice at the

---

[1] For modern classicism, see p. 30 above.

opposite extreme from Falla, and an achievement that has no feel whatever of the unfinished about it, there is the obsessive miniaturist Federico Mompou (1893–1987), whose Satie-like primitivism yields 'an extraordinarily haunting, exquisitely melancholy elegance'.[2]

Francis Poulenc (1899–1963) also owed much to Satie, and yet managed to effect a transition to more 'mainstream' genres and a more varied expressive palette. Uneasy with even Ravel's degree of alignment with symphonic music, Poulenc blended melancholy and wit to considerable effect, as in the Sextet for piano and wind (1932–9) and the Oboe Sonata (1962). Nor was he incapable of more serious, dramatic gestures when these seemed appropriate (Organ Concerto, 1938). But Poulenc is at his best when engaging the limpid eloquence of French texts (*Tel jour, tel nuit*, 1936–7, *Figure humaine*, 1943). His later, large-scale scores, like the opera *Dialogue des Carmélites* (1953–6) and the *Gloria* (1959), also have their admirers, though they lack the more strongly focused ambiguities to be found in Poulenc's most personal work—what Wilfrid Mellers defines as 'an idiom that is modern in being modally ambiguous and tonally precarious, while preserving the sense of wonder and purity of heart typical of Poulenc's earliest master Erik Satie'.[3] Poulenc, like another of his enthusiasms, Chabrier, may have been 'civilized, witty, sensuous', yet, 'as with all true hedonists "les plaisirs de Poulenc" are shadowed with impermanence',[4] and it is the technical resource with which such impermanence is realized that gives his music memorability and depth.

In its relatively disciplined shape, Poulenc's output contrasts with the sprawling prodigality of Charles Koechlin (1867–1950), Darius Milhaud (1892–1974), and Heitor Villa-Lobos (1887–1959). As a result, their work is less well-known and, in the cases of Milhaud and Villa-Lobos, at least, there is the added drawback that their earlier works are the best. Milhaud never surpassed *Saudades do Brasil* (1920–1) or *La Création du monde* (1923), while Villa-Lobos never matched his early, pre-1930 evocations of 'an unmistakably Brazilian landscape' in the orchestral compositions *Amazonas* and *Uirapurú* (1916).[5] Like Falla, Villa-Lobos's determination to aspire to synthesis rather than relish the differences between local and international styles was not necessarily a wise one for so instinctive a creative mind, and helps to account for the more derivative and less disciplined qualities of his later work—though in a positive reading this displays 'an idealized, mellow, and mature depiction of national antiquity', with a 'national idiom' that is 'made to be internationally understood'.[6]

---

[2] Lionel Salter, 'Mompou', *The New Grove Dictionary of Music and Musicians*, ed. S. Sadie (London, 1980), xii. 476.

[3] Wilfrid Mellers, *Poulenc* (Oxford, 1993), 76.   [4] Ibid. 34.

[5] Simon Wright, *Villa-Lobos* (Oxford, 1992), 13.   [6] Ibid. 80–1, 123.

The early Hindemith

There can be few composers whose first decade of mature creative activity is as remarkable as that of Paul Hindemith (1895–1963). There is less agreement about the quality of his later music, especially the compositions completed after 1940 in America, and about the extent to which his 'even greater stylistic differentiation and refinement of technique'[7] led to dryness of manner and monotony of expression, at least when compared to his earlier achievements. Even David Neumeyer, an advocate who makes consistently high claims, finds 'subtler harmonic-tonal structures' offset by 'poorer chord definition'[8] in the late works, suggesting that, like others, Hindemith had difficulty in sustaining his personal brand of modern classicism at a time when the new, post-war radicalism left his earlier theory and practice seeming dated and, in some ways, ill-defined. It is therefore difficult to resist the conclusion that, even if some of those later works have been unfairly neglected, it is in the compositions of the inter-war years that Hindemith was at his best.

In the early String Quartet in F minor, Op. 10 (1919), essentially traditional elements of form, tonality, and texture are projected with a vigour and purposefulness going well beyond mere youthful exuberance and indicating a formidable combination of intellect and sensibility. This quartet was completed before Stravinsky's first neo-classical work, *Pulcinella* (1919–20): there can be no question of any influence. Yet Hindemith's opening shows an equal facility for translating baroque gestures into modern terms (Ex. 7.1)

The harmonic sweep of the music is boldly shaped, with clear bitonal conflicts emerging at a fairly early stage. The forceful energy could indicate a knowledge of Bartók, and a particularly impressive feature of the quartet's first movement is the presence of strongly contrasted lyric material. There is none of the monotony, the resistance to lyric contrast, to be found in some of Hindemith's more ambitious later projects.

Hindemith was lucky in the short term, for the cultural atmosphere in post-war Germany favoured brittle, sardonic, parodistic, yet far from superficial creative work, in alignment with the 'linear-contrapuntal manner of the New Objectivity (*Neue Sachlichkeit*)'[9] that other German composers, including Weill, adopted. A large proportion of the flood of compositions Hindemith produced between 1918 and 1930 is of high quality, but the Sonata for Cello and Piano, Op. 11 No. 3 (1919) is an exception, the neo-classic/post-romantic stylistic range less well motivated than in the F minor Quartet, and weakened by an overextended structure (an ill omen). At the other extreme, all but one of the seven works called *Kammermusik* are attractive and interesting, the occasional brashness tolerable simply because there is an unmistakable sense of fun in the treatment of baroque and classical devices: for example, the throwaway cadences which are

---

[7] David Neumeyer, *The Music of Paul Hindemith* (New Haven, 1986), 5.
[8] Ibid. 240.   [9] Ibid. 4.

Ex. 7.1. Hindemith, String Quartet No. 1, 1st movt., opening

particularly prominent in Nos. 3 and 4. Neumeyer argues convincingly that it was 'only in the *Kammermusiken* Op. 36, the Concerto for Orchestra Op. 38, and *Cardillac*', written between 1925 and 1927, that Hindemith brought 'all the elements of style and technique together, laying the foundation for the synthesis of the early 1930s'.[10] The *Kammermusik* No. 4, Op. 36 No. 3 (1925), for violin and chamber orchestra, is probably the best of the set: one only needs to compare it with the later, more orthodoxly planned Violin Concerto (1939) to sense the lowering of temperature and loss of vigour which had taken place in little more than a decade. The main fault to be found with individual movements of the *Kammermusik* set is the same as that of the 1919 Cello Sonata: unduly protracted formal schemes, where the material is simply not interesting or imaginative enough to warrant such thoroughgoing exposure of its properties. In particular, the slow movement of the Organ Concerto (*Kammermusik* No. 7, Op. 46 No. 2, of 1927) is as dull as anything from later decades.

Apart from the *Kammermusik* series, to which we might append the unambiguously neo-classical Concerto for Orchestra (1925), Hindemith wrote three more string quartets during the 1920s, of which No. 3, Op. 22 (1922) is the most highly regarded. It is a work which merits close study both for the way it shows the composer's confidence and flexibility in the treatment of traditional forms and tonal relationships, and also for its clear anticipations of weaknesses which were to increase in later years.

String Quartet No. 3

The Third String Quartet is in five movements and has a main tonal centre of F sharp, which is firmly established only in the finale. Clearly defined 'progressive' tonal schemes can work very well (Nielsen's Fifth Symphony was also completed in 1922) but Hindemith seems to be attempting an ambitious dual scheme here: first, a conflict between a gradual progression towards F♯ by way of both relatives and opposites (e.g. C♯ and C); and also a more general process of clarifying tonality out of atonality and bitonality. The work begins with a Fugato which can, in retrospect, be seen to hint at F♯ at cadence points, but which, in its own terms (the terms imposed by the contradictory directions of the two phrases of the fugato theme itself), has no clear tonal centre at all (Ex. 7.2).

The second movement provides strong contrast in every respect, being fast, vigorous and securely anchored on C♯. Ironically, the weakest moment is the only contrapuntal passage, a *quasi-stretto* (from four bars before letter M) which marks the transition at the end of the middle section of the ternary scheme. If this is a structural miscalculation, expanding what would be better compressed, the final C♯ major triad sounds an inconceivably tame outcome of the toughly discordant idiom which the movement employs for most of its length (hints of

---

[10] Neumeyer, *The Music of Paul Hindemith*, 114.

Ex. 7.2. Hindemith, String Quartet No. 3, 1st movt., opening

Bartókian influence, specifically the oscillating minor-third motive of the second movement of his String Quartet No. 2, are strong here).

The central movement of the work is the weakest, a leisurely, meandering, and repetitive affair, which seems to be aiming at a kind of nonchalant serenity, but alternates an oddly toothless bitonality—'bite' being usually easy to achieve by combining clashing keys—with an equally uningratiating modality. The restraint is evidence of Hindemith's overconfidence, the rhythmic monotony robbing the ultimate arrival on the bimodally coloured F♯ triad of all conviction (Ex. 7.3).

After this, the brief, improvisatory fourth movement comes as a relief, with its distinct suggestion of the *Kammermusik* style. Though centred on C, the music creates a sense of progressive conflict which carries over into the blander rondo-finale with its much more explicitly neo-classical material. This is a well-balanced movement with ample internal contrasts, but the conclusion again seems tame, perhaps because a full, pure (if pizzicato) F♯ major triad two bars from the end actually precedes the final thematic statement (in octaves).

As a whole this quartet displays a disturbing tendency to lose focus, both in its diversity of thematic character (the lyric material so much less convincing than the energetic, neo-classical shapes) and in its range of harmonic language, with resolutions seeming forced and unearned. With hindsight it is all too easy to diagnose the symptoms of later disease: but even in the immediate context of the early 1920s this quartet shows that Hindemith could not always sustain the ideal balance between a desire to exploit traditional forms and the employment of a flexible tonal musical language involving a high degree of chromaticism. The more serious the intention, the less successful the result.

Hindemith after the Third String Quartet

The best of Hindemith's neo-classical works is probably the opera *Cardillac* (1926), 'a composition in which we find assembled and perfected all the techniques and stylistic idioms of Hindemith's early career'.[11] Unambiguously a

---

[11] Ibid. 168.

Ex. 7.3. Hindemith, String Quartet No. 3, 3rd movt., last six bars

number opera, its pugnacious vitality ensures that its 'synthesis' does not preclude the 'surprising juxtaposition of stylistic and expressive components',[12] and its reconciliation of 'the Baroque esthetic with the demands of an expressionistic dramatic subject'[13] does not drive the music into a bland stability.

Hindemith's second major opera, *Mathis der Maler* (1934–5), while not totally dissimilar in subject-matter to *Cardillac*, is less obviously divided into separate numbers, and gains in fluency and continuity, the grandeur of its subject-matter well matched in music of often visionary fervour which is, arguably, Hindemith's most fully realized expression of a modern classicism from which most elements of parody or pastiche have been purged.

At a much later date, Hindemith attempted another large-scale study of the relationship between the artist and society (*Die Harmonie der Welt*, 1956–7), in

[12] Neumeyer, *The Music of Paul Hindemith*, 171.
[13] Ibid. 172, citing Ian Kemp, 'Hindemith', *The New Grove*, ed. S. Sadie (London, 1980), viii. 579.

which the principal character is the Renaissance philosopher Johann Kepler. From the purely dramatic point of view the opera is weighed down by the absence of a conventionally unfolding plot, and while it is firmly structured musically as a gradual, systematic progress towards the ultimate E major, there is little of the compelling vitality of *Cardillac* or the exalted expressiveness of *Mathis*. Hindemith's very different final opera, *The Long Christmas Dinner* (1960), based on the play by Thornton Wilder, has much more direct dramatic appeal.

It might seem naive to relate Hindemith's retreat from the vitality and abrasiveness of his early style to a response to the political disaster which afflicted Germany at the end of the 1920s. Yet there can be no doubting the affiliation between the social and political instability of the post-war, pre-Hitler period and the at times aggressive, at times morbidly languid music of Hindemith, Weill, and others. Culture and society were very much of a piece in the Weimar Republic, and Hindemith's later music exhibits all the symptoms of an attempt to exalt Apollo and resist Dionysus: to provide, whether intentionally or not, a spiritual antidote to the poison of fascism. In these terms, that music fails when it seems too negative, avoiding issues, going through the motions. It is certainly no mere matter of a retreat from the avant-garde to modern classicism, with a return to diatonic tonality and explicitly traditional forms. What is lacking in many of Hindemith's later works is not only the fundamental tensions of a modernist aesthetic, but also the urgent eloquence of the best modern classicism, such as *Mathis der Maler* has in abundance.

The kind of calm resignation that is so moving at the end of *Mathis* is also to be found, on a smaller scale, at the end of the Second Piano Sonata (1936), and the special mood of serenity which Hindemith could create reappears in the ballet *Nobilissima Visione* (1938), as well as at the end of the keyboard cycle *Ludus Tonalis* (1942). Geniality can also play a positive part, as in the finale of the Cello Concerto (1940) or the deservedly popular *Symphonic Metamorphosis on Themes of Carl Maria von Weber* (1943); and in works like the Violin Concerto (1939) and Clarinet Concerto (1947), where leisurely, lyric flow is the predominant quality and one longs for a touch of the old eccentricity or vulgarity, the climaxes are nevertheless imposing and skilfully placed. The Sonata for Cello and Piano (1948) has a first movement, marked 'Pastorale', in which effective, if gentle, tension is generated by flexible harmonic direction and changes of accent, as well as by a fugato texture which is, for once, more fanciful than ponderous. Even in as prosaic and soporific a work as the *Harmonie der Welt* Symphony (1951), the music may suddenly, briefly, spring to life with a weirdly orchestrated episode (bars 150–67 of the finale) which recalls the old (young) Hindemith. Yet his last chamber work, the Octet (1958) is a sad ending to a career which had begun with the F minor Quartet. In the Octet there is ample geniality, and the occasional flicker of true creative imagination (the ghostly march ending of the second movement, with its scurrying string figuration). Yet as the melody at letter C of the third movement shows, composers stand or fall by the appropriateness of

their material, and the pedestrian protraction of this unimaginative idea is ultimately what counters the effectiveness of other parts of the work.

A simple way of summarizing Hindemith's career is to say that he progressed
from Kokoschka to Kepler. It is a far cry from the modish, garish expressionism
of Kokoschka's *Mörder, Hoffnung der Frauen*, which Hindemith set as a one-act
opera in 1919, to the grand philosophical issues of the much later dramatic work,
Die Harmonie der Welt. Hindemith was the complete practical musician, as his
skill as violist, teacher, and conductor proved. But his delight in theoretical
speculation, allied to a conviction that tonality was a universal, indestructible
law of nature, never inspired a practical compositional breakthrough which
would have excused all the theoretical inconsistencies and inaccuracies.[14]
Rather, having progressed, between *Cardillac* and *Mathis der Maler*, towards a
majestic and personal classical conservatism, he was unable to sustain the level
of inspiration marking the works that preceded and embodied that progression.

Prokofiev

At first, Sergei Prokofiev (1891–1953) seems conveniently similar to Hindemith—
a brilliant prodigy whose creative growth was redirected at midpoint by the
inescapable political and social factors encapsulated in his declaration of 1934,
after his return to the Soviet Union, that 'we must seek a new simplicity' based
around melody which is 'comprehensible without being repetitive or trivial'.[15] In
Prokofiev's case, however, it is far less justifiable to praise his early, more radical
compositions at the expense of the later, more conservative ones: the operas and
symphonies which form the most important part of his output in the 1920s (he
had left Russia in 1918 and lived mainly in Paris) are all surpassed by those he
wrote after his return to Russia in 1933. Perhaps the only genre in which his earlier
achievement is superior is the concerto, No. 3 for piano (1917–21) being in many
ways his best.

Prokofiev in the later years certainly had less difficulty than Hindemith in
sustaining a style which accepted the need to resist, if not wholly reject, the more
explicitly modernist qualities of his earlier work. Writing in 1941, he saw the
origins of his style in the interaction of five distinct features—classical, modern,
toccata, lyrical, grotesque[16]—which neatly implied a governing dialogue
between tradition and innovation, along lines not too dissimilar from those
found in Bartók. His later music is less innovative harmonically, its contrasts of
mood less extreme, as the 'modern', 'toccata', and 'grotesque' strands of his style
lose their expressionistic overtones. At the same time, however, subtlety of form

---

[14]   See Paul Hindemith, *The Craft of Musical Composition*, i, trans. A. Mendel (New York, 1945).

[15]   Sergei Prokofiev, *Soviet Diary 1927 and Other Writings*, trans. and ed. O. Prokofiev and C. Palmer
(London, 1991), 297.

[16]   See Neil Minturn, *The Music of Sergei Prokofiev* (New Haven, 1997), 24–5. See also Prokofiev, *Soviet
Diary*, 248–9.

and distinctiveness of character persist into the later years, not least in many particularly straightforward and therefore 'comprehensible' melodic ideas, as Prokofiev continued to assess the extent to which traditional forms and tonal structures were suited to the individual cast of his thematic thinking.

The contrast between hectic drama and more restrained lyricism which he could encompass was already marked in the 1920s: the opera *The Fiery Angel* (1927) and the associated Symphony No. 3 (1928), together with the ballet *Le Pas d'acier* (1927), represent the limit of Prokofiev's aggressive anti-romanticism, reflecting similar preoccupations in Stravinsky, Bartók, and Hindemith while never sounding like mere imitations. Yet the ballet *The Prodigal Son* (1929) and the related Fourth Symphony (1930) operate at a much cooler temperature. These works opened the way for a more positive blend of lyrical and dramatic qualities which Prokofiev was to explore in several of his finest compositions: the ballet *Romeo and Juliet* (1936), the Fifth and Sixth Symphonies (1944 and 1947), and the opera *War and Peace* (first version 1942).[17]

Analysis: Symphonies Nos. 5 and 6

It was not until 1944, eleven years after his return to Russia and fourteen years after his last essay in the form, that Prokofiev returned to the symphony as such; but there is a remarkable sense of confidence in the fact that the Symphony No. 5 was composed in only one month. The principal virtue is precisely that which was lacking in Nos 2, 3, and 4: a disciplined control of tonal and thematic relationships which owes nothing to programmatic schemes. Yet the most impressive thing of all is the extent to which the debt to a traditional four-movement plan serves to enhance the originality of the result. In many respects this is a truly 'classical' symphony, but there is no pastiche or parody of classical style. The music is utterly personal to Prokofiev in its characteristic moods of wistfulness and wit, and its certainty of purpose, however instinctive, gives it the stamp of genius.

The least 'classical' feature is that the first, sonata-form, movement[18] is an Andante rather than an Allegro, and the only possible structural miscalculation lies in the use of a faster tempo for the second subject (Poco più mosso, Fig. 6), which is difficult to gauge effectively in performance, and can undermine the steady growth of the movement rather than acting as a truly dynamic contrast. Since the first subject is basically lyrical, Prokofiev creates tension by harmonic means, with the simplest and most orthodox of background tonal relationships (the exposition ending in the dominant), coloured by chromaticisms which are always just prominent enough to disturb the main tonality without obscuring it unduly. The richness of the orchestration is a further factor making for

---

[17] For the operas, see Ch. 4 above, pp. 86–9.
[18] This movement is also discussed in Minturn, *Music of Prokofiev*, 111–20.

purposeful monumentality, but the use of E♮s in the spare harmonic support for the opening B♭ major melodic phrase is the clearest statement of intent: even if the traditional hierarchy of the cycle of fifths is preserved, the anti-diatonic, tonality-enriching tritone has an increasing part to play (Ex. 7.4).

The first-subject paragraph unfolds organically, with varied statements of the main theme, and the second subject, itself far more chromatic melodically than the first, leads to the main climax of the exposition at Fig. 8, with the firm establishment of the dominant F in the bass for the first time. Only at the end of the exposition, in the codetta between Figs 9 and 10, is there a clear contrast of thematic character, an 'afterthought' which is to grow in significance as the work proceeds.

There is a fine development section in which increasing dramatic excitement is achieved by a thorough exploration of all the thematic ideas, and a widening of tonal perspective culminates in an emphasis on E major which is the most impressive fulfilment of tritonal polarity (five bars before Fig. 17). The tonic key of B♭ remains the essential foundation throughout the recapitulation, but the more agitated mood, revived by the return of the codetta theme six bars after Fig. 22, inspired one of Prokofiev's finest passages, the thirty-six-bar coda, in which the lyric-epic character of the main material is transfigured and reinforced with compelling logic as the phrases climb up from their B♭ pedal bass. The final cadence might seem slightly self-conscious in its avoidance of conventional plagal or perfect harmonies, but it concentrates chromatic tensions—with E♮s in a suitably prominent position—and diatonic resolution into the smallest possible space (Ex. 7.5).

Ex. 7.4. Prokofiev, Symphony No. 5, 1st movt., beginning

Ex. 7.5. Prokofiev, Symphony No. 5, 1st movt., last four bars

The scherzo (Allegro marcato), which comes second, provides the first truly fast music in the symphony. Yet the first two bars indicate that this is not going to be an entirely lighthearted affair. It is a *danse macabre*, whose obsessive ticking accompaniment achieves symphonic rather than balletic status by virtue of its flexible support for a cumulative construction with much variety of harmony and phrase-length. The 'trio' is more conventionally dance-like, and the bright-eyed innocence of its opening and closing statements (Meno mosso, Figs. 36 and 47) makes the more heavily orchestrated return of the scherzo at Fig. 48 the more sinister. The diabolical intensification of this recapitulation never becomes over-elaborate, however, and the driving direction of the harmony issues ultimately in a discordant, chromatic but undoubtedly final cadence in D minor.

The Adagio in F major begins with one of Prokofiev's most beautiful melodies. The three-bar ostinato introduction proposes a strong tritonal element (F–B–C in the bass), which the melody itself incorporates along with other chromatic features. As the Adagio proceeds, however, it is clear that a more fundamental alternation between E major and F major is involved, which, in terms of the basic tonic of the whole work, is nothing if not dramatic. The middle section of the movement has a rather formal rhetoric which does not attain to the same very high level as the outer parts, but the ostinato-dominated transition from its climax at Fig. 71 to the return of the main idea at Fig. 72 is telling in its very simplicity. With the main theme there also returns the F/E alternation. The conflict is resolved in a closing paragraph of the greatest lyrical beauty, the decisive harmonic moment being at Fig. 76, where the E as root of E major becomes the bass of a first-inversion C major triad. This effect shows with particular pertinence that triadic harmony can still function with validity and originality when apparently 'non-functional' tonal relationships are involved.

The finale is marked Allegro giocoso, and begins with an introduction whose uncomplicated smile is barely clouded by quotation of the earnest first subject of the first movement (Fig. 79). Even when the main Allegro theme is launched, tritonal and other chromatic infiltrations at first impinge little on its diatonic good humour. The danger, then, is that the movement may seem to have too little to do with what has gone before, and that, in seeking to be unambiguously life-enhancing in orthodox Soviet fashion, it may sever its connections with the truly symphonic essence of the work as a whole. Prokofiev avoids that pitfall triumphantly by allowing the material to generate its own inexorable momentum—a technique which is the most positive relic of his early manner and which has already worked well in the second movement. Simple exuberance becomes fierce energy, with any potential monotony resulting from motoric rhythmic assertions kept at bay by the tonal argument between diatonic and chromatic elements around the fundamental B♭. The ending is at once exhilarating and disturbing. Since this was a wartime symphony, associations between vigour and violence need not be suppressed, but the finale has no need of programmatic props to justify it: it succeeds because it concludes the whole work in an appropriate way, continuing its arguments and resolving its tensions.

Prokofiev's Sixth Symphony was first performed in Leningrad on 11 October 1947. Its main musical ideas were to some extent inspired by the war but the titanic conflicts expressed so uncompromisingly may owe at least as much to an intention of Prokofiev's to dedicate the symphony—his Op. 111—to the memory of Beethoven: although Prokofiev makes no attempt to match the Olympian serenity of the Arietta of Beethoven's Op. 111, his last Piano Sonata, the terse forcefulness of the sonata's opening Allegro con brio ed appassionato can be sensed behind the more expansive but no less tragic character of the symphony's Allegro moderato.

The achievement of the Sixth Symphony is the more remarkable in view of an approach to both structure and key relationships which is considerably more original than that of No. 5. It is in only three movements, with an apparently extreme contrast between the first and third dramatically undermined with the reappearance of the first movement's second subject near the end of the finale— a very different effect from the incidental reminiscence of the first movement's first theme in the introduction to the finale of the Fifth Symphony. On one level, the Sixth Symphony is more diffuse than the Fifth: contrasts within movements tend to be greater. Such is the composer's skill, however, that the result is never episodic, and the cumulative approaches to perorations which avoid the conventional diatonic affirmations so beloved by Soviet 'aestheticians' are structured with a master hand.

The first movement (Allegro moderato) is a large-scale sonata design, in which the modifications are the result of perceptions about the character and potential of the artless yet eloquent main theme.[19] On its first appearance it is framed by an introduction and a continuation, both of which are more decisive in character: the 'questions' raised by the theme itself concern its tonality or modality (A♭? E♭? B♭?) and also its capacity, as a melodic rather than motivic entity, for symphonic development (Ex. 7.6). Prokofiev's answer is to develop the theme at

---

[19] This movement is also discussed in Minturn, *Music of Prokofiev*, 122–32.

Ex. 7.6. Prokofiev, Symphony No. 6, 1st movt., beginning

once in an extended, tonally fluctuating context, which finally comes to rest in the region of B minor (the enharmonic submediant of E♭ minor) for a second subject ('moderato') of even more tragically lyrical cast than the first (Fig. 10). With only the briefest exceptions, this paragraph is in a pure Dorian mode on B, creating the atmosphere of a kind of epic pastoral. So the first really dramatic surprise—and the act which generates the central conflict of the movement—is that which ensues at Fig. 13. A further related idea, though more assertive, fails to launch the development, but prepares the return of the first theme, rooted on G♯ (Fig. 15). After another statement on D♯ (i.e. the tonic) at Fig. 16, the exposition ends on to the original dominant: B♭.

The home key is regained, but with a new tempo (Andante molto) and a new theme (Fig. 17), more expansively lyrical than anything heard so far, for which the typically ticking accompaniment is a perfect background. With a shock of surprise, this is countered (Fig. 20) with an allegro faster than the original, and the main theme centred on G. The central section of the sonata scheme is now under way, and there is no longer any question of the capacity of the main theme to bear developmental processes. In perspective, the delaying role of the

Andante (could it not be the 'real' second subject?) is shown to be dramatically essential, the goad stirring the main material from reflection into action. At Fig. 29 a mighty dominant pedal is heard, and the most hectic assertions of main-theme motives surround it. This is the crux. The first subject has the capacity for development of the kind that reveals its latent intensity, but it cannot be trans-formed into a convincingly triumphant assertion. With superb control, as the dominant pedal persists and harmonic tension crystallizes around it, Prokofiev slows and quietens the music. What is prepared is the recapitulation of the 'second subject' in the tonic key (Fig. 33), which then links up at Fig. 36 with the Andante molto theme, whose greater chromatic density had earlier provoked the main development. For the second time, the first theme follows on from it, but now at the *original* tempo and, of course, in E♭ minor (Fig. 37). The first bar is again 'developed' to achieve an overwhelming *harmonic* climax on the sub-mediant major chord (C♭). A coda then ends the movement, with dark timbres undermining the otherwise positive presence of the major third in the final tonic chord.

The extent to which Prokofiev has risked incoherence in the interests of ambi-guity in this movement may be apparent from the above analysis. It is far less 'safe' a structure than that of the first movement of the Fifth Symphony, but it succeeds because it shows that the Andante molto theme has a positive function of contrast, which in the recapitulation leads to its enclosure by the two main ideas of the exposition. Of course, in the most concentrated sonata-form move-ments such additional perspectives are not needed, but, given the lyric nature of Prokofiev's initial material, his skill in the creation of such a profoundly dramatic design is difficult to overpraise.

Even more daring was his decision not to insert a lightweight Scherzo at this point, but to deepen the tragic atmosphere still further with an extended Largo. The taut chromaticism of the A♭-centred opening is as uncompromising harmonically as anything in Prokofiev's works of the 1920s, yet the singing theme for trumpet and violin (one bar after Fig. 1 [42]) has a self-confidence which anti-cipates an ultimately serene ending. It is therefore possible to feel that the violent eruption at the end of the first part of the movement is less organic and inevitable than the climax of the first movement; yet it still acts as an effective foil to the more relaxed central episode. This in turn is grafted on to a compressed reca-pitulation in which the main theme precedes its original introduction. The music calms down, but the harmonic issue remains ambiguous until the last two bars restore the tonic chord of A♭ major.

The opening theme of the finale (Vivace) seems much more straightforwardly playful than that in the Fifth Symphony, not least because of the virtually exclu-sive diatonic use of E♭ major. After only ten bars, however, the insertion of a more earnest and aggressive dotted rhythm outlines a conflict which is to have extra-ordinary repercussions (Ex. 7.7).

At this early stage we might expect a simple battle between 'good' and 'evil',

Ex. 7.7. Prokofiev, Symphony No. 6, 3rd movt., beginning

ending in the triumphant enthronement of the playful main theme, well equipped as it is with the potential for triadic fanfares. Most of the movement proceeds in a way which makes this probability a real one; nor would it be very difficult to compose an ending comparable to that of the Fifth Symphony, with a less bland but still essentially affirmative fantasia on the opening theme. Only when the recapitulation is launched does it become clear that Prokofiev is composing a disintegration of the main theme rather than an apotheosis. Under the guise of development, the direction becomes hesitant and the main key is lost. All seems well again when the chief contrasting theme returns in the dominant key (at Fig. 34 [94]) but increasingly hectic development of the initiating motive of the first subject destroys that security, and what might once have been the clinching tonic-key return of the main theme has undeniably ominous overtones. When, at Fig. 49 [109], the accompanying rhythm for the contrasting theme comes round again, there is at first no theme at all, just the sustained clash of A♮ against B♭. When thematic statement does return, it coincides with the gradual loss of rhythmic impetus and a descent towards minor tonality. At Fig. 53 [113] the second subject of the first movement returns, marked Andante tenero, and it sounds almost consolatory in spite of its E♭ minor modality. It yields to a harmonic outburst of unparalleled intensity but unclear direction, with thematic roots back in the main body of the finale. After a pause the menacing dotted rhythms return, merging not into 2/4 joviality but into remorseless 6/8 reiterations of harmonies which, in a final cadence, resolve on to a major triad as conclusive but as untriumphant as any major triad can be.

The Sixth Symphony was Prokofiev's last great orchestral work and it was a worthy climax to a career which, whatever it may have initially tried to reject, ultimately succeeded in confirming the continued relevance of the most fundamental traditional techniques. In affirming the roots of his language, and of his own profound romanticism, Prokofiev, at the cost of baffling his Soviet colleagues, transcended the limitations of his own earlier experiments and fulfilled himself through reinterpretation rather than rejection.

Shostakovich

Dmitri Shostakovich (1906–75) came to creative maturity at precisely the time when tonal sonata form might justifiably have been felt to have no future save as a vehicle for affectionate or sardonic parodies like Prokofiev's Classical Symphony (1916–17). Yet he first achieved fame with a four-movement symphony (No. 1, Op. 10), written in 1926 when he was still a student, and when he died his huge list of works was dominated by fifteen symphonies and fifteen string quartets, with several concertos and substantial chamber works (notably a piano quintet and two piano trios). Coupled with the pressures of his situation as a Soviet composer, this contribution can easily be interpreted as evidence of arch-conservatism, suggesting that, even within his own stylistic terms of reference, Shostakovich failed to explore alternatives, or to adapt to changing circumstances.[20] Yet one of the most remarkable things about his output is the absence of carbon copies, the sheer variety of forms employed. Not all are equally successful, but it is precisely because Shostakovich achieved a distinctly personal manner and continued to explore its structural implications that he can be regarded as one of the great modern symphonists in the romantic tradition as well as, in Richard Taruskin's phrase, 'a heroic classicist'.[21]

Shostakovich's acceptance of that tradition was clear from the first, even if it took him a decade to work out how to continue it in a positive, coherent way. The broad dimensions of the First Symphony enabled a large number of obvious influences—the early Stravinsky, Prokofiev, Hindemith, and Mahler among them—to survive without eliminating all traces of emerging originality. It was

[20] For a vivid portrait of the composer and his life, see Elizabeth Wilson, *Shostakovich: A Life Remembered* (London, 1994). On the controversial nature of the composer's 'memoirs'—Solomon Volkov (ed.), *Testimony: The Memoirs of Dmitri Shostakovich* (London, 1979)—see David Fanning (ed.) *Shostakovich Studies* (Cambridge, 1995), 4.

[21] See Richard Taruskin, 'Public Lies and Unspeakable Truth: Interpreting Shostakovich's Fifth Symphony', in *Shostakovich Studies*, 17–56.

probably the conscious effort to achieve greater concentration in combination with political 'relevance', which led to the less than totally coherent single-movement plans of the Second and Third Symphonies (1927 and 1931). In the same year as the First Symphony, Shostakovich had composed the single-movement First Piano Sonata, which provides plentiful evidence of his openness to the more radical composers of the West—Bartók and Berg for example. The sonata barely keeps its feet on the solid ground of tonality; and traditional structural relationships, even such as a study of single-movement sonatas by Liszt and Skryabin might suggest, are obviously not of the greatest importance. The dramatic intensity of the sonata makes it entirely appropriate that much of Shostakovich's time between 1927 and 1932 should have been devoted to opera (*The Nose* and *Lady Macbeth of Mtsensk*), and ballet (*The Golden Age* and *The Bolt*). Had the cultural climate permitted *Lady Macbeth* to remain in the repertory after its première, Shostakovich's development might well have been very different. As it was, the often frantic concentration carried over from the Second and Third Symphonies must have seemed a major contributory factor to the 'decadence' of the opera. And even though the Fourth Symphony (1935–6) is a much more deliberate and expansive conception than Nos. 2 or 3, it too was felt to be too strongly tarred with the brush of formalism and was withdrawn at the rehearsal stage, not to be heard of again for a quarter of a century.

As is well known, Shostakovich's way out of this crisis was to compose 'a Soviet artist's practical creative answer to just criticism'—the Symphony No. 5 Op. 47 (1937). Some Western commentators, in whose veins the blood of democratic liberalism surges so freely, would be overjoyed if it were possible to regard this work not merely as a failure in its own terms, but as a marked decline after the achievements of the more radical, Western-influenced works of the previous decade. Unfortunately for ideology, however, the Fifth, that shameful product of compromise and conformism, is a masterpiece, and one of the greatest of all modern symphonies. In it the composer achieved a new clarity and certainty of purpose by simplifying and expanding where he had previously tried to compress and complicate. The Fifth Symphony expresses not the inevitable superiority of Soviet aesthetics, but the particular truth that this particular composer could find his deepest expressive resources only through less experimental, eccentric channels. Not that the work is palely orthodox in form, but it does show a grasp of how traditional features may be adapted, rather than merely copied or stood on end, which is new in Shostakovich's work.

The breakthrough which the first movement of the Fifth Symphony represents was achieved by means of a crucial sacrifice, the abandonment of the attempt to write that 'real symphonic allegro' to which Shostakovich attached such importance in his own self-critical comments. Just as Prokofiev was only to attain true greatness as a symphonist in works whose first movements are not merely 'economical' but also have basically broad tempos, so Shostakovich found it difficult to combine breadth and profundity, in Beethovenian, or even

Tchaikovskian or Sibelian, fashion, with forceful energy. The further challenge was to avoid hyper-romantic self-indulgence in a slow first movement, and here too the Fifth Symphony, with its potentially austere but deeply moving thematic material, succeeds completely.

The finale is commonly regarded as the weakest movement of the work, and is often described as a crudely turbulent march which achieves an embarrassingly empty apotheosis in an endless belt of D major triads. It has even been claimed that such over-emphasis was a deliberate attempt to expose the essential banality of the Soviet 'paradise' which the work was dedicated to praise. The movement undeniably forms a perfectly logical final stage in the evolution of the symphony from 'darkness' to 'light'.[22] Even if we regard such an ending as organically inevitable, however, we may well prefer the earlier, less optimistic, more introspective music of the first and third movements, which move slowly but never meander. Whatever the relevance or quality of Shostakovich's optimistic perorations, his mastery of the public projection of essentially intimate, personal feelings never faltered, and gradually gained greater emphasis, first through the series of string quartets begun in 1938, and later, in response both to a degree of liberalization in post-Stalinist Russia and to a sense that with increasing age and ill-health he had little to lose, in the outstanding symphonies Nos. 13, 14 and 15. The Symphony No. 14 (1969) is particularly novel in form: a cycle of eleven songs, pessimistic in tone—the subject-matter is death—and less conservative in language. Indeed, the concentration and chromaticism of his early music of the 1920s are recalled, though the context is immeasurably more controlled and pertinent, the remarkably abrupt, non-triadic ending inexorably prepared by all that comes before. Concentration and chromaticism are even more satisfyingly integrated in the single-movement scheme of the String Quartet No. 13 (1970). No fewer than five of the earlier quartets (Nos. 5, 7, 8, 9, and 11) are played without a break, though distinctness of the separate stages—in No. 11 (1966) there are no fewer than seven of them—is as important as the underlying unity. Even when the basic form is more conventional, the skill and sensitivity with which Shostakovich shapes it are exemplary (as with the handling of sonata form in the first movement of No. 2). Yet there is particular satisfaction in observing the way in which the composer returned at a late stage of his career to the issue of strongly unified single-movement symphonic form, an issue he first tackled in the First Piano Sonata written a mere two years after Sibelius's Seventh Symphony, but which then led to the impasse of the over-ambitious and ill-defined Second and Third Symphonies. The name of Schoenberg has been invoked to account both for the formal plans of the Twelfth and Thirteenth Quartets and for the presence of twelve-note successions—though Shostakovich was still far from 'pure' atonality: the more consistent chromaticism which twelve-

---

[22] For discussion of the finale, including its quotation from Shostakovich's setting of Pushkin's 'Rebirth', see Taruskin, in *Shostakovich Studies*, 17–56.

note succession involves is used simply to create greater perspective for the ultimate tonal resolutions on which Shostakovich's forms normally depend for their
coherent completion. As the ending of the String Quartet No. 13 illustrates (Ex.
7.8), there is still a key signature to indicate the essential focus, and, in context,
the arrival of that final B♭ is not a precarious and previously unforeseen point of
closure but the confirmation of a fundamental structural feature evident from
the outset.

The increasingly melancholy tone of the later works reinforced the essential
romanticism of a style whose strongest roots were in the symphonies of Mahler.
Like Mahler's, Shostakovich's wit had a bitter, wellnigh frantic edge to it, and this
sardonic, self-conscious trait entered a new phase with the use of quotations
(Rossini's *William Tell* overture, some of Wagner's more doom-laden motives)
in the Symphony No. 15 (1971). Shostakovich became increasingly willing to
quote himself, and to use a musical motto—D, E♭, C, B♮—based on the
German transliteration (DSCH) of his initials. This was first consciously
employed in what is probably his greatest single work, the Symphony No. 10,
Op. 93 (1953).

Analysis: Symphony No. 10

That greatness is certainly not the result of structural compression, but of the
way in which a natural tendency to expansiveness is not merely controlled, but
turned to dramatic—symphonic—account. This is partly a matter of overall
structural proportion, with the longest, slowest, most intense movement coming
first. In basic outline, this could be a textbook example of sonata form, but it
is remarkable how little of it is clearly in the tonic key of E minor or any of its
conventionally close relatives. Not only is the main melodic material chromatic,
but the entire harmonic motion of the movement involves hints rather than
affirmations, implications rather than clarifications. The long first and second
subject sections in the exposition enable the music to evolve through the development of smaller thematic units, and the harmonic character is of progress
without stability. Ambiguity begins to intensify with the appearance of the
second subject (Fig. 17), whose supporting harmony seems designed to contradict an underlying tonic rather than to enrich or obscure it, and it is not until the
return of this second subject in the recapitulation (Fig. 57), differently accompanied, that true stability is reached. Even now, the music remains extremely
chromatic, but at least the background of E major and, later, E minor harmony
is preserved. The coda—which is also the 'real' restatement of the first subject,
since the beginning of the recapitulation is neatly conflated with the later stages
of the development—provides the clearest definition of the essential language
of the whole work, the tension between chromatic and diatonic factors never
more explicit than at the final 'perfect' cadence (Fig. 69) (Ex. 7.9).

(Adagio)

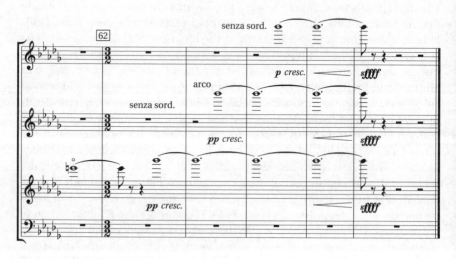

Ex. 7.8. Shostakovich, String Quartet No. 13, ending

Ex. 7.9. Shostakovich, Symphony No. 10, 1st movt., from six bars before Fig. 69

The second movement, Allegro, is an obvious opponent of the first: it is brief, violent, rooted in the key a tritone distant, B♭ minor. Even though its main thematic idea begins with the same ascending steps (tonic, supertonic, mediant) as that of the first movement, there is little sense of an argument being continued in a new context. Rather, it is the task of the remaining two movements both to continue these thematic and tonal arguments, and to resolve them. The third movement, Allegretto, takes its tonal stance the other side of the basic dominant from the Allegro, on C (minor). Once more the main thematic idea begins with the rising steps, but the mood, while still uneasy, is less aggressive, so it is possible to progress naturally to a point at the centre of the movement where a direct reminiscence of first-movement material is heard (Fig. 115). Another prominent thematic element in this movement is the DSCH motive—a permutation of the principal theme's first four notes—and this will be dramatically recalled at the climax of the finale.

The last movement, Andante–Allegro, for all its exuberance, is no mere dismissal of the serious issues raised by its three predecessors. First, there is an extended slow introduction of a profoundly tragic character, chromatic but centred in the dominant, B minor. Some of this material reappears during the course of an immense dominant preparation during the closing stages of the movement (Fig. 185), and, together with the DSCH motive, contrives to give a serious dimension to the otherwise exuberant E major ending. Yet even the light-hearted main allegro theme rarely remains firmly in its tonic key for long: the contrast of mood between first movement and finale does not imply a change of language, and the consistency with which the chromatic elements in all the themes radiate out into the underlying structural tonal organization is one of the reasons for the work's success. So, while there can be no mistaking the finality and centrality of E in the later stages of the finale, the constant presence of chromatic 'irritation' and brilliantly placed rhythmic cross-accents ensure that there is nothing the least perfunctory about the inevitable outcome.

David Fanning takes the lack of perfunctoriness in the Tenth Symphony's finale further, arguing that the movement is 'deliberately unbalanced'; its 'failure to observe symphonic good taste is not mitigated by the conflicting elements that arise during its course but actually gives them a profound raison d'être'.[23] In these terms, there is in Shostakovich 'a coexistence of the Mahlerian poles of utopia and catastrophe, of idealism and nihilism. The Doublethink of the Stalin years is countered with a devastating brand of Doublespeak.'[24] Nevertheless, what Fanning describes as Shostakovich's 'brand of ambivalence'[25] is the more powerful for its ability to resist the technical, tonality-undermining fractures of modernism. As 'one of the great modern symphonists in the romantic tradition' he remained committed to 'heroic classicism', and that commitment, Richard Taruskin claims, 'was his personal *perestroyka*; it was real, it was permanent, it was necessary—and it was tragic',[26] simply because, by 1930, the heroic-classic age was past. It is nevertheless perfectly possible that the twenty-first century will value those 'tragic' attempts to preserve 'heroic classicism' during the second half of the twentieth century more highly than the various attempts to destroy or ignore it.

Other Symphonists

In Europe and America many other composers born between 1880 and 1920 wrote fine symphonic works, often under the influence of obvious models. Ernest Bloch (1880–1959), a near-contemporary of Bartók and Stravinsky, had roots in Teutonic late romanticism, and his major symphonic compositions— the Piano Quintet No. 1 (1921–3), the Violin Concerto No. 2 (1987–8), the Concerto Symphonique for piano and orchestra (1947–8), the String Quartet No. 3 (1952)— all display a skilled structural sense at the service of material which is rarely sufficiently memorable to warrant such full-blooded treatment. Bloch is best known for his less ambitious but passionately expressive 'Rhapsody' for cello and orchestra, *Schelomo* (1915). The enormous output of the Czech composer Bohuslav Martinů (1890–1959) includes six symphonies and six string quartets, all of the former postdating his strongly neo-classic phase. Two of his operas, *Julietta* (1936–7) and *The Greek Passion* (1956–9) have enjoyed some success in the years since his death. Among the orchestral works the Double Concerto for

---

[23] David Fanning, *The Breath of the Symphonist: Shostakovich's 10th* (London, 1988), 72.
[24] Ibid. 76.   [25] Ibid.
[26] Taruskin, in *Shostakovich Studies*, 55.

two string orchestras, piano, and timpani (1938) is a powerfully wrought response to contemporary political tensions, and a sympathetic commentator regards Symphony No. 5 (1946) as 'in a sense . . . the most classical and perfectly balanced of the symphonies: the perspectives are precisely judged and the control over detail and its relation to the work as a whole is complete'.[27] It is a typical example of a 'conservative-modern' symphony: the form was always there for a sufficiently able composer to employ. But Martinů, for all his fluency and skill, was less successful than, for example, Prokofiev at imposing a strongly personal vision on the form, and the result is pleasingly efficient rather than compulsively memorable.

The five symphonies of Arthur Honegger (1892–1955) belong to the last twenty-five years of his life and represent a gradual retreat from an emphasis on dramatic works, including the 'dramatic psalm' *Le Roi David* (1921) and the 'stage oratorio' *Jeanne d'Arc au bûcher* (1934–5). The concentrated, contrapuntal energy of his most characteristic compositions is appealing, and bears out the accuracy of his own comment that 'a symphonic work must be built logically; . . . one must give the impression of a composition in which all is linked, the image of a pre-determined structure'.[28]

Tonal symphonic form exercised as great a fascination in the United Kingdom as it did elsewhere. Tippett's work is discussed in Chapter 12, but it was never very likely that he would follow for long in the stylistic footsteps of Vaughan Williams or Holst. Benjamin Britten was an even less likely disciple, although his Sinfonia da Requiem (1940), Spring Symphony (1949), and Cello Symphony (1963) are characteristically well-made responses to the concept, as 'programme symphony', 'choral cantata', and 'concerto'. The inter-war years saw the production of the two best symphonic works by William Walton (1902–83): the Viola Concerto (1929) and the Symphony No. 1 (1935). Both are unapologetically romantic yet finely constructed compositions, and the very confidence of their manner makes Walton's subsequent failure to match them the more regrettable. Walton was no more able to follow up his success with *Belshazzar's Feast* (1931) in the realm of oratorio.

Of the three American symphonists born in the 1890s—Walter Piston (1894–1976), Howard Hanson (1896–1981), and Roy Harris (1898–1979)—Harris is generally regarded as the best, and of his fourteen symphonies it is the Third (1937) which has made the greatest impact, its single-movement form and broadly diatonic manner recalling Sibelius, but not being dwarfed by the comparison. Harris's idiom exploits national roots through the medium of a personal approach to elements of traditional structure.

The career of Aaron Copland (1900–90) typifies the problems and rewards of pursuing the tonal symphonic structure in the modern age. Spending a crucial

---

[27] Robert Layton, in Robert Simpson (ed.), *The Symphony*, ii (Harmondsworth, 1967), 228.
[28] Arthur Honegger, *I am a Composer*, trans. W. O. Clough and A. A. Willman (London, 1966), 79.

period of study in France between 1921 and 1924, he seemed from his earliest works to have been ideally suited to the task of revitalizing tonal forms without recourse to any extremes, whether neo-classical or 'nationalist'. The Symphony for Organ and Orchestra of 1924 begins delightfully, but its more ambitious later movements are relatively dull. The orchestral *Music for the Theatre* (1925) uses simple forms in a brilliantly effective way to sharpen the focus of a wholly personal style, whose rhythmic energy avoids mere imitation of Stravinsky and whose delicate lyricism, while obviously 'French', is still given an individual cast. There is a joyful jazziness in places, and little or none of that later, portentously homespun manner which Copland was to cultivate so intensively.

It was the attempt to expand this marvellously instinctive idiom to fill larger forms which was to occupy, and often frustrate Copland in the years ahead. The Piano Concerto (1926) was in many ways an unpropitious omen, with its exhilarating, but ultimately unrewarding confrontation between 'popular' and 'symphonic' elements. The 'Dance' Symphony (1928) is very much better, even if the slow movement seems a little too long. It has great lyric charm, and well-made climaxes generated by rhythmic activity of goodhumoured 'hoe-down' persistence, rather than 'Rite-of-Spring' savagery. After this, the next piece is another disappointment: indeed, the single-movement *Symphonic Ode* (1928, revised 1955) is in most respects the crudest of all Copland's larger works, especially in its over-emphatic repetition of irregular rhythmic patterns, a technique which palls with great rapidity. In so far as the failure of the *Ode* may have urged Copland to greater concentration, however, it was worthwhile: certainly the Piano Variations (1930) and the 'Short' Symphony (1933) are more purposeful, the chromatic elaboration of basic tonal relationships better controlled. The approach to 'all-thematicism' in the Variations is especially noteworthy, in view of Copland's later use of serial techniques (in the Piano Quartet (1950) and other instrumental works of the 1950s and 1960s).

Copland's genius as a writer of ballet music was fully displayed between 1935 and 1945, in *El Salón méxico* (1936), *Billy the Kid* (1938), *Rodeo* (1942), and *Appalachian Spring* (1944)—the last a truly miraculous rediscovery of the essential simplicity of his earliest works in terms of a much more confident and personal style. In following it up with the grandiose Symphony No. 3 (1946), Copland dramatized the entire structural issue which his music had faced with startling clarity, for a basic simplicity is here stretched to breaking point by a scheme which almost 'out-Soviets' Shostakovich in its progress towards a diatonic paean provoked by a 'Fanfare for the Common Man'.

This symphony is the last word in great achievements against the grain, for Copland's later instrumental works displayed as ambivalent an attitude to tonality as they did to sonata form. The Piano Fantasy (1955-7), Nonet for Strings (1960), *Connotations* for Orchestra (1961-2), and *Inscape* (1967) represented Copland's hope that tonality could survive revitalized by a fusion with twelve-note technique. As it happens, tonality has survived and also adapted itself in other ways, often with no input from serial thinking. But the possibilities explored by Copland and other contemporaries continue to offer models for composers, even when their concern is more with confrontation than with fusion.

Schoenberg in Transition

On 7 December 1917, slightly less than two months after his forty-third birthday, Arnold Schoenberg (1874–1951) was finally discharged from the Austrian Army. His first period of military service had lasted from December 1915 until October 1916 and this second short spell had begun in September 1917. The disruption to his creative work was considerable. He was able to write the fourth of the Orchestral Songs Op. 22, in July 1916 (Nos. 1–3 had been composed while he was still in Berlin, between October 1913 and January 1915), but his main project during the war was the oratorio, *Die Jakobsleiter*. He completed the first draft of the text as early as January 1915 and began the music of Part One in June 1917, only to be interrupted by the second call-up three months later. Although he returned to the score as soon as his final discharge came through, and continued to work on it until 1922, the work was never finished. But for the wartime interruptions, the oratorio might stand—complete—as the most mighty and absorbing of transitional works. Certainly there is an element of tragedy in the picture of a genius at the height of his powers forced to let a major composition languish while providing a potboiler like 'The Iron Brigade', the march for piano quintet which Schoenberg wrote for a 'festive evening' at his army camp in 1916. From his early years as an orchestrator of other men's operettas to his late years as a university teacher in America, Schoenberg suffered from the supreme frustration: the regular necessity to set his own work aside and perform other tasks in order to support his family. The sympathy for, and efforts on behalf of, other composers in a similar plight which his letters reveal are therefore as understandable as his often extreme irritation and impatience with bureaucracy and officialdom in all forms. For Schoenberg, in life as in music, inflexible systems were anathema.

Perhaps the most fundamental of all Schoenberg's creative decisions had been taken ten years before the end of the war—though to describe it as a decision is to minimize the instinctive, impulsive forces at work when he found himself moving away from the traditional tonal techniques he had used so powerfully and imaginatively in works like *Verklärte Nacht, Pelleas und Melisande*, the First String Quartet and the First Chamber Symphony. All the later quibbling—it is still going on—about whether 'atonality' is possible or meaningful is really beside the point, for a situation had arisen in which tonal structures—the relationships between keys and between those types of harmony which had expressed them—no longer seemed to Schoenberg to represent the living language of music. There would be occasions when he chose to revive the traditional tonal structures themselves (e.g. the Suite for Strings of 1934) or when the nature of the material and its treatment in a twelve-note work might suggest that a single note or chord is being given 'tonal' emphasis (*Ode to Napoleon Buonaparte*, Piano Concerto, both 1942). But the development and use of the twelve-note system was intended, in Schoenberg's own words, 'to replace the no longer applicable principle of tonality'.[1] It established a new principle, and however much importance we may attach to those occasional tonal stresses and triadic harmonies which occur in Schoenberg's twelve-note works, we cannot demonstrate that they represent a continued commitment to the principle of tonality. At most they are references to elements associated with that principle—references usually justified by the closeness of texture and form to the texture and form of tonal works. Indeed, as subsequent discussion will show, it is possible that Schoenberg modelled certain twelve-note works on specific tonal compositions.

Schoenberg explained in a letter how, from about 1915 onwards, he was consciously seeking ways of founding musical forms 'on a unifying idea which produced not only all the other ideas, but regulated also their accompaniment and the chords, the "harmonies"'.[2] If this phrase is surprising, it is simply because he had already achieved such a technique in one of his early non-tonal compositions, the Piano Piece, Op. 11 No. 1 (1909), which, as many analysts have shown, uses a three-note cell to form both thematic motives and accompanying chords.[3] This 'cellular serialism' was, in essence, the technique still being employed a decade later in the first four of the Piano Pieces, Op. 23 (1920). In Schoenberg's hands it is a technique of great subtlety and flexibility, which might seem to offer all the balance of unity and diversity which any composer could require. Yet Schoenberg ultimately saw it only as a step along the road to the true method: eventually, he came to feel that short motives should not function as background as well as foreground. Rather, the background should be provided by continually rotating cycles of all twelve chromatic semitones in an order (changing from piece to piece), which would probably have been suggested by a motivic or melodic shape shorter or longer than itself, but which would be to an extent independent of that shape and more capable of projecting and supporting a musical form of the most substantial proportions.

Schoenberg never expected this new method to provide a substitute for the harmonic functions of tonality; many years later he wrote of chord progressions in twelve-note music that 'as such progressions do not derive from roots, harmony is not under discussion and evaluation of structural functions cannot

[1] *Arnold Schoenberg Letters*, ed. E. Stein, trans. E. Wilkins and E. Kaiser (London, 1964), 104.
[2] Willi Reich, *Schoenberg, a Critical Biography*, trans. L. Black (London, 1971), 131.
[3] For a detailed survey of the analytical issues, see Ethan Haimo, 'Atonality, Analysis, and the Intentional Fallacy', *Music Theory Spectrum*, 18 (1996), 167–99.

be considered. They are vertical projections of the basic set, or parts of it, and their combination is justified by its logic.'[4] But his musical inheritance and his creative instinct combined to convince him that, while an underlying unity was a basic necessity, the diversity of a complex, extended form must be the ultimate goal of any worthwhile compositional technique. On the one hand he was content to be able to 'provide rules for almost everything': on the other his consciously assumed role as the composer of 'really new music which . . . rests on tradition' ensured that only when all twelve notes were given a precise position in a scheme could a form of sufficient power and range be generated. The result at times seems to involve a loss of both the visionary radicalism of the monodrama *Erwartung* and the elaborately moulded yet undoctrinaire total thematicism of the Piano Pieces, Op. 23 Nos. 1–4 (1920–3). Yet in certain late works (the String Trio of 1946, for example) both virtues were regained: and Schoenberg was able to show not merely that the new method 'worked', but that he had achieved a new fluency, and a new integration of those traditional and structural textural elements by which he set such store.

Schoenberg's Twelve-Note Practice

The material for a twelve-note composition comprises a 'prime' [P] set (row, or series), and its eleven possible transpositions; the inversion of this set [I] and its eleven transpositions; and the reversals or retrogrades of the twelve prime [R] and twelve inverted [RI] forms. This makes a total of forty-eight versions of a set, although in certain cases, where retrogrades turn out to be identical to transpositions of primes, the total will be twenty-four.[5] By convention, the first pitch-class of the four untransposed set forms is designated 'o', with each transposition (from 1 to 11) represented by the distance in semitones from this untransposed basis. The identity of 'o' itself will therefore vary from work to work, at least until such time as all commentators agree to regard C as 'o', irrespective of whether that pitch-class is fundamental to the composition's material or not. In the absence of clear instructions from the composer, early analysts of twelve-note music tended to choose the first pitch-class of the first set-form used in the piece, or the first to be given melodic prominence, as 'o'. Yet increasing musicological work on sketch materials, particularly Webern's, has reinforced the point that the transposition levels with which the finished work begins are often not those which the composer himself thought of as fundamental when he began the work. In other words, 'o' is relative, but in the following discussion it is usually attached to a pitch-class which is in some way fundamental to the work in question.

---

[4] Arnold Schoenberg, *Structural Functions of Harmony*, ed. L. Stein (London, 1969), 194. The analytical issues raised by such perspectives are regularly aired in the specialist literature. For a particularly cogent discussion of the topic, see Timothy Jackson, review of Silvina Milstein, *Arnold Schoenberg: Notes, Sets, Forms* (Cambridge, 1992), *The Journal of Musicological Research*, 15 (1995), 285–311.

[5] See analysis of Webern's Op. 28, Ch. 10 below, pp. 212–7.

Twelve-note composers are obliged to accept that all forty-eight (or twenty-four) forms of the basic set are available. There are, however, no rules compelling them to *use* all of this material. Nor need they attempt to use all the elements of a twelve-note set with strict equality, in order to reinforce the essential difference between atonality and the inherently hierarchical features of tonal compositions. The impulse to formulate the twelve-note method was undoubtedly provided by Schoenberg's desire to organize the so-called 'total chromaticism' which was the natural product of the nineteenth century's increased emphasis on chromatic harmony. Yet simply because of the way Schoenberg himself composed (it was rather different, as we shall see, for Webern), any sense of the constant and absolute equality of every pitch is virtually ruled out—if not through specific melodic or harmonic emphasis then through the ways in which the twelve-note material itself is used. Such emphases in Schoenberg's music are not necessarily audible: but they are a result of accepting the fact that, of the forty-eight versions of a set, some will bear closer internal resemblances of pitch order than others, and if the form of the work involves hierarchical elements (distinctions between main and subsidiary themes, for example) it will be logical to treat the twelve-note material in a hierarchical manner also.

The practical implications of this can be followed easily enough in the succession of completely twelve-note works which Schoenberg finished in a remarkable five-year creative outburst between 1923 and 1928.[6] There are two movements (the fifth piece of Op. 23 and the central Sonnet in the Serenade Op. 24) which are based solely on single, untransposed twelve-note sets, but in the first work to involve transpositions and inversions, the Piano Suite, Op. 25 (1921–3), the sets employed are P-0, I-0, P-6, I-6 and their retrogrades. The choice of transpositions at the sixth semitone—the tritone—may seem the consequence of a desire to hint at 'tonic-dominant' relationships, and the occurrence of the tritone G/D♭ in all four sets is a hierarchical feature which Schoenberg exploits in several places: see the inner *ostinato* at the start of the Intermezzo and, most obviously, the 'double drone' of the Musette (Ex. 8.1).

What is important here is not the actual occurrence of these 'common features' or 'invariants' within the composer's chosen forms of the set—the nature of the twelve-note system makes some such invariants inevitable—but Schoenberg's decision to use them. In the Piano Suite the invariants are rendered audible as emphases on specific pitches; in later works, even if single-pitch emphasis occurs, invariance will come to play more of a background role, through the exploitation of certain set-forms, usually in pairs.

The Piano Suite is also significant for its use of forms primarily associated with the baroque keyboard suite, and although the music is scarcely neo-classical in the Stravinskian sense, it shows that allusion to the textures of the past was no

---

[6] See Ethan Haimo, *Schoenberg's Serial Odyssey: The Evolution of his Twelve-Tone Method, 1914–28* (Oxford, 1990). Also Martha M. Hyde, *Schoenberg's Twelve-Tone Harmony: The Suite Op. 29 and the Compositional Sketches* (Ann Arbor, 1982).

Ex. 8.1. Schoenberg, Suite for Piano, 'Musette', bars 20–31

less important to Schoenberg. There is an expressionistic concentration and forcefulness to the music, nowhere more obvious than in the final Gigue. And when Schoenberg employs canonic imitation most explicitly (the Trio section of the Minuet) it is with strutting, sardonic effect. In several of these early twelve-note works he seems to be expressing savage mockery of his own capacity to employ such traditional textures as imitation and such traditional structures as sonata or rondo form. To regard this as a bitter admission of failure to develop completely new forms exploring all the potentialities of the new serial method and finally throwing off the dead weight of the past is to ignore the tremendous sense of creative liberation which the conjunction of serial technique and traditional structural background reveals. In four large-scale works: the Wind Quintet, Op. 26 (1924), the Suite Op. 29 (1926), the String Quartet No. 3, Op. 30 (1927), and the Variations for Orchestra, Op. 31 (1928), Schoenberg displayed a truly awesome fluency and a phenomenal resourcefulness, not simply in using the new technique on a large scale, but in adapting forms originally developed during the tonal period to serve a very different function.

As a group, these four works triumphantly affirm the central role of thematicism—it is only in the Wind Quintet that the composer's polyphonic dexterity, nourished by the medium itself, seems to have inhibited the generation of well-defined and colourful thematic material. In the Suite there is even a wittily projected series of serial variations on a simple tonal melody ('Ännchen von Tharau'). The result is perhaps heavy-handed as a piece of music, but it serves, even at its most incongruous, to prove Schoenberg's willingness not only to write thematically, but to incorporate a very traditional kind of thematicism into a twelve-note texture. Such direct melodic ideas are used more satisfyingly and more coherently in the Third Quartet and the Variations, however. The Quartet starts with finely controlled lyric melody set off by dynamic accompanimental counterpoints, while the Variations are based on a twenty-four bar theme, mainly in the cellos, whose phraseology and rhythmic character are rooted in the romantic language of the fairly recent past (Ex. 8.2).

Given such a commitment to thematicism, decisions about form became decisions about thematic treatment. Since Schoenberg's tonal works had shown his ability to intensify and extend the role of developmental processes within the sonata-form scheme, it is fascinating to observe this skill in contexts where the underlying logic of tonal relationships has been replaced by the firm association between thematic ideas and certain versions of the basic set. As early as the first movement of the Wind Quintet, begun on 21 April 1923, Schoenberg had attempted a conventionally proportioned sonata design in which the relationship between exposition and recapitulation is as close (yet as subtly varied) as one would expect in a post-Brahmsian, tonal sonata-form movement. Schoenberg had not merely rejected athematicism: he had chosen to regard sonata form as valid in view of its overriding thematic connotations—valid even when the tonal system itself had been abandoned.

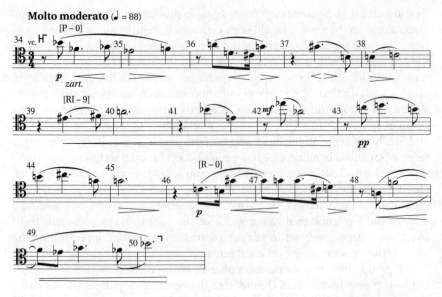

Ex. 8.2. Schoenberg, Variations for Orchestra, bars 34–50

All the movements of the Quintet, the Suite, and the Third Quartet establish associations with traditional form, ranging from the expanded binary design of the Gigue (finale of Op. 29) to the sonata rondo of the finale of the Third Quartet. The *precise* associations may be matters of argument—Schoenberg himself disliked the suggestion that the first movement of the Third Quartet was in a straightforward sonata form[7]—but their essential dependence on the statement and elaboration of clearly delineated thematic ideas cannot be denied. In many ways the best and most ambitious of all these works is the large-scale Orchestral Variations (Op. 31), his first orchestral twelve-note work. The opportunity for relatively dense textures demanded a particularly skilful control of serial technique, and this makes one basic decision of the composer's, with regard to the twelve-note material, all the more fascinating. The theme itself comprises three set statements: P-o, RI-9 and R-o, and the two halves, or hexachords, of RI-9 have the same notes (in a different order) as the two hexachords of P-o; the one actual interval which is common to both their first hexachords is the tritone Bb/E, while in their second hexachords it is the tritone G/C♯. Schoenberg is simply associating sets which have a significant permutational feature in common, something which establishes a degree of unity between them beyond the mechanical transpositional relationship of interval sequence. It is a similar technique to that of the Piano Suite, and its use can be traced in all the intervening compositions.

---

[7] Arnold Schoenberg, 'The Third and Fourth String Quartets', in U. Rauchhaupt (ed.), *Schoenberg, Berg and Webern. The String Quartets: A Documentary Study* (Hamburg, 1971), 51.

Schoenberg had enjoyed himself as early as the first movement of the Wind Quintet with the 'punning' associations possible between transpositions closely related in the actual order of pitches, but the more far-reaching implications of such relationships took time to work out.

As far as the Variations for Orchestra is concerned, we can extend the area around P-0 and I-9 to include no fewer than six other sets containing that pivotal pair of tritones B♭/E and G/C♯; these are P-3, P-6, P-9, I-0, I-3, and I-6. Schoenberg's compositional exploitation of their association is already evident in the introductory section of the work, where they predominate, and in the first three variations. Yet the whole work, while involving many rapid changes of set-form, is dominated, not simply by the theme, but by the theme *at its original pitch*. In view of the association of seven other sets around P-0, Schoenberg could have divided the forty-eight possible versions into three subgroups of sixteen sets each, those sharing their pairs of tritones with P-0, or with P-1, or with P-2. Such comprehensive schematization might be felt to involve the creation of unreal distinctions, fundamentally different from the concept of a basic area which is departed from and returned to (the last thirteen bars of the Variations use only P-0 and its close associates). Nevertheless, Schoenberg did establish a principle for the combination or close association of sets and gave it its first full compositional statement in the same year as the Variations were completed, 1928. In the Piano Piece Op. 33a we have a form clearly derived from the classical sonata or ternary design, though the recapitulation is much compressed. We also have a fixed association between P-0 and I-5 which is grounded in the fact that their first hexachords together provide all twelve notes. This association is fixed and applies to all transpositions (P-1 with I-6, etc.). Schoenberg was to remain committed to it for the rest of his life.

Because of its brevity and simplicity Op. 33a provides a convenient summary both of Schoenberg's adaptation of traditional form and of his newly achieved technique of 'combinatoriality' (Milton Babbitt's term for the fixed-association technique).[8] The ideas are not among the composer's most appealing, but the particularly obvious differentiation between the main elements of the first and second thematic groups makes the form more clearly audible than is the case with some of Schoenberg's more elaborate works.

As the first few bars show, 'combinatoriality' can involve the juxtaposition of the set-pair as well as their combination. Each of the main subject-groups is cast in a miniature ternary form of radically different proportions (first subject $2 + 7 + 2$ bars; second subject $5 + 2 + 2\frac{1}{2}$) and both have appendages, the first a two-bar transition and the second a four-bar codetta. In the whole of this $26\frac{1}{2}$-bar exposition, only P-0, I-5, and their retrogrades are used. The last thirteen bars of the piece are divisible into five bars of elaboration and eight and a half of recapitulation. The development concerns the chordal material of the first

---

[8] Milton Babbitt, 'Some Aspects of Twelve-Tone Composition', *Score*, 15 (1955), 52–61.

subject-group and 'modulates' away from the basic set-pair, employing P-2 and I-7 (bars 27–9) and P-7 and I-0 with retrogrades (bars 29–32). The abbreviated and varied reprise then restores the primacy of P-0 and I-5. The 'sonata-ness' of the piece is as much in the dramatic-lyric alternations as in any more precisely proportioned resemblances to the classical form. We shall see later how in his last String Quartet and the two concertos Schoenberg further refined the process of composing 'serial sonatas'. But his main concern during the period 1928 to 1932—his last years in Europe—was with another long-established musical form: opera.

Twelve-Note Music and the Voice

Schoenberg's first twelve-note vocal piece has already been mentioned in passing—the Sonnet which forms the fourth movement of the Serenade, Op. 24. In 1925 he composed two works for mixed choir, Four Pieces, Op. 27, and Three Satires, Op. 28. More than two years then elapsed until, in October 1928, he began the first twelve-note opera, *Von Heute auf Morgen* ('From one day to the next'), and that same month produced the first sketch for the text of *Moses und Aron*. From then until March 1932, when the composition of Act II of *Moses und Aron* was completed, he was absorbed by these musico-dramatic projects, though he did turn aside to write a further set of choral pieces, Op. 35, as well as two short instrumental compositions, the *Accompaniment to a Film Scene* for orchestra, Op. 34 (1930) and Piano Piece, Op. 33b (1931).

This shift of emphasis away from the instrumental works of the early twelve-note years confirms that Schoenberg was a creative artist whose ideas could not find complete expression in abstract musical forms. For all his resource in the handling of instrumental designs, and for all his delight in the pedagogic explication of compositional techniques, his need to express ideas through words in the sceptical, often anti-emotional inter-war era seems to have been even greater than his desire to express deep inner feelings through the medium of paint on canvas during the heyday of expressionism before the First World War. The attempt to marry a philosophical text and music in *Die Jakobsleiter* had met with frustration, but the 1925 choral pieces, in an obviously less ambitious way, provided an outlet which in turn revived the desire to undertake a more ambitious project. In 1926 Schoenberg completed the first version of his drama *Der biblische Weg*, which he described as 'a very up-to-date treatment . . . of the story of how the Jews became a people'. A further remark could equally well apply to *Moses und Aron*: 'It is highly dramatic . . . and, although its profundities offer the superior kind plenty of food for thought, is vivid and theatrical enough to fascinate the simpler sort.'[9] Thus, although Schoenberg finally embraced the Jewish

<hr>

[9] Reich, *Schoenberg*, 159. See also Alexander L. Ringer, *Arnold Schoenberg: The Composer as Jew* (Oxford, 1990).

faith only in July 1933, shortly before his arrival in America, his preoccupation with the issues raised by his own race and religion was of great importance throughout the 1920s. The path from *Der biblische Weg to Moses* is clear. By contrast, *Von Heute auf Morgen* was a fuller working-out of the humorous side of Schoenberg's creative personality, which had found recent expression in the Satires and the 'Ännchen von Tharau' movement of the Suite Op. 29. The very title suggests another important link with the Satires and with Schoenberg's desire to argue that his own invention, the twelve-note technique, was no modish flash in the pan but a genuine, inescapable and irreversible step forward. His aim, and therefore that of his librettist 'Max Blonda' (alias his wife Gertrud), was 'to show, using everyday figures and goings-on, how . . . the merely modern, the fashionable, lives only "from one day to the next", from insecure hand to greedy mouth—in marriage, but at least equally in art, in politics, and in people's views about life'.[10]

The fifty-minute score, which was completed on New Year's Day 1929, may even be seen as a kind of comic parallel to *Erwartung*. As a case-history of a rela-tionship—and most commentators agree that the plot must have originated in the Schoenbergs' own experience—it shows a keen awareness of the importance which fantasy, role-playing, and jealousy can take on even in a well-established marriage. The basic situation, the husband and wife returning home from a party where each has been attracted by someone else, develops into an attempt by the wife to 'win back' the interest of her husband, first by dressing up in an exotic costume, then by flirting over the telephone with her admirer from the party, a famous but fatuous operatic tenor. The husband is by now thoroughly resentful, and the wife, though she has agreed to meet the tenor in a nearby bar, senses that her victory is close. By transforming herself back into the attitude (and costume) of a submissive wife, and helped by the opportune appearance of their small child, she ensures a rapid reconciliation. The final stages of the opera begin with the arrival of the tenor and the woman to whom the husband had been attracted at the party. The married couple survive the mockery of the more liberated, 'fashionable' pair, and the opera ends with a cosy domestic scene at the breakfast table.

The psychological factor is especially evident in lines such as the wife's question to her husband, 'soll ich wieder ich sein?' ('shall I now be me again?') (bars 851–2). One way in which Schoenberg draws attention to it is to associate two linked statements—the wife's 'Man will doch schliesslich auch sein eignes Leben leben' ('one wants, after all, to lead one's own life') (bars 294–300) and her later remark 'So will ich schliesslich doch mein eignes Leben leben' ('Thus shall I live at last a life that is my own life') (bars 493–9)—with broad, melodic state-ments of the opera's basic set (transposed). Yet the musical coherence of the work depends not only on such obvious thematic recurrences but also on the skilful

<hr />

[10] Reich, *Schoenberg,* 168.

characterization of individuals and situations in such a way that a balance is struck between tendencies to 'recitative' and tendencies to 'aria'. Hans Keller defined a 'formal scale of recitatives, ariosos and actual numbers', evidence that 'the organization . . . can simply be called classical'.[11] In spite of the elaborate orchestration, there is very little purely orchestral music in the opera: the hectic momentum of the comedy requires consistent vocal dominance. Even with such exacting comic requirements, however, there are several moments of great lyric beauty, like the wife's confession of interest in the tenor (bars 177ff.) or, much later, the moment of reconciliation (bars 919ff.). Nor is rhythm uniformly complex from start to finish: waltz patterns and parodies of popular dances emerge from time to time, and the empty-headed tenor is deliciously characterized by simple scalic phrases—first heard in an imitation of him by the wife (bars 198ff), but coming into their own with his 'appearance' on the telephone (bars 689ff.). Appropriately a rapid semiquaver figure portraying the anger of the married couple is a clear derivative of the music associated with this potential threat to wedded bliss.

Schoenberg's pervasive contrapuntal dexterity can be found at such incidental moments as the brief four-in-one canon in the orchestra (bar 569) but the device plays a more explicit dramatic role in the couple's anger duet (bars 254ff.) and in the final ensemble for the four singers, ending with an amusing canon at the unison for the tenor and the other woman, which, no doubt intentionally, seems to lie too low for her and too high for him.

The ending is finely calculated to keep both sentimentality and seriousness at bay. Domestic harmony restored, the couple lapse into *Sprechgesang* in a context as different from *Pierrot lunaire* as from the imminent *Moses und Aron*. The child has the last word, with the question 'Mama, was sind das, moderne Menschen?' ('Mummy, what's up-to-date people?'), and the last notes are a restrained yet luscious orchestral cadence, satisfyingly conclusive despite the absence of traditional concord (Ex. 8.3).

The composition of Acts I and II of *Moses und Aron* occupied Schoenberg from May 1930 to March 1932, but only a little of Act III was sketched at this time, and it was never finished. As late as 1950 the composer wrote, 'it is not entirely impossible that I should finish the third act within a year,' and shortly before his death he allowed that 'it is possible for the third act simply to be spoken, in case I cannot complete the composition.'[12] 'Possible', but not essential; it is generally agreed that the first two acts alone make a satisfying dramatic whole, whereas merely to speak the short surviving text of Act III would be more of an anti-climax than a consummation, though it may add something to one's appreciation of Acts I and II to know that Aaron is subsequently imprisoned by Moses, and falls dead at the moment of his release. Above all, the image at the end of Act II is

[11] Hans Keller, 'Schoenberg's Comic Opera', *Score*, 23 (July 1958), 33.
[12] See appendix to study score of *Moses und Aron*, Mainz 1958.

Ex. 8.3. Schoenberg, *Von Heute auf Morgen*, ending

surely the most moving portrayal of a desolate and despairing heroic figure since Wagner completed the third act of *Die Walküre* in 1856. The parallels are far from exact, but the central characters are both shown in full realization of their own limitations, and the poignancy of Wotan's 'farewell' music is matched by the less resigned but equally eloquent arches of the superbly fashioned tutti violin line that supports Moses' final outburst: 'O Wort! Du Wort! Das mir fehlt!' ('O word, thou word that I lack!').

It is this ending which also clinches the *musical* justification of Schoenberg's decision to make Moses primarily a speaker and only briefly, in Act I, Scene 2, a singer (conversely, Aaron is allowed one brief moment of speech). The philosophical or symbolic basis for this decision seems obvious enough, with the contrast and conflict between Moses and Aaron stemming from Moses' grasp of inner essence and Aaron's of outer representation. Aaron works miracles, while Moses lacks not merely the song but the words which will convey Divine Truth convincingly to all the people. The Tables of the Law stand in opposition to the Golden Calf, and at the end of Act II both are destroyed, yet it is Aaron whom the Israelites follow towards the Promised Land. To imagine a final scene in which Moses sang—even if he had sung throughout—is impossible; or rather, a scene in which he sang could not possibly convey the same degree of deprivation, the same conviction of impotence, isolation, and failure. In that Moses' dominant mood is righteous anger (at Aaron's foolishness and at his own inability to prevent it), the heightened speech as notated by Schoenberg is entirely appropriate. But in practice it seems better for the performer to underplay the role: Moses is more convincing as a cold, even remote academic than as a demonic, apparently deranged dictator. Aaron is characterized by long melodic lines of great lyric power, the people by choral textures which may often be polyphonically complex yet which can achieve the direct simplicity of the canon which ends Act I. The orchestra is handled with sovereign virtuosity, most obviously in the wild rout during the Dance round the Golden Calf, but such hectic elaboration is ultimately purged in the single, supremely eloquent melodic line which ends the work.

As a twelve-note composition the opera displays interesting hierarchical features. There is some disagreement about the pitch level of P-o. Some favour that initiated by the first chord of the whole work (A/B♭/E etc.); others (notably Milton Babbitt) argue that it should start on C♯, since this is the level at which it is first presented melodically, on Aaron's entrance in Act I, Scene 2.[13] As Babbitt notes, this is the only place in the opera where Schoenberg uses the succession of combinatorial relatives (P-o, I-3, R-o, RI-3), a process found at the start of instrumental works like the Variations for Orchestra, the Fourth String Quartet, and the Piano Concerto, though here, for once, the combinatorial pair is not P-o and I-5, but P-o and I-3.

Babbitt's essay draws attention to other significant structural features; for example, the reason for beginning Act I, Scene 4 with the Inversion form on D is that this has a 'middle tetrachord' (F♯/E/B♭/G♯) in common with the set which ends Scene 3—the prime form on C. Of greater aural significance—especially in view of the increasing freedom of note-order within the hexachord in the later stages of the opera—are the larger thematic and textural recurrences at dramatically relevant points. Within Act I, Scene 2, the way in which a lower line of bars 148 ff. achieves melodic prominence at bars 162 ff. is a good example of the logical manner in which a scene may be structured around thematic recurrence (there is a third 'variation' at bar 187 and a fourth at bar 218).

By the last scene of the first act it is possible to claim that 'by-now-familiar musical materials or clear derivations from them are shaped into an intricate formal mosaic of cross-references to preceding events and within the scene itself'. Material from Scene 2 returns at bar 879 'and it is with this music in the orchestra that the scene closes'.[14]

In the first two scenes of Act II, Aaron's music again refers back to that of Act I, Scene 2, and there is a particularly significant relationship between the end of the long third scene (the Dance round the Golden Calf) and the very start of Act I. The interrelationships between the two acts and the sense in which the whole opera thematically elaborates premises stated in its early stages are confirmed in the links between the first two scenes of Act I and the final scene of Act II. Conscious perceptions of the strong unifying factors at work in *Moses und Aron* may always be subservient to absorption in the inevitability of the unfolding

---

[13] Milton Babbitt, 'Three Essays on Schoenberg' in B. Boretz and E. T. Cone (eds.), *Perspectives on Schoenberg and Stravinsky* (Princeton, 1968), 55.
[14] Ibid. 59.

drama but with familiarity it comes to contribute substantially to an awareness of the superbly controlled intellectual substructure of this richly expressive masterpiece.

One further resonance of Moses' defeat and dejection at the end of Act II is its parallel to the feelings of the Jewish people as Hitler came to power. Little more than a year and a half after the completion of Act II Schoenberg and his family arrived in New York, fortunate to have escaped but faced with the inevitable practical aftermath of such an upheaval. The need to earn a living as a teacher and the problems of finding a permanent post absorbed most of the composer's energies until, in 1936, he was established as a professor at the University of California in Los Angeles, and moved into the house at Brentwood Park where he would spend the rest of his life. Here at last he was able to make rapid progress with his first substantial twelve-note instrumental compositions since the *Accompaniment to a Film Scene* of 1930, the Violin Concerto, Op. 36 (1934–6), and the String Quartet No. 4, Op. 37 (1936).

Schoenberg in America

The first work of any kind which Schoenberg completed in America was the five-movement Suite for Strings (1934), a tonal composition intended for student orchestras, which follows on from the two 'concerto-arrangements' he had made in 1932–3: that for cello and orchestra deriving from a harpsichord concerto by M. G. Monn and that for string quartet and orchestra deriving from Handel's Concerto Grosso, Op. 6, No. 7. Like them, the Suite for Strings has points of contact with 'the old style'; the title on the manuscript is actually 'Suite im alten Stile'. Yet Schoenberg's avowedly didactic intention did not demand the mere imitation, much less parody, of an earlier manner. His primary purpose was practical:

within a harmonic idiom conducive to modern feelings—and without, for the moment, putting students in jeopardy through the 'poison of atonality'—I had here to prepare them for the modern technique of playing.... But hints of modern intonation, composition technique, counterpoint and phrase structure were also needed, if the student is gradually to acquire a sense that melody, to count as such, need not mean the kind of primitive symmetry, lack of variation and lack of development such as are the delight of the mediocre in every land and among all peoples; rather that here, too, there already exist higher forms, belonging not merely technically but spiritually and intellectually in a higher artistic category.[15]

Such thinking was likely to have been behind all Schoenberg's later non-twelve-note works, whether specifically 'educational', like the Theme and Variations for Wind Band (1942), or not, like the Variations for Organ (1941). Thus his confession

[15] See Reich, *Schoenberg*, 198.

that 'a longing to return to the older style was always vigorous in me'[16] was not an admission of neo-classical tendencies, but an explanation of his delight in still occasionally demonstrating that worthwhile tonal compositions could exist alongside twelve-note ones—and have similar textural and structural features.

Schoenberg had composed the first movement of the Violin Concerto before the Suite in 1934, but the work was not finished for another two years, soon after the Fourth String Quartet. Dedicated to Webern, perhaps in response to Webern's dedication of his own Concerto for Nine Instruments, Op. 24, to Schoenberg on his sixtieth birthday, this is Schoenberg's first twelve-note concerto, though it is safe to say that in texture and thematic treatment it profits directly from the Handel and Monn adaptations. The Violin Concerto certainly confirms that, after a seven-year abstention from multi-movement, twelve-note, instrumental com-position, Schoenberg was proposing to continue his commitment to traditional forms. Since 1927 the major technical development had been the establishment of the combinatorial relation, with all its consequences with regard to invariant factors within the set-group. The hierarchical employment of the set-group elements in the concerto is indicated by the structural pre-eminence of two sets, P-0 and I-5, which are used throughout the first fifty-eight bars of the ninety-two-bar first section of the first movement. They are also present at the start of the finale and end both movements. Parallels with traditional harmonic processes extend further when we examine another pair of sets, P-7 and I-0. As Milton Babbitt has noted, P-7 'is that set which, by a traditionally tested and rea-sonable criterion of relatedness, carries the work away from the opening area to the most closely related area' (in bar 59). 'This transpositional relation may suggest a parallel with the dominant region of tonal "second subjects," but—be that pertinent or not—this particular transposed form . . . has a singular hexa-chordal relationship [to P-0] in that it preserves the greatest number of pitches (four) between corresponding hexachords of any set not in the initial complex.' It follows that this relatedness, whatever its associations with traditional tonic-dominant links, 'is determined completely by the . . . intervallic structure of the hexachords of the set'.[17]

The neatness of these tonal-serial parallels can create confusion if they encourage the assumption that the composer intended identity rather than allusion. But all Schoenberg's twelve-note works show that there can be no true analogy between harmonically functional modulation and the change of transposition levels within a set-group. Both processes involve departure, both predicate eventual return, but Schoenberg's decisions about when to change transposition levels and which level to move to at any given point do not seem to have been the result of reference to an all-embracing functional principle such as decisions about modulation in tonal music can involve.

[16] Arnold Schoenberg, *Style and Idea*, ed. L Stein (London, 1975), 109.
[17] Babbitt, 'Three Essays', 49.

The challenge to aural perception which Schoenberg (like many other composers generally regarded as 'complex') presents, and which is particularly apparent in the Violin Concerto and Fourth String Quartet, arises less from the absence of tonal coherence or traditional harmonic progression than because of the composer's belief in the necessity for thematic evolution—the kind of thematic process to which he referred in his remarks on the Suite for Strings. This 'higher form' of melody can certainly be traced in the Violin Concerto, and it means that exact repetition of significant motives or melodic shapes is much less evident than in those symphonic works from the classical and romantic past to which, in form and texture, Schoenberg's concerto remains in many respects beholden.

The concerto and the quartet mark the beginning of a change in Schoenberg's treatment of thematic processes and traditional forms, and in the String Trio (1946) he devised a more overtly modernist structure, less backward-looking than any of his earlier twelve-note schemes, and enabling his thematic techniques to attain a new range, concentration, and vitality. Thematic diversity and recurrence were given new purpose in the Trio by being made far less dependent on associations with tonally functional structures and traditional processes of thematic organization and development. Even so, the Violin Concerto and Fourth Quartet are works of great sophistication and power, and the perceptibility and pre-eminence of thematic working in a traditional formal context are particularly well demonstrated in the shortest movement in either, the Largo from the quartet.

Analysis: String Quartet No. 4 (Largo)

The underlying binary (ABAB) scheme for this movement naturally excludes the kind of 'separate development' involved in orthodox sonata form, and on first acquaintance the main fascination of the structure is likely to be on account of the almost 'recitative–aria' relationship of the two main ideas.[18] Schoenberg himself referred to the five-bar unison theme with which the Largo opens as a 'recitative', the rhapsodic character of which is continued for a further ten bars of diverse comments which do not agree on any single thematic or textural way of continuing, or answering, the clear-cut lines of the recitative.[19] Instead, the indications 'ad libitum' and 'rubato' confirm the almost improvisatory, preludial quality of the music up to bar 629 (the bars of all four movements are numbered consecutively).

The second main idea of the movement begins at the Poco adagio (bar 630)

[18] See Silvina Milstein, *Arnold Schoenberg: Notes, Sets, Forms* (Cambridge, 1992), 99–100, and Jackson, review, on the possibility of a Beethovenian model for this movement.

[19] Schoenberg's notes on the Fourth String Quartet are published in Rauchhaupt (ed.), *Schoenberg, Berg and Webern*, 61.

and is described by Schoenberg as 'a cantabile melody, formulated in the form of a period, antecedent followed by a consequent, very simple and regular, comprising six measures' (Ex. 8.4).

As the example shows, this, unlike the recitative, is not a twelve-note melody, nor a single horizontal articulation of the basic set. It shares an ascending perfect fifth with the first part of the recitative theme, but in isolation the first bar and a half have an unmistakably 'tonal' cast, the C# cadence confirming the diatonic trend of the previous notes. This tendency is undermined both by the melodic continuation and by the supporting parts, but the 'leading-note/tonic' associations of the phrase are an important aid to recognition in the process which follows. The rest of the first half of the movement (up to bar 663) is concerned with 'varied repetition', elaboration and development of the cantabile melody.

The second half of the Largo begins with the unison recitative in free inversion, but its 'rhapsodic continuation' is replaced by what Schoenberg rather

Ex. 8.4. Schoenberg, String Quartet No. 4, 3rd movt., bars 630–5

unguardedly calls a 'modulatory elaboration'.[20] The thematic content is, obviously enough, derived from the recapitulated recitative, using the same pair of sets: P-10 and I-3. The texture is fugal, with the 'answers' starting on the 'dominant' and inverting the subjects. After the climax of this 'insertion' the return of the second theme is prepared with the help of hints of the exposition's rhapsodic episode (e.g. compare first violin in bars 622 and 678).

The second theme itself returns on the same pitches as at its first appearance, but the continuation differs.

The deviation from the first formulation of this part is far-reaching, because of the difference in purpose. The first time it served as a lyric contrast to the dramatic outbursts of the recitative, which it had to overcome by virtue of its intrinsic warmth. The second time, when the insertion of the [fugal] section has already reduced the tension of the beginning, its purpose is to prepare for an ending.[21]

The process whereby that purpose is achieved is summarized in Ex. 8.5. The richness of the elaboration, even in a relatively small-scale movement, is never such as to obliterate the first principles of the idea being elaborated, and the movement as a whole is an excellent example of that typically Schoenbergian blend of spontaneity and intensity, rhapsody and rigour, which is all the more gripping in view of the unambiguously romantic opening. The rhetoric of the recitative can seem disconcerting, but, as Schoenberg himself explained, it is the ideal foil for the rich restraint of the 'subordinate' theme.

Late Works

The most noteworthy feature of Schoenberg's last decade is the contrast between its two most important works, the Piano Concerto, Op. 42 (1942) and the String Trio, Op. 45 (1946). The concerto is the culmination of all that is most recreatively traditional in the composer's handling of twelve-note technique. The single-movement form comprises four distinct sections and to this extent recalls the one-movement schemes of forty years earlier, the First String Quartet and the First Chamber Symphony, though the concerto begins with an Andante rather than a hectic fast section. The concerto may initially make a rather more relaxed impression than any of Schoenberg's other twelve-note works, but the melodic breadth of its opening—a thirty-nine-bar theme in the solo instrument—is only one element. More dramatic material appears in the Molto Allegro (section two), provoking in turn a still more restrained Adagio. The work ends with an energetically good-humoured, rondo-like Giocoso, the main theme of the Andante reappearing not long before the end (bar 443).

The nature of the keyboard writing itself is quite traditional in the Liszt-

---

[20] Schoenberg's notes on the Fourth String Quartet are published in Rauchhaupt (ed.), *Schoenberg, Berg and Webern*, pp. 58–64.
[21] Ibid. 63.

Ex. 8.5. Schoenberg, String Quartet No. 4, 3rd movt. From bar 679, melodic line only

Brahms manner which Schoenberg never completely abandoned. Since this involves much octave doubling and figuration with a considerable amount of internal repetition, the links between the concerto and its nineteenth-century precursors are manifest enough. In all respects, however, it seems like an end rather than a beginning. The treatment of the material shows no loss of invention, but the nature of that opening theme is problematical. With its lilting rhythms and arpeggiated accompaniment it can sound dangerously neo-tonal—perhaps the initial perfect fourth is primarily responsible for this effect—or rather like an attempt to test just how close to traditional functions a twelve-note texture could approach. For some the result is an appealing quasi-*rapprochement*; for others, an uneasy compromise, in which the inevitable appearance of cycles of twelve notes seems to be curiously at variance with the musical impulse, and even to make what is fundamentally a purposeful tonal theme aimlessly atonal.

The concerto was written at a time when Schoenberg was much concerned with tonal composition. Not merely had he finished the Second Chamber Symphony in 1939, returning to the score after a lapse of thirty years, but, as mentioned earlier, the Variations on a Recitative for Organ, Op. 40, and the Theme and Variations for Wind Band, Op. 43, are also elaborately chromatic, fundamentally tonal works. Even the twelve-note *Ode to Napoleon Buonaparte*, Op. 41 (1942), is freer in its use of the technique than any of the other late works, and introduces triadic harmonies for illustrative purposes, letting them emerge naturally from a texture—the instrumentation is for piano quintet—in which octave doublings and late romantic figuration are, if anything, even more prominent than in the Piano Concerto.

There is no evidence to suggest that Schoenberg was experiencing some kind of crisis of confidence in serialism as he approached his seventieth birthday. The works composed after the Piano Concerto are in general very different from those of the first American decade, but a change is not necessarily caused by a crisis. It would perhaps be surprising if the Piano Concerto did not reflect to some extent the degree of concern with tonal tradition that the other works of those years display; and as Schoenberg's last large-scale composition in a traditional form, its particularly involved stylistic relationship with the past is appropriate and intriguing. What we do not know is whether Schoenberg wrote nothing else on similar lines because of a sense that the concerto was a kind of conclusion; because of a positive decision not to pursue the kind of *rapprochement* the concerto adumbrates; or whether such thoughts never occurred to him. Certainly the String Trio seems to have owed its origin less to thought than to a particular physical experience: a heart attack, on 2 August 1946, which almost killed him. The trio was begun only eighteen days later, and finished on 23 September.

There is a danger of exaggerating the differences, of course. The trio is *not* everything which the concerto is not: it is not athematic, totally fragmented, utterly new in form. For a start, it too is in one continuous movement, with restatement of earlier material rounding the work off. The use of repetition within the five individual sections is the mark of pre-existing structural principles: so too the fundamental lyric-dramatic conflict, though both elements create strikingly new effects simply because of the nature of the thematic material itself. It is here that the contrast with the Piano Concerto is most apparent, for whereas the earlier work begins with ordered, serene melody, the trio starts out in a state of virtual incoherence, searching for thematic stability through a hail of instrumental effects. The trio does not lack melody: passages in the First Episode and in Part Two are as melodious as anything in Schoenberg; yet these passages occur, not in places prescribed by predetermined structural moulds, but simply where they are most appropriate for the continuously

Ex. 8.6. Schoenberg, String Trio, Part Two, bars 159–62

unfolding lyric-dramatic conflict in which the work is rooted, as in Ex. 8.6, from Part Two.

It is the long-term continuity of the sonata scheme which the trio has most obviously abandoned, but its own short-term confrontations do not add up to an incoherent sequence of arbitrary juxtapositions. There is still a thematic process at work, variation ultimately rounded off by selective recapitulation in the final Part. The trio is not proposing a fully-fledged 'alternative' to the sonata design rejected after the valediction of the Piano Concerto, but it does represent a decisive break with some of the most fundamental features of all essentially tonal forms, aligning itself with those aspects of early twentieth-century modernizers which would prove particularly attractive to successive generations of the post-1945 avant-garde. The twelve-note combinatorial factor is present: but the serial process itself is still in no sense the primary determinant of the form.[22] The new flexibility of thematic evolution is reflected in the reorderings of the set which are brought into play, amounting as these do to an eighteen-note succession, and the residually hierarchical principle whereby the combinatorial pair, P-0 and I-5, return in the closing stages is still employed. But Schoenberg's thematicism is never the slave of prearranged serial schemes and ultimately it is the

---

[22] For a discussion of the special characteristics of the trio's twelve-note processes, see Milstein, *Schoenberg*, 162–79.

enlargement of the whole issue of unity and variety in essentially thematic terms which makes the trio so fascinating.

The same concentrated expressive range and structural fluidity recur in Schoenberg's last instrumental work, the Phantasy for Violin with Piano Accompaniment, Op. 47 (1949). The purely timbral tension between the two instruments ensures that in some respects this seems even more the ultimate recreation of Schoenberg's early expressionist impulse than the String Trio. Yet here, too, pure melody (the *Lento*, bars 40–51) can emerge as a powerful contrast to—and a clear thematic relative of—the vehement framing material. As in the trio, the last of the Phantasy's five sections is a varied recapitulation—here, exclusively of first section material. But internal repetitions in the other sections are still a primary factor in ensuring audible coherence.

Schoenberg also wrote some vocal music in his last years. *The Ode to Napoleon Buonaparte*, a setting of Byron's diatribe against tyranny, was a bold and angry wartime gesture, but in many respects *A Survivor from Warsaw*, Op. 46 (1947), for which Schoenberg provided his own text, is more immediate, more economical, and more moving. The last pieces of all, a *De Profundis* and a *Modern Psalm* (the latter unfinished), are religious. Schoenberg was, above all, a man of strong beliefs. His long struggle with external circumstances may at times encourage the conviction that internally all was certainty and security. Yet the twelve-note method itself is an objectification of tension, a law not to eliminate destructive chaos but to control and filter high emotion. As it happens, emotion has been as much in evidence in scholarly studies of the composer as in the best performances of his music.

The Schoenberg Debate

As part of his typically hard-hitting claim that 'as a cultural phenomenon' twelve-note composition 'has not yet begun to be investigated', Richard Taruskin has sought to underline not merely those 'classicizing tendencies'[23] rendering it analogous to Stravinskian neo-classicism, but also that chauvinistic aspect which might be interpreted as sustaining a belief that German music (especially Bach) was effortlessly superior to all other music. Taruskin also asserts that those he associates with such beliefs could not be wholly unsympathetic to 'National Socialism's metaphysical organicism'.[24]

Since Taruskin's quarrel is more with musicologists who have aimed to stress the evolutionary, innovatory vitality of inter-war dodecaphony to the virtual exclusion of any acknowledgement of its 'classicizing tendencies' or (involuntary?) complicity in dubious ideologies, it should be noted that recent musicology has made significant efforts to do justice to relations between old and new

---

[23] Richard Taruskin, 'Revising Revision', *Journal of the American Musicological Society*, 46 (1993), 134.
[24] Richard Taruskin, 'Back to Whom? Neoclassicism as Ideology', *19th Century Music*, 16 (1993), 299.

in Schoenberg and others. Martha Hyde, following up cues in the work of Charles Rosen and Joseph Straus, has made an intricate but absorbing study of the 'intense and far from comfortable dialogue with the past' that takes place in Schoenberg's Third String Quartet, modelled as this is on Schubert's A minor Quartet, D804.[25] Here, as in the possible relation between the third movement of Beethoven's first 'Rasumowsky' Quartet and the Largo of Schoenberg's Fourth Quartet, the kind of classicization involved is more a matter of sustained structural analogy than intermittent stylistic allusions of the kind employed so brilliantly by Stravinsky in a neo-classical score like the Symphony in C,[26] and Schoenberg achieves as coherent a 'modern classicism' in those works of his which might be shown to have specific models in Beethoven or Schubert as he does in those which do not. Schoenberg's 'classicizing' is nevertheless not literally comparable to that of those neo-classical composers who retained a sense of tonality, if only the more effectively to challenge it. Schoenberg's combinatorial twelve-note textures, in which superimposed strata complement each other, offer quite different perspectives on the dialogue between conflict and homogeneity from those to be found in Stravinsky, Bartók, and many others in the years between 1920 and 1950. The classicizing aspirations of Schoenberg's twelve-note music are expressed through the range of possible associations between Schoenberg and other, earlier composers, creating a finely balanced and specially subtle equilibrium between possible model and actual realization.

The sustained equilibrium between older and newer factors in Schoenberg's twelve-note compositions therefore suggests that the 'cultural phenomenon' of any analogies to be drawn between their apparent 'organicism' and contemporary political or social developments is of dubious validity. Art and Life cannot be made to fit together so neatly, and least of all in the case of a composer with Schoenberg's complex responses to possible relations between forms of belief and matters of technique. Christopher Hailey's perceptive observation, that 'Schoenberg's emancipation of the dissonance served not only to colonize new terrain within our universe of artistic expression but also to acknowledge that that universe might include irreconcilable difference as a constructive principle',[27] cannot be used simply to promote the argument that Schoenberg's music embraces modernistic fragmentation and discontinuity as wholeheartedly as that of Ives or Berg. As Hyde shows, when Schubert ultimately 'disappears', in the first movement of the Third Quartet, as Schoenberg attempts 'to give integrity to an entirely twelve-tone form',[28] the constructive principle of irreconcilable dif-

[25] Martha M. Hyde, 'Neoclassic and Anachronistic Impulses in Twentieth-Century Music', *Music Theory Spectrum*, 18 (1996), 223.
[26] See Ch. 6 above, pp. 125–9.
[27] Christopher Hailey, 'Introduction', in Juliane Brand and C. Hailey (eds.), *Constructive Dissonance: Arnold Schoenberg and the Transformations of Twentieth-Century Culture* (Berkeley and Los Angeles, 1997), p. xv.
[28] Hyde, 'Neoclassic Impulses', 234, 235.

ference in the background nevertheless promotes a consistent, logical, controllable process on the surface of the music. Even in the religious affirmations of the late work, *A Survivor from Warsaw*, there is a balance between divergent tendencies which resist rather than implement synthesis, and a mood of defiance in face of death which is not as utterly different from that found in *Erwartung* as might at first appear. In neither are the roles of 'victim' and 'victor' easily distinguished, and any 'truth' is inherently ambiguous, the product of oscillations between hope and despair. The polarity between tonality and atonality was also that between classicism and modernism, and Schoenberg's heroic struggle to balance the opposites—the conservative and the revolutionary—is what makes his work so challenging and so rich.

Wozzeck

Alban Berg (1885–1935) studied with Schoenberg from 1904 to 1911, and although their subsequent relationship was nothing if not complex,[1] Berg was able to achieve significant creative independence without rejecting the association between an expressionistic atmosphere and intricate structures based in traditional concepts of musical design which Schoenberg himself had favoured in his most radical works. Although Berg's early compositions, from the many songs and the Piano Sonata Op. 1 to the Three Pieces for Orchestra Op. 6, are far from negligible, it was his first opera *Wozzeck* which fully revealed his originality and greatness for the first time. Berg began it in 1914, soon after seeing the play by Büchner from which he adapted his own libretto, and it occupied him until 1922: it was first performed, with great success, in Berlin in 1925. On one level *Wozzeck* continues the progress away from Wagnerian heroics begun by Richard Strauss in *Salome* and *Elektra*. Wagner's last music drama dealt with Parsifal, the saviour in spotless armour, the fool who becomes wise. Wozzeck is a fool who goes mad, a common soldier who saves no one but kills his mistress and, apparently, commits suicide. The three acts of *Wozzeck* together are shorter than the first act of *Parsifal*. The contrast would be even greater had Berg adopted the kind of musical approach which emerged in the 1920s in the more determinedly anti-romantic operas of Hindemith and Weill, but he had no desire to keep his audience at a distance from the drama. Rather, the justification for showing so much squalor and brutality was to evoke feelings of compassion even more intense than those usually inspired by Wagner's larger-than-life mythological characters.[2]

Wozzeck's fate is held up as something for the observer not merely to contemplate, but to regret, and throughout the work, though most specifically in the final orchestral interlude of Act III, Berg expresses his own acute sympathy with this pathetic protagonist, driven to self-destruction. The musical means by which this sympathy is conveyed—a build-up to a twelve-note chord which then resolves into a D minor perfect cadence, and the use of overtly Mahlerian material, derived from one of Berg's early, unfinished piano sonatas—suggest

[1] See *The Berg–Schoenberg Correspondence: Selected Letters*, ed. Juliane Brand *et al.* (London, 1987).
[2] The principal studies of Berg's first opera are George Perle, *The Operas of Alban Berg*, i. Wozzeck (Berkeley and Los Angeles, 1980); Douglas Jarman, *Alban Berg: Wozzeck* (Cambridge, 1989).

that the composer was involved to a point where it became essential for him to invest the character of Wozzeck with heroic as well as tragic qualities. Nevertheless, in the theatre such extravagance seems all of a piece with the musical attitudes expressed throughout; the final interlude is no arbitrary imposition but a gesture calculated to ensure that the opera achieves a shattering climax with a sense of revelation: *lux facta est*, but for the audience, not for Wozzeck.

A degree of objectivity is then restored, in the final scene, at the point where sentimentality could overflow and swamp the entire enterprise. (Did Berg know *Madama Butterfly*, with its climactic and embarrassing use of a small child?) The closing scene of *Wozzeck* understatedly depicts the vulnerability of the orphan, seen playing with other children when the discovery of his mother's body is announced, and the ending embodies that archetypal musical multivalence, matching the mixed feelings being represented, which has helped to make Berg the most immediately accessible of the 'atonal' modernists from the years before 1940, and immensely influential on many later composers.[3] Most authorities on Berg's music now accept that there are inherent continuities which can be traced through the various distinct phases of his work: tonal, 'freely' atonal, twelve-note. In particular, modes of structuring involving consistent patterns (interval cycles), as well as interactions between residual elements of tonal thinking and features which counteract that thinking, provide an appropriately consistent foundation for the diverse textures and often tempestuous emotional landscapes of all his mature compositions.[4] The conclusion of *Wozzeck* demonstrates this technique in the most unambiguous way, combining a sense of closure with a more floating, open-ended effect. As the strings play soft fifths, G and D, in cadential fashion, a chordal ostinato is superimposed, decorating and clouding the finality of the ending, so that the music seems to stop rather abruptly, fulfilled and frustrated at the same time. The effect is not to suggest that *Wozzeck*, as a whole, moves towards some kind of extended tonality of G, but rather that its fundamental atonality can encompass hierarchically superior harmonic entities alongside freer configurations, entities which evoke, if only to resist, the more stable, lost world of diatonic tonality.

Another powerful, and very un-Wagnerian kind of conjunction in *Wozzeck* stems from the fact that the music's unremittingly expressionistic atmosphere is rooted in a succession of separate, clearly delineated formal structures. Act I has five character pieces: Suite, Rhapsody, Military March and Lullaby, Passacaglia, and Rondo; Act II is a Symphony in five movements, and Act III comprises six Inventions, on a theme, a note (B), a rhythm, a six-note chord, a key (D minor), and a constant quaver movement. Given the opera's sequence of short scenes,

---

[3] See Arnold Whittall, 'Berg and the Twentieth Century', in A. Pople (ed.), *The Cambridge Companion to Berg* (Cambridge, 1997), 247–58.

[4] On interval cycles, see George Perle, 'Berg's Master Array of the Interval Cycles', *Musical Quarterly*, 63 (1977), 1–30. Also Dave Headlam, *The Music of Alban Berg* (New Haven, 1996).

the internal structure of each could have been relatively free: provided that some sense of overall unity was achieved, contrasts between the scenes themselves would easily be established. Yet Berg needed the contrast of passing such explosive, grotesque, and tragic events through a more constrained formal process than that which is found in the later Wagner, Strauss, or in Schoenberg's *Erwartung*. It is difficult to argue that the forms are satisfying, or even perceptible, in their own right: their justification lies in the way they enabled Berg to exploit the story's grim and potentially hysterical dramatic content without lapsing into incoherence. We may not perceive the background structures as such, but we do perceive the coherence and implacable sense of inevitability to which they give rise. Despite its potent, modernist complexity, *Wozzeck* has the directness and clarity of a classical tragedy.

Chamber Concerto

In his next major work, Berg again constructed an elaborate framework involving the treatment of traditional schemes in new ways. The Chamber Concerto for piano, violin, and thirteen wind instruments (1925) lasts for nearly forty minutes, and its purpose—a fiftieth-birthday present for Schoenberg—demanded something special in intellectual content. Study of Berg's sketches and drafts for the work has revealed the characteristic feature of a biographical subtext, with the three movements respectively designated 'Friendship', 'Love', and 'World'. The first movement depicts Schoenberg and his pupils, the second is a tribute to Schoenberg's first wife, Mathilde, who died while Berg was composing the movement, and the finale blends these topics in what one commentator terms 'a kaleidoscopic reprise'.[5] In character, the concerto lacks the immediate appeal of the later *Lyric Suite* and Violin Concerto. What it has in abundance, apart from purely technical virtuosity, is dramatic excitement, for all the carefully plotted symmetries of its design. Appropriately, given its dedicatee, it shows awareness of the new twelve-note technique, without itself being serial, and the elaboration of its rhythmic structuring, which Berg proudly described in an open letter to Schoenberg, is a particularly clear indication of one way in which Berg had achieved independence of his formidable master.[6]

The first movement is simultaneously a three-part theme with five variations and a sonata design with double exposition, the whole preceded by a five-bar motto which translates the names of Berg (horn), Schoenberg (piano), and Webern (violin) (Ex. 9.1). The second exposition of the theme, which doubles as Variation 1, is for piano solo, depicting the Schoenberg pupil Edward Steuermann. Variation 2 ('development' in the sonata scheme) portrays the

[5] Brenda Dalen, ' "Freundschaft, Liebe und Welt": The Secret Programme of the Chamber Concerto', in D. Jarman (ed.), *The Berg Companion* (London, 1989), 142–50.
[6] *Berg–Schoenberg Correspondence*, 334–7.

Ex. 9.1. Berg, Chamber Concerto, beginning

violinist Rudolf Kolisch in Berg's favourite slow waltz time, and deals with the
three thematic elements in reverse order (the elements themselves appear in
retrograde). Variation 3 (Josef Polnauer) continues the development by introducing inversion, the thematic elements now restored to their original sequence,
while Variation 4 (Erwin Stein) uses retrograde inversion. These proto-serial
procedures do not, however, determine every detail of the complex texture: in
1925 Berg was still more interested in the ambiguities that could arise when 'old'
and 'new' were brought into confrontation, in matters of pitch-structuring
no less than in formal organization. With Variation 5 the tempo of the original
statement of the theme is restored, and the variation can therefore be regarded,
in sonata-form terms, as a free recapitulation. The thematic elements also
reappear in their original order, and the variation ends with the soft entry of the
violin signalling the start of the Adagio.

Each half of the second movement is in three main sections, with the central
part of each half further divisible into three, and three times the length of each
of those that flank it: thus the five distinct segments of the first half total 30, 12,
36, 12, and 30 bars. This symmetry is further reinforced by the fact that the second
half is a free retrograde of the first. Moreover, the Adagio as a whole contains the
same number of bars as the first movement: 240.

The violin begins the movement with a twelve-note phrase of characteristically stifled intensity, but perhaps the most prominent thematic idea—only
freely derived from the Berg-Schoenberg-Webern motto—is presented at the
start of the central episode (bar 283). It is restated later in augmentation (bar 303)
and, later still, in inversion (bar 314). One final symmetrical feature of the Adagio
is that the third main section of the first half inverts the material of the first main
section. Not surprisingly, scholars aware of the programmatic resonance of the
movement, and recognizing its references to Schoenberg's *Pelleas und Melisande*

as well as to *Wozzeck*, have discussed the symbolic meaning of Berg's various compositional procedures. No less important is the possibility that it was the experience of composing this movement which predisposed Berg to avoid such a high degree of predetermination when he did eventually adopt the twelve-note technique—or at any rate to ensure that the music itself projected less of the precompositional contrivance that lay behind it.

The expansive, exuberant finale of the Chamber Concerto is a suitably complex blend of sonata and rondo schemes, incorporating thematic features from both previous movements and containing a total of 480 bars, the same as the first two movements put together. The grand total for the whole work is therefore 960.

Lyric Suite

Berg's numerical obsessions—especially with 10 and 23—find similarly consistent expression in the *Lyric Suite* for string quartet (1926). Five of its six movements have bar-totals which are multiples of 23: 69 in the first, with the second thematic group beginning in bar 23; 138, subdivided as 69, 23, and 46 in the third; 69 in the fourth, 460 in the fifth, and 46 in the sixth. Tempos are also related, as with the crotchet 69 principal tempo of the fourth movement, the dotted crotchet 115 of the fifth, and the alternation between crotchet 69 and crotchet 46 in the finale. Berg gave increasing play to such potentially counter-productive constraints as their ability to stimulate his creative imagination became more evident. They were in any case only a part of a nexus of extra-musical factors which he took delight in weaving into the fabric of such apparently 'abstract' compositions.

The *Lyric Suite* is dedicated to Schoenberg's mentor and brother-in-law Alexander von Zemlinsky (1872–1942), and the fourth movement contains brief quotations of a theme from his *Lyric Symphony*, while the sixth movement introduces Wagner's *Tristan* chord-progression (bars 26–7): Ex. 9.2. But the

Ex. 9.2. Berg, *Lyric Suite*, Zemlinsky quotation, *Tristan* chord, and associated intervals

discovery that the work was a secret celebration of Berg's affair with Hanna Fuchs-Robettin, and that the finale was a setting of Baudelaire's poem 'De profundis' with the text suppressed, meant that scholars were able to uncover other special features, not least the prominence of the lovers' initials (A, B[♭], H [B], F) in the work's pitch materials.[7] The suite is a partially twelve-note composition (Berg had first used the method for a complete piece in his second setting of 'Schliesse mir die Augen beide' of 1925) but Berg seized on the opportunity to underline that consistency with his earlier procedures which most directly represented his hard-won independence of Schoenberg and the true focus of his own musical identity.

The referential richness of the *Lyric Suite*'s material may be gauged from the fact that the Zemlinsky fragment quoted in the fourth movement employs a five-note segment of the whole-tone scale plus an added note (the initial B♭) which is equivalent to a collection often used by Berg, for example, in the String Quartet Op. 3 and *Wozzeck*. The suite's basic set also contains the tritone-plus-major third unit which can be regarded as a permutation of the whole-tone motive, and the same unit appears within the *Tristan* chord itself, thereby 'legit-imizing' the Wagnerian association through which Berg's sought to dramatize his feelings for Hanna, as well as the most imposing historical context for his own musical voice. The suite therefore mediates between old and new, private and public, strict and free, in a remarkably rich and engaging way.

The first and last movements, the outer sections of the third and the tenebroso sections of the fifth are serial: the second and fourth movements, the central part of the third and the framing sections of the fifth are 'free'. This in itself suggests a symmetrical design, but Berg imposes upon it a structure in which each movement employs an intensification of the speed and atmosphere of a prede-cessor, to form two interlocking 'trichords':

1 Allegretto giovale

    2 Andante amoroso

3 Allegro misterioso
  (Trio estatico)

    4 Adagio appassionato

5 Presto delirando

    6 Largo desolato

The *Lyric Suite*'s intimate scenario of a progress from happiness to despair led Berg away from the grandiose symphonic structures of the Chamber Concerto, and he was able to reinforce the impression, already created by the early Op. 3 Quartet, that the medium was in some ways even more appropriate for the focused expression of his naturally discursive and proliferating musical mind

---

[7] See George Perle, 'The Secret Programme of the *Lyric Suite*', *Musical Times*, 118 (1977), 629–32, 709–13, 809–13.

than larger forces, with constructive and spontaneous elements in perfect equilibrium.

This is evident from the start in the way the twelve-note technique is used to underline the closeness to tonal features (as well as the distance from them) that can be achieved. The set takes three distinct forms in the first movement—scalar, chordal, and melodic (Ex. 9.3). The two scalar hexachords a tritone apart make easily audible appearances at the ends of both parts of the movement (bars 33–5, 67–8): the chordal arrangement in two cycles of fifths provides the harmonies in the first bar (a device foreshadowing the arpeggiated opening of the Violin Concerto), and these introduce the first melodic statement, arranging the hexachords into two all-interval sequences, the second forming R-6 to the P-0 of the first.

Much has been made of the differences between Berg's technique here (and of the transformation processes which provide the new sets for later twelve-note passages in the suite) and the stricter serial methods of Schoenberg and Webern. Of course the difference is aurally arresting in the first movement, because of the fifths and scales employed there: Berg's intentions, building bridges between tonal and post-tonal worlds in order to promote a dialogue of similarities and differences, are more transparent even than Schoenberg's. In particular, his varied orderings within the hexachord can create harmonic perspectives which retain certain hierarchic qualities, even some sense of distinction between

Ex. 9.3. Berg, *Lyric Suite*, 1st movt., (i) bar 33; (ii) bar 1; (iii) bars 2–4

relatively consonant and relatively dissonant sonorities: or they can be deployed to promote harmonies that seem to float in space, freed from all the gravitational and functional attributes which they had during the tonal era.

The *Lyric Suite* may shun the symphonic ambitions of the Chamber Concerto, but its reliance on structural compression—the conflation of development and recapitulation, for example—ensures that there is no loss of richness or intensity. These qualities have naturally been enhanced with the revelations about the work's extra-musical associations, especially in the heart-rendingly valedictory finale, though even here the 'purely musical' factors are ultimately what matter most. The Largo seems in one respect a farewell to the musical world of *Wozzeck*, with its approaches to triads of G major or minor and its dissolving coda, another invention on a continuous quaver movement which has such power precisely because of the feeling we have of reaching this point as the result of an insistent yet far from inflexible progress throughout the work from beginning to end. Above all, purely on the level of compositional technique, a detailed comparison of the two halves of the first movement—exposition and varied recapitulation—shows just how vital the presence of clearly defined thematic elements remains. Most of the later movements involve substantial amounts of easily perceptible recapitulation, in keeping with their predominantly ternary structures, but only in the third movement, when the repeat of the Allegro misterioso is a retrograde of the original, is there anything the least mechanical about the process. The freest forms and the most heartfelt emotional expression are found in the fourth and sixth movements—those involving the Zemlinsky and Wagner quotations. Perhaps at this stage the way was still open for Berg to move into much more flexible structures in which thematic development and repetition would have played little part. In reality, however, Berg's last purely instrumental composition was to show even greater reliance on traditionally structured thematic process, filtered through an individual treatment of serialism, than that found in the *Lyric Suite*. Nothing of emotional immediacy is lost in the Violin Concerto, and the overall form is as satisfying in its confrontations between old and new as Berg ever achieved.

Der Wein

Berg's next completed composition after the *Lyric Suite* was written when he had already begun work on his second opera, *Lulu*. *Der Wein* (1929), a concert aria for soprano or tenor and orchestra, is a setting of three of Baudelaire's poems in German versions by Stefan George. The entire work has a ternary form, since Part 3 (bars 173–216) is a varied recapitulation of Part 1 (bars 1–87), and the central episode is itself tripartite, the third section (bars 141–72) retrograding the second (bars 112–41). In purely technical terms *Der Wein* qualifies as Berg's first wholly twelve-note work of any substance, and it also confirms his own personal, undogmatic attitude to the technique, which he developed here with increasing consistency and confidence.

The basic set, like that of the *Lyric Suite*, has definite tonal associations, so that if it and its close relatives were used consistently throughout it would be possible to create the effect of a chromatically coloured D minor whenever this was desired. The opening seven bars do just this, linking tonal and post-tonal worlds through the employment of set forms which share the trichord D, E (or E♭), and F to generate the ostinato bass parts (bass clarinet, double bassoon, harp). Thereafter, the reorderings of the basic set and the creation of four subsidiary sets, or tropes, ensure that the musical character established at the opening is able to persist and evolve with appropriate flexibility. Such development of, and from, the basic set itself remains an essential part of Berg's serial technique, and the main difference between his technique and Webern's. (Schoenberg's use of free ordering within the hexachord, and of derived sets, in the String Trio, for example, is also a significant indication of the value of troping, adumbrating the kind of procedures which many late twentieth-century serial composers have employed.)

Berg's manipulations of an already tonally orientated set in *Der Wein* provided a systematically controlled diversification of the properties of that set. Three of the four derived tropes are actually less tonally explicit than the set itself, so that although traditional harmonic elements are admitted—the 'dominant' A major triad at the start of Part 2 (bar 89), for example—they are not allowed to function in the way they would in a traditionally tonal texture. Nor is there any quotation of pre-existent tonal material in *Der Wein*, though the presence of an alto saxophone and the prominence of tango rhythm reflects Berg's interest in the sound of popular dance music, already heard in *Wozzeck* and to achieve new importance in *Lulu*. *Der Wein* demands rather less vocal and instrumental virtuosity than any other work of Berg's maturity (it was written quite quickly to fulfil a lucrative commission), and its main value for him may have been to clarify processes which he would elaborate in the new opera.[8]

Lulu

Lulu was the main focus of Berg's attention from 1928 until his death.[9] If it is not universally accepted as the crowning achievement of his short career, on grounds of variable musical quality, especially in Act III, it is nevertheless an appropriately many-sided compendium of his technical developments and expressive concerns, using its tonally allusive twelve-note language to represent

---

[8] See Anthony Pople, 'In the Orbit of *Lulu*: The Late Works', in Pople (ed.) *Cambridge Companion to Berg*, 204–26.

[9] For major studies of *Lulu*, see George Perle, *The Operas of Alban Berg*, ii. Lulu (Berkeley and Los Angeles, 1985); Douglas Jarman, *Alban Berg: Lulu* (Cambridge, 1991); Patricia Hall, *A View of Berg's Lulu through the Autograph Sources* (Berkeley and Los Angeles, 1996).

a world in which exalted and decadent feelings seem increasingly interdependent. That tonal allusiveness, it must be stressed, emerges only occasionally, though to great effect, and despite the fact that the hexachords of the opera's basic set can be ordered to provide scale segments of B♭ major and (with one gap) E major, such relationships are not of great structural importance in the work. As with *Der Wein*, the basic set functions as the source of new twelve-note collections by means of various transformation processes—for example, choosing every fifth or seventh note from successions of the set. Hierarchies and symmetries of various kinds help to determine the opera's structure—not least, those pairs of characters performed by the same singer—but there is no sense of a single note like *Der Wein*'s D, or a single 'tonal' relationship, like the Violin Concerto's G and B♭, exercising fundamental dominance over the entire musical fabric. Even more intensely than those shorter and in many ways simpler scores, *Lulu* is concerned with the interaction of opposites: synthesis is resisted, not embraced.

It is easy to link the subject-matter of *Lulu*—the progressive degradation of a *femme fatale* and her victims, ending when she herself becomes a victim of Jack the Ripper—with that of *Wozzeck*, and to focus on an inherent 'decadence', with Lulu placed alongside Salome, Elektra, and Turandot in the gallery of twentieth-century operatic sadists, who stand for everything that the pure romantic heroine would find unspeakable. Even if the essential point of Wedekind's play is that it is Lulu's lovers who are truly decadent, not Lulu herself, neither the opera nor the plays are concerned with the more traditionally romantic conflict between nobility and evil, but with honest intensity of experience versus the postures of assumed feeling. The brief final eulogy of the lesbian Countess Geschwitz over the dead Lulu is moving, and justified, not because any heroic status is claimed for Lulu herself, but because Geschwitz, dying as the prostitute's last sacrificial victim, has been true to true feelings (Ex. 9.4). At the same time, it would not be true to Berg if there were not an element of ambiguity. As Douglas Jarman has written,

the music that comes back at this point of the opera is music that brings with it a host of complex and conflicting associations [and the] difference between the luxuriant, elegiac music and the events on stage produces an emotional disorientation that is deeply disturbing: it can also, if we respond to the music and are prepared to give these characters the understanding and compassion that the humanity of Berg's score demands, be humanly restorative.[10]

That this is true, whether or not one regards the tonally allusive serialism of the opera's ending as subversively parodistic (of Mahlerian romanticism[11]) or simply as representative of Berg's own modernist idiom, gives a telling indication of why

[10] Jarman, *Berg: Lulu*, 100–1.
[11] See Judy Lochhead, 'Lulu's Feminine Performance', in Pople (ed.), *Cambridge Companion to Berg*, 227–44.

Ex. 9.4. Berg, *Lulu*, ending

Ex. 9.4. (*cont.*)

Ex. 9.4. (*cont.*)

it is that Berg has become one of the most important influences on the century's later developments, achieving a 'unity which does not conceal the fragmentary and chaotic nature of the handed-down musical material, and yet which does not simply mirror fragmentation . . . but . . . is able to embody, negate and transcend it'.[12]

The structure of *Lulu* is less tightly bound by the kind of formal frameworks that serve for the more economical *Wozzeck*, although plenty of generic references can be discerned. Much of the second and third scenes of Act I is organized as a sonata, with exposition and repeat in Scene 2 (bars 533–668), development and recapitulation in Scene 3 (bars 1209–1355). The sonata is preceded, and interrupted, by smaller structural units, some of them vocal character-pieces (Canzonetta, Arioso) and some dance-forms (Ragtime, English Waltz). Berg also uses less obviously predetermined structures when the dramatic design dictates: most notably in the section of Act I Scene 2, after the sonata exposition, called 'Monoritmica' (bars 669–957). Though most of the prominent thematic motives appear, the basic material is a four-unit rhythm which in the first half (culminating in the painter's suicide) is progressively accelerated (from quaver 84 to minim 132 at bar 842). The pace then gradually slackens (though the music is not otherwise palindromic), reaching the original pulse again at around bar 956.

In Act I Dr Schön replaces the Painter as Lulu's husband: in Act II it is Schön's son Alwa, a composer, who replaces his father (shot by Lulu). In Act II the equivalent of Act I's sonata is a rondo which is divided into two main sections (bars 243–336; 1001–96) representing Alwa's 'conquest' of his father's murderer. In Act I the sonata was interrupted by the Monoritmica and a sequence of

---

[12] See Max Paddison, *Adorno's Aesthetics of Music* (Cambridge, 1993), 158.

other short forms culminating in a palindromic sextet (bars 1177–208). In Act II the two rondo sections are divided by Dr Schön's 'aria in five verses', which is itself interrupted by Lulu's song, and by other segments, notably the Film Music interlude (bars 656–718), which, as a palindrome, is an equivalent to the Act I sextet.

Act III traces Lulu's fate after her flight from Vienna, with Alwa and other associates in tow. It is divided into two scenes, the first set in Paris, the second in London. Scene 1 is spanned by three ensembles which surround other distinct form-types, including two song-like Intermezzos, the second a reprise of Lulu's aria from Act II, Scene 1. Scene 2 involves the recall of music from the set of Variations on a banal tune written by Wedekind, evoking a barrel organ, which forms the Interlude between the two Scenes. But there are many other re-capitulatory references, in keeping with Berg's decision to have the roles of Lulu's clients duplicated by the singers of her earlier lovers, the Professor of Medicine, the Painter and Dr Schön respectively. This device helps to reinforce the musical power as well as the dramatic irony of the final scene, so that, even if Scene 1 of Act III seems more diffuse and featureless in places than the earlier parts of the opera, the final stages still create an overwhelming impact.

Until 1979 only the first two acts of *Lulu*, with brief extracts from Act III, could be performed, but in that year Friedrich Cerha's completion of Act III was heard for the first time. Despite some inevitable controversy, it soon established itself as the only viable version, not least because Berg's intentions were so fully set out in the surviving sketches and materials.

Violin Concerto

Berg would probably have finished *Lulu* before his death had he not agreed to compose a Violin Concerto in memory of Manon Gropius, a swansong of very different character, if no less ambiguity, than the closing bars of the opera.[13] Though betraying certain signs of haste, the concerto is organized with all Berg's scrupulous concern for structural proportion. The explicitly tonal, triadic harmonic possibilities of the basic set (Ex. 9.5 (i)) render the exploitation of ambiguities all the more attractive, of course, and the last thing Berg wanted was a final, clarifying, reductive resolution of contemporary post-tonal tensions into archaic diatonic closure (e.g. Ex. 9.5 (ii)). As the actual ending of the work shows (Ex. 9.5 (iii)), it was more satisfying and appropriate to contrive a cadence in which a whole-tone chord resolves on to a major triad in one stratum, while contradictory whole-tone ascents and descents in other strata establish a note (G) which, even if it is heard as the added sixth of the B♭ triad, resists classification as an all-embracing, all-resolving tonic of the kind used by Mahler at the end of

---

[13] See Anthony Pople, *Berg: Violin Concerto* (Cambridge, 1991).

(i) solo violin, bars 15–18

Molto adagio

(ii) chords derivable from basic set in retrograde

(iii) ending (bars 227–30)

Ex. 9.5. Berg, Violin Concerto: (i) solo violin, bars 15–18; (ii) chords derivable from basic set in retrograde; (iii) ending (bars 227–30)

Das Lied von der Erde. In twelve-note terms, Berg devised a perfect illustration of how tension between hierarchical features in a set-group need not actually achieve explicit diatonic resolution in order to provide an appropriately ambivalent yet still satisfyingly conclusive ending.

It was on 22 April 1935 that the 18-year-old daughter of Alma Mahler and Walter Gropius died, and the short score of the concerto was finished three months later, on 23 July. Five more months later, on Christmas Eve, Berg himself was dead, at the same age as Mahler when he died in 1911.

The concerto is a requiem, its dedication 'to the memory of an angel' underpinned, as we would expect with Berg, by other, hidden references and associations. The use of a Carinthian folksong is now known to refer to Berg's own memory of a teenage girl, Marie Scheuchl, with whom, a teenager himself, he had a brief affair which resulted in a child. In addition, sketches show that the four-part plan reflects the motto of the right-wing, nationalist Deutscher Turnverein—*Frei, Fröhlich, Fromm, Frisch* (Free, Happy, Pious, Lively)—but retrograded, presumably in order to symbolize Berg's actual rejection of such distasteful sentiments.[14]

The form of the work is very different from that of the earlier Chamber Concerto, while showing a similar capacity for the reshaping of traditional schemes. There are two movements, each in two parts, the slower parts (Andante and Adagio) enclosing the faster ones (Allegretto and Allegro) in a shape whose intensifying progression recalls the plan of the *Lyric Suite*. The Andante is a seven-sectioned arch. The introduction anticipates the ordered form of the basic set in its open-string arpeggios (it also foreshadows the conflicts between B♭ and G as referential centres). The three main sections, including a bridge passage, have distinct thematic ideas, the last, as centre of the arch, being the most extended. The bridge is recapitulated in shortened inversion and the remaining sections are also abbreviated. The Allegretto is another arch form and the first section is itself a miniature arch. The whole movement has a light, dance-like character which modulates into exquisite nostalgia, with the quotation of the triadic folksong just before the coda.

The most violent part of the concerto embodies the greatest extremes. The Allegro is an extended cadenza, but at the moment when we might expect the most improvisatory elements to dominate, Berg introduces a four-voice canon to provoke the return of the opening music of the movement, creating the main climax and completing a ternary shape.

The ternary form of the concluding Adagio comprises the introduction and initial statement of Bach's harmonization of Ahle's chorale melody 'Es ist genug', whose whole-tone opening coincides with the last four notes of the basic set, but whose tonal harmony is an alien presence in a score that rejects tonality even as it alludes to it. A middle section of three variations with a central climax and reminders of the folk tune in its final stages leads to a coda in which there is another full statement of the chorale tune, now harmonized by Berg according to twelve-note criteria, and extended by just two bars to achieve the concluding, ambiguous cadence already discussed. The fact that the work ends at bar 230 is of course a further indication of Berg's obsession with numerical control.

It is also typical of Berg that in bar 222 of the coda the instructions 'religioso' and 'amoroso' should appear simultaneously. Other composers after Berg would attempt to evoke essentially Mahlerian moods. Other post-tonal serialists have continued to explore conjunctions with tonal forms and late romantic expression; but none have surpassed Berg's achievement. His emotional intensity never seems excessive simply because it was moulded and controlled by one of the most skilled musical architects of the century. He explored new kinds of tension between freedom and rigour, between volatile expressiveness and strict, often symmetrical structures, the erection of traditionally derived, all-embracing formal schemes acting as a framework and a discipline for

[14] See Douglas Jarman, 'Secret Programmes', in Pople (ed.), *Cambridge Companion to Berg*, 167–79.

material which might otherwise have run riot. Berg's consciousness of the past was as great as Stravinsky's, but his use of quotation and allusion is far from neo-classical in spirit. Rather it is post-romantic and often expressionistic in its modernism—the personal memory, the personal nostalgia breaking through the ordered surface which the new techniques imposed as a necessary basis for coherence.

The Path to Twelve-Note Music

About 1911 I wrote the Bagatelles for String Quartet (Op.9), all very short pieces, lasting a couple of minutes—perhaps the shortest music so far. Here I had the feeling, 'When all twelve notes have gone by, the piece is over'. . . . In my sketchbook I wrote out the chromatic scale and crossed off the individual notes. Why? Because I had convinced myself, 'This note has been there already'. . . . The inner ear decided quite rightly that the man who wrote out the chromatic scale and crossed off individual notes *was no fool*. . . . In short, a rule of law emerged; until all twelve notes have occurred, none of them may occur again.[1]

The series of lectures which Anton Webern (1883–1945) gave in Vienna in 1932 and 1933 have survived through the shorthand notes of one of the audience. They present a fascinating picture of a composer utterly convinced of the intuitive rightness of Schoenberg's formulation of twelve-note technique because, as the quotation shows, it matched his own experience completely. At the same time, Webern shared Schoenberg's deep involvement in the reinterpretation of traditional concepts, notably of the way in which unity may be expressed through the use of contrapuntal textures and symmetrical forms. In Webern's own words, 'We want to say "in a quite new way" what has been said before'.[2]

Webern remained closely associated with Schoenberg long after ceasing to be a pupil, and long after establishing that compressed, fragmented style so different from Schoenberg's own. His acceptance of atonality was complete and total—he could see little point in retaining any links at all with something 'really dead'. Yet atonality as such was not a 'law' and the quotation at the head of this chapter shows Webern's own later realization of how the 'law' of serialism had been anticipated—necessarily—for it could not have emerged simultaneously with atonality but only through a gradual exploration of atonality. Webern never claimed that he either anticipated or prompted Schoenberg's discoveries. In the lectures he describes an event

in the spring of 1917—Schoenberg lived in the Gloriettegasse at the time, and I lived quite near—I went to see him one fine morning, to tell him I had read in some newspaper where a few groceries were to be had. In fact I disturbed him with this, and he explained to me

---

[1] Anton Webern, *The Path to the New Music*, ed. W. Reich, trans. L. Black (Bryn Mawr, 1963), 51.
[2] Ibid. 55.

that he was 'on the way to something quite new'. He didn't tell me more at the time, and I racked my brains—'For goodness' sake, whatever can it be?'[3]

During the next six years (1918–23) Webern worked on a succession of vocal compositions, completing the three sets of songs Opp. 13, 14 and 15.[4] These pieces employ wide-ranging, rhythmically flexible vocal lines, with supporting instrumental textures which occasionally perform an accompanimental function but more often present thematic figures of their own. This is contrapuntal music, but it is only in the last song of Op. 15, a double canon in motu contrario, that traditional imitative techniques of the kind on which Webern was to rely so heavily in his twelve-note music are found.

Op. 15 No. 5 is rather atypical in another respect, too, for the vocal line employs narrower intervals and simpler rhythms than those of most of the other songs of this period: the opening texture recalls that of the baroque chorale-prelude. Yet neither this nor its successor, the Five Canons, Op. 16 (1923–4) for high soprano, clarinet and bass clarinet, are actually twelve-note. None of the vocal phrases presents a succession of the twelve chromatic semitones, and most of them contain prominent pitch repetitions (e.g. the Gs in bars 2 and 4). There is also little of that internal motivic repetition (of three- or four-note cells) within individual lines which Webern's methods of set construction made so important in later years. The prominence of the interval of the major third in both main parts at the start may nevertheless reflect that conscious concern with unity which Webern would explore so creatively through the twelve-note technique, and the pairs of canonic parts both have the same specific pitches in common—a kind of invariance which Webern would carry over into his combinations of twelve-note sets.

One curiosity about this canon is the change in the interval of imitation between the accompanying parts in bar 7, where the flute's major sixth (bar 6) is answered by a minor sixth (trumpet, bar 7). This must be simply to avoid too E-majorish an atmosphere, which the ear might detect if an E instead of an F supported the E, F♯, G♯ ascent in harp and clarinet. The point is significant because it shows that Webern was perfectly prepared to sacrifice strict exactness. He was never a blindly dogmatic composer, imprisoned by laws imposed from outside. Rather, he came to believe that the twelve-note technique was the result of an inevitable historical process which ensured that, even within the new world of atonal serialism, 'one works as before'.[5]

By the early months of 1923 Schoenberg was using the new method on quite a large scale—he began the Wind Quintet in April. Webern's instinct led him to try out the technique on his own much smaller scale, and the years 1924 and 1925

---

[3] Webern, *Path to the New Music*, 44.

[4] For an outstanding study of these transitional years, see Anne C. Shreffler, ' "Mein Weg geht jetzt vorüber": The Vocal Origins of Webern's Twelve-Tone Composition', *Journal of the American Musicological Society*, 47 (1994), 275–339.

[5] Webern, *Path to New Music*, 54.

were largely experimental, the 40-year-old composer seeking ways in which to move naturally from his freely atonal technique to the new twelve-note method. In one sense the distance was small. If we look at one of the 1922 songs—Op. 15 No. 4, for example—we find that the vocal line begins with a twelve-note statement: yet in the remaining phrases internal repetitions have become more and more significant, and the accompanying parts contain prominent repetitions (the B♭s and A♭s in bars 1 and 2). So this is still a case of all twelve notes being kept freely in play, and the avoidance of tonal tendencies, rather than of a consistent ordering of the notes. We may feel that all twelve notes are more or less equal in importance, but the 'law' whereby they are employed is indefinable save in terms of instinctive rightness. A comparison between this and a simple example of Webern's early use of the twelve-note method itself is therefore instructive. In the autumn of 1924 he composed his *Kinderstück* for piano solo, the only completed piece from a projected cycle for young players. This seventeen-bar miniature presents six successive statements of a twelve-note set which, while having none of the internal symmetries so characteristic of his mature sets, reveals a significant interest in the interval of the minor second. As a composition this piece is little more than a doodle. Yet it has a simple progressive form (rather than a ternary or binary shape) moving from sober to skittish rhythms, from a single line (with typically wide intervals) to a five-note chord at the start of the final set statement. The dynamic range is narrow—between *pp* and *mp*—but a variety of registers is used, only one note, B♭, appearing in the same octave on all six occasions.

Of much greater musical interest are the *Three Traditional Rhymes*, Op. 17, for voice, violin (viola), clarinet, and bass clarinet (1924–5) and the Three Songs, Op. 18, for voice, E♭ clarinet, and guitar of 1925. In particular, Op. 17 Nos 2 and 3 reveal a virtuosity in the handling of one untransposed, uninverted, unretrograded twelve-note set that proves just how resourcefully Webern was now responding to Schoenberg's discoveries. There are no dramatic differences in style and texture between these songs and their immediate non-twelve-note predecessors, and Webern already shows how the twelve-note successions can be submerged into the phrase rhythms of the music rather than mechanically determining those rhythms. There are twenty-three statements of the basic set in the twenty-two bars of Op. 17 No. 2, the longest of which is the first (two bars), the shortest the fifteenth (one beat—the second of bar 15). Here the accompanying trio of instruments shares each set statement with the voice in the exact order of notes, so to this extent the piece is a more accurate forerunner of Webern's mature technique than Op. 17 No. 3, where the voice has its own independent twelve-note successions and the instruments supply the missing notes for each phrase in a freer overall ordering (the song actually starts with note 7).

Webern gradually expanded his serial technique to include inversions and retrogrades of the basic set (Op. 18 Nos 2 and 3) and then, in the Two Songs for Mixed Chorus, Op. 19 (1926), transpositions of prime and inversion at the sixth semitone (the tritone)—the same transposition level as Schoenberg had used in his first fully twelve-note work, the Piano Suite, Op. 25. These choral songs, settings of short poems by Goethe, bring to an end the long series of vocal works which had occupied Webern for more than a decade. Already in 1925 he had composed two short instrumental pieces, the binary-form *Klavierstück im tempo eines Menuetts*, and a movement for string trio. Both use single untransposed sets—the piano piece nineteen times, the trio thirty-five times (three of the statements are incomplete). Of themselves they are of only minor significance, though the trio movement turns out to be a preliminary study for Webern's first substantial instrumental twelve-note work, the String Trio, Op. 20 (1927), which is also the first of that remarkable succession of instrumental compositions which dominated the remainder of his output. There were to be more vocal works, too, but the all-important problem of form could best be confronted in instrumental terms: in tackling it, Webern was to achieve one of the most thorough-going renovations of traditional modes of thought in the entire history of music.

The discovery of Webern's sketchbooks[6] has yielded the interesting fact that his first three mature twelve-note instrumental compositions—the trio, the Symphony, Op. 21, and the Quartet for violin, clarinet, tenor saxophone, and piano, Op. 22—were all planned in three movements, yet ended up with only two. This has pointed up the apparent differences between the kind of overall form which satisfied Webern and Schoenberg. Webern presumably studied Schoenberg's serial works with close attention, yet of his own early essays in the method, only the Piano Piece of 1925, which suggests a knowledge of Schoenberg's Piano Suite of the previous year, has much stylistically in common with the music of the master.

The String Trio is rather a different matter. When Webern came to write it, in the summer of 1927, Schoenberg had completed his first two large-scale twelve-note instrumental works, the Wind Quintet (finished August 1924) and the Suite, Op. 29 (finished May 1926), and he was to finish the Third String Quartet during that same year (it was first performed on 19 September). These compositions demonstrate in the clearest possible way Schoenberg's own commitment to forms and, to some extent, textures relating quite closely to those of the tonal, thematic music of the classic and romantic periods. Of course Webern himself had a far less impressive early tonal *œuvre* than Schoenberg, and his only wholly successful early instrumental work to use key relationships was a passacaglia, not a sonata movement. Webern may have sensed that what made Schoenberg's serial-sonata structures appropriate was the type of material invented and the

[6] One substantial selection of sketches has been published: *Anton von Webern: Sketches (1926–45). Facsimile Reproductions from the Composer's Autograph Sketchbooks in the Moldenhauer Archive*, commentary by Ernst Krenek, foreword by Hans Moldenhauer (New York, 1968). These and other significant sketches have been widely discussed in the subsequent Webern literature. See in particular Kathryn Bailey, *The Twelve-Note Music of Anton Webern* (Cambridge, 1991), and Bailey (ed.), *Webern Studies* (Cambridge, 1996).

manner of its employment, elements seen in fully realized form in the first movement of the Third Quartet, where the second main theme, in particular, has a
romantic expansiveness quite foreign to Webern's manner, however intense the
lyric atmosphere of some of his songs. Even if more of Webern's forms involve
some kind of background relationship with sonata schemes than is often perceived, his instrumental textures tend to employ, or aspire to the condition of,
canon, as the most logical way of ensuring the equal distribution of thematic
material between all the parts. In general the material is motivic, just as the sets
from which it is drawn are subdivisible into units of similar interval-content; the
texture is contrapuntal with only rare examples of a melodic line with subordinate accompaniment; and the form will be clearly subdivisible into stages likely
to observe the basic symmetry of a ternary scheme and, on occasion, to invite
comparison with sonata or other traditional designs as well.

The String Trio, Op. 20 is the work in which Webern comes closest to a Schoenbergian structure. Yet even here a rondo form comes first, and a sonata form
second. As the relatively large scale requires, Webern for the first time uses more
than a single transposition of his set: in the first movement eighteen of the available forty-eight are employed. Analogies with tonal process are pursued to the
extent that the restatement of the principal rondo material in the exposition
(bars 16–21) uses the same group of sets as the first statement (bars 4–10), while
the entire recapitulation (bars 44–65) repeats the set sequence of the exposition.
None of these repetitions is exact with regard to rhythm, register, or instrumentation, however, so that in a context where melodic continuity is less evident than
motivic interplay, variation becomes the principal structural feature. The music
is skilfully shaped on a larger scale by effects like the unmistakable climax (bars
38–40) at the end of the central episode and the carefully balanced contrasts of
the tripartite outer sections, leading in the later stages to the neatly engineered
cello cadence (F/E, bars 59–60, repeated bar 61), which helps to focus the ear on
a fundamental thematic interval.

The rondo contains fifty-four successive set statements: twenty in each of the
outer sections, fourteen in the middle. The sonata-form finale is longer and more
complex, not least because from bar 40 onwards Webern starts to use two sets
in combination. He marks off the various sections of his exposition by tempo
modification and rhythmic contrast, while the second subject (violin, bars 41–4)
has the phrase of greatest melodic continuity, which is echoed later by the cello
(bars 51–4). The exposition is marked for repetition, and is carefully differentiated from the start of the development, yet the nature of Webern's material tends
to invalidate the presence of a *separate* development: motivic interplay (violin,
cello, violin, viola from bar 84 onwards, for example) is obvious enough, but
in general the constant process of variation overrides the broader structural
divisions which grew up in classical music under the pressure of the need for
tonal conflict as well as thematic manipulation. There is, however, a full, and fully
varied, recapitulation (in terms of sets it starts in bar 115, in terms of structure in

bar 118), the first fourteen sets of which are the same as those of the exposition, but which diverges after bar 136, during the transition to the second group.

Twelve-Note Mastery

The Trio is a *tour de force* of concentration and flexibility. Yet in comparison with Webern's later works it might seem that the contrapuntal impulse has been inhibited by the use of extended rondo and sonata forms. In the Symphony, Op. 21 (1928), a less hectic atmosphere prevails: all is lucidity and symmetry, and in choosing the most resonant of classical genres Webern stressed the extent to which it could still be relevant to a work in which only certain fundamental structural principles remain valid. Since he now fully understood the principles of serialism, and how he personally could use them to his own satisfaction, he began a far-reaching reinterpretation of the principles of symphonic composition. If tonal symphonic organization was rooted in the concept of hierarchy, for Webern

considerations of symmetry, regularity are now to the fore, as against the emphasis formerly laid on the principal intervals—dominant, subdominant, mediant, etc. For this reason the middle of the octave—the diminished fifth—is now important. For the rest one works as before. The original form and pitch of the row occupy a position akin to that of the 'main key' in earlier music; the recapitulation will naturally return to it. We end 'in the same key!' This analogy with earlier formal construction is quite consciously fostered; here we find the path that will lead us again to extended forms.[7]

It was precisely because Webern attached such importance to the 'analogy with earlier formal construction' that an element of tension between old hierarchies and new symmetries remained. As Kathryn Bailey has noted, while the symphony is 'perhaps . . . the most eloquent expression of symmetries in all of his *œuvre* . . . perfect reflections are continually thrown out of focus by a variety of means' in order to achieve a 'perfectly judged . . . balance between identity and variety'.[8]

As background frameworks, the forms used in the two movements of the symphony approach the palindromic, and in his choice of set-forms Webern demonstrates a concern, not merely with unity, which is unavoidable, but with *similarity*. The symmetrical nature of the basic set of the symphony ensures that P-0 and R-6 (and equivalent transpositions) are identical, thereby reducing the number of set-forms available from forty-eight to twenty-four. The fact that the last interval of the set is an inversion of the first is used as a means of linking set statements (e.g. P-0 to I-3 and I-0 to P-9), and the combination of P-4 and I-4 at

[7] Webern, *Path to New Music*, 54. For a full discussion of the way Webern uses 'old forms in a new language' in Op. 21, see Bailey, *Twelve-Note Music*, 163–71 and 199–201.

[8] Kathryn Bailey, 'Symmetry as Nemesis: Webern and the First Movement of the Concerto, Opus 24', *Journal of Music Theory*, 40 (1996), 246.

the start of the first movement reveals a strong degree of similarity, four of the six pairs of notes being identical in both, though in a different order. Even so, as Bailey's comment implies, the last thing Webern aspired to in this work was a mechanically predictable succession of palindromes, in which the second half of each movement is as literal a mirror as possible of the first. Such obviousness could not be expected to appeal to a composer of such motivic concentration and subtlety as Webern, for it would in effect eliminate the sense of constantly evolving variation which his best movements possess. So even in the ninety-nine-bar second movement of the symphony, with a theme, seven variations, and a coda, and a chain of set-forms which goes into reverse at bar 50, Variations 5, 6, and 7 complement rather than merely reverse Variations 3, 2, and 1, with subtle textural allusions that add a further dimension to the concept of variation form.

Both movements of the symphony display a fine control of the tension between underlying symmetry and continuous, evolutionary change. In both there is a return to the set-forms from which the movement started out, but this degree of parallelism serves purely as the basis against which the foreground variants are composed. The more concentrated, the more dependent on inversion and retrograde the local motivic interplay in a Webern movement becomes, the more important it is that the overall form, while logical and well-proportioned, should not be naively predictable or obviously predetermined.

The symphony is no less important for its refined and imaginative use of instrumental colour. This was Webern's first work for more than a few instruments since the orchestral songs of the First-World-War period, and from now on subtlety of motivic argument can scarcely ever be separated from delicate shading of instrumental timbre: indeed, it was from the intimate relationship between the two that the possibility of serializing dynamics and tone colour was born.

Whereas the two movements of Op. 21 avoid direct associations with sonata form, those of the Saxophone Quartet, Op. 22 (1930) invite them. In the first movement a basic symmetry focuses on the tritone F♯-C, a factor Webern is careful to draw early aural attention to by the repetitions in bars 3 and 4. Such apparently hierarchical processes create coherence without ever suggesting even the kind of tonal centrality which some of Schoenberg's twelve-note works imply—the focal notes are never associated with any diatonic relatives.[9]

Webern was to pursue the link between canon and sonata further in later works, but the second movement of Op. 22 (the first to be composed) is more in the nature of a glance back at the first movement of the String Trio. Whereas in the first movement of the quartet C and F♯ act as foci without actually beginning

[9] One analyst in particular has attempted to disprove this assertion. See Graham Phipps, 'Tonality in Webern's Cantata I', *Music Analysis*, 3 (1984), 125–58, and 'Harmony as a Determinant of Structure in Webern's Variations for Orchestra', in C. Hatch and D. W. Bernstein (eds.), *Music Theory and the Exploration of the Past* (Chicago, 1993), 473–504.

or ending any of the sets employed, in the second they initiate and end the move-ment with appropriate emphasis—an emphasis aided by the combination of P and I set-forms at the same transposition level.

It has already been noted that in the Two Songs for Mixed Chorus, Op. 19 (1926), where Webern for the first time employed transpositions of P-o and I-o, he selected P-6 and I-6, the same level as Schoenberg in the Piano Suite. When Webern returned to vocal composition in the Three Songs, Op. 23 (1933–4), he adopted the same grouping of sets: P-o, P-6, I-o, and their retrogrades.

For the first time, Webern set texts by Hildegard Jone, and all the vocal works of his last decade used her verse. Webern had first met her in 1926 and she and her sculptor husband Josef Humplik became, as Webern's letters to them show, greatly valued friends. The mystical imagery yet straightforward syntax of the poetry make it an acquired taste, but its appeal for Webern must have lain pre-cisely in its concentration, which is closely akin to the spirit of his music. As Webern wrote to Hildegard Jone in August 1928:

I understand the word 'Art' as meaning the faculty of presenting a thought in the clearest, simplest form, that is, the most 'graspable' form. . . . That's why I have never understood the meaning of 'classical', 'romantic' and the rest, and I have never placed myself in oppo-sition to the masters of the past but have always tried to do just like them: to say what it is given me to say with the utmost clarity.[10]

It was nevertheless not until 1930 that Webern confessed to Frau Jone that 'ever since I have known your writings the idea has never left me of setting something to music' and three more years elapsed before he was able to report: 'I have been working well. One of your texts is already done. . . . How deeply they touch me. And I am happy to have arrived at this position at last (of making a composition on your words). I have wished for it so long.' In September 1933, Webern seemed convinced that the two songs he had composed 'shall remain alone *in themselves* for a while at least. Musically they combine to form a *whole*; in the sense that they constitute a certain antithesis.' But on 6 January 1934 he announced that work on a third setting—'Das dunkle Herz'—had begun, and this, completed in March, became the first of the three published Op. 23 songs. Webern wrote that 'it has got quite long, and in its musical form it is really a kind of "aria", consist-ing of a slow section, and a faster one . . . which nevertheless bears the tempo indication "ganz ruhig". . . . After a great upsweep in the first part, there is suddenly quiet, peace, simplicity.'[11]

The refined allusiveness of 'Das dunkle Herz' is reflected in music of appro-priate subtlety and economy. Both parts preserve their initial time signature throughout, and the first treats its basic metre more flexibly than the second (see bars 19 and 22, where triplet patterns are superimposed, though even here the

[10] Anton Webern, *Letters to Hildegard Jone and Josef Humplik*, ed. J. Polnauer, trans. C. Cardew (Bryn Mawr, 1967), 10.

[11] For citations in this paragraph, see ibid. 15, 21, 22, and 25.

primary accent of each bar is preserved). The lyric nature of the vocal line is such as to ensure the subordination of obvious motivic correspondences in the broader sweep of phrases, which evolve in a natural, unforced manner, confirming the spontaneity of Webern's response to his chosen texts.

The vocal line has its own succession of twelve-note sets, but these are not completely independent of the parallel successions in the piano, which may on occasion 'borrow' a note from the voice or lend one to it. When such interchangeability coincides with the overlapping function—the last note of one set statement acting simultaneously as the first note of the next—intriguing situations arise which must have given the ingenious composer great pleasure. Thus in bar 9 of the first song, the D in the voice part is, primarily, the fifth note in the voice's own complete statement of R-0; but it also 'completes' the piano's statement of R-6 and initiates (without being repeated) the next set in the piano part, I-6. Similarly, the C♯ in the voice part on the first beat of bar 33 has a triple function: as note 3 of P-6 (voice), note 11 of RI-0 (piano: note 12 is the simultaneously sounded G♯) and note 2 of RI-6, the next set in the piano part! Such interchangeability is reinforced at the end of the song, when the voice with its last note completes the piano's R-0, leaving the piano to round off the last set begun by the voice, R-6.

Simultaneously with the Op. 23 songs, Webern worked on a new instrumental piece, the Concerto for Nine Instruments, Op. 24, which was dedicated to Schoenberg for his sixtieth birthday in September 1934. Here there is an even greater delight in using similarities of interval and pitch-class order between different transpositions of the basic set, a delight which continued to determine the type of material employed without ever imposing an inflexibly symmetrical organization on the work. Indeed, as Bailey has shown in an absorbing study of the evolution of the first movement, from preliminary sketches to finished score, while Webern first tried to match the symmetries built into the row as fully as possible, he gradually came to appreciate the need to resist rather than merely reflect such properties. 'In the final analysis', the first movement 'begins and ends with clear expressions of the symmetrical relationships inherent in the row; elsewhere, and overall, the clear realization of these unique relations is avoided. This is the compromise he came to in his quest for the balance between expression and concealment which was a necessary condition of the work's success.'[12]

Along with symmetry, the set for Op. 24 offers consistent invariant relations between certain transpositions, and although the concerto's basic materials could theoretically be divided equally into those sets whose hexachords contain the same pitch-classes, variously ordered, as those of P-0 and I-0 respectively, the succession of sets used in the individual sections indicates no desire to exploit such alternations in any systematic way. Similarity is used to great punning effect in the last section of the finale, however, where P-6, RI-1, and

---

[12] See Bailey, 'Symmetry as Nemesis', 298.

Ex. 10.1. Webern, Three Songs Op. 25, no. 1, bars 1–3

R-0 (later P-0), all of which share the same four trichords in different orders, are brought together as a kind of 'tonic' group for a free recapitulation of the first section of the movement.[13]

The simplest of Webern's later works is the set of Three Songs, Op. 25, for high voice and piano (1934–5), his last composition for the medium. It was on 9 July 1934 that Webern first mentioned to Hildegard Jone that he was working on the first of the songs 'Wie bin ich froh!'. After the completion of the Concerto, Op. 24, he tackled 'Sterne, Ihr silbernen Bienen', which was eventually to come third, and reported its completion on 17 October 1934. The final (second) song, 'Des Herzens Purpurvogel', 'will soon be finished', he wrote on 9 November.[14]

While not abandoning the wide intervals so common in Webern's earlier vocal collections, these songs have a directness and clarity making them particularly attractive. The first and third use only P-0, I-0, and their retrogrades, and the opening of the first song (Ex. 10.1) shows how clearly Webern acknowledges the resulting invariance, as voice and piano share the pitches of the same set-form.

This is a good example of what we might term 'anti-combinatorial' technique: not the simultaneous statement of two sets with complementary hexachordal content, but two simultaneous statements of the same set-form. Such quasi-heterophony is unusual in Webern, but actual pitch doublings are not uncommon, and he evidently had no inhibitions about using them, confident that no inappropriate 'tonal' effect would result. The third song of Op. 25 also makes sophisticated use of Webern's favourite technique of double functioning; for example, the B♭ and C in the vocal line in bars 15–16 are the ninth and tenth notes of the voice's statement of P-0, but the piano is also using P-0 at this point, and simply 'borrows' the two notes without stating them independently.

[13] See Bailey, *Twelve-Note Music*, 202–7.
[14] Webern, *Letters*, 28.

The central song of Op. 25 transposes the P-o/I-o relation to P-5/I-5, supplying the collection as a whole with an underlying symmetry, and the return to the original P-o/I-o combination in the third song is enhanced by the way in which, after the first two notes, the first vocal phrase uses the same pitches, at the same register, as that of the first song, though with different rhythm and accompaniment.

In the immediacy and delicacy of their response to the imagery of the text, these songs represent an important aspect of Webern's later manner, which was to find its most refined embodiment in his last completed work, the Cantata No. 2, Op. 31. Yet he also remained fascinated by the issues involved in achieving a purely instrumental structure which would allow the contrapuntal nature of his material, and the particular properties of the set-forms to which that material gave rise, to reach their fullest and most coherent expression. One of the most concentrated, extreme results of this process can be found in the second movement of the Variations for piano, Op. 27 (1936), which has received a great deal of attention from analysts on account of the high degree of invariance which it displays—an invariance which anticipates the development of a stricter, more comprehensive serialism, particularly as applied to the register of pitches.

This twenty-two-bar movement is a canon by inversion disguised as a rhythmic monody, a succession of single notes with a few pairs of chords as the only 'harmonic' events. Each half of the movement is marked for repetition, and both halves are very similar. Each uses two pairs of sets, one each for the right and left hands of the performer. The four pairs are chosen because they either begin or end with G♯ or B♭, and all the pitches are disposed in strict mirror symmetry about the pivotal A above middle C (Ex. 10.2). The pivotal nature of the As and E♭s is reinforced by the circumstance that in all four pairs of sets A coincides with A and E♭ with E♭; furthermore, in all four pairs of sets B♭ coincides with G♯, C♯ with F, G with B, E with D, F♯ with C.

All this information might lead one to expect a totally predetermined piece, which is 'set in motion' rather than composed. That it is not is the reason for its particular relevance in a set of variations. The same pairs of notes appear in each

Ex. 10.2. Webern, Piano Variations Op. 27, 2nd movt., pitch symmetry

of the four pairs of sets: but they never appear in the same order. The composer's variation technique is also brought into play in respect of the three-note chords: there are two of these in each pair of sets (four in each half of the movement) and since they always combine and juxtapose different pairs of pitches the surrounding context is kept as flexible as is consistent with the clear characterization of the individual cells and groups by rhythm, dynamics and phrasing as well as register.

This technique derives from that used in the first movement of the Symphony, Op. 21, but Webern never constructed an entire work in this way. As far as the Variations for piano is concerned, the larger outer movements are more relaxed, and the complete difference in character between the first movement of the symphony and the second of the variations is evidence enough that Webern did not reserve registrally symmetrical substructures for a particular type of movement. He apparently did not believe that they should achieve the status of a principle, as all-determining and as sophisticated as the pitch-set itself.

Analysis: String Quartet Op. 28

The Variations is a fascinating work, yet the String Quartet, Op. 28 (1938), is an altogether finer achievement, meriting the closest study.[15] In the late vocal works, a new lyric quality emerges even in the most concentrated movements, and this spirit is also evident in the rapt intensity of the quartet, for all its variety of timbre and severity of motivic working. More important, however, the quartet is a potently dramatic, and ultimately symphonic, conception, in which Webern's preoccupation with the tension between symmetry and variation reaches its most complex and satisfying stage.

The work consists of three movements, each tripartite in form, and based on a set which is also tripartite: three versions of the same four-note motive (B [Bb], A, C, H [B♮]). The process of variation is already at work within the basic set: if we chose to analyse the work in terms of a four-note set, the twelve-note prime form (P-0) would consist of P-0, I-5, and P-8. Equally basic to the conception of the work, therefore, are the degrees of similarity between certain transpositions of the set, which reduce the number of possible versions from forty-eight to twenty-four, while also proposing their own continuation or succession. In the first respect, P-0 is identical with RI-9, which means it is possible to discuss the set-forms employed exclusively as either P or I forms with their retrogrades; in the second respect, the last 'tetrachord' of P-0 can be deployed simultaneously

---

[15] See Bailey, *Twelve-Note Music*, 215–22 and 256–61. Webern's own detailed comments on the work can be found in various sources, including Hans Moldenhauer and Rosaleen Moldenhauer, *Anton von Webern: A Chronicle of his Life and Work* (London, 1978), 751–6.

Ex. 10.3. Webern, String Quartet Op. 28, invariant relations (t4)

as the first of P-8—an extension of the kind of overlapping used so often by Webern. Or the last dyad of P-0 can be the first of P-10 (not forgetting that the last note of all can be the first of P-9). Moreover, if we pursue the question of overlapping by four notes, and place P-8 alongside P-0, we see that while the first tetrachord of the former is identical with the third of the latter, the second tetrachord of P-8 is a retrograde of the first of P-0, and the third of P-8 retrogrades the second of P-0—a high degree of invariance in which P-4 also shares (Ex 10.3).

Slightly less close, but more significant in the actual composition of the quartet, is the relationship between sets three semitones apart, e.g. P-0 and P-3, P-9 and P-0. Each equivalent tetrachord in both pairs has three notes in common: for example, the first of P-0 with the third of P-3 and the second of P-9 (Ex. 10.4)

Such a network of interrelationships (equally applicable, of course, to all transpositions of P-0) would make it only too easy to achieve a mechanical, anti-musical result. But Webern's genius lay, not in devising these invariants, but in employing them to serve the purposes of a gradually evolving, comprehensible musical discourse.

The 'double function' of the quartet's basic set, as P-0 and RI-9, is reflected in the double structure of the first movement.

VARIATION FORM	TERNARY FORM	BAR NUMBERS
Theme	First subject	1–15 (minim *c.*66)
Variation 1	Repeat of first subject	16–32
Variation 2	Transition	33–49 (minim *c.*84)
Variation 3	Second subject	47–65 (minim *c.*56)
Variation 4	Repeat of second subject	66–78
Variation 5	Reprise of first subject	80–95 (minim *c.*66)
Variation 6	Coda	96–112

The main divisions in this scheme are made audible by means of rests and ritardandi, as well as by textural differences; the most explicit division consists of

Ex. 10.4. Webern, String Quartet Op. 28, invariant relations (t3)

seven crotchet beats of silence before the reprise of the first subject (Variation 5), which is also more dynamic in character (and faster in tempo) after the relatively relaxed middle section.

The Theme (bars 1–15) is the only part of the movement to use one set at a time, and it exploits tetrachordal overlapping. As Ex. 10.3 indicates, consistent use of such overlapping would result in a 'loop' of only three sets (P-0, P-8, P-2, P-0 etc.), or, in the transpositions chosen by Webern for his first-movement Theme, P-6, P-2, P-10, P-6. Having used this loop, Webern changes the degree of overlap from four notes to two, thereby introducing P-4 in bar 11. The main body of the movement is then exclusively concerned with pairings of the type shown in Ex. 10.3, starting with P-2/RI-2 in bar 16.

Another aspect of serial technique which needs some elucidation is the overlapping of set statements. Variation 1 does not overlap with either the Theme or with Variation 2: its own set-pairs overlap by four notes. In Variations 2 and 3 no overlaps are involved, though the actual *texture* of Variation 3 starts before the end of Variation 2 (second violin, bar 47). This central section of the seven-part movement is the only one not to employ P-6: indeed, neither of the pairings involved in Variation 3 are used elsewhere in the movement. Variation 4 parallels Variation 1, with overlapping tetrachords. In Variation 5 the overlaps are by dyads and finally, in the coda, by tetrachords again. It is in the coda, too, that Webern allows the common pitches between tetrachords (which are the result of superimposing sets four semitones apart—see, again, Ex. 10.3) to become explicit (for example, the C♯s and Es in bars 98 and 99, F♯s in bar 101, Cs in bar 103, etc.).

The form of the first movement can be discussed in yet another way, for the texture is not merely contrapuntal but canonic. Ex. 10.5 shows that, at the beginning of Variation 1, there is an exact rhythmic canon between the Dux or leading voice (RI-2, beginning in the viola, bar 16) and the Comes or following voice (P-2, beginning seven beats later in the cello, bar 17). The canon is regular to the extent that the Dux allocates each of the set's trichords to a different instrument, in the order viola, first violin, second violin, cello, while the Comes has the sequence cello, viola, first violin, second violin. Differences between the two canonic lines arise in dynamic markings (the Dux's three minims in first violin, bars 17–18, are marked *f* diminuendo, while the Comes for viola, bars 19–20, has *p*, then crescendo/diminuendo) and, most crucially, in intervallic sequence. As the abstract presentation of the two sets involved in Ex. 10.5(ii) indicates, the pitch intervals in the two canonic voices are sometimes the same (e.g. the descending major sevenths between notes 5 and 6), sometimes the same but with a distinction between simple and compound forms (ascending major tenth in Dux, notes 8 and 9, ascending major third in Comes), and sometimes inverted in the sense that a descending minor ninth in one voice is mirrored by an ascending major seventh in the other (notes 1 and 2). The effect—often the result of practical necessity in terms of what each of the instruments can actually play— is that the Comes is not simply imitating the Dux, but varying it, carrying the movement's large-scale formal principle down into the smallest thematic details.

Later in Variation 1 there is a canon between first violin and cello (from bar 23, see Ex. 10.6: the music for the other instruments is not shown), but the distance in crotchet beats between their entries changes suddenly in bar 26 from seven beats to three (Ex. 10.6). Such procedures ensure that the first movement of Op. 28 is one of Webern's most fascinating explorations of the interaction between a

Ex. 10.5. Webern, String Quartet Op. 28, 1st movt., bars 16–21

time-honoured principle (canonic variation) and a radical new practice—the twelve-note technique.

In the second and third movements of Op. 28, Webern's canonic wizardry is employed with breathtaking nonchalance. What in the first movement was a tension between twos (the pairs of sets) and threes (the underlying ternary form) now develops explicitly into threes and fours—not merely four instruments but four, simultaneous sets. The double canon of the second movement's outer sections uses trios of tetrachordally overlapping sets: P-3, P-7, P-11, and their retrogrades. (P-3 and R-11 have invariant tetrachords, as have P-7 and R-11, and P-11 and R-3.) The same sets are also employed in the rhythmically more diverse canon of the 'trio'.

In the finale, however, Webern reshapes the association principle of the first movement, so that we start with P-0 combined with P-6 (the tritone at last appearing to assert its basic structural role) and, simultaneously, with both their retrogrades (R-0 and R-6). This movement, a scherzo with a double fugue for its middle section, is the playful climax to Webern's synthesis of polyphonic and classical structures. The pointlessness of such concerns in the absence of any specifically harmonic structural determinants will always be argued by some, but it was the essential symmetry of classical ternary form which Webern was adapting, not its dynamic tonal processes. Webern's own view of the lengths to which symmetry should go may be gauged from his account of the way in which the violin's consequent phrase in the exposition (bars 8–14) reverses the rhyth-

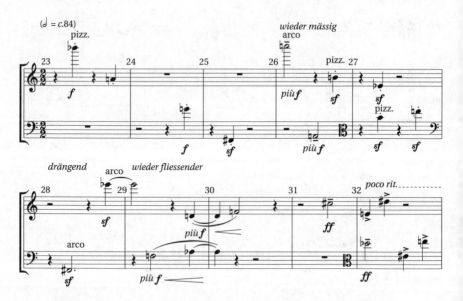

Ex. 10.6. Webern, String Quartet Op. 28, 1st movt., bars 23–32

mic scheme of the antecedent phrase (bars 1–7). There is no question of an exact mirror-image.[16] The *concept* of mirroring always stimulated Webern, but the technique of variation drove it into a subordinate position (Ex. 10.7).

Webern after Op. 28

Since the above discussion of Webern's String Quartet was undertaken in the light of the aesthetic judgement that this is remarkably passionate as well as exceptionally refined music, it might seem pointless to mention the very different response of Richard Taruskin, whose assessment—'Webern's most stringently constrained and dehumanized work'—stems from Taruskin's linkage of 'the BACH cipher' with a nationalistic commitment to 'a heritage dogmatically viewed as extreme' and a predisposition to 'fall easy prey to National Socialism's metaphysical organicism'.[17] The argument is not simply that Webern (like Stravinsky and many others) was complicit in the prevailing fascist, anti-Semitic ideology of the inter-war years, but that this complicity is inherently and inevitably embodied in the musical compositions produced in those years.

There is evidence to support the argument that Webern had right-wing sympathies, and this has been used to promote the hypothesis that Webern's death—shot by a nervous American soldier when lighting a cigarette outside his house—was a kind of assisted suicide, the result of his disillusionment with right-wing politics and despair at his son's death during the war.[18] Given the difficulty of proving such arguments with respect to a composer's life, the application of similar judgements to his work is even more problematic. When the evidence is impressive—as in the case of the relation between Wagner's anti-Semitism and certain methods of characterization in his music dramas—then it is possible to understand that some admirers of the work will turn totally against it, while others will take the line that the strengths and beauties of the music outweigh (even if they do not eliminate) the negative ideological element. One's love of *Die Meistersinger* may cease to be unconditional if one accepts that Beckmesser is portrayed, and caricatured, as a Jew: but the positive aspects of the drama continue to make their effect. In the case of Webern's Op. 28, however, the evidence of taint is far less concrete. Taruskin can only offer opinion, supposition, not fact, and to see the music quite so abjectly reduced to the status of a sonic sponge absorbing external, cultural factors—though common in New Musicological writing—is unpersuasive to anyone who feels that, at the very least, the music's qualities transcend rather than helplessly implement its ideological context.

---

[16] U. Rauchhaupt (ed.), *Schoenberg, Berg and Webern. The String Quartets: A Documentary Study* (Hamburg, 1971), 132–6.
[17] Richard Taruskin, 'Back to Whom? Neoclassicism as Ideology', *19th Century Music*, 16 (1993), 299.
[18] David Schroeder, 'Not Proven', *Music Times*, 137 (1996), 21–3.

Ex. 10.7. Webern, String Quartet Op. 28, 3rd movt., bars 1–7, 8–14

Webern's own attitude to Op. 28 was unambiguously positive. Shortly after completing it he wrote, 'I must confess that hardly ever before have I had such a good feeling towards a completed work. It almost seems to me that this is altogether my first work.'[19] Its 'suitability for study', as a compendium of Webern's serial techniques in full maturity, should not blind us to its musical qualities, of course, and analytical explorations like the foregoing are worthless if they do not ultimately serve to enhance the experience and appreciation of the music.

In his last completed instrumental work, the Variations for Orchestra Op. 30 (1940), Webern exploited the double-function form of the first movement of the String Quartet on a larger scale. In a well-known letter,[20] he described the blend of variation and 'overture' form, and the result can be laid out in a similar way to the first movement of the quartet:

VARIATION FORM	OVERTURE FORM	BAR NUMBERS
Theme	Introduction	1–20
1st variation	1st subject	21–55
2nd variation	Transition	56–73
3rd variation	2nd subject	74–109
4th variation	1st subject recap.	110–134
5th variation	Intro./Transition recap.	135–145
6th variation	Coda	146–180

[19] Rauchhaupt (ed.), *Schoenberg, Berg and Webern*, 127.
[20] Webern, *Path to New Music*, 60.

Ex. 10.8. Webern, Cantata No. 2, Op. 31, 6th movt., set structure

The later work, since it is not part of a larger whole, contains greater contrasts within itself, and the constant changes of metre and tempo in the first section are an immediate indication of the considerable difference in character between the two compositions.

Certainly Webern continued to explore the implications of a serialism rooted in traditionally derived textures until his death. It is appropriate, too, that the last movement of his last completed work, the Cantata, Op. 31, should be a double canon by inversion thrice repeated, each pair of parts employing three sets each. Schematically, this works as follows:

Tenor	P-8	RI-10	RI-4
Alto	I-4	I-10	R-8
Soprano	P-0	P-6	RI-8
Bass	I-8	R-6	R-0

The basic set is not, in fact, symmetrical or subdivisible in the archetypal Webernian fashion. It does, however, span six semitones (C to F♯) and if the combinations are set out in simple form it will be seen that in each pair G♯s and Ds always coincide (Ex 10.8). There are other invariants with respect to note order, and overlapping is also involved: by one note only between the first and second pairs, then by three notes between the second and third. This movement, then, is the ultimate expression of Webern's all-inclusive yet freely unfolding serial method.[21] The properties of the material are unfailingly perceived and exploited; the polyphonic essence of a system which has no self-sufficient harmonic properties is rooted in traditional contrapuntal textures, giving them new meaning. The vision and integrity with which all this was done ensure Webern's place among the greatest of all twentieth-century masters, as a genius in whom radical and conservative meet and interpenetrate: and although the consistent homogeneity of his later twelve-note textures, as individually wide-ranging lines balance one another to achieve a well-nigh

---

[21] See Bailey, *Twelve-Note Music*, 315–17.

classical coherence, is very different from the overt modernism found in many of his progressive contemporaries, Webern's consistent use of small-scale structures could still prove a seminal as well as radical influence on the music of the future.

As 'the Second Viennese School', Schoenberg, Berg, and Webern are conventionally accorded collective credit for the establishment of the twelve-note technique as an important factor in twentieth-century music, and the story of composition since 1950 is largely one of reactions to that factor—positive, negative, equivocal. Whereas Webern, and Schoenberg in some of his late works, indicated the basis for a fuller exploration of the conjunction between strict serial technique and atonal expressionism, Schoenberg's earlier serial pieces, and all those by Berg, opened up the very different prospect of associations between traditional forms and procedures and twelve-note methods which involved tension as well as connection. The continued influence and development of twelve-note composition after 1950 therefore helped to intensify the already vigorous pluralism of style and aesthetic that had been evident in twentieth-century music from the beginning, and most composers of significance who have emerged since mid-century have been concerned to some extent with the basic principle of consistently ordered pitch structuring (though often with fewer, or more than twelve notes) that lies at the heart of the Schoenbergian concept. Such composers will feature in all the later chapters of this study, illustrating the extreme diversity to which types of serial thinking, in a post-tonal context, can give rise.

This chapter considers five composers born between 1882 and 1916, whose contribution to the continuation and development of serialism in the 1950s and 1960s was particularly substantial. The fact that Stravinsky only turned to twelve-note composition after Schoenberg's death is often commented on, and even though Webern's influence on Stravinsky's tersely contrapuntal twelve-note textures is undeniable, a Schoenbergian trait can be perceived in the tendency of such works as *Abraham and Isaac* and *Requiem Canticles* to preserve an element of harmonic centricity—a factor even when the music also seems to embody a response to the concentrated athematicism of Boulez and Stockhausen. Webern also had a decisive influence on Dallapiccola, although an expressionistic lyricism recalling Berg is no less evident from time to time.

While it was from Webern rather than Schoenberg that younger European composers such as Boulez and Stockhausen gained the primary stimulus for exploring the possibility of serializing durations, dynamics, and registers as well as pitch, several of Schoenberg's pupils, of whom Roberto Gerhard was one, remained active after 1945 in promoting their personal interpretations of their teacher's style and techniques. In America, the Schoenbergian influence manifested itself in two quite different ways. The starting-point for Milton Babbitt's uniquely rigorous exploration of serialism lay primarily in Schoenbergian combinatorial procedures. Roger Sessions, by contrast, was encouraged to emulate the strong continuity between full-blown late romantic chromaticism and the richly inflected harmonic progressions he found in Schoenberg's twelve-note works.

As if in direct response to the radical intellectuality of such initiatives, the 1940s and 1950s also saw the rapid growth of indeterminate or aleatory music, and of other forms of experimentalism which, as the precursors of minimalism, provided the most thoroughgoing reaction, not merely against serialism, but against the whole idea of a musical composition as something fixed and fully written-out in form, as well as complex in texture and technique. The fragmentation of the musical spectrum has grown steadily more extreme since 1950, and one result of this process is that the serial music of the five composers considered in this chapter seems even less 'mainstream' in its significance at the end of the century than it did during the 1970s.

Stravinsky

In adopting serialism, Stravinsky had to validate not merely the series in his own terms, but also atonality; and, like Schoenberg in his early exploration of atonality, he had to decide whether and in what sense thematicism could survive. Stravinsky shared Schoenberg's dislike of the word 'atonal', expressing it with characteristic sharpness in *The Poetics of Music*, and somewhat more cautiously in the first volume of *Conversations*. Just as in the *Poetics* Stravinsky was concerned to establish a broader definition of tonality as 'the polar attraction of sound, of an interval, or even of a complex of tones', so in the *Conversations* he was willing to admit that 'we can still create a sense of return to exactly the same place without tonality . . . form cannot exist without identity of some sort'. Thematic identity is structurally more significant in Stravinsky's twelve-note works than the fact that 'the intervals of my series are attracted by tonality', and this type of motivic focus is his most obvious debt to Webern. As the same passage in the *Poetics* asserts, however, 'musical form would be unimaginable in the absence of elements of attraction',[1] and it is true that the serial processes may be manipulated by Stravinsky just as they were by Schoenberg to admit pitch-emphasis as that element of attraction (the C♯ in *Abraham and Isaac* is a good example): it is by means of such polarities, between pitch-emphasis and its absence, that Stravinsky reformulates his essential modernism to suit the

---

[1] Igor Stravinsky, *The Poetics of Music*, trans. A. Knodel and I. Dahl (New York, 1947), 40–1. Igor Stravinsky and Robert Craft, *Conversations with Igor Stravinsky* (London, 1959), 24.

twelve-note technique. Understandable though it is that early commentators on Stravinsky's serial pieces should have seized on the chance of declaring that at last the great synthesis between tonal and serial had been achieved, the sober remarks of Milton Babbitt, pointing out the incompatibility of the two processes, are ultimately more relevant to Stravinsky's twelve-note works: 'The formal systems—of which the tonal system and the twelve-tone system are, respectively, instances—are, under no conceivable principle of correspondence, equivalent; they are so different in structure as to render the possibility of a work being an extended instance of both unthinkable.'[2]

What Roman Vlad describes, in his analysis of the ending of *Threni*, as 'tonal polarization'[3] is merely the arrangement of sets in combination to achieve a concordant cadence. Even if Stravinsky has added together 'the diatonic impli-cations of the various series', the result is neither diatonic nor tonal, but polar-ized to 'resolve' on to this particular interval. Most importantly, since this polarization is of purely local significance (though conclusive), it cannot be held to confirm the tonal direction of the work as a whole (unlike the C of the *Cantata*, 1951–2, or the A of the Septet, 1952–3). Stravinsky himself accepted that *Movements* for Piano and Orchestra (1958–9), the work which followed *Threni*, 'has a tendency towards *antitonality*'. In his own terms, therefore, several of the later twelve-note works are distinctly less anti-tonal, just as they are consider-ably more thematic: and even Stravinsky himself used the term 'a kind of triadic atonality' to describe the harmonic situation in *Threni*.[4]

Threni (1957–8), with a text from the *Lamentations* of Jeremiah, is not merely Stravinsky's first wholly twelve-note composition, nor is it simply the longest (thirty-five minutes): it is seminal in both form and atmosphere, the form episodic but held together by varied repetitions, the mood elegiac in a manner at once ritualistic and intensely expressive.

The most fundamental unifying feature in the work is the regular occurrence of the Hebrew letters introducing the separate verses of the text. These punctu-ate the form and articulate the smaller divisions within the larger framework, even though the letters are by no means all set in an identical manner. It is the first of the work's three main parts ('De Elegia Prima') which makes the most substantial use of exact repetition to construct an overall 'rondo' form.

The 'De Elegia Prima' establishes the importance of canonic writing and irregular accentuation, the latter a long-standing Stravinskian trait, which depends just as much on the reiteration of small numbers of pitches as it did in *The Rite of Spring*. Because of this, it is possible to sense polarization on to F♯ amounting almost to 'tonal centrality' in this part of the work (as the final pitch

[2] Milton Babbitt, 'Remarks on the Recent Stravinsky', in B. Boretz and E. T. Cone (eds.), *Perspectives on Schoenberg and Stravinsky* (Princeton, 1968), 184. Another important contribution by Babbitt to the study of Stravinsky's twelve-note music is 'Stravinsky's Verticals and Schoenberg's Diagonals: A Twist of Fate', in E. Haimo and P. Johnson (eds.), *Stravinsky Retrospectives* (Lincoln, Nebr., 1987), 15–35.

[3] Roman Vlad, *Stravinsky*, 3rd edn. (Oxford, 1978), 219.

[4] Igor Stravinsky and Robert Craft, *Expositions and Developments* (London, 1962), 107.

of P-0, F♯ clearly represents a culmination). Yet however strong such centrality seems in this first part it is not confirmed in the remainder. Only the final section of the 'Sensus Spei' (the second 'movement' of Part Two) gives some emphasis to F♯ as a pedal in the bass.

Similarly, exact repetition is less significant in the two other main parts of *Threni*. Part Two, 'De Elegia Tertia', is itself tripartite, and each part is episodic, with repetition important within the individual episodes. The central section, 'Sensus Spei', contains eight distinct episodes, each focusing on a different element set up in connection with each successive Hebrew letter. There is sufficient internal repetition to ensure the distinct thematic character of each episode, however. For example, the section between bars 231 and 245 ('Nun') begins with two two-bar phrases, and these are immediately repeated in varied form before the final seven bars, which are different. Naturally, the derivation of all material from the basic set (though its original identity is not strictly preserved throughout) means that familiarity can suggest ever-increasing similarities of thematic shape to the ear. The perception of such invariants inevitably creates a far richer sense of the work's unity than the simple awareness of virtually exact repetitions will do.

Since *Threni* is longer by ten minutes than any of Stravinsky's later twelve-note works, it is not surprising that substantial repetitions on the scale of 'De Elegia Prima' are not found again.[5] The repetitions therefore seem in retrospect to have more in common with the symmetries of transitional refrain structures like the *Cantata on Old English Texts* (1951–2) and *In Memoriam Dylan Thomas* (1954) than with the more consistently evolutionary later scores, while the episodic organization of the 'De Elegia Tertia' section is an anticipation of some aspects of later developments—notably the quasi-stanzaic form of *Abraham and Isaac*. Certainly the *Movements* for Piano and Orchestra presents a remarkable 'alternative' in almost every respect: athematic fragmentation is rife, in spite of some characteristic rhythmic reiterations, and the articulating divisions of the form (five movements linked by interludes) are hard to hear, as is the justification for repeating the 'exposition' of the first movement (bars 1–22).

By comparison, *A Sermon, a Narrative and a Prayer* (1960–1) seems almost artless in its lyricism and rhythmic simplicity. Yet it is not a complete contrast to *Movements*, as the instrumental counterpoint on the very first page shows: there is simply a more appealing expressive range, befitting the return to vocal music on a broader scale.

In the four substantial works which Stravinsky completed between 1962 and 1966—*The Flood, Abraham and Isaac, Variations Aldous Huxley in memoriam* and *Requiem Canticles*—the structural role of repetition, and of thematic

---

[5] For an excellent general discussion of technique and style in the late works, see Stephen Walsh, *The Music of Stravinsky* (London, 1988), 245–76.

identity, remains of paramount importance. As the longest and most loosely constructed, *The Flood* (1961–2) is nevertheless the only one of these late works to include an example of that most unified and symmetrical of Webernian structures, the palindrome, in the fifty-six-bar orchestral movement called 'The Flood'. This is firmly anchored in regular repetitions of a seven-note chord (D♯/D/C/F♯/F/B/E) which contains enough semitonal clashes to inhibit any tonal feeling, as does the 'Jacob's Ladder' music which appears four times (bars 6, 179, 496, and 582). On the other hand, the way in which the phrases of the Te Deum near the beginning and the repeat of the Sanctus near the end start out from C♯ (with D♯ and G♯ in close attendance) is more obviously focused, and the two settings of God's words (bars 80 ff. and 181 ff.) inhabit a comparable area.

Abraham and Isaac (1962–3) is far more concentrated, though in its acknowl-edgement of a degree of centrality for C♯ it follows on from *The Flood*. With the concentration goes a vast expansion of the number of available set-forms, for Stravinsky here makes use of hexachordal rotations, starting, say, with the fifth note, and continuing with 6, 1, 2, 3, 4, which increases the number of six-note sets theoretically available from 96 to 576. Far from ensuring the complete non-recurrence of any single set and the absolute avoidance both of thematic repetition and of pitch-emphasis, however, this technique is so used that *Abraham and Isaac* is still a thematic twelve-note work in which the note C♯ is given clear primacy (F is also emphasized to some degree). Thematic repetition and pitch-emphasis are at their clearest in the fourth of the work's ten short sec-tions (bars 105–35), where the hypnotic chant of the vocal line establishes close links with the melodic style of many much earlier works of Stravinsky (Ex. 11.1). Elsewhere, a more fragmented, less obviously directional, or centric vocal line makes this one of his least appealing pieces and notably difficult to perform. Yet in its cool, conscious handling of the multifarious choices open to a composer who rotates his sets systematically it is a *tour de force*.

Like *Abraham and Isaac*, the orchestral *Variations* (1963–4) has less obvious thematic repetition than *Threni, A Sermon, a Narrative and a Prayer*, or *The Flood*. Here, however, there is a broader structural use of varied recurrence, for while the ten sections of *Abraham and Isaac* are all new stages in the thematic process, the twelve sections of the *Variations* include three which are basically identical in texture and material, though not in timbre. Sections 2, 5, and 11 are all in twelve parts (for twelve violins, ten violas and two basses, and twelve woodwind respectively), so that, even though no thematic process or internal repetition of any kind can readily be discerned within them, they do neverthe-less act as clearly recognizable unifying features, set off as they are by the more open texture of the surrounding sections. Other unifying features relate the beginning and the end (compare the chords in bars 2–5 and 137–40), while sections 7 (bars 73–85) and 9 (bars 95–100) divide into two related phrases. The thematic process of section 10 (bars 101–17) is particularly clear.

Ex. 11.1. Stravinsky, *Abraham and Isaac*, bars 112–35 (vocal line only)

Perhaps it was only in the fifteen-minute *Requiem Canticles* (1964–6) that Stravinsky recaptured an ideal balance between repetition, contrast, and variation, as well as the polar opposites of pitch-emphasis and its absence, making this the most immediately communicative of his twelve-note works after *A Sermon, a Narrative and a Prayer*.[6] The instrumental Prelude is itself a marvellously uncluttered example of the process in action. It is fifty-four bars long, and can be subdivided into four phrases and a coda (the coda restores the harmonic basis of the first phrase, but excludes its melodic material). With respect to pitch focus, the Prelude starts out from a brief emphasis on F, establishes a much stronger emphasis on F♯ (bars 20–33), then 'modulates' back to F via D (bars 35–46). Thematically, the second, third, and fourth phrases are expanded variations of the first.

All the other movements can be analysed along similar lines, without for a moment suggesting a mechanical reliance on the processes of the Prelude. In the

---

[6] Richard Taruskin has discussed the possibility of specific connections, primarily in relation to octatonic usage, between *Requiem Canticles* and much earlier works: see *Stravinsky and the Russian Traditions* (Berkeley and Los Angeles, 1996), 1648–75.

Lacrimosa, for example, which has six short phrases for the contralto soloist separated by miniature ritornelli for three trombones, the vocal phrases finally lose the security of sustained harmonic support, and with it the possibility of any clear pitch-emphasis emerging. The instrumental Postlude confirms that, although pitch polarization around a particular bass note may be sensed for a significant part of the work (here, as with the Prelude, there is a movement away from F and back again), it is the thematic content of phrases and the relationship between which constitute the most vital traditional feature of this music (Ex. 11.2). Thematicism has replaced tonality as its central identity, and variation has replaced modulation as the primary structural agent of meaningful change and progress. In the Postlude of the *Requiem Canticles* what is thematic may be little more than a particular timbre associated with a particular rhythm, but it is enough to create that continuity, that sense of concern with an 'Idea', which is the essential quality of pitch-serialism for Stravinsky, Schoenberg, and Webern alike.

Sessions

Of native-born American serialists, Roger Sessions (1896–1985) was the most distinguished exponent of the more traditional, Schoenbergian manner. His music is relatively little known, at least outside the United States, but it has considerable appeal, confirming in its fluency and clarity that the Schoenbergian example could be followed without pious imitation or purposeless parody.

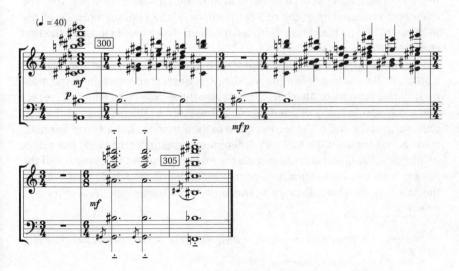

Ex. 11.2. Stravinsky, *Requiem Canticles*, 'Postlude', last seven bars

Sessions was well into his fifties before producing his first twelve-note work, the Violin Sonata of 1953. To a far greater extent than Stravinsky, whose conversion took place around the same time, Sessions had moved towards the technique gradually, explaining that

my first use of it was, at the beginning, quite involuntary. I had at various times, for my own self-enlightenment, carried out quite small-scale exercises with the technique, but I still envisaged it as not applicable to my own musical ideas. It was therefore a surprise to me when I found the composition of the Sonata flowing easily and without constraint in its terms.[7]

Such a natural transition ensured that in those later works where Sessions used twelve-note techniques he was able to continue the exploration of large-scale structures begun earlier. Before 1953 he had already contributed to all the major traditional genres: sonata, symphony, string quartet, concerto, opera; and the serial works reinforce that commitment, notably to the symphony, of which there are eight, six composed after 1953.

The Eighth Symphony, completed in 1968, is a fine example of a style in which an elaborate evolutionary process, often of considerable rhythmic complexity, maintains sufficient contact with memorable recurrences. The two-movement form—Adagio e Mesto and Allegro con fuoco—proposes a fairly extreme basic contrast, and the symphonism of the work involves in large part the creation of associations between the movements, preparing an ending which recalls the opening.

Sessions's own straightforward note on the symphony[8] describes the first movement as dividing into three episodes, and a background of traditional ternary design may well be evoked in the third episode with its 'melodic fragments reminiscent of the quieter portions of the opening episode of the movement' and its conclusion with a dark chord which also belongs in the first episode.

Strategic recurrence is no less important in the Allegro, which follows without a break. As the composer comments, 'the two fast sections which form the main body of this movement are characterized by a three-note motif which . . . recurs frequently and in many different guises'. The return to the first idea of the first movement at the end of the second is not in itself an indication of deep thematic associations between the two very different movements of the work, but rather a satisfying demonstration of reversal: the Adagio 'prepares' the Allegro and the Allegro itself can lead logically back to a reminder of the Adagio to dramatize the fact that the sheer distance between the two entities can possess its own coherence.

[7] Roger Sessions, 'Schoenberg in America', in *Roger Sessions on Music: Collected Essays* (Princeton, 1979), 360.
[8] Issued with the original LP recording , ZRG702.

Gerhard

Roberto Gerhard (1896–1970) was born in the same year as Sessions, and studied with Schoenberg in Vienna and Berlin between 1923 and 1928. A native of Catalonia, Gerhard emigrated to England after the Spanish Civil War, and lived there for the rest of his life, though he paid several visits to America to teach, and to learn about the more rigorous serial techniques being pioneered by Milton Babbitt. Gerhard's music progressed from the impressionistic nationalism of the Piano Trio (1918), and preliminary essays in serialism (Wind Quintet, 1928), to the fully mature, unusually well-varied manner of the opera *The Duenna* (1946–7), which has strong claims to be regarded as his finest single work. The idea of alternating between tonal and atonal styles, between music with Spanish roots and a more austere, international modernity could have generated mere incongruity and self-contradictory improbability. In *The Duenna*, however, it proves the ideal way of bringing to musical life the inherent ambiguities and tensions in Sheridan's play, and the opera complements its vivid comedy and attractive lyricism with a disturbing sense of unresolved social conflict, as in the final scene where the happy lovers are contrasted with a chorus of beggars.

After *The Duenna* Gerhard pursued a more radical and consistent twelve-note technique in his works of the 1950s, until the final period in which serialism, while pervasive, is used with sovereign flexibility within a style of the widest resonance. The last melody heard in his final work *Leo* (1969) is a folk tune, and this kind of polarity between simple modality and freshly invented post-tonal material has remained a fruitful feature of later twentieth-century British modernism—for example, in the music of Peter Maxwell Davies.[9]

Like Babbitt, Gerhard developed ways of relating pitch and duration serially,[10] although in practice it appears that such processes were little more than a background against which other freer, and often much more traditional factors, could operate. The Schoenbergian principle of permutation within the hexachords of the twelve-note set was therefore of more direct importance to Gerhard than any consistent correlation between pitch, duration, and other compositional elements in determining the later stages of his stylistic evolution.

In conformity with Schoenberg's own practice, Gerhard affirmed that 'the identity of the series will be maintained in spite of permutation, provided that this takes place exclusively within the constituent units (hexachord, tetrachord, etc.)'. But he went on to declare that 'this seems to me to confirm the view that the fundamental idea of the twelve-tone technique is in fact a new formulation of the principle of tonality',[11] a conclusion strongly at variance with that of Babbitt, quoted above in relation to Stravinsky, and the clearest indication one

[9] See below, Ch. 17, pp. 375–6.
[10] See R. Gerhard, 'Developments in Twelve-Tone Technique', *Score*, 17 (Sept. 1956), 61–72.
[11] R. Gerhard, 'Tonality in Twelve-Tone Music', *Score*, 6 (May 1952), 34.

could have of Gerhard's reluctance to regard his novel twelve-note techniques as divorced from the characteristics and even the functions of tradition. Once again, however, it is an attitude similar to Gerhard's which has greater appeal to more recent composers, especially those who, like Gerhard himself, have remained committed to the symphonic forms and genres of earlier traditions.

In a note on his Symphony No. 1 (1952–3) Gerhard described his concern with

the possibility of evolving a large-scale work as a continuous train of musical invention that would progress much as a poem progresses—by the strength and direction of its inherent potentialities alone, growing and branching out freely, without being forced into predetermined channels. In other words, I discarded the traditional symphonic framework, with its exposition, themes, development and recapitulations. . . . Admittedly the appearance and recurrence of themes provide land-marks that help the listener to find his formal bearings. But today a theme may become a period piece of musical furniture, and it is possible to imagine an infinite variety of land-marks of an entirely different type that will orientate the listener equally well.[12]

This is an admirably clear statement of the way Gerhard thought it possible to advance beyond Schoenbergian precepts, in which thematic recurrence (in varied rather than literal form) as a means of articulating symphonic structures remained crucial. Yet, like some of Gerhard's other analytical comments, these seem to refer as much to a future ideal as to his own practice. Certainly, from 1959 onwards, when Gerhard worked exclusively with single-movement schemes, the music demonstrates resourceful and consistent continuations of the kind of structural and thematic processes found in Schoenberg's late single-movement works, the String Trio and the Violin Phantasy. And in the Symphony No. 4 (1967), one of the best of these pieces, the thematic process can be perceived as a sequence of distinct stages in the evolution of complementary hexachords, a process which has a good deal in common with traditional thematicism.

The amount of imitation, ostinato, and repetition in this symphony is more than enough to build strong traditional associations, and if the work has a weakness, it is in creating the impression that its successive stages occasionally attempt to evade crystallization into the more fully shaped contours of conventional thematic material. More positively, we may respond to an extremely wide range of thematic elements—improvisatory coruscation to lyrical, extended melody—through an awareness of their common serial basis.

As a simple example, we can compare the cadenza-like clarinet entry in the eighth bar of the work—the symphony's first melodic idea—which states two complementary hexachords in close position, each filling out six adjacent semitones, with a passage near the end at Fig. 103, where the oboe and violas outline another close-position hexachord (E♭ to A♭) and violins and cellos provide the complementary six notes, A to D. (Ex. 11.3)

[12] Issued with the original LP recording, ALP2063.

Ex. 11.3. Gerhard, Symphony No. 4: (i) bars 8–9; (ii) from Fig. 103

Examples of similar processes can easily be multiplied. In the passage before Fig. 29 a twelve-note string chord separates out into the hexachords A♭ to D♭ and D to G. But a very different thematic adaptation of the close-position hexachords can be found at Fig. 35, where the violins initiate a typically dense semiquaver passage with A–E and E♭ to B♭ (descending), while at Fig. 53 the trumpet presents a new version of the G–D hexachord, with the harps sustaining the complement.

The thematic interrelationships of the work seem stratified according to whether close- or open-position hexachords are involved—certainly the connection between the trumpet theme at Fig. 53 and the oboe theme at Fig. 93 is clear despite the absence of obvious repetition. It is not merely that 'the identity of the series will be maintained in spite of permutation',[13] but that the links between stages in a thematic process (the series shaped in a particular way) are made explicit. The possibility of creating such unambiguous links could, in turn, have encouraged Gerhard to explore the no-less-vital musical element of strong thematic contrast, as found in *The Duenna* and *Leo*, for example, and which contributes so significantly to the effectiveness and originality of his most fully realized works.

Dallapiccola

Like all the composers considered in this chapter, Babbitt excepted, Luigi Dallapiccola (1904–75) was a 'late' convert to twelve-note techniques. While, broadly speaking, Sessions and Gerhard continued to explore the Schoenbergian commitment to substantial instrumental forms, Dallapiccola attempted a still more difficult task, the extension of Webernian lyricism, and the pursuit of that most demanding prize, the convincing full-length twelve-note opera. Both Sessions and Gerhard wrote operas—Sessions, in particular, labouring over his three-act *Montezuma* for more than two decades (1941–62)—but neither showed such exclusive devotion to vocal forms, or such obvious lyrical gifts in non-operatic vocal music as Dallapiccola.

[13] See Gerhard, 'Tonality', 34.

His advance towards complete acceptance of atonal serialism was as gradual as that of Gerhard or Sessions, and the influence of local, more traditional composers—Casella, Malipiero—was paramount until the mid-1930s. Then, at the Prague ISCM Festival of 1935, Dallapiccola heard the first performance of Webern's Concerto, Op. 24. He wrote: 'We are confronted here with a man who expresses the greatest number of ideas in the fewest possible words. Though I did not understand the work well, it seemed to me to have an aesthetic and stylistic unity on which one could not wish to improve.'[14] This immediate attraction was to a truly 'foreign' music—'a composition of unbelievable brevity... and truly extraordinary concentration. Every decorative element is eliminated.' The impact made by Webern's work was no short-lived phenomenon. Three years later, at the London ISCM Festival of 1938, Dallapiccola attended the first performance of *Das Augenlicht*, which was, in all probability, an even greater revelation, simply because it was a vocal work. He wrote at the time that the twelve-note system is 'a language which contains within itself exceedingly varied possibilities, whose total realization we shall not perhaps live to see'.[15] Yet he did not immediately reject every aspect of his earlier style and plunge into the imitation of Webern. The transitional period, which roughly spans the years 1936 to 1948, contains what may eventually be seen as his finest works, and their quality is the result of positive compromise.

The major works of this period are both operas. *Volo di notte*, with the composer deriving his own libretto from the book by Saint-Exupéry, was composed between 1937 and 1939, and *Il Prigioniero*, again to Dallapiccola's own libretto, between 1944 and 1948. Purely as convincing theatrical presentations of thoroughly modern subjects—the personality of the pilot-explorer, the horror of psychological and political tyranny—these operas, if given the widest circulation when they were new, should have established Dallapiccola as the most important opera composer since Berg, and as the obvious continuer of Bergian eclecticism. *Volo di notte* is a compromise-work in the most obvious sense: it begins and ends tonally (B major–E major) but uses twelve-note processes in between. More obviously Bergian features are the distinct forms used for the different scenes and the use of *Sprechgesang* (Dallapiccola, along with Puccini, had heard and admired *Pierrot lunaire* in 1924). *Volo di notte* incorporates material from the slightly earlier *Tre Laudi* for soprano and chamber orchestra, whose reliance on canon is a more explicit link with Webernian practice.

It is nevertheless in the smaller-scale vocal works of this period, principally the *Liriche Greche* (1942–5), settings of Italian translations of Sappho, Anacreon, and Alcaeus, that the most refined expression of Dallapiccola's lyrical gift may be found (Ex. 11.4). Here, as in the *Canti di prigionia* (1938–41), later to be used in the second opera, Dallapiccola seems to achieve new depth and focus in spite of

---

[14] Luigi Dallapiccola, 'Meeting with Webern: Pages from a Diary', *Tempo*, 99 (1972), 2.
[15] Ibid. 3.

Ex. 11.4. Dallapiccola, *Sex carmina Alcaei*, opening

the flexibility of style, and this style reaches its apogee in *Il Prigioniero*, where Dallapiccola's 'variety of rows and motives, his evocative use of traditional chord structure, his mingled echoes of Verdi, Debussy and Berg, all offend against *a priori* conceptions of serialism; but his right to profit as he chooses from serial discipline is vindicated by the powerful impact the work has continued to make'.[16]

Dallapiccola dedicated the *Sex carmina Alcaei* to the memory of Webern, and it may be that his very faithfulness to that memory was the principal reason for the relative failure of his later music. It is not solely a matter of form—of trying to do what Webern did on a much larger scale—but of a different kind of compromise. After 1948 tonal reminiscence diminishes and disappears. Within

[16] Peter Evans, in M. Cooper (ed.), *The Modern Age, 1890–1960: The New Oxford History of Music*, x (London, 1974), 421.

234   THE SPREAD OF SERIALISM

the atonal-serial residue the opposition between 'lyrical' and 'cerebral' elements becomes increasingly marked and, whether the two confront each other or either dominates, the earlier momentum, ensured by the tendency of serially derived harmonies to move towards tonal resolutions, is no longer to be found. As a result, Dallapiccola's later works, including his only full-length opera *Ulisse* (1960–8), have been less often heard, and the impression remains that he was at his best on a relatively small scale, whether in purely serial miniatures or compositions in which the tensions between tonal and post-tonal tendencies are palpable.

Babbitt

Milton Babbitt (b. 1916) is the most notable of those composers whose theoretical explorations of the twelve-note system were intended from the first to realize its full, inherent potential. Not, for Babbitt, the preferred option of so many other recent composers, exploring serialism's compatibility with, or capacity to interact with, other quite different compositional principles. From his base at Princeton University, he progressed in an appropriately logical and consistent manner through three broad phases (1947–60, 1961–80, after 1980) in which the serial principles essential to his work have been progressively elaborated.[17] During the 1940s he laid the foundations for a 'synthesis of Schoenbergian and Webernian practices'[18] which enabled him to move beyond a relatively conventional, even thematic kind of writing, to one whose central rationale built on the capacity of the 'combinatorial' method pioneered by Schoenberg[19] to generate more complex structures, built from superimpositions of complementary set-forms, and known as 'arrays' of 'aggregates'.[20]

The early *Three Compositions for Piano* (1947–8) is still thematic: the continuity of the pieces is not merely the result of rhythmic and textural factors, and the recurrence of related melodic shapes, within clear-cut formal frameworks, can easily be perceived. Even the first piece goes beyond Schoenberg or Webern, however, since a simple kind of serialization of rhythmic patterns is employed, involving units of 1, 2, 4, and 5 semiquavers in prime (5, 1, 4, 2), inversion (1, 5, 2, 4), R, and RI forms. This technique, in combination with the pitch serialism, helps to place the piece in the Schoenbergian tradition of developing variation. A more thoroughgoing kind of variation, to exclude rather than promote thematic process, was not long in coming, however, as Babbitt tried out various other applications of serialism to the time factor. One such application is the 'attack-point' set, in which the distance (in semiquavers) between instrumental

---

[17] For a fascinating account of aspects of Babbitt's life and work see S. Dembski and J. Straus (eds.), *Milton Babbitt: Words About Music* (Madison, 1987).

[18] See Andrew Mead, *An Introduction to the Music of Milton Babbitt* (Princeton, 1994), 54.

[19] See above, p. 167.

[20] For full discussion of these terms, see Mead, *Introduction to Babbitt*, 20–5.

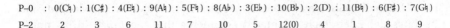

Ex. 11.5. Babbitt, *Composition for Twelve Instruments*, opening

attacks relates to the distance in semitones between the first pitch of a given pitch-class set and its eleven successors. The opening of Babbitt's *Composition for Twelve Instruments* (1948) shows the association between a P-2 attack-point set and the initial aggregate, formed from the first pitches of the twelve different pitch-class sets in use (one for each instrument) (Ex. 11.5).

There can still be an element of linear continuity in such music, and one must emphasize that, in all phases of Babbitt's work, certain statements are likely to stand out as more melodic than others, simply by virtue of longer note-values and legato phrasing. But Babbitt himself is quite clear that, for example, the single, eighteen-minute span of the String Quartet No. 3 (1969–70) 'does not instance any cherished "formal" pattern created by conjoined repetitions'. There is recurrence beneath the surface: 'there is a fundamental and—I trust—helpful articulation into four "parallel" sections, created by the pitch structure, for—to within familiar transformations—the linear dispositions and ordering of the pitch-classes, the linear consistency of the aggregates and the order of aggregate progression of these sections are identical'.[21] The problem of perception entailed

---

[21] Note issued with the original LP recording, TV34515S.

in such deeply submerged continuities has been widely acknowledged, and Babbitt's defenders have countered arguments that too much in his music depends on inherently inaudible intellectual contrivance by raising the possibility of a kind of 'aggregate hearing' which, while it 'marks a profound reinterpretation of musical information, a fundamental shift in the construal of what we hear', is not fundamentally different from 'tonal hearing' in its dependence on 'two interrelated ways of indexing pitch events: by content and by order'.[22] One positive judgement is that Babbitt's work 'appears to have extended the musical universe in a multitude of directions and respects and has taken it near to the bounds of human conceptual and perceptual capacity, while taking it near as well to the heights of contemporary intellectual accomplishments',[23] and this view has been reinforced more recently in Andrew Mead's conclusion concerning the virtues of a music in which

nothing is unconnected. . . . Compositional decisions at any level will ramify into every level, so that our sense of progression invokes not just our immediate sense of the moment but how that moment is echoed and reflected through the depths. . . . Babbitt's music depends on the tension between levels, the interplay between the specifics of a moment, or a passage, or a piece, and their contexts within a passage, a piece, or his work as a whole, and ultimately within the chromatic world of the twelve-tone system. It is this inclusiveness that makes his work most deeply and affectingly human.[24]

Understandably, admirers of Babbitt's music have refused to accept the dangerous historical argument that the initiatives composers take in the direction of new technical complexity must always and inevitably render their music incomprehensible to their immediate contemporaries.

Babbitt's account of the attempt to perform his *Relata I* (1965) is a classic tale of the mutual incomprehension which can arise between a traditionally constituted orchestra and a total serialist.[25] Predictably, in view of the difficulties (of rhythm, in particular) which his music usually presents to performers, Babbitt was involved, during the 1960s and 1970s, with electro-acoustic techniques. Nevertheless, like Xenakis and other pioneers, he has been reluctant to deny himself the sophisticated sound-resources available from traditional instruments, and his later works have consistently shunned the synthesizer and the tape. It is his vocal compositions, like *Philomel* for soprano, recorded soprano, and synthesized accompaniment on tape (1963-4), and *The Head of the Bed* for soprano and four instruments (1982), with their vividly projected texts, which offer the most direct and dramatic demonstrations of that 'humanity' celebrated by Mead. Yet the total interconnectedness of a Babbitt score remains a challenge

---

[22]   Mead, *Introduction to Babbitt*, 13.
[23]   Benjamin Boretz, 'Babbitt', in *Dictionary of Twentieth-Century Music*, ed. J. Vinton (London, 1974), 48.
[24]   Mead, *Introduction to Babbitt*, 263.
[25]   Milton Babbitt, 'On *Relata I*', in R. S. Hines (ed.), *The Orchestral Composer's Point of View* (Norman, Okla., 1970), 11-38.

Ex. 11.6. Babbitt, *Canonical Form*, bar 304 to the end

to performers and listeners alike, even though there is something more classical than modernist about the way his compositions—while they embrace remarkable diversity of detail, such as the clearly perceptible contrasts in the third quartet between traditionally consonant and dissonant intervals—celebrate order and exult in rationality. For all its abundant nervous energy, its twitching, febrile surfaces, this music never sounds neurotic; the microscopic motive-forms suggest a positive, powerful life-force, and, at his most imaginative, as in *Canonical Form* (1983) for piano, Babbitt balances playfulness and reflection in beguiling equilibrium. Expectations can be contradicted just as explicitly as in earlier classical music, by surprising intervallic combinations, novel rhythmic gestures, strongly contrasted spacings. But the predominant unity of the whole is never in doubt, and as an example of what Mead terms the 'grand synthesis' of Babbitt's later manner, the 'interplay among three different registral continuities' in *Canonical Form* can be heard, and enjoyed, even without a more sophisticated perception of the intricacies of its 'superarray structure'.[26] In context, the focus on the lower register which is sustained at the end, together with the extensive use of repeated notes, creates a satisfying sense of completion, of logical arrival (Ex. 11.6).

On a larger scale, and with its demonstration of Babbitt's willingness to align himself with well-established classical genres, the Piano Concerto (1985), 'perhaps the most elaborate work Babbitt has ever undertaken',[27] offers a still more formidable technical display. Mead has described the concerto's use of 'a twelve-part all-partition hyperaggregate array type',[28] and this super-rational framework underpins the predominant aural impression of volatile atoms of material tamed and moulded by a mind, and an aural imagination, to which total, yet constantly diversified integration is the only valid source of both beauty and memorability. The Concerto is not forbiddingly opaque to the ear: there are perceptible distinctions between sections which emphasize particular registers and tone-colours: there are also well-characterized contrasts between the sustaining orchestra and the skittering, capricious piano. Yet these diverse elements never break free of that single, controlling sensibility which prevents contrast from growing, modernistically, into sustained and all-pervading tension. It is on these grounds, rather than the music's extreme elaboration of detail, that few if any other composers of significance have followed the sustained rigour of Babbitt's unremittingly precise charting of serialism's inherent properties. His chosen path has proved to be a very personal one, and most other composers, even those who more than match him in textural complexity, have been less inclined to carry through so consistently such intricately integrated precompositional strategies in their pursuit of that uncompromising immediacy of feeling which lies at the heart of late twentieth-century modernism.

---

[26] Mead, *Introduction to Babbitt*, 213.
[27] Ibid. 228.   [28] Ibid.

12   THREE INDIVIDUALISTS

Michael Tippett (1905–98), Olivier Messiaen (1908–92), and Elliott Carter (b. 1908) have been highly regarded throughout the second half of the twentieth century for their integrity and individuality. All three began as relatively conservative, tonal composers. Then, after 1945, they moved away from an overriding reliance on tonality and traditional formal designs, though without making any significant commitment to the kind of post-tonal structuring available through the twelve-note technique. Both Tippett and Messiaen reintroduced elements of tonal thought during their later years, while Carter did not, but all three maintained an essentially modernist approach to style and structure.

In each case that essential modernism resides in the balance between stratified textures and juxtaposed formal segments on the one hand, and the coherence of consistent stylistic qualities and harmonic procedures on the other. It is therefore primarily in matters of musical character that differences are to be found. With Messiaen, his Roman Catholic faith is the defining attribute, promoting a music in which the turbulence and torments of individual human concerns are dissolved into timeless contemplation: 'his music exudes a joy that the old chains of cause and effect have been forgotten, and that chords can be moved about in a symmetrical universe that imposes no single flow of time'.[1] While by no means depriving the music of all ambiguity—Paul Griffiths shrewdly notes that 'there is a profound ambiguity between the personal and the universal in his work'[2]—this means that the discontinuous coherences of Messiaen's works are utterly different in effect from the less stable, more directly human qualities present in both Tippett and Carter. Ultimately, nevertheless, all three composers share the ability to transcend the pessimism that is the most pervasive of all emotional states in later twentieth-century 'high' culture. Though without Messiaen's Catholic certainties, Tippett and Carter both retain the elements of an idealistic belief in the capacity of humanity to prosper and even progress, and in the power of art to celebrate human achievements rather than merely to reflect on human failings. Carter's later musical style is more attuned to solemn eulogy—as in 'Remembrance' (1988: No. 2 of *Three Occasions*)—than to anguished lament. Tippett's late setting of Yeats, *Byzantium* (1991), although considerably more sceptical and circumspect in its celebration of the human

---

[1] Paul Griffiths, *Olivier Messiaen and the Music of Time* (London, 1985), 16–17.
[2] Ibid. 74.

capacity to increase self-understanding than the unequivocally optimistic hymn to spiritual, psychological rebirth that ends his first opera *The Midsummer Marriage* (1945–52), is also far from the unsparing confrontation of despair (no less human, far less hopeful) found in many younger modernist composers.[3]

Tippett 1

In strong contrast to his younger English contemporary, Benjamin Britten, Tippett matured slowly as a composer, and his early interests (especially the instrumental music of Beethoven) proved to be of lasting importance.[4] Long study and severe self-criticism combined to ensure that the first works he allowed to survive date from the late 1930s, but the last of these, the Concerto for Double String Orchestra (1939), is not merely evidence of a newly matured composer's freshness of style and sophistication of technique: it is one of the finest works for the medium ever written, and one of the best British compositions of the century.

The concerto is, in the broadest sense, neo-classical: a modern but formidably well-integrated recreation of older stylistic elements which are, historically, pre-classical. The flexible rhythms and vigorous contrapuntal textures recall the English madrigals and fantasies of the sixteenth and seventeenth centuries, transmuted through a jazz-inspired exuberance and a pervasive modality suggested by folk music itself and those modern British composers influenced by its idioms. The uninhibited melodiousness and radiantly diatonic sheen of the texture at the end clearly proclaim a composer committed to positive statement, and even if nothing were known about Tippett's involvement in amateur music-making, or his pacifism, it would be possible to assert with confidence that this was the work of no ivory-tower composer (Ex. 12.1).

Yet the sheer passion of Tippett's commitment to ideas, as well as his openness to musical inspiration, created problems of transmission and translation which he had to fight hard to solve. In the oratorio *A Child of our Time* (1939–41), the timely theme of racial persecution could be expressed in music of maximum directness—hence the incorporation of Negro spirituals, and here the strong contrasts between the spirituals and Tippett's own music offer a foretaste of the fully fledged modernism he would embrace after 1960. Moreover, when Tippett moved on from public to more private concerns in his first opera, *The Midsummer Marriage* (1945–52), the subject-matter and its mode of verbal expression became more complex, risking both incongruity and incoherence. The dramatic theme is still a very simple one: maturity, fulfilment, and the ability

---

[3] See Arnold Whittall, '*Byzantium*: Tippett, Yeats and the Limitations of Affinity', *Music and Letters*, 74 (1993), 383–98.

[4] The most substantial study of Tippett's life and works is Ian Kemp, *Tippett: The Composer and his Music*, rev. edn. (Oxford, 1987). For Tippett's writings, see *Tippett on Music*, ed. M. Bowen (Oxford, 1995).

Ex. 12.1. Tippett, *Concerto for Double String Orchestra,* 3rd movt., ending

to relate to others can only be attained through self-knowledge and self-acceptance; and Tippett's music is fortunately capable of illustrating how such a state can be attained much more directly and convincingly than his words or stage directions. The richness and spontaneity of the musical language employed in the opera—and in the two major instrumental works of this period:

Ex. 12.1. (*cont.*)

the Symphony No. 1 (1944–5) and the String Quartet No. 3 (1945–6)—proved that the Concerto for Double String Orchestra was no happy accident: the manner presented through such an appropriate medium in the concerto was capable of considerable extension and enrichment, and it found its apotheosis in *The Midsummer Marriage* with its satisfyingly positive conclusion depicting the joyful union of two lovers who have completed their psychological rites of passage.

Only a composer with supreme confidence in his musical language could have used it to express such supreme confidence, and for most of the next decade Tippett's music was dominated by the principle of the ultimate, positive major triad. The Piano Concerto (1953–5) and the Symphony No. 2 (1956–7) both reflect the richness of the world created for the opera, though in the symphony the lyric impulse yields its pre-eminence to a more forceful rhythmic profile and sharper thematic outlines. A transition had begun, and *King Priam* (1958–61), Tippett's second opera, reveals the elements of a new manner: the ultimate possibility of tonal resolution is finally stifled by a curious, disembodied cadence (Ex. 12.2). Instrumental colours and groups alternate and conflict in mosaic-like rather

Ex. 12.2. Tippett, *King Priam*, ending

than developmental contexts, and the lyric impulse is compressed and burnished to yield a new, uncompromising clarity.

Tippett's use of tonality had been no more literally imitative of classical and romantic practice than that of most other modern masters, but he could only abandon his reliance on the expressive power of the triad as the embodiment of positive resolution at the cost of entering a different, darker world of expression. In the years after the completion of *King Priam* the implications of this new situation were worked out with characteristic single-mindedness and resource.

Messiaen 1

For Messiaen, as for Carter, the late 1940s were the critical years of change. When Messiaen's career began, with the short organ piece *Le Banquet céleste* (1928), and the *Préludes* for piano (1929), Debussy had been dead for little more than a decade. Messiaen acknowledged Debussy as his most important musical forebear, even though he had little sympathy for Debussy's way of life and lack of serious Christian concerns. For Messiaen it was not enough to be a religious composer; he saw himself as a theological composer, dedicated to the task of reconciling human imperfections and divine glory through the medium of art.

Such an aim might easily have led to the cultivation of a popular, or at any rate conservative, style. Yet Messiaen was never concerned to provide liturgical material for average choirs, organists, and congregations, and his approach—the use of relatively radical techniques to express an unquestioning acceptance of Catholic dogma—contrasted markedly with that of equally didactic Marxist composers who used conservative techniques to express supposedly revolutionary social and political concepts. In a revealing interview, Messiaen voiced his detestation of most aspects of modern life, both social and political, and summed up his view of the present in terms of a pervading bad taste.[5] He much preferred the idea of the ancient Assyrian or Sumerian civilizations, and it

[5] Olivier Messiaen, *Music and Color: Conversations with Claude Samuel*, trans. E. T. Glasgow (Portland, Oreg., 1994), 33.

therefore made sense for him to exploit certain aspects of non-Western music, as well as relying extensively on such a purely natural, non-human, musical phenomenon as bird-song.

Just as Debussy was decisively influenced in his formative years by both Russian and French masters, so Messiaen's early work owed something to the erotic mysticism of Skryabin as well as to the sensuous religiosity of Gounod and Franck. The example of Debussy himself was paramount, however, and although Messiaen once believed that it was no longer possible to compose operas, he always claimed that *Pelléas et Mélisande* had influenced him more than any other single work. Messiaen was well able to continue and intensify the rapt, contemplative moods and the timeless reticence typical of much of *Pelléas*. Yet, like Debussy, Messiaen was by no means exclusively attached to understatement: nor was he concerned to pursue the organic integration of the diverse materials he used in his larger scale works. The contrast between meditation and jubilation is likely to be more evident in these compositions than any sense of gradual transition from one to the other.

The technical importance of Debussy's example was far-reaching, and Messiaen responded to it with that keen analytical intelligence which made him much sought after as a teacher. In particular, his system of pitch modes, whereby seven different scales and those transpositions of them which do not merely present the same pitches in a different order can be used to produce 'non-functional' tonal harmony, represented both an extension and a codification of Debussian chromaticism, whose own relationship to systematic modality had been so fruitfully ambiguous.[6]

A simple example of the extended tonality which these modes of limited transposition make possible occurs in the seventh movement of Messiaen's *Quatuor pour la fin du temps* (1941) (Ex. 12.3).[7] This passage uses the first version of Mode II, an octatonic scale which makes conventional cadential progressions impossible; any triad treated as tonic cannot be supported by its regular dominant or subdominant. Even so, the phrase-structure of this extract is conventional, with the second three bars a sequential repetition of the first a minor third lower, and the final six bars an extended sequential repetition, another minor third lower. In addition, although no 'pure' triads are employed, in each phrase there is a clear distinction between relatively tense or dissonant chords—those including the clash of a minor second—and the less tense added sixths with which each phrase ends. These 'resolutions' enable the successive tonalities of A major, F♯ major, and E♭ major to be hinted at rather than firmly established, but at this stage of his development Messiaen still retained a fundamental allegiance to tonality as an ultimate structural force.

Messiaen shared Debussy's dislike of sonata form, though his view of rhythm

---

[6] See Ch. 2, pp. 22–7.
[7] Olivier Messiaen, *Technique of My Musical Language*, trans. J. Satterfield (London, 1957), ii. 54, Ex. 359.

Ex. 12.3. Messiaen, *Quatuor pour la fin du temps*, 7th movt., beginning (reduction used in Messiaen's *Technique of My Musical Language*)

'as arising from an extension of durations in time rather than from a division of time'[8]—a result of his close study of *The Rite of Spring*—was a new factor of considerable significance. Debussy also had a notably ambivalent attitude to Wagner, and Messiaen in turn established certain Wagnerian associations through his interest in the Tristan story. Messiaen made it clear that this archetypal account of the strengths and weaknesses of human love attracted him only to the extent that, even at its greatest, human love palely reflects divine love, thus providing a link between life and death, man and God. In a trilogy of works composed between 1945 and 1949, Messiaen provided an elaborate treatment of this 'theology of love'. The song cycle *Harawi* (1945), the *Turangalîla* Symphony (1946–8) (Turangalîla is the Hindu word for love song), and the *Cinq rechants* for twelve unaccompanied voices (1949) are a formidable theologico-aesthetic statement, but they are also a stylistic turning-point. As the symphony shows, Messiaen was content to employ quite simple structures, often involving the alternation and repetition of self-contained sections, on a very large scale. Already, too, there was a great variety of material, ranging from florid ornamental lines deriving from transmuted bird-song to a rhythmic 'series' and

---

[8] Robert Sherlaw Johnson, *Messiaen* (London, 1975), 32.

simpler, chordal, triadic themes. Messiaen may have sensed that the expressive and structural weight being placed on these triadic 'resolutions', not only in the symphony, but also in large works like the *Visions de l'Amen* for two pianos (1943) and the *Trois petites Liturgies de la Présence Divine* (1944), was not sufficiently justified in a purely linguistic sense; or he may simply have decided to give the more complex harmonic elements already present greater prominence, just as bird-song and chant-like thematic material, densely harmonized, began to oust more traditional melodic phrases. The end of the war meant for many European composers the chance to discover serialism: for many it was to lead to conversion, and even for Messiaen, at a time when his pupils included young firebrands like Pierre Boulez,[9] it demanded serious consideration and left permanent effects.

Carter 1

It was in a Paris dominated by the neo-classicism of Stravinsky that the young Elliott Carter studied from 1932 to 1935.[10] As a friend and admirer of Charles Ives, Carter could never have felt as close to the great European tradition as either Tippett or Messiaen, yet he was equally cautious about imitating the exuberant and often chaotic experimentation of Ives, with his dense atonal polyphony, his constant quotations of hymn tunes, popular songs, and other borrowed material, ranging from *Sir Roger de Coverley* to Beethoven's Fifth Symphony. Carter opted for discipline and clarity, so that during the 1930s and early 1940s he seemed to be treading a path roughly similar to that of the leading American neo-classicist, Aaron Copland. Yet this cautious beginning was the foundation of one of the most complex and imaginative stylistic transformations in twentieth-century music. Messiaen's religious beliefs continued to shape his musical subject-matter after the dogma of serialism had failed to compel his adherence; Tippett's voracious absorption of literary, philosophical, and psychological imagery stimulated more far-reaching musical explorations than a musical language framed by triadic rhetoric could contain; and Carter, too, was decisively influenced by extra-musical factors:

Before the end of the Second World War, it became clear to me, partly as a result of re-reading Freud and others, and thinking about psychoanalysis, that we were living in a world where . . . physical and intellectual violence would always be a problem, and that the whole conception of human nature underlying the neo-classic esthetic amounted to a sweeping under the rug of things that, it seemed to me, we had to deal with in a less oblique and resigned way.[11]

---

[9] See Pierre Boulez, 'Olivier Messiaen', in *Orientations*, ed. J. J. Nattiez, trans. M. Cooper (London, 1986), 404–20.

[10] The standard study of Carter's work is David Schiff, *The Music of Elliott Carter* (London, 1998). See also *Elliott Carter: Collected Essays and Lectures, 1937–95*, ed. J. W. Bernard (Rochester, NY, 1997).

[11] Allen Edwards, *Flawed Words and Stubborn Sounds: A Conversation with Elliott Carter* (New York, 1971), 61.

After his return to America in 1935 Carter's style in works like the ballets *Pocahontas* (1939) and *The Minotaur* (1947) resembled Hindemith and Stravinsky as well as Copland. As long as he remained committed to some kind of tonality these were likely to remain his most basic influences, yet they did not inhibit the evolution of a vigorously confident manner nor the use of substantial forms. The Piano Sonata (1945–6), for all its tonal framework, is far from palely neo-classical, and suggests an almost epic imagination, a confrontation of major expressive issues of the kind acknowledged in the above quotation. Elsewhere, Carter defined the neo-classic aim as to make music 'anti-individualistic, to sound almost machine-made', and the basic impulse in his move away from such concerns after 1946 was a desire to rethink 'the rhythmic means of what had begun to seem a very limited routine used in most contemporary and older Western music'. So it was to African, Indian, Arab, and Balinese music that he turned, as well as very un-neo-classical Western composers like Skryabin and Ives. 'The result was a way of evolving rhythms and rhythmic continuities, sometimes called "metric modulation":' a further result was the abandonment of neo-classical structures with their 'static repetitiveness', and with the loss of traditional forms came the loss of tonality itself.[12] The parallel with Messiaen's increasing involvement with aspects of Eastern culture needs no stressing.

All these tendencies and tensions are found in the fine Sonata for Cello and Piano (1948), a transitional work in which only the second of the four movements uses key signatures. This was apparently written first—the first movement certainly came last—and the key signatures are the result of a musical character described by Carter as 'a breezy treatment of a type of pop music, [which] verges on a parody of some Americanizing colleagues of the time. . . . It makes explicit the undercurrent of jazz technique suggested in the previous movement by the freely performed melody against a strict rhythm.'[13]

The Cello Sonata is remarkable for its anticipation in admittedly simple form of many of the principal features of Carter's later, more explicitly modernist masterpieces. Thus it begins and ends with 'extreme dissociation' between the two instruments: the cello plays 'a long melody in rather free style, while the piano percussively marks a regular clock-like ticking'. As Carter said, these differences of character are 'one of the points of the piece'. They are nevertheless differences which are so far from being immutable as to be interchangeable, and the whole work ends with the cello using the ticking rhythm and the piano recalling the expressive melody. The drama of changing characters is significantly exploited at the end of the second movement, where the piano 'predicts the notes and speed of the cello's opening of the third', and also at the end of the third movement, where the cello 'predicts . . . the piano's opening of the fourth'. In the simplest terms, then, the texture of the sonata is concerned with mediation between relative dissociation and relative association, a process which can be clearly observed in the first movement itself. 'Association' begins at the point

---

[12] Carter, *Collected Essays*, 228–9.   [13] Ibid. 230.

where the piano echoes the last three notes of the cello's first long phrase, and reaches unity of character and rhythm at the climax just before what can still be defined as the recapitulation (Ex. 12.4).

Tippett 2

After the completion of *King Priam* in 1961, Michael Tippett began to work out the implications of his new style in the most direct way by using music from the opera in two further works, the Piano Sonata No. 2 (1962) and the Concerto for Orchestra (1963). *King Priam* is a heroic tragedy, and its study of men caught in the web of violence and conflict is as intelligent and compassionate as—perhaps—only someone dedicated to non-violence could achieve. To this extent it has more in common with *A Child of our Time* than with *The Midsummer Marriage*, but the stylistic innovations—the juxtaposition, repetition (usually in varied forms), and combination of specific types of material and colour—raised structural issues which stimulated further exploration. The Piano Sonata No. 2, a single ten-minute movement, uses eight different types of material (including motives from Act II of the opera), alternating and intercutting in a sequence which might seem highly arbitrary, when set out diagrammatically, yet creates a satisfying psychological progression in performance. The great danger of this kind of form is that its wholehearted modernism might produce an episodic succession in which there is no decisive reason why *one* sequence of events should be preferable to any other. Yet Tippett's instinct ensures essential coherence; as he himself commented, 'the formal unity comes from the balance of similarity and contrast'.[14] Tippett avoids a static effect through the dramatic excitement engendered by the unpredictable interaction of easily identifiable thematic elements; the sonata's material ranges from highly dissonant and percussive chords to a lyrical, quasi-tonal melody which recalls the world of the Piano Concerto and *The Midsummer Marriage*. It is certainly possible to dispute the assertion that the work is atonal, for the composer's technique of repeating material at the same pitch, and of allowing occasional chords to approximate to triadic formations, can create at least a residue of tonal feeling, even if, as in *King Priam* itself, the ending avoids any obvious sense of resolution.

After pursuing these techniques on a larger scale in the Concerto for Orchestra, and creating a particularly telling contrast between the florid melodic continuity of the central Lento and the more disparate, variously coloured elements of the flanking movements, Tippett returned to vocal composition in a work which is extremely difficult to perform yet is one of his most remarkable. *The Vision of St Augustine* for solo baritone, chorus, and orchestra (1966) is a

---

[14] Tippett's note issued with the original LP recording, Philips 6500 534.

Ex. 12.4. Carter, Sonata for cello and piano, 1st movt., bars 95–105

three-part setting of a text which combines Augustine's own words with quotations from the Latin Bible and other sources. Augustine was deeply concerned with the meaning of Time—and Eternity—and Tippett prefaced his score with T. S. Eliot's line 'and all is always now', adding in his introductory notes that 'we cannot in this temporal existence experience a true present'. Time-structure is of great importance to the work, and the page facing the first bars of the score sets out the fourteen tempos (ranging from crotchet $c.56$ to dotted crotchet $c.168$) which operate during its course. *The Vision of St Augustine* projects a great melodic and thematic richness which is fully equal to its ambitious 'programme'; and this richness, and an ease in the handling of a 'new' idiom, display satisfying links with the ecstatic lyricism of Tippett's earlier manner. The new style achieves its clearest definition, and most ambitiously proportioned form, in conjunction with fundamental features of the old.

Tippett's third opera, *The Knot Garden* (1970), is another parable of the need for self-knowledge and an account of its attainment by a diverse group of characters (including a musician and a psychoanalyst), whose stylized environments and inter-reactions are projected through music as economical and intense as that of *The Vision of St Augustine*. The text is not without a characteristic awkwardness: jarring quotations, slang, high-flown imagery, jostle together in an idiosyncratic mixture which is nevertheless vindicated by the force of its need for just this particular dramatic form and musical setting.

The progress of the characters towards positive self-realization is dramatized through music of extraordinary imagination, often hectically disjointed, but equally capable of the simplest lyrical phrases. Arias, ensembles, and brief orchestral interludes provide a framework of precisely the right degree of formality, and the music is often disruptively critical of both formality and convention, as in the hysterical coloratura of Denise's long scena (Act I, Scene 13) (Ex. 12.5).

Equally ambiguous is the role of tonal stress, with the note B exercising an underlying force which rises most obviously to the surface in Act II with the quotation of Schubert's song 'Die liebe Farbe'. This technique of reminiscence is carried further in *Songs for Dov* (1971), an offshoot of the opera in the form of an extended cycle for one of the characters, and is also crucial to the Symphony No. 3 (1972).

While even less tonally explicit than *The Knot Garden*, the symphony is closer to the opera and also more remote from traditional formal types than is the Third Piano Sonata (1973). The first of its two parts presents a polarity between the concepts of 'Arrest' and 'Movement', immobility and propulsion. These entities alternate five times each, getting progressively longer until the fifth recurrence of the 'Movement' material is cut short to make way for a combination of the two elements (Fig. 87). The remainder of Part One is a Lento in which there is a change of polarity, with the elements now representing Discontinuity and Continuity—discontinuity in the sense of the constant repetition of rather static shapes. The repetitions of the viola melody which represents Continuity grow shorter until, on the fifth and last appearance, the original thirty bars are reduced to two. The movement ends, not with the two elements combined, but with a sixth reference to the Discontinuous material.

The first part of the symphony therefore involves two very different kinds of opposition but a similar means of simple structural intensification in each

Ex. 12.5. Tippett, *The Knot Garden*, from Act 1, Scene 13, finale

case: a more convincingly symphonic procedure than that of the works written immediately after *King Priam*, with their greater number of short contrasting segments. Part Two is more sectional in structure, beginning with a turbulent Allegro molto based around five contrasted types of material. Apparently Tippett originally intended to follow this with a sequence of purely instrumental Blues, but his inclination to parallel what he called the 'abstraction' of Part One with the 'dramatics' of Part Two led him inevitably to vocal music. In that the four of his own poems which he sets are songs of innocence and experience, the structural dualities of Part One may have generated the dramatic contrasts of Part Two. Further dualities involve the quotation and distortion of the finale of Beethoven's Ninth Symphony (Tippett's fourth poem recalls Schiller's *Ode to Joy*) as a kind of goad to Tippett's own propulsive style, and the contrast between the transfigured Blues idiom of the first three settings and the 'original' Tippett of the last—complete with references to Part One of the symphony. Yet the grand affirmation ending Tippett's text—'We sense a huge compassionate power/To heal, to love'—is still not matched by the sort of transcendentally lyrical peroration and triadic resolution most memorably achieved in *The Midsummer*

Marriage. Instead, a sequence of orchestral chords (alternately loud and soft, and all discords) intone a 'coda' in which alternative gestures seem frozen into immobility. The power is sensed: it cannot yet be used for, as Tippett said, 'at the very end, I wanted to preserve the underlying polarities'.[15]

The Third Symphony employs the symphonic principle in a very personal way. The Third Piano Sonata is, at least in outline, more traditional, for its three continuous movements are, respectively, a 'fast sonata-allegro, i.e. . . . a statement of contrasted materials', a slow set of four variations on a theme comprising 'a succession of seventeen elaborate chords', and a fast finale which is 'an ABA-shaped toccata'.[16] In place of the shifting contrasts and cumulative superimpositions of the symphony, Tippett adopted more formal, symmetrical procedures suggested by the visual mirror-image of a pianist's hands moving inwards and outwards between the extremes of the keyboard. Thus 'the independence of the hands is explored chiefly in the outer fast movements and the unity in the middle'. In the slow movement, each of the four variations transposes the basic sequence of chords up a minor third, 'thus returning in Variation Four to the initial level'. Then, in the finale, the central section repeats the first in mirror form. Such a comprehensive rediscovery of traditional structural features is satisfying, since, far from displaying a dilution of Tippett's musical language, the Third Sonata is characteristically forceful and eloquent. For a composer with Tippett's associative mind, it never seemed that compositions which proceeded entirely 'by statement' (like the Second Sonata) would prove permanently attractive. The dramatic nature of *King Priam* suggested a musical approach which had a powerful effect on Tippett's style, but his finest music is more wide-ranging and ultimately more appealing.

Messiaen 2

Messiaen's short piano composition *Mode de valeurs et d'intensités* (Mode of Durations and Dynamics), written in 1949, is often loosely described as 'totally serial', but the title itself suggests that the piece presents an extension of Messiaen's own modal techniques. It does not even follow the Schoenbergian principle of fixing the twelve pitches in sequence; as in all Messiaen's earlier modal works, the notes of the mode need not appear in any specific order: some may be omitted altogether, others used as often as the composer desires. More significant in terms of serialism in this piece is the association between certain registers, durations, and dynamics. The keyboard is divided into three regions, which overlap to a considerable extent. The lowest region has the longest durations (quaver to dotted semibreve), the highest the shortest (demisemiquaver to dotted crotchet), but some durations recur in two or three regions. Messiaen

---

[15] *Tippett on Music*, 100.
[16] Tippett's notes, issued with the original LP recording, Philips 6500 534.

employs twelve different durations and twelve different types of attack (including 'normal'), but only seven dynamic markings (*ppp* to *fff*)—a more realistic arrangement than the twelve, ranging from *ppppp* to *fffff*, which are theoretically possible.

As a reaction to the delayed exploration of serial music in Europe in the late 1940s, this piece, along with its close contemporaries *Cantéyodjayâ*, *Neumes rythmiques* (both 1949), and *Île de Feu* I and II (1950), has undeniable historical importance. We know that, 'as early as 1944, during the course of his discussions of Berg's *Lyric Suite* in his composition classes, Messiaen spoke out against the tendency of the second Viennese school to experiment exclusively with pitch structures while adhering to traditional conceptions of rhythm and form:'[17] yet Messiaen's style was never likely to turn permanently in the direction of such uncompromisingly unified pattern-making. Twelve-note pitch serialism had a permanent effect on his later music, but his only orthodox twelve-note piece was the fifth movement of *Livre d'orgue* (1951), and his use of various kinds of rhythmic motives, modes, and series, which predated *Mode de valeurs et d'intensités*, was more a result of his continuing interest in Eastern music—principally the 120 deçi-tâlas of Sharngadeva—than an outcome of Western pitch-serialism as such. The major works of the 1950s, with their increasing concentration on the atonal polyphony of bird-song and the colours of tuned percussion, were consistent in their rejection of any all-embracing serial system: *Réveil des oiseaux* (1953) derives its material entirely from thirty-eight different bird-songs, and the gigantic seven-volume *Catalogue d'oiseaux* (1956–8) brings together elements as potentially disparate as tonality, modality (of pitch and rhythm), and twelve-note sets in free permutations. *Chronochromie* (1960) is characteristic in its presentation of extremely complex textures in terms of simple formal outlines involving much repetition, and in *Et Exspecto Resurrectionem Mortuorum* (1964) the emphasis on more monumental thematic outlines and simpler rhythmic patterns was primarily the result of a conception which envisaged open-air performance—the work is scored for wind, brass, and metal percussion. Each movement is prefaced with a biblical quotation and the finale, 'and I heard the voice of a great multitude', is a rare example of a Messiaen movement entirely founded on a regular pulsation. An almost unbearable tension results from this inexorable reiteration. The bonds of the small form were burst, and Messiaen embarked on three works on a much larger scale than anything since the *Turangalîla* Symphony of twenty years earlier.

La Transfiguration de Notre Seigneur Jésus-Christ (1963–9) is an oratorio in two seven-part sections, or septenaries. Once again all the typical stylistic elements are present: the repetitive forms, the chant-like monody, bird-song, Greek metres, colour chords. In this work there is also a greater use of tonal concords, most explicitly of all in the massive chorales which end the two septenaries.

---

[17] Johnson, *Messiaen*, 105.

The simplification of thematic outline and rhythmic pattern which *Et Exspecto* displayed is therefore extended here to harmony, and it is confirmation of the sureness of instinct with which Messiaen composed that these triads should sound like a rediscovery, not a retreat, proclaiming his ability to associate and control the most diverse elements without incongruity.

Such interactive diversity is also to be found in Messiaen's first major organ work for almost two decades, the nine *Méditations sur le Mystère de la Sainte Trinité* (1969) and in the huge *Des canyons aux étoiles* (1974) for solo piano, horn, and orchestra. With their references to the text of the *Summa Theologica*, the *Méditations* present a parallel summation of Messiaen's musical language, covering the widest range from simple tonal and triadic progressions to the metrically complex, anti-tonal textures of the 1950s and 1960s. Yet the summation itself generated a new technique, for Messiaen had ceased to be entirely content with a musical language of explicit symbolism, and had devised an actual alphabet of pitch and duration in order to translate specific words into tones. The partial use of this alphabet is evidence of its experimental nature. With it, Messiaen associated musical figures for grammatical cases and also for the twin concepts of 'being' and 'having' (the latter an inversion of the former). Such 'translations' of texts occur only in two movements, however, and of greater musical importance to the work as a whole are the motto themes representing various aspects of God, the presence of three tritones in the principal version of which suggests that Messiaen was impervious to the traditionally diabolical associations of that interval. As a contributory stylistic aspect of the composition as a whole the alphabet exists on one extreme of a spectrum primarily notable for structural simplicity, the avoidance of extended contrapuntal textures, and the admission that modality can engender tonality.

The seventh movement is particularly suitable for detailed study in that it brings together virtually all the important features of Messiaen's style. The composer described it as falling into three parts, the outer sections an introduction and a coda which unfold the same basic sequence of events, three in all.

The first segment of the Introduction presents a series of seven chords with durations of 6, 7, 5, 8, 9, 11, and 13 semiquavers respectively. Messiaen explained that the chords employ pitches from two modes of limited transposition, 3^2 and 3^1. Combined, these modes provide all twelve chromatic semitones, and only the first of the chords belongs exclusively to either mode (3^2). Other *Méditations* use the third mode more systematically, especially with regard to the triadic elements present in its first and fourth transpositions.

The second segment of the Introduction, *Oiseau de Persépolis*, is a characteristic episode of bird-song—an unidentified bird which Messiaen heard at Persepolis—continuing the irregular rhythmic motion of the first segment, and with much internal repetition. The Introduction then ends with a pedal B (the dominant of the E major which will end the whole movement), over which four dense 'horn-chords' are heard; the first belongs to Mode 3^1, the second and third blend 3^1 and 3^2, and the last, a dominant aggregate in E major, belongs to 3^2.

The Coda of this seventh *Méditation* is one of Messiaen's typically varied recapitulations. The opening chords have the same sequence of durations as those of the Introduction but the pitch sequence is reversed, so that the notes of the Introduction's first chord appear in the Coda's last, and so on. The second section—*Oiseau de Persépolis*—begins with the identical pair of double statements, continues differently, but returns to the original material in the last group of demisemiquavers: the cadence in the Coda is a transposition (down a perfect fifth) of that in the Introduction. Segment Three adds an E to the original B pedal, and this time the horn-chords resolve on to a pure E major triad. All the chords in this final segment of the Coda belong to Mode 3^1 (Ex. 12.6).

These outer sections of the seventh *Méditation* are either harmonic or monodic in character, but the main body of the movement is considerably more complex, and closer in style to the more radical works of earlier years. It is a trio, with the thematic material concentrated in the middle voice. This material 'translates' a sentence from Aquinas—'the Father and Son love, through the Holy

Ex. 12.6. Messiaen, *Méditations*, No. 7, ending

Ex. 12.7. Messiaen, *Méditations*, No. 7, p. 61

Spirit [the love which proceeds] themselves and the human race'—in the following way (Ex. 12.7).

Père	8-note theme (begins as 'Being')
Fils	8-note theme (inverts 'Père': begins as 'Having')

Aiment	10-note theme ('aimer': to love)
Père	repeated
Fils	repeated
par	motto for ablative case
Saint Esprit	prime and retrograde of 'God' motto
Amour	'Aimer' theme repeated
Procédant	each letter 'translated'
Père/Fils/aiment	repeated as before
Race Humaine	each letter 'translated'
par/Saint Esprit	repeated as before
Amour	as before
du	motto for genitive case
Père/du/Fils	repeated as before

This thematic statement involves considerable internal repetition, and the texture is completed by decorative counterpoints, each organized in a different way. The right hand is exclusively occupied with bird-song (the Moroccan Bulbul) which, while thematic in its own terms, is not related by the incidence of its internal repetitions to the text. The pedal part involves a rhythmic ostinato which, while apparently not a specific deçi-tâla (these can be found elsewhere in the work), uses a rhythmic series of the following semiquaver values: 5, 5, 4, 4, 3, 3, 2, 2, 1, 1, 1; followed by a longer value, the duration of which varies on each appearance. This series appears six times in all, with extended, irregular pauses between each statement.

The overall effect of this trio is therefore to suspend any sense of regular rhythmic succession or tonal direction. In terms of the movement as a whole, it is a contrast, but it clearly carries the meditative essence, suspended in both space and time.

Carter 2

It was with the Second String Quartet (1959) that Elliott Carter finally established those stylistic principles which were the logical result of the process of exploration begun in the mid-1940s. This quartet is not merely atonal; 'dependence on thematic recurrence . . . is replaced by an ever-changing series of motives and figures having certain internal relationships with each other'. The single movement is symmetrically divided into nine sections: an Introduction and Conclusion frame four principal movements which in turn are linked by cadenzas for viola, cello, and first violin respectively. The four main movements are each dominated by a single instrument, each of which is given a particular expressive character and its own repertory of speeds and intervals. Thus the Allegro fantastico focuses on the 'whimsical, ornate' first violin, with its

Ex. 12.8. Carter, String Quartet No. 2, beginning

predominant minor thirds and perfect fifths: the Presto scherzando on the 'moderating influence' of the second violin, with emphasis on major thirds: the Andante brings forward the 'almost lamenting' viola (the tritone), and the Allegro the 'romantically free' cello (perfect fourths). 'The separation of the instrumental characters is kept quite distinct throughout the first half of the work but becomes increasingly homogenized up to the Conclusion, at which point the separation re-emerges.'[18]

The opening of the quartet (Ex. 12.8) shows the way in which the character and intervallic material of each instrument is defined. It will be clear that the overall form of the work does not sever all links with the traditional four-movement sequence, just as the decision to define material in terms of certain intervals is still, in the broadest sense, 'thematic'. As far as the listener is concerned, Carter

[18] Carter, *Collected Essays*, 234–5.

is exploiting one of the most basic of all perceptions—the ability to distinguish between the primary intervals, and he is using that fundamental fact as the foundation for his vividly dramatic scenarios, which involve the conflict and interaction of 'thematic' elements in a state of constant transformation.

The dynamic concept of diverse elements gradually coming to fusion, then diffusing to the point of maximum diversity again, is also the groundplan of the Double Concerto for Harpsichord, Piano, and Two Chamber Orchestras (1961). This time, the available intervals are divided into two groups, and since each interval is associated with a certain metronomic speed, a further level of differentiation between the groups becomes possible. As with the Second String Quartet, the single-movement form has a quasi-symmetrical layout, with the Introduction and Conclusion presenting the material in a state of maximum differentiation while the two ensembles come closest to fusion in the central Adagio.

In the Piano Concerto (1966) there is again a division of the available material into two, between a 'concertino' comprising the piano solo and seven other instruments and the 'ripieno' of the rest of the orchestra. The work is in two movements, the first stressing the similarity between the material of both groups, and the second the dissimilarity, a process which obviously shuns the more symmetrical scheme of the Double Concerto, with its return to the original diversity after the greater homogeneity of the central Adagio. The Concerto for Orchestra (1969) has a form which elaborates the basic scheme of the Second String Quartet, with its four distinct 'temperaments', one for each instrument. The Concerto for Orchestra has four main movements, each at a different speed, each featuring a different combination of instruments. Instead of following one another, however, the four movements interpenetrate throughout, each coming into focus successively, but always against the background of the other three.

Carter's three major works of the 1960s, with their enthralling and exhilarating feeling for the ebb and flow of richly detailed instrumental drama, may seem the ultimate in polyphonic complexity, but the Third String Quartet (1971) develops the simultaneous statement of different movements a stage further. Here the basic duality (first violin and cello, second violin and viola) is exploited to the extent that 'the two duos should perform as two groups as separated from each other as is conveniently possible, so that the listener can not only perceive them as two separate sound sources but also be aware of the combinations they form with each other'.[19] The first duo plays four 'movements' or types of material, initially (and always 'quasi rubato') in the order Furioso (A), Leggerissimo (B), Andante espressivo (C), and Pizzicato giocoso (D), which alternate to form this sequence: A B C D B A D C B D A C A. The second duo, 'playing in quite strict rhythm throughout', has six 'movements', which move through a different sequence. Each of the ten 'movements' emphasizes a particular interval, with the

---

[19] See Carter's note in the score.

eleventh interval, the major second, being a shared resource, and the polyphonic process is such that each of the Duo I movements is heard at some stage in combination with each of the Duo II movements.

Carter 3

In the works of the 1960s and the early 1970s Carter came closest to a kind of turbulent, fragmented expressionism in which images of disorder and anxiety could on occasion overwhelm the essentially positive view of the world and of humanity embodied in his intricately balanced structures and subtly rational procedures for the organization of pitch and rhythm. The importance of a rational approach to the composer–listener relation is evident in Carter's remark that 'while I believe that music should be continuously surprising, I believe it should be so in the sense that whatever happens should continue an already perceived ongoing process or pattern', and he declared it his business as a composer 'to be sufficiently aware of the probable predictive expectations of the listener who has grasped the process I have begun'.[20] Such a concern with the listener's 'probably predictive expectations' could be one reason why, in the mid-1970s, and after many years of writing large-scale instrumental or orchestral compositions, Carter sought to focus more on music's lyric dimension, and to undertake a series of vocal works: *A Mirror on which to Dwell* (1975), *Syringa* (1978), *In Sleep, in Thunder* (1981), and *Of Challenge and of Love* (1994). In the last of these, Carter sets verse by John Hollander, and the 'focal text' is 'Quatrains from Harp Lake', 'with its brief, vividly contrasting quatrains that have an undercurrent of irony and deep anxiety'.[21] To have ended the work with this poem would nevertheless have been rather too solemn for Carter, and so he actually concludes it with a short, very different movement called 'End of a chapter', in which a flowing yet angular vocal line is punctuated by gruff chords in the piano (Ex. 12.9). The text is prose: 'But when true beauty does finally come crashing at us through the stretched paper of the picturesque, we can wonder how we had for so long been able to remain distracted from its absence.' The effect of Carter's setting is to distance us from the more solemn proposals of 'Quatrains from Harp Lake' while at the same time affirming with a complete lack of ambivalence a belief in the power of art—a belief ironized by the rueful acknowledgement of our regrettable ability to endure the absence of beauty, as well as to rejoice in its presence.[22]

These vocal works, and the parallel series of short pieces for solo instruments or small ensembles beginning with *Changes* for guitar (1983), did not involve any radical changes of technique or style, since Carter continued to exploit his ability to generate freely flowing melodic lines which project a sure sense of direction,

---

[20] Edwards, *Flawed Words*, 87–8.
[21] See Carter's note in the score.
[22] See Arnold Whittall, 'Summer's Long Shadows', *Musical Times*, 138 (Apr. 1997), 14–22.

Ex. 12.9. Carter, *Of Challenge and of Love*, 'End of a chapter', ending

despite the absence of clear-cut motivic processes. Nevertheless, their generally less aggressive atmosphere, compared to such imposing predecessors as the Piano Concerto and the Duo for violin and piano, led David Schiff to speak of a reformulation 'of the relationship between the modern and the classic'.[23] Schiff is a perceptive commentator, yet the overriding quality of Carter's major works of the 1980s and 1990s, including two orchestral trilogies and three concertos, for oboe, violin, and clarinet, as well as the Fourth and Fifth Quartets and other substantial chamber works, is more appropriately thought of as a further refinement of the dialogue, fundamental to modernism, between tendencies to continuity and discontinuity, fragmentation and integration. The musical representation of what Carter himself, in the score of *Penthode* (1985), termed 'the experiences of connectedness and isolation' reaches back to his earliest mature works; these experiences persist, and continue to interact, even if the theatre of their interaction is less explicitly violent and disruptive than it was in the Piano Concerto or the Third Quartet. Schiff's search for a new classicism in the later Carter seems to have been motivated by what he perceives as a change of musical tone—a shift from epic, tragic concerns to a contentment with the utopian vision of ideal equality. Yet the music, in its post-tonal essence, cannot achieve the hierarchic integrity of truly classical, tonal composition. It sustains, with tremendous energy and imagination, a dialogue between similarity and difference, rather than making any decisively classicizing shift from difference to similarity. It is his ability to turn these strategies to such engagingly positive expressive account that defines Carter's achievement, and his music's greatness.[24]

Messiaen 3

Whereas Carter's music since the mid-1970s has embodied a substantial new stage in his development, Messiaen's might be thought to comprise a series of epilogues—alternatively grand and unassuming—to the achievements of his earlier years. Even so, the period includes what many regard as the grand summation of his entire career, the opera, subtitled 'scènes franciscaines', *Saint François d'Assise* (composed 1975–9, orchestrated 1979–83). Though not technically innovatory in terms of Messiaen's own style, this work's transformation of 'opera' into an imposing, pageant-like celebration of spiritual values in confrontation with the worldly and the mortal was a triumphant demonstration of Messiaen's ability to turn modern, secular genres to his own purposes. Although other major composers, since Stravinsky in *Oedipus Rex*, have written innovatory 'anti-operas' which nevertheless work best in an environment normally dedicated to conventional opera, *Saint François* has the vitality and the assur-

---

[23] David Schiff, 'Carter's New Classicism', *College Music Symposium*, 29 (1989), 115.
[24] See Arnold Whittall, 'Modernist Aesthetics, Modernist Music: Some Analytical Perspectives', in J. M. Baker *et al.* (eds.), *Music Theory in Concept and Practice* (Rochester, NY, 1997), 157–80.

ance to equal those achievements, confirming Messiaen's mastery of an harmonic language in which consonance and emancipated dissonance coexist (Ex. 12.10). The originality of Messiaen's materials, and the conviction with which he uses them, enabled him to deploy similar ideas and effects from work to work in ways that would seem self-indulgently repetitive in a lesser talent. So the opera confirms the ritual, ceremonial core, uniting nature and humanity, that powers all Messiaen's compositions, as well as an approach to form-building that raises discontinuity into a force of nature.

Eight years of work on the opera left the composer exhausted, yet two large-scale instrumental scores were to follow. *Le Livre du Saint Sacrement* (1983) is his farewell to the extended cycle for solo organ, while *Éclairs sur l'Au-Délà* (1987–91) is his last major orchestral piece. This sixty-five-minute, eleven-movement contemplation of Christ in majesty is certainly no epilogue. Indeed, it could come to be regarded as the crowning glory of Messiaen's orchestral works, for, while it lacks the sacred/secular, rarefied/vulgar confrontations of *Turangalîla*, and the pungently abstract modernist tensions of *Chronochromie*, it combines rich sonic imagination, spiritual conviction, and grandly conceived, episodic yet cumulative structural design so persuasively (and with none of the opera's sense of using a genre simply because no other was available) as to make it Messiaen's true *summa*.

Tippett 3

Messiaen's preference for the mosaic, his rejection of through-composition (even though the textures of individual formal units are highly homogeneous), indicates an approach to form-building which was shared by Tippett in his later compositions: these include the operas *The Ice Break* (1976) and *New Year* (1988), the large-scale work 'for voices and instruments' *The Mask of Time* (1972–84), a vocal 'scena', *Byzantium* (1989), a fifth string quartet (1990–1), and a valedictory

Ex. 12.10. Messiaen, *Saint François d'Assise*, from Act 3, Tableau 8

Ex. 12.11. Tippett, *Byzantium*, ending

'song without words' for orchestra, *The Rose Lake* (1991–3). The personal overview of issues in politics and philosophy embodied in *The Mask of Time*, and culminating in the humanistic yet utopia-resisting affirmation, 'O man, make peace with your mortality, for this too is god', is a more generalized but no less urgent continuation of the concerns evident in many earlier works, including the Symphony No. 3 and *The Ice Break*, where the possibility of a kind of rebirth, or recovery from the most destructive kind of personal and social conflict, is affirmed. What seemed to be a certainty in *The Midsummer Marriage* is now, as the ending of *New Year* confirms, only a possibility, yet the way in which Tippett's music revived features from its tonal past without rejecting the hard-won developments of later years enabled the composer to present an essentially positive image in his last works. The ending of *Byzantium*, setting Yeats's final line, 'That dolphin-torn, that gong-tormented sea' is both strongly rooted and, in its use of dissonance, unresolved (Ex. 12.11). The inference is that, even if society is doomed to remain persistently unstable and inchoate, as different concepts of liberty and necessity struggle to coexist, humanity itself is capable of acting altruistically, for what it sees as the greater good. Human individuals also remain capable of dreaming, of imagining forms of transcendence—of experiencing moments of vision. It is difficult not to read an element of self-analysis in Tippett's tribute to Holst as managing, 'even early on . . . the sort of odd intermingling of disparate ingredients which, when also properly cohesive, attests to the quality of a vision'.[25] Tippett's formulation manages to link modernism of technique to a visionary quality of expression—an appropriate image with which to conclude this account of Tippett's own achievements.

[25] *Tippett on Music*, 75.

One of the attractions of 'radicalism' as a critical concept is its flexibility, the questions it raises about what it means. Since the 1920s, has it been more radical for composers to attempt to ignore traditional styles and systems, or more radical to aim at conserving those styles and systems as completely as possible? Radicalism is always relative, and matters of perspective are no less significant when other general terms, such as avant-garde and experimental, are brought into the debate. Within the twentieth century as a whole, it is probably the case that the initiatives most generally recognized as radical have been those which distanced themselves most dramatically from contemporary norms, as in the work of John Cage and his followers after 1940, which aimed to dispense with the accepted image of the art-work by facilitating the production of parallel events and experiences—comparable to, yet very different from, events and experiences normally associated with art.

In a conception like $4'33''$[1] Cage sought to transform the nature of composition by questioning the nature of the creative act itself: to replace composition as a particular kind of decision-making—to put it crudely, deciding which note comes next—Cage turned instead to methods (like dice-throwing or using the *I Ching*) which would make all the necessary choices, free from the constraints of human rationality or instinct.[2] This initiative shares certain attributes with that identified in André Breton's Surrealist Manifesto of 1924 as 'thought dictated in the absence of all control exerted by reason, and outside any aesthetic or moral preoccupation'.[3] As will be evident later, however, the consequence was not automatically to render the musical result of the new processes more easily accessible than that of more conventionally composed, but tradition-resistant composition. Nor did Cage wish it to be, since he was well aware of earlier composers—notably Satie and Varèse—who had pioneered new kinds of music, either by setting aside the traditional notion of high art or, in Varèse's case, by searching for new kinds of sound. Nevertheless, and even when his compositions had an extremely attenuated, pared-down quality, Cage was very different from those minimalist contemporaries who sought a radical simplification of sound structures themselves, and for whom repetition, slow rates of change in

---

[1] See below, pp. 278–9.
[2] For a full description of these procedures, see James Pritchett, *The Music of John Cage* (Cambridge, 1993), 70–1.
[3] André Breton, *Manifestes du Surréalisme* (Paris, 1962), 40.

melody and harmony, and a reaffirmation of the essentially consonant, diatonic basis of tonality were the most effective ways of countering avant-garde complexity, and of suggesting degrees of compatibility with the often hypnotic, quasi-narcotic effect of commercial popular music.

Carmina Mundana

As a preliminary to the main concerns of this chapter, it is instructive to consider the work of a pioneering simplifier, whose life and work is something of a cautionary tale when the matter of music's relation to social and political factors is explored. The most familiar composition by Carl Orff (1895–1982), *Carmina Burana* (1937), is 'a work of driving rhythm and exultant hedonism',[4] and the fact that it is entirely devoid of the kind of edgy socio-political critique found in other German seekers after forms of direct musical expression of the inter-war period (notably Kurt Weill and Hanns Eisler) has done little to reduce its popularity. Orff's concerns, 'to create a spectacle' and 'to make the most immediate impression possible', are those of commercial art, and have more in common with the rituals of Nuremberg Rallies than of the Bayreuth Festival. *Carmina Burana* is certainly 'music of powerful pagan sensuality and direct physical excitement', yet it cannot escape the accusation of having taken a particular work as model— Stravinsky's *Les Noces*—and of having 'coarsened and vulgarized' that model.

There were other, arguably more positive aspects to Orff, especially when his work as an educationist is considered. But *Carmina Burana* was only the beginning of a sustained attempt 'to achieve the maximum theatrical intensity through the minimum of means'[5] which remains a feature of quite different kinds of music later in the century. The fact that primitivism, like radicalism, has taken so many different forms is one of the more disconcerting aspects of twentieth-century pluralism.

Edgard Varèse (1883–1965)

Varèse was born and studied in France, but it was only after his move to America in 1915 that he began to achieve maturity as a composer. He lived for another half-century, well into that era of electronic music which he had foreseen and foreshadowed, yet he completed relatively few compositions in his later years, and it is for the rather primitive grandeur of works like *Intégrales* (1924–5) and *Déserts* (1954) that he is remembered, rather than for purely technical innovations or initiatives.

---

[4] For this and subsequent citations in this paragraph, see Hanspeter Krellmann, 'Orff', *The New Grove*, ed. S. Sadie (London, 1980), xiii. 707–10.

[5] Erik Levi, 'Orff', *The New Grove Dictionary of Opera*, ed. S. Sadie (London, 1992), iii. 751.

Varèse, whose early contacts were with Strauss and Busoni, and whose style was grounded in Debussy and Stravinsky, was never as determinedly progressive as Ives or Satie.[6] His works of the 1920s and 1930s, with their up-to-date, science-based titles, their abrasive timbres and concentrated structures, now seem more like bracing but peripheral alternatives to the prevailing density and allusiveness of then-current serial and neo-classical music than potent correctives laying the foundations for future progress. Cage, in a shrewd critique, paid tribute to Varèse's laudable 'acceptance of all audible phenomena as material proper to music',[7] while suggesting that he lacked the technical assurance—even the creative courage—to realize the full implications of his own innovations. (A parallel here with Boulez's critique of Schoenberg is worth noting.[8]) Cage correctly observed that, in Déserts, in which orchestral music and taped sections of 'organized sound' alternate, Varèse 'attempts to make tape sound like the orchestra and vice versa, showing again a lack of interest in the natural differences of sounds, preferring to give them all his unifying signature'.[9] Yet even if we don't reproach Varèse for wishing to follow the traditional path of a composer in seeking the consistent expression of a personal identity, and even if we make due allowance for the fact that much later music involving interaction of acoustic and electronic sound also pursues the possibilities for 'punning' overlaps and interactions of identity between the two types of material, the sheer primitiveness of the musical materials themselves in Déserts is undeniable. Yet Cage's diagnosis, of a 'need for continuity' failing to 'correspond to the present need for discontinuity',[10] is not entirely correct. The problem with Déserts, which is discussed more fully below, is rather that the musical rewards of Varèse's exploration of tensions between continuity and discontinuity are relatively meagre. Even so, the kind of flexible consistency, with respect to symmetrically disposed pitch-formations, which Jonathan Bernard has demonstrated in Déserts and other works, identifies a compositional technique that is far from random or unsystematic. Moreover, Varèse's vision of 'musical space' as something more concerned with symmetrical centredness than hierarchic rootedness actively associates him with one of the twentieth century's most important procedural innovations.[11]

The personal nature of the works written between 1918 and 1936—Varèse declared in 1916 that 'I refuse to limit myself to sounds that have already been heard'[12]—is a clear indication of radical intent, even though certain influences on structure if not style (Debussy and Stravinsky, in particular) are also impor-

[6] See above, pp. 19–21, 34–6.
[7] John Cage, Silence (Cambridge, Mass., 1967), 84.
[8] Pierre Boulez, 'Schoenberg is Dead', in Stocktakings from an Apprenticeship, trans. S. Walsh (Oxford, 1991), 209–14.
[9] Cage, Silence, 83.   [10] Ibid.
[11] See Jonathan W. Bernard, The Music of Edgard Varèse (New Haven, 1987). This is the most substantial technical study of the composer to date.
[12] Louise Varèse, A Looking-Glass Diary (London, 1975), 123.

tant. Melodic lines evolving through internal repetition are an 'impressionist' feature which becomes no less relevant to Varèse's more scientific, crystallographic techniques. Yet such evolutionary processes, the presence of which makes it dangerous to assume that Varèse's structures are essentially inorganic, had to find their place in a satisfactory form. Just at the time when more mainstream composers, Stravinsky, Bartók, and Schoenberg among them, were rethinking the basic elements of sonata form, Varèse questioned the whole nature of musical continuity from a more radical base, offering an approach with more of expressionism than neo-classicism about it.

Speaking in later years of Debussy's *Jeux*, Varèse commented that in it 'we find a higher state of tension than in any work before it',[13] and the exploitation and control of high tension dominate his own most characteristic works. The terminology with which he described his techniques in 1936 is also closely linked to such considerations:

taking the place of the old fixed linear counterpoint, you will find in my works the movement of masses, varying in radiance, and of different densities and volumes. When these masses come into collision, the phenomena of penetration or repulsion will result. Certain transmutations taking place on one plane, by projecting themselves on other planes which move at different speeds and are placed at different angles, should create the impression of prismatic aural (auditory) deformations.[14]

With such preoccupations, it is not unexpected to find Varèse remarking that 'in neoclassicism, tradition is reduced to the level of a bad habit'.[15] Yet he praised the discipline provided by the twelve-note method, and his refusal to abandon all sense of continuity and organic interconnectedness, even when electronically generated sound-sources were at last available to him, is further evidence that his roots in late romanticism were never totally severed.

These roots were detectable in Varèse's first American compositions, *Amériques* (1918–21) and *Offrandes* (1921), and the four-minute work for wind and percussion called *Hyperprism*, completed in 1923, his first fully realized statement of radical intent. The title presumably means 'intensifying a prismatic function', and therefore implies a basic unity strongly refracted by surface contrasts. It is not difficult to perceive that the interval of the major seventh possesses a primary thematic function which unifies pitch procedures throughout, and Bernard's analysis has demonstrated the role of 'unifying forces' in the creation of 'continuity' in *Hyperprism* as a whole.[16] Yet the diversity of tempo and thematic shape within the short single movement is ultimately more disruptive than integrative, and the music is closer to the disconcerting juxtapositions of a Satie ballet than to the dynamically interconnected units of *Jeux* or the

[13] Fernand Ouellette, *Edgard Varèse: A Musical Biography*, trans. D. Coltman (London, 1973), 178.
[14] Ibid. 84.
[15] Louise Varèse, *Looking-Glass Diary*, 257.
[16] Bernard, *Music of Varèse*, 193–217.

Ex. 13.1. Varèse, *Intégrales*, from Fig. 16

Symphonies of Wind Instruments. Thematically, too, the contrasts between single-note reiterations, a sinuous flute melody (after Fig. 2), and an initially chorale-like brass phrase (Fig. 4) emphasize the dangers of producing too episodic a scheme in the attempt to elaborate very simple basic elements without completely submerging them.

As if in response to these issues, *Octandre*, for seven wind instruments and double bass (1923), is cast in three separate movements which have clear thematic cross-references. Then, in *Intégrales* (1924–5), in which Varèse returns to a single-movement design for wind and percussion, the control of form and thematic process is even more assured, the surface thematic diversity firmly projected from the fundamental unifying factors. The opening section, Andantino, is an exposition involving much repetition of a thematic idea which is little more than a reiterated monotone. The music verges on the static, despite constantly changing time signatures, but in view of the frequent variation of tempo in the middle of the work, such changes provide an appropriate foundation. After a somewhat slower second section, marked Moderato, in which the monotone of the Andantino with its two-note anacrusis remains the central thematic feature, the tempo changes, first to Allegro, then to Presto, and the material becomes more conventionally melodic. With the establishment of a slow tempo which dominates the rest of the work until the coda, melodic material is related to monotone material in a manner which is truly 'integral', and allows for explicit reminiscences of earlier moments[17] (Ex. 13.1).

The coda, which starts as a Presto, also looks back, confirming that Varèse was able to achieve a satisfactory balance between evolutionary and recapitulatory factors in a work which is thematic without obvious adherence to traditional structural proportions and convincingly coherent, despite the tendency to rely on short-breathed phrases, with many climactic emphases and restarts. This later quality is even more evident in the longer orchestral work *Arcana* (1926–7),

[17] For a fuller analysis, see Bernard, *Music of Varèse*, 7.

a score notable for its explicit references to the Stravinsky of *Firebird* and *The Rite*. But even *Arcana* employs the large percussion section which is the most obvious evidence from these years of Varèse's radicalism, his interest in new kinds of sound, since without new instruments the composer was forced to exploit new combinations and unusual selections of existing instruments. In *Ionisation* (1931) Varèse wrote for percussion alone, and the whole piece up to the coda uses unpitched instruments (the siren, strictly speaking, is an exception, though its pitch is in a constant state of change). 'Ionisation' is another scientific term, denoting the 'electrophoresis', or migration, of electrically charged particles. In the composition, the particles are rhythmic cells, or 'sound masses', and even in the absence of pitch a textural thematic process can be observed—a traditional feature underlined by the fact that the basic pulse remains stable until the slower concluding section, when pitched percussion (piano, bells, glockenspiel) enter for the first time. It is therefore far from inappropriate that the published score of *Ionisation* should include an analysis (by its dedicatee and first conductor Nicholas Slonimsky) of the work as a sonata-form movement.

In his next composition, *Ecuatorial* (1934), Varèse used electronically generated sound—a pair of Ondes Martenots—for the first time. As with *Ionisation*, the phrase-structure is far from revolutionary, and the vocal line contains significant amounts of varied repetition (Ex. 13.2). After *Ecuatorial*, twenty years were to elapse before another substantial work—*Déserts*— was completed, and that would use pitch without 'themes', and organized sound

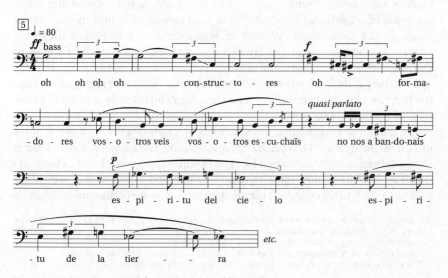

Ex. 13.2. Varèse, *Ecuatorial*, from Fig. 5 (vocal line only)

on tape alongside live orchestral sound. Only the short solo flute piece *Density 21.5* (1936) and the *Étude pour espace* (1947: performed, but never published and not surviving in a definitive form) were composed during the intervening period.[18]

Speaking of Varèse's last completed work, the *Poème électronique* (1958), Karlheinz Stockhausen noted that

anyone living today—Varèse was at the time living in New York—is confronted daily with the hurtling together of all races, all religions, all philosophies, all ways of life . . . of all nations. In works by the musician Varèse this bubbling of the cauldron is aesthetically portrayed. . . . Ideas one might have about possible integration, about a coherent unification, or about possible syntheses of the influences issuing from all parts of the globe, all these must be tested against living experience if they are to lay claim on any truth.[19]

These remarks are also relevant to *Déserts*, which occupied Varèse from 1950 to 1954, and which is, arguably, a portrait of an urban desert, a 'bubbling cauldron' like New York. *Déserts* can be interpreted as an unremittingly pessimistic work, more a commination on the whole of modern civilization than a celebration of technical and social progress. Yet it is also the logical outcome of the more radical tendencies in Varèse's earlier works.

Like them, *Déserts* has vital organic features: a 'continual process of expansion, penetration, interaction and transmutation accounts for the immense sense of growing organicism in the entire score, and illustrates Varèse's concept of "sound as living matter" '.[20] What focuses the music's radical credentials is the sense that this 'organic process' is not in any traditional way a thematic process. At last Varèse's own term, 'sound mass', seems precisely right to define the 'idea, the basis of an internal structure'.[21] The successions of sound masses which surround the three taped episodes of organized sound in *Déserts* present a process in which single pitches are successively brought into focus. Yet even in this athematic context, a residual sense of hierarchy survives, and nowhere more openly than at the end, when a 'rich but subdued' horn E♭, prolonged through the last two bars by piano, vibraphone, and flute, forms a clear point of focus, even of resolution (Ex. 13.3).

The danger of exaggerating the structural function of a series of pedal notes in a thematically featureless pitch texture is obvious. The athematicism of *Déserts* recalls those statically conjoined blocks of sound-matter employed in the early stages of *Intégrales*, and the alternation of live and taped sound, with their radically different associations, may heighten one's sense of discontinuity, while

---

[18] *Density 21.5* has been the object of much analytical scrutiny. See e.g. Jean-Jacques Nattiez, 'Varèse's *Density 21.5*: A Study in Semiological Analysis', *Music Analysis*, 1 (1982), 243–340, and Jonathan W. Bernard, 'A Response to Nattiez', *Music Analysis*, 5 (1986), 207–31.

[19] Karl H. Wörner, *Stockhausen, Life and Work*, trans. G. W. Hopkins (London, 1973), 139.

[20] See Chou Wen-Chung, 'Varèse: A Sketch of the Man and his Music', *Musical Quarterly*, 52 (1966), 161.

[21] Edgard Varèse, 'The Liberation of Sound', in B. Boretz and E. T. Cone (eds.), *Perspectives on American Composers* (Princeton, 1971), 30.

Ex. 13.3. Varèse, *Déserts*, last fifteen bars

274 RADICALS AND RITUALS

also underlining the distinctly primitive nature of the musical thought. In aiming for an elemental yet organic effect, with monumental rather than complex textures and formal processes, Varèse risked simplistic reductiveness. Cage was right to claim that Varèse was attempting to make the tape sound orchestral and vice versa: the object was to bring the new world of concrete and electronic sound into the orbit of the old, and mediate between them, not to use the new to demonstrate the redundancy of the old. But by the mid-1950s Varèse lacked the creative energy to exploit interactions and confrontations in a way that fulfilled the potential richness of his long-standing radical vision. In the late 1950s it was nevertheless entirely justifiable for Stockhausen to honour Varèse's pioneering role as a modernist conquering his own organicist inclinations, declaring with respect to the *Poème électronique*, that 'Varèse is alone in his generation in having composed a work of electronic music and furthermore in having heralded in this *Poème* a modern formulation of compositional relationships whose true significance can only today be recognized: namely the sequential presentation and superimposition—even though sometimes abrupt and unmediated—of events of a heterogeneous nature.'[22]

The work was created for the Philips Pavilion at the 1958 Brussels World Fair, designed by Le Corbusier and Xenakis, for the simultaneous presentation of projected visual images and 'organized sound' through 425 loudspeakers. The diversity and realism of many of the sounds employed categorizes the *Poème électronique* as *musique concrète* (a term coined in 1948 by Pierre Schaeffer for recorded sound material which, even if electronically modified, originates in nature or man-made environments), rather than the kind of studio-generated, abstractly conceived electronic music which Stockhausen himself was working on, for example in his *Studie I*, composed during the summer of 1953. It is not the least of the ironies created by the contemplation of Varèse's remarkable initiatives that later twentieth-century composers (including Stockhausen) have come to favour the kind of allusive, interactive approach, whose early stages he represented, to the possibilities available from the less open-ended world of 'pure' electronic composition.[23] The tragedy for Varèse was that the new techniques were not available to him thirty years before. As it is, his last work seems like a retreat, or even a pessimistic confession of disillusionment: *Nocturnal* for soprano, chorus, and orchestra (1961), survives only in fragmentary form, does not use any electronic elements, and the prevailing atmosphere is sombre and doom-laden. Perhaps *Ecuatorial* is Varèse's most fully realized achievement: a passionate, primitive prayer for survival, it has the quality of an enigmatic, gripping ritual, and is utterly remote in spirit from the kind of radical experimentation which was shortly to gain ground in America, and in which John Cage was for nearly half a century the leading light.

[22] Wörner, *Stockhausen*, 139.
[23] See Bernard, *Music of Varèse*, 16.

A Context for John Cage

As a prominent figure in the new-music scene in 1920s New York, Varèse worked alongside composers who were rather more conscious of the prospects for radical and distinctively American developments, laying the foundations for attitudes which Cage would find sympathetic and stimulating. Henry Cowell (1897–1965) was the most important; as early as 1912 (the year of Cage's birth) he had begun to question received beliefs as to how traditional instruments like the piano could be exploited, and to employ extremely discordant clusters for which he devised a new kind of notation. In 1919 Cowell completed a short book called *New Musical Resources* (not published until 1930) which, although predating many of his most influential experimental compositions like the 'Mosaic' String Quartet (1934), an early example of so-called open form, is a remarkable anticipation of the spirit of root-and-branch questioning of accepted ideas about music which would become much more widespread after 1950.[24]

Cowell was also a tireless supporter of Charles Ives, who undertook virtually no new creative work after his heart attack in 1918, and several of Ives's works were published in Cowell's *New Music Edition*. In all these respects he was more closely involved in American musical life than the other great innovatory figure Harry Partch (1901–74). It was in the late 1920s that Partch wrote the first draft of what was to become a more radical attempt than Ives's, or Cowell's, to create a completely new music. *Genesis of a Music* (not published until 1949) is an enormous, rambling tome that provides both a critique of the entire history of musical theory and composition from Partch's own very personal viewpoint, and also a primer in the new techniques of 'Corporeal Music' which reject equal temperament and are rooted in just intonation with a scale of forty-three steps to the octave. What makes Partch such a consistently radical figure is not his rejection of old traditions so much as his determination *not* to create a new tradition. His compositions are not intended to provide 'a basis for a substitute tyranny, the grooving of music and musical theory into another set of conventions. What I do hope for is to stimulate creative work by example, to encourage investigation of basic factors, and to leave all others to individual if not idiosyncratic choice. To influence, yes: to limit, no.'[25]

In discussing musical instruments which attempt 'better intonations', Partch ruefully noted that they tended to survive only in museums, and the efforts required to gain access to, and learn to play, his own instruments—which have such evocative titles as the Marimba Eroica and The Spoils of War—seem certain to guarantee that his work will remain of fringe rather than mainstream interest. Yet Partch, in works with titles like 'A soul tormented by contemporary music finds a humanizing alchemy' (Scene 4 of *The Bewitched*, 1955), remains a revered

---

[24] See Henry Cowell, *New Music Resources*, ed. D. Nicholls (Cambridge, 1996). See also David Nicholls, *American Experimental Music, 1890–1940* (Cambridge, 1990), 134–74.

[25] Harry Partch, *Genesis of a Music*, 2nd edn. (New York, 1974), p. xviii.

example and inspiration to many more recent American composers who have achieved more of an accommodation with the mainstream of musical activity than he could ever have done.

Cage

Harry Partch was never tested by success, but John Cage (1912–92), who was, showed indomitable resilience in the face of sustained exposure to the full glare of acclaim and ridicule as a cult figure. In the American musical scene after 1945, Cage stood at the opposite extreme from the arch-systematizer Milton Babbitt, and it is therefore ironic that it was Cage, not America's leading serialist, who actually studied with Schoenberg, between 1935 and 1937. Cage also took lessons from Henry Cowell, who stimulated an interest in non-Western ideas; and this interest, later to embrace aspects of Buddhist philosophy, did much more to mould Cage's development as a composer than the high-art, harmony-orientated convictions of Schoenberg and the European classical masters.

Cage first gained attention in the 1940s as an explorer of new sound-sources, carrying on from what Varèse had achieved in *Ionisation* at a time when Varèse himself was virtually silent. One of Cage's earliest characteristic works is the *First Construction in Metal* for percussion ensemble (1939), and in the same year he also produced *Imaginary Landscape No. 1* for two variable-speed gramophone turntables, frequency recordings, muted piano, and cymbal. This is not only a precursor of electronic music, but also employs the modification of a traditional sound-source with which Cage became most closely associated, the 'prepared' piano. In view of the Dadaist expectations aroused when audiences see a pianist plucking the strings, using drum sticks, inserting screws, pieces of paper, and other objects to deaden resonance, it is important to stress that Cage's most substantial composition for prepared piano, the seventy-minute *Sonatas and Interludes* (1946–8), involves quite rigorous rhythmic structuring.[26] Radicalism did not mean complete and utter randomness, and it was only after 1950 that the experimental concept with which Cage was principally associated was fully established and explored.

The Cageian aesthetic ideal involved not so much the fusion as the peaceful coexistence of differences. Cageian quietism is evident in his remark that 'I don't think that the notion of "being in opposition" is beneficial to our society. I think that the opposites must come together',[27] and it follows that 'Cage tried to operate outside the polarities the West has produced in self-conscious ricochets between ideals of critique and transcendence. He wanted to avoid . . . all

---

[26] See Pritchett, *Music of Cage*, 29–35.
[27] Joan Retallack (ed.), *Musicage: John Cage in Conversation with Joan Retallack* (Hanover, NH, 1996), 163.

polarities, dichotomies, dualities, either/ors.'[28] It nevertheless remains doubtful if such an ideal can be adequately realized in any actual compositional practice, at least one located in the twentieth-century Western world. The best Cage could do was to pursue experiment rather than routine, and to remain open to features best defined as 'indeterminate'.

Appropriately enough, 'indeterminacy' has been variously defined, but in essence it involves a shift of emphasis away from the idea of a musical composition as a sequence of fixed and fully realized elements to an approach seeking a significant degree of freedom and flexibility in both structure and notation. With the liberation of music from the principle that every performance of a particular piece would be substantially the same, experimentalism achieved one of its most striking twentieth-century breakthroughs.

Indeterminacy encouraged greater spontaneity through performer-participation in determining both the course of events in a work and the content of those events, and it was soon possible to observe parallels with those surrealistic dramatic happenings often known collectively as the Theatre of the Absurd. Similarly, the more imprecise, graphic methods of musical notation may well resemble abstract or surrealist painting more than traditional musical notation. While it was possible for composers to use these new techniques without the resulting work losing all points of contact with the traditional concept of composition, Cage himself pursued a still more radical goal. For him the distinction between art as an activity and other areas of human life was no longer valid, and the old concept of creating a work of art as something different in kind from other human activities was to be set aside. It followed that the authority of the composer as decision-maker must be challenged, and the traditional idea of a concert as an event governed by distinct functions—composer, interpreter, listener—should be resisted. Cage first attempted to displace the responsibility for creative decisions by such random procedures as employing the *I Ching*, as in his *Music for Changes* for piano (1961). Later he came to favour Dadaist activities like those envisaged in *Musicircus* (1968) in which his role was confined to that of an initiator of events which were likely to possess certain characteristics but in which the gulf between what was prescribed in the 'score' and what took place at a performance was, intentionally, immense.

Cage was always perfectly willing to discuss his motives—the thinking behind the new freedom from control and logic—and to function as a consistently engaging performer of his own creative concepts. He even made 'compositions' out of his lectures, as in *45' for a speaker* (1954), the seventh minute of which is laid out as shown in Ex. 13.4.[29] Cage's writings, and his many published conversations, are as full of recurring themes as a classical set of variations: 'I attempt to let sounds be themselves in a space of time . . . I do not object to being

---

[28] Retallack (ed.), *Musicage*, p. xl.   [29] Cage, *Silence*, 155.

7' 00"   Composers are spoken of as having
          ears for music which generally
          means that nothing presented
          to their ears can be heard by them.
          Their ears are walled in
          with sounds
  10"   of their own imagination
                    Of five aspects
          observe
  20"   *two.*

          The highest purpose is to have no purpose
          at all. This puts one in accord with nature
          in her manner of operation. If someone comes
          along and asks why? there are answers.
  30"   However there is a story I have found very help-
          ful. What's so interesting about
          technique anyway? *What if there are twelve tones in a*
          row? What row? This seeing of cause and effect
          is not emphasized but instead one makes an
          identification with what is here and now. He
  40"   then spoke of two qualities. Unimpededness and Inter-
          penetration.

          The relationship of things happening
          at the same time is spontaneous
          and irrepressible.
  50"   It is you yourself
          in the form you have
          that instant taken.
          To stop and figure it out
          takes
          time.

Ex. 13.4. Cage, *45' for a speaker*, seventh minute

engaged in a purposeless activity';[30] 'more and more in this global electronic world that we are living in, I think this experience of non-knowledge is more useful and more important to us than the Renaissance notion of knowing ABCDEF what you are doing'.[31] At the same time, Cage's often complex sound-events can call on many of the resources of modern electronic technology. While his work was in most respects spontaneous and improvisatory, it had little in common with the repetitive rhythmic routines and warm, connected sonorities of much minimalist composition, which is experimental, and ritualistic, in very different ways.

The work from Cage's earlier years that most fully enshrines his radical aesthetic is *4'33"* (1952), the score of which

presents, by means of the roman numerals I, II and III, a three-movement work; each movement is marked 'TACET'. A footnote . . . indicates that at the first . . . performance David Tudor chose to take four minutes and thirty-three seconds over the three sections. Since 'tacet' is the word used in western music to tell a player to remain silent during a

---

[30] Richard Kostalanetz (ed.), *John Cage* (London, 1971), 116–18.
[31] John Cage, *A Year from Monday* (London, 1968), 42.

movement, the performer is asked to make no sounds; but . . . for any length of time, on any instrument.[32]

The whole point of the piece therefore lies in its contradiction, graphic and dramatic, of what normally happens at a concert when a pianist enters and sits down at the instrument. In these terms, it may irritate or amuse. After all, those decisions which the composer *has* made are still very important, and the implication that any noises which occur during the time of the (non-)performance—audience shuffles, laughter, traffic outside the hall, air-conditioning systems, and the like—can in some way be compared with a Bach suite or a Boulez sonata, presents the kind of challenge to perception of which any strongly creative personality might be proud.

It is entirely appropriate that Cage's most consistent trait should have been unpredictability, even allowing for tributes to the memory of a revered precursor. *Cheap Imitation* (1969) arose as a practical solution to the problem of mounting a ballet prepared to fit the phrase-structure of Satie's *Socrate* after the copyright holders refused permission for the use of Cage's two-piano arrangement of the score. What Cage did in consequence was 'make a piece with the rhythms and phrases of *Socrate*, but with the pitches so altered that he could stay clear of any copyright problems. . . . In *Cheap Imitation*, Satie's symphonic drama is reduced to a single melodic line played on the piano',[33] a line arrived at by subjecting Satie's notes to transformational procedures using the *I Ching* (Ex. 13.5). The effect, especially when the intervals within each bar tend to shadow Satie's, is like a gentle distillation of the grave original.

As Pritchett notes, *Cheap Imitation* is different from other works by Cage from the 1960s in being 'a composition . . . in the old sense of the word'.[34] It may be so in technique, yet in atmosphere it shares with Cage's more radical concepts a general austerity, a lack of Western purposefulness, and it is for these qualities, rather than any obvious, fundamental rejection of the concept of creativity as such, that Cage's works are likely to remain a potent presence within the musical world he sought to transform so radically.

All commentators on the later stages of John Cage's career as a composer note its richness and diversity, the contrasts between sustained simplicity (*Ryoanji*, 1983–5) and the surrealistic allusiveness of the *Europeras* (1985–91). In one sense at least this diversity can be read as asserting an essential modernism. For example, as David W. Bernstein has stressed, Cage's concept of ' "anarchic harmony" allows dissonant harmonies and harmonic configurations that are surprisingly conventional to coexist and remain free from a central "dominating" tone'[35]—the kind of flexible motion between opposite poles of compositional technique that is found in many distinctive modernist styles from Xenakis

[32] Michael Nyman, *Experimental Music* (Cambridge, 1999), 3. See also Pritchett, *Music of Cage*, 59–60 and 208–9.
[33] Ibid. 164–6.   [34] Ibid. 164.
[35] David W. Bernstein, review of Pritchett, *Music of Cage*, in *Music Theory Spectrum*, 18 (1996), 272.

Ex. 13.5. Cage, *Cheap Imitation*: (i) I, bars 11–20; (ii) II, bars 7–12. Satie's vocal line is superimposed for comparison.

to Maxwell Davies, and whose twentieth-century manifestations may be traced back at least as far as those emblematic Bergian confrontations between older and newer musics.

Bernstein also offers an interesting comparison between Cage and his one-time teacher Schoenberg, suggesting that 'in composing, Cage, like Schoenberg, began with a musical idea; the difference lies in that the former did not express his ideas in terms of organically integrated compositions'.[36] Once

[36] Bernstein, review of Pritchett, 273.

again, this formula might seem to claim Cage for mainstream modernism, were it not for the sense created by Cage's purposeless purposes that modernism's inherent tension between aspiration to organicism and resistance to it, played out in a world of intensely human feelings and actions, is not a prime concern. In choosing to describe Cage's music as 'effortless and transparent', with primary qualities of 'concentration, spaciousness, simplicity',[37] James Pritchett highlights not so much an absence of 'anarchy' as its ultimate subordination to the evocation of a sublime detachment, even a ritualized state of trance, a transcendence from which the impulses of the human will seem to have been purged.

The Forceful and the Passive: Nancarrow, Feldman

If the Cageian ethos embodies a radical, experimental aesthetic in its purest, most extreme form, it is hardly surprising that few other composers have chosen to follow the same path, at least with such consistency. A very different kind of single-mindedness distinguishes the music of Conlon Nancarrow (1912–97), whose body of work centres on more than fifty studies for player piano, the first composed in 1947 or 1948.[38] The belated discovery, mainly through recordings, of these works led to Nancarrow being hailed as a great original, a heroic figure who lived a life of principled exile from his native USA in Mexico, working in dedicated isolation, and labouring over the routine mechanical work of punching his piano rolls with sublime indifference to fame and fortune. More than that, the zany exuberance of the music, the instantly attractive combination of chirpily unresonant player-piano sound with fantastically convoluted rhythmic patterns, in canonic combinations beyond the capacity of human hands and brain to execute, seemed like a parable of liberation from outworn traditional techniques and aesthetics. Nancarrow transformed a musical idiom deriving from jazz and folk music into an elaborate yet never forbiddingly aggressive language that could appeal to devotees of minimalism and complexity alike. However many strata accumulate in a Nancarrow study, there is always a coherence to the harmony, a resistance to textural chaos that has a well-nigh classical power: the mechanical is transformed into the magical, and even if the expressive world of Nancarrow's music excludes the meditative and the lyrical there is a special fascination in the sense of danger the music can create, confronting and conquering the risks of disintegration. Even if tragedy and lament are generally absent, there is an abundance of ebullient melodic invention, and with it a strong feeling for the tensions and epiphanies of drama, the sense of human triumph over adversity.

---

[37] Pritchett, *Music of Cage*, 204.
[38] For a comprehensive technical study, see Kyle Gann, *The Music of Conlon Nancarrow* (Cambridge, 1995).

Ex. 13.6. Nancarrow, Study No. 11, transcription of the beginning

Ex. 13.6, from a transcription of Nancarrow's Study 11, gives a good indication of his ingenuity (the use of repeated, isorhythmic patterns) and his immediate appeal, which in this instance owes much to the recurrences of basic triadic notes: G, C, E, flat or natural. As Kyle Gann observes, 'like so many of Nancarrow's lengthy melodies . . . this one starts out in a clear key (C major/minor) and becomes increasingly atonal, though it returns to the tonic at structural points'.[39] Described in this way, Nancarrow's basic musical language was evidently not, in itself, original or innovative. It is the textural, timbral context of its use that makes the results so remarkable. Nancarrow was able to live his musical life with relatively little involvement with traditional instruments, and with little variety of compositional genre, yet his radicalism did not require him to experiment with fundamentally new kinds of musical notation. By contrast, Morton Feldman (1926–87) was affected in his early years by the New York experimental ambience in which painters were particularly influential, and composers

[39] Gann, *The Music of Conlon Nancarrow*, 97–8.

embraced graphic notation as a way of escaping from the overdeterminate oppressiveness, as they saw it, of post-war avant-garde composition. But even Feldman eventually found his way back to the five-line stave.

For the experimental aesthetic at its purest—that is, its most quixotic—there is no better text than Feldman's *Essays*.[40] Here we find the aspiration, similar to Cage's, to let sounds be themselves, and not to push them around. Given that a composer has to make some decisions about the identity of sounds, he can still avoid putting them on trial, subjecting them to processes, forcing them into relationships, making them live a life of logic and goal-directed determinism. When Feldman says in an interview that 'one of my problems about Ives is that the work is just too literary',[41] he is not simply resisting the capacity of music to align itself with pictorial imagery, but its engagement with concepts and, through concepts, feelings. Feldman sought the kind of transcendent detachment—leaving the sounds (once invented) alone—that goes as far as it can to prevent the listener from coercing the music into conceptual, emotional scenarios. As Feldman's later works indicate, it is possible to sustain a 'state' of apparently inconsequential detachment, unassertive, not arguing about ideas or displaying strong feelings in the way that 'personalities' will tend to do, and in this way to let the sounds live in peace. These sounds are realities, not abstractions, however, and by their very existence they represent the desire of their inventor to elevate understatement, feeling as something delicate and unobtrusive, into the single principle of their being. Feldman attempted to make the stretched similarities of these compositions seem unwilled, to reduce intention to a minimum without actually abandoning his personal responsibility for the sounds. The result is the supreme modernist paradox, music that is consistently singular, yet also anti-organic, music whose governing purpose (or controlling mechanism) is to reject coercion.

Feldman was perfectly prepared to accept his own role as initiator, and as an initiator with particular cross-cultural insights: it was, he claimed, 'the new painting' that 'made me more desirous of a sound world more direct, more immediate, more physical than anything that had existed heretofore'.[42] Even if absolute indeterminacy was not an option, and systems and controls could not be totally rejected, they could be consistently, gently resisted: 'only by "unfixing" the elements traditionally used to construct a piece of music could the sounds exist in themselves—not as symbols, or memories which were memories of other music to begin with'.[43] The aim was to situate the sounds in a perpetual present, a music of 'extreme quietude' which would be happier with a 'dead' audience than a living one.[44] The ideal is 'anonymity', a 'beauty without biography'.[45] But how can beauty be distinguished from something else? We must have an idea of how we feel when we encounter beauty and its absence. Feldman is certainly right when he accepts that 'the most difficult thing in an art experience is to keep

[40] Morton Feldman, *Essays*, ed. W. Zimmerman (Kerpen, 1985).
[41] Ibid. 234.   [42] Ibid. 38.   [43] Ibid. 49.
[44] Ibid. 62.   [45] Ibid. 71.

Ex. 13.7. Feldman, *palais de mari*, beginning

intact this consciousness of the abstract', as something that is 'not involved with ideas'. And he goes on: 'whereas the literary experience of art, the kind we are close to, is involved in the polemic we associated with religion, the Abstract Experience is really far closer to the religious. It deals with the same mystery—reality—whatever you choose to call it.'[46] In these phrases, the implicit conjunction of the radical and the ritualistic is unmistakable.

Feldman used graphic notation in various works written up to the early 1970s, but he was always wary of the kinds of choices it conferred on performers, and it is clear in retrospect that the freedom he sought was less from notational strictness than from emotional exhibitionism. Like Cage, Feldman aspired to a kind of contemplative purity, a sustained, trance-like concentration which can be aligned with minimalism in its emphasis on repetition and constraints on contrast, but is quite different in its rhythmic passivity and avoidance of tonal-sounding harmony.

Feldman's later, conventionally notated works often sustain their meditative rituals for hours at a time, and the music is notable for its use of steadily evolving change, shunning obvious and explicit contrast, and centring on very gradual, barely perceptible degrees of variation. With their reliance on gently

---

[46] Feldman, *Essays*, 103–4.

articulated, repetitive processes these pieces invite the kind of straightforward analytical narrative found in Wes York's patient parsing of *For John Cage* (1982) for violin and piano, with its abundance of tree diagrams and charts, and its exploration of Feldman's notion of 'crippled' (varied) symmetry. While the character of the music resists the kind of hierarchized essentialism that the diagrams seem to suggest, it is far from random or passive in technique. Whether or not it offers, as York claims, a 'unique sense of coherence',[47] its 'balancing of order with disorder' not only 'opens up the closed system of the symmetry to new transformations of the material', but sets up a discourse between ambiguity and clarity that associates itself with the dialectic of more traditional thematic and developmental composition. The music's strength of character lies in its resistance to the expressive consequence of this association, and because tendencies to anti-directionality are countered, from the outset, by transformational 'cripplings' of what would otherwise be literal mirrorings, a dynamic approach (however gentle) counters static self-reflection. The sounds may, as York insists, be 'radically new', but the formal structures and compositional techniques are not. Thomas DeLio observes that in Feldman's music 'differences are not *oppositions*, but shiftings, on-going displacements, de-centerings, unfixings'.[48] One could just as well say that the oppositions in Feldman's music are unusually, if not uniquely, delicate, tender, seeking to persuade by stealth rather than by insistence.

Even on the relatively small, twenty-five-minute scale of the late piano piece *palais de mari* (1986), these qualities are evident. On the one hand this is an integrated conception, unified by the persistence of certain dynamic, textural, and harmonic materials (Ex. 13.7). On the other hand, the composer resists the kind of coercive strategies that the more active rhythms and transformational routines of mainstream minimalism project. Listening, one can imagine that the player is choosing the order in which events occur, that the notation is more flexible than it really is; and the absence of bass-orientated harmony is crucial in effecting this quality of slowly shifting suspense, a detached yet far from arid reflection on time circling in space.

The refined understatement that is fundamental to Feldman's expressive world is the more austere for resisting association with any particular political or religious system. Indeed, Feldman's detachment, like Cage's, can be interpreted as a lack of engagement, a limitation, as something irresponsible and even decadent, if one prefers the politically and socially sensitive minimalist dramas of Steve Reich and John Adams, or the Christian rituals of Arvo Pärt and John Tavener. This very different, parallel musical world, in which rituals tend to be more explicit and 'engaged', will be considered in Chapter 15.

[47] Wes York, 'For John Cage', in T. DeLio (ed.), *The Music of Morton Feldman* (Westport, Conn., 1996), 148.
[48] DeLio, *Morton Feldman*, 11.

Change of focus from America to Europe inevitably involves some change of aesthetic and technical perspective. It is not that the composers considered in this chapter have escaped all contact with the distinctively iconoclastic radicalism found in Cage, Feldman, and Nancarrow. But in their attitudes to traditional genres, and their relations with well-established forms of public music-making and promotion, the seven (very different) composers considered here offer powerful confirmation of the adaptability of modernism, and its ability to contribute to a rich and diverse twentieth-century 'mainstream'. The distance between the unambiguous commitment to symphonic music found in Lutosławski and Henze and the innovative projects of Xenakis or Stockhausen is, self-evidently, immense, and the co-fertilization between radicalism and a sense of ritual is no less palpable here than in the composers actually considered under those headings. Inevitably, my groupings are as much a matter of convenience as of coherence. A relatively restricted range of birth-dates (1913 to 1928) may promote an elementary feeling of connection among the seven Europeans, but, in the end, the polarities cannot be suppressed.

Witold Lutosławski (1913–1994)

Lutosławski's earlier works, such as the Symphonic Variations for orchestra (1936–8) and the Symphony No. 1 (1941–7), display a wide range of influences from among those twentieth-century composers who retained an ultimate commitment to some kind of tonality. Of their very nature, however, those influences tended to stimulate further exploration rather than mere imitation, and the music of Szymanowski and Bartók was of particular importance in providing Lutosławski with ideas about how he might develop a more personal, more radical style, at least partly from sources in folk music.[1]

Well before the Polish political 'thaw' of 1956, Lutosławski had encountered some of the recent music of Cage, Boulez, and Stockhausen, and witnessed the eager involvement of younger Western radicals with 'total' serialism, as well as the speedy reaction in favour of indeterminacy. Lutosławski's reaction to these

[1] For a comprehensive survey, see Charles Bodman Rae, *The Music of Lutosławski* (3rd ed., London, 1999). A fuller technical study of the works up to the later 1970s is Steven Stucky, *Lutosławski and his Music* (Cambridge, 1981).

two phenomena was determined principally by his awareness of what remained potent in his own earlier idiom. Thus, although around 1960 he began to engage with aspects of twelve-note structuring, and of aleatory processes, it was with clear consciousness of the limitations both of orthodox serialism and of the more Dadaist forms of indeterminacy. With regard to the former, and its extension into total serialism, Lutosławski believed that, because of the inaudibility of its essential processes, 'it places the experience of a musical work outside the realm of human sensibility';[2] as for the latter, it became no less futile as soon as it reached the point where the composer could not 'foresee all possibilities which could arise within the limits set beforehand'.[3] Lutosławski was suspicious of extremes, and his finest later works, from *Paroles tissées* (1965) to *Mi-parti* (1976) and the Symphony No. 4 (1992), are those in which the need to constrain progressiveness is turned to personal and positive account.

In the Five Songs (1956–8), and many subsequent works, Lutosławski built his basic structures from 'elementary' twelve-note chords containing 'one, two or three types of intervals'. Such chords

have for me a distinct, easily recognisable character, while twelve-note chords comprising all types of intervals are colourless—they lack a clearly defined individuality. Elementary twelve-note chords enable the use of strong harmonic contrasts, a possibility which is denied, for example, in the serial technique . . . The only thing that links me with this technique is the almost continuous flow of the twelve notes of the scale.[4]

One primary result of Lutosławski's search for harmonic character and colour was the preservation of a sense of hierarchy, even of tonal centricity, particularly in the compositions of his last decade, but also in earlier works: for example, in the *Trois poèmes d'Henri Michaux* (1960–5), a focus on F♯ emerges in a way which does not evade the connotations of a 'resolution', yet avoids anything remotely suggestive of traditional tonal functions. Lutosławski came closest to orthodox serialism in the *Funeral Music in memoriam Béla Bartók* (1958), parts of which use a melodic twelve-note set containing only two different intervals, minor second and tritone (interval classes 1 and 6). Even at the beginning, however, this set is presented in two different orderings, and the climax of the work, 'based on chords comprising all the twelve tones' which 'are gradually drawn towards the middle register where they form a unison',[5] is a clear adumbration of the technique which Lutosławski later developed and expanded, in order to integrate a sense of pitch-focus into the structure of twelve-note chords. For example, the Preludes and Fugue for thirteen solo strings (1972) ends with a two-interval twelve-note chord (built from interval-classes 2 and 5), the last of twelve twelve-note chords which help to define the structure of the concluding Fugue as a progress towards the final, C-based harmony (Ex. 14.1).

It was in the orchestral *Jeux vénitiens* (1961) that Lutosławski used 'aleatory

[2] O. Nordwall (ed.), *Lutosławski* (Stockholm, 1968), 54.
[3] Ibid. 88.   [4] Ibid. 109, 112.   [5] Ibid. 57.

Ex. 14.1. Lutosławski, *Preludes and Fugue*, ending

counterpoint' for the first time. The term is exact, for it is the contrapuntal relationship between simultaneously played parts which is no longer strictly controlled by precise rhythmic notation. Instead, a period of time is defined either by gestures from the conductor, by signals from other players, by listening for other players to start new material, or by 'space-time' notation, which allots a certain amount of space on the page to an approximate duration, usually marked in seconds. The individual performer then repeats the group of notes provided for the period in question, and during that period there is no fixed co-ordination between the various performers.

This treatment of the element of chance consists above all in the abolition of classical time division, which is consistent for all members of an ensemble. . . . [It does not] affect in the slightest degree the architectural order of the composition or the pitch organization. . . . In composing my piece I had to foresee all possibilities which would arise within the limits set beforehand. This, in fact, consisted of setting the limits themselves in such a way that even 'the least desirable possibility' of execution, in a given fragment, should nevertheless be acceptable. This guarantees that everything that may happen within the previously set limits will fulfil my purpose.[6]

[6] Nordwall (ed.), *Lutosławski*, 88.

Lutosławski was able to relax this principle, for example in the Preludes and Fugue, allowing that 'any number of Preludes in any order can be performed with or without a shortened version of the Fugue'. Even so, as his later large-scale compositions demonstrated, he would normally seek to employ the element of 'mobility' to enhance rather than reduce the sense of gradual, dramatic evolution fundamental to the symphonic concept. Just as Lutosławski's technique centred not solely on twelve-note chords but on the relationships and polarities between such chords and single-note pitch-emphases, so his forms involved an attempt to balance, and even integrate, fixed and freer factors. For Lutosławski, the unambiguously unattached juxtapositions and superimpositions of material exploited by some composers were always suspect. Rather, modernism offered him the opportunity for particularly intense interactions between opposing tendencies: connection and fragmentation, progressiveness and conservatism, polarity and synthesis.[7]

Lutosławski's own ideas about the whole question of devising appropriately large-scale forms for works in which fixed and free materials coexist were well expressed in his fascinating essay about his Symphony No. 2 (1965–7). He regarded 'a very restricted and strictly controlled aleatoricism' as the best way in which to make 'old' instruments sound 'in a fresh and stimulating way',[8] and this revisionist approach to traditional instrumental resources was paralleled by his mixed feelings about traditional 'closed' musical forms. Lutosławski believed that forms which were at their peak in the baroque and classical periods 'are today cultivated mostly in their ossified and degenerate form'. Yet even if sonata form, rondo, and so on could not be validly revived as such, 'a long process of evolution' might still be ahead for the closed-form principle. Lutosławski's own works, from the Symphony No. 2 to the Symphony No. 4 written a quarter of a century later, are indeed 'inseparably bound [up] with the closed form', even if, for the Second Symphony, he decided to use the traditional title, not because the work had anything in common with 'the classical or the neo-classical form', but because 'it is a work for symphony orchestra composed in a large closed form'.

This symphony, whose two movements chart an archetypal Lutosławskian progress from 'hesitant' first movement to more 'direct', and dramatic, second movement, is one of his more radical conceptions, with little in the way of pitch-focus to offset the atonal flux, even though the climax of the second movement does reiterate E♭ and F, the pitches which begin and end the entire work. In the single-movement Cello Concerto (1969–70), by contrast, there is a rather more consistent balance between tendencies towards pitch-focus and tendencies to keep all twelve notes in play. This work is also a particularly successful rethinking of the traditional concerto principle of alternately polarized and interactive

[7] See Arnold Whittall, 'Between Polarity and Synthesis: The Modernist Paradigm in Lutosławski's Concertos for Cello and Piano', in Z. Skowron (ed.), Lutosławski Studies (Oxford, forthcoming).

[8] The quotations from Lutosławski's essay in this paragraph are from the English version published in R. S. Hines (ed.), The Orchestral Composer's Point of View (Norman, Okla., 1970), 145–51.

dialogues between soloist and orchestra: dialogues in which distinctive thematic ideas and freshly imagined textures were equally significant.

As Lutosławski's later works revealed, the purposes of a suitably substantial symphonic process were not always well served when the music sounded more like a counterpoint of textural ostinatos than an ongoing thematic and harmonic argument. That the composer himself found it difficult to sustain large-scale structures is evident from the long gestation of the Symphony No. 3, begun in the early 1970s but not completed until 1983, and the rather uneasy balance it seeks to establish between his characteristically volatile textural writing and more stable, more traditionally shaped thematic and melodic features.

In the early 1980s, Lutosławski developed his ideas about aleatory counter-point into what he termed the 'chain' principle, in which independent, comple-mentary strands of material are juxtaposed and interwoven: but this did not promote a more overtly modernist resistance to the progressively intensifying convergence of strands, and even goal-directedness, found in the Third Sym-phony and the Piano Concerto (1987). To an even greater extent than the Third Symphony, the concerto explores the possibility of links with romantic styles, extending its generic associations back through Rakhmaninov to Chopin with results that risk stylistic diffuseness, even though the balance between approaches to tonal focus and assertions of total chromaticism still works to good effect. But it was in his last substantial work, the Symphony No. 4, that Lutosławski achieved the most satisfying, large-scale balance between those older and newer factors that had often seemed at odds in his later years. Although not as rhythmically flamboyant as many of his earlier successes, it has a firmly sculpted bipartite single-movement structure, the symphonic argument eloquently as well as energetically sustained in the last of his adaptations of the fruitful 'preparatory-leading-to-principal movement' scheme. The harmony has an abrasive edge, its capacity for yielding moments of tonal focus almost ironi-cally deployed (as the final Es, echoing those of the Third Symphony, indicate). Yet the build-up to the main climax reveals that Lutosławski's capacity for gen-erating personal, urgently expressive melodic spans is fresher and more persua-sive than ever (Ex. 14.2).

Ex. 14.2. Lutosławski, Symphony No. 4, from Fig. 82, melodic line only

That melodic gift was no less richly revealed in a pair of works for solo voice and orchestra, *Paroles tissées* and *Les Espaces du sommeil* (1975), in which Lutosławski sets surrealistic yet refined texts by the French poets Jean-François Chabrun and Robert Desnos. Together with what is probably the finest of all his orchestral compositions before the Symphony No. 4, the relatively brief *Mi-parti*, these indicate that Lutosławski's greatest strengths were in robust formal concentration, and poetic allusion, rather than in expansive symphonic dialectic. Indeed, it seems increasingly clear that, for creative energy and textural resourcefulness—despite its obvious conservatism—he never surpassed his early Concerto for Orchestra (1954) in any of his later, full-scale symphonic compositions. As with Tippett and Carter, it is the case that the undoubted achievements of Lutosławski's radicalized style after 1960 did not, in the end, render his earlier, more traditionally conceived work redundant.

Iannis Xenakis (b. 1922)

Lutosławski's mature style was rooted in positive compromises between the divergent impulses to conserve and to change. Xenakis's music may seem to involve a comparable underlying ambition to integrate the 'fixed' and the 'free', but the results could scarcely be more different. Xenakis's radicalism has thrived on standing aside from all traditions and all other contemporary initiatives. He has rejected all familiar genres (symphony, concerto) even if he has made frequent use of traditional musical media from the string quartet to the *a cappella* choir. Xenakis believes that 'to escape from the trivial cycle of relationships in music, the musician, the artist, must be absolutely independent, which means absolutely alone'.[9] Even if, strictly speaking, such absolutes are impossible, Xenakis seeks to work as if they were attainable, and this iconoclasm aligns him at least as closely with the more overt radicalism of composers discussed in the previous chapter as with the European modernists considered here.

A Greek born in Romania, who moved to France in 1947, Xenakis was still able to claim in 1966 that 'I am always rediscovering in the civilisation of ancient Greece the germ of the most advanced ideas of contemporary life.' At 18, after a youth 'saturated' with 'classicism, antiquity, philosophy, poetry', he became directly involved in the anti-Nazi resistance and, as with Ligeti, Henze, and Stockhausen, the influence of his wartime experiences was profound and long-lasting.

In my music there is all the agony of my youth, of the Resistance, and the aesthetic problems they posed, with the street demonstrations, or even more the occasional, mysterious, deathly sounds of those cold nights in December 1944 in Athens. From this was born my conception of the massing of sound events, and therefore of stochastic music.[10]

---

[9] Bálint András Varga, *Conversations with Iannis Xenakis* (London, 1996), 211–12.
[10] Mario Bois, *Iannis Xenakis: The Man and his Music* (London, 1967), 9–16.

On this basis, the desire to create a completely new world *on* the ruins of the old, rather than *from* those ruins, becomes understandable, but those experiences created a persistently pessimistic rather than idealistic frame of mind. As Xenakis has said in later years, 'no-one can create a new world. It is impossible to create something really different—no example of that exists in the history of art. It's sad; we are prisoners of ourselves.'[11] In such an environment, not least that in which 'too much music is nice',[12] Xenakis offers as his 'contribution to the development of music' the use of 'ideas in composing that are completely alien to music'.[13] In that way, at least, the illusion of creating 'something really different' may for a while be sustained.

Xenakis's early training was as a mathematician, engineer, and architect, and for more than a decade after arriving in France (as well as for several years after musical studies with Honegger, Milhaud, and Messiaen) he worked with Le Corbusier. In an early indication of iconoclasm he rejected the European total serialism of the 1950s, using his mathematical skills to develop a technique with which it was possible 'to attain the greatest possible asymmetry . . . and the minimum of constraints, causalities and rules'.[14] This 'stochastic' principle is derived from the law of large numbers as defined by Jacques Bernouilli in 1713. The usual, informal explanation of the law instances the tossing of a coin; toss it once, and the result is unpredictable, within the obvious limits of the two alternative possibilities. Continue to toss it, and the number of heads and tails will increasingly tend towards equality. The consequences of this, in Xenakis's music, can indeed involve some sense of an ultimate equilibrium between clearly defined, massively deployed alternatives: stochastic laws, he has said, 'are the laws of the passage from complete order to total disorder in a continuous or an explosive manner'.[15] In these terms, the principle can be productively aligned with the kind of modernist confrontations and interactions explored throughout this study, as well as those disconcerting shifts between extreme expressive states and textural characteristics that seem, ultimately, to embody an expressionistic aesthetic.

Two of Xenakis's early stochastic works which use identical basic material can scarcely not be heard other than in terms of contrasts between relatively regular and irregular patterns. *ST/4-1, 080262*, and *ST/10-1, 080262*, were both completed in 1962. The titles mean the first piece of stochastic music for four and ten instruments respectively, using calculations made by computer on 8 February 1962. Example 14.3 shows two extracts from *ST/4* for string quartet, displaying the extreme contrast between constantly changing durations, dynamics, and dynamic patterns, and a far simpler texture which includes a descending chromatic scale with regular note values and a uniform dynamic level. Such

[11] Varga, *Conversations*, 71.   [12] Ibid. 62.   [13] Ibid. 79.

[14] Iannis Xenakis, *Formalized Music* (Bloomington, Ind., 1971), 23.

[15] Christopher Butchers, 'The Random Arts: Xenakis, Mathematics and Music', *Tempo*, 85 (Summer 1968), 5.

Ex. 14.3. Xenakis, *ST/4*: (i) beginning; (ii) bars 224–30

contrasts are a regular feature of Xenakis's stochastic works; *Morsima-Amorsima* (*ST/4-1, 030762,* for violin, cello, double bass, and piano) begins with immense diversity of register, duration, and dynamics, with relatively rapid pitch succession, but after six bars a much sparser texture ensues; the rest of the piece alternates these two basic elements.

In his long and productive composing career, Xenakis has remained faithful to his interest in computer calculations and mathematical strategies—including game theory and the symbolic systems derivable from set theory. In addition (an interest stemming from his early contacts with Varèse in connection with the building of the sound-space for *Poème électronique* at the Brussels World Fair in 1958) he has also made extensive use of electro-acoustic techniques, in a whole series of works involving tape and sound projection. It is in these works, in particular, that Xenakis's music advances beyond theoretical abstractions, and engages with archetypal dramatic themes, as in his music drama *Oresteia* (1965–6) or the much later *Bacchae* (1993). In addition, the violent energy and vertical density so characteristic of his music has not precluded the use of scalic figures, melodic shapes, and microtonal inflections that evoke the idioms of folk music, as in *N'Shima* (1975), which specifies 'two peasant voices' for the music's ritualistically repetitive response to a Hebrew text: HA-YO means 'to be', HA-YA 'being' (Ex. 14.4).

♯ indicates a quartertone sharp, ♯ three-quarters sharp

Ex. 14.4. Xenakis, *N'Shima*, beginning

Such a development is not as surprising as may at first appear. At an early stage of his career Xenakis declared that his strongest desire was for a closer association between Greek folk music and certain aspects of Western art music, and that ambition is given impetus by his continued reliance on forms assembled, stochastically, from widely diverse components, as can be heard in such characteristically pugnacious later compositions as *Dikhtas* for violin and piano (1979) and *Keqrops* for piano and orchestra (1986). That Xenakis is never likely to retreat into mellow gentility is especially clear in the turbulent *Dämmerschein* (1994) for orchestra, a score that amply bears out the composer's confession that 'I do lack lyricism. Maybe life killed it in me—but it's also possible that I was born without it.'[16] At the same time, Xenakis has not found it necessary to shun simplicity, and in *Plektó* (1993) and *Sea-Change* (1997) there is an intensity that is the result not only of relatively unelaborate textures but also of strong human feelings, most notably of sorrow and regret. Although he rejects with contempt 'the pathos of German music', which in his view Schoenberg and Webern carried 'to an extreme',[17] he has nevertheless created some of the later twentieth century's most piercing musical laments. For all his feeling for science and technology, his compositions often evoke dark and primitive rituals.

György Ligeti (b. 1923)

One consequence of Xenakis's uncompromising radicalism, for the listener, is the virtually complete absence of more relaxed moods, as well as of much that can be called witty or humorous. Very occasionally, as in the bouncy rhythmic patterning of *Rebonds B* for percussion (1988), an enlivening exuberance counters the prevailing darkness, but this is an exception. The musical world of György Ligeti is, in this respect, not only more diverse but also closer to tradition. Like Lutosławski, he manages to be eminently individual while giving prominence to expressive archetypes which have been present in music for many centuries.

Ligeti's capacity for lightness of touch can be gauged from his comment, in 1973, that 'many of my pieces have an underground connection with *Alice in Wonderland*.'[18] Yet it is the often disconcerting quality of fantasy, of conflicts between reality and dream, or nightmare, that Ligeti admired in Lewis Carroll. Recalling wartime experiences as traumatic as those of Xenakis, he once observed, in very un-Xenakis-like terms, that 'anyone who has been through horrifying experiences is not likely to create terrifying works of art in all seriousness. He is more likely to alienate':[19] and elsewhere he speaks of a music where 'the comic elements, fear, buffa and seria are not only inextricably mixed

---

[16] Varga, *Conversations*, 63.   [17] Ibid. 53.

[18] Richard Steinitz, 'Connections with Alice', *Music and Musicians*, 22 (Dec. 1973), 42.

[19] *György Ligeti in Conversation* (London, 1983), 21.

up in it, they merge and become one and the same thing. What is serious is at the same time comical and the comical is terrifying.'[20] Similarly, we might suggest with respect to Ligeti's later work that what is 'mechanical', connected to specific ideas deriving from science and mathematics, is also intensely human and deeply felt; not for nothing is this composer attracted by the coexistence of turbulence and coherence that fractal geometry seeks to highlight.[21]

Ligeti was born in Romania but studied in Hungary and taught at the Liszt Academy in Budapest from 1950 to 1956. There the acceptable modern style was closer to Bartók than to Webern, but just as, in Poland, Lutosławski's idiom had begun to change even before political upheavals gave such changes impetus and legitimacy, so from about 1950 onwards Ligeti had begun to explore alternatives to the prevailing nationalist-cum-neo-classical manner, and his String Quartet No. 1 (1953–4) shows just how accomplished and well-characterized such relatively conservative music could be.

The brief liberalization which preceded the savagely repressed Hungarian uprising in 1956 enabled Ligeti to hear some of the most recent and progressive Eastern European music, and when he arrived in West Germany soon after the revolt was crushed he took refuge in Cologne, first with Herbert Eimert, the pioneer of electronic music, and then with Stockhausen. In the mid-1950s increasing enthusiasm for aleatory procedures and electronic techniques was leading many younger composers away from serialism. Like both Lutosławski and Xenakis, Ligeti could see no point in continuing Schoenbergian or Webernian types of twelve-note technique, and his rejection of the kind of total serialism found in Boulez's Structures Ia (1951–2) was complete.[22] He did write two electronic works, Glissandi and Articulation (both 1958), but soon abandoned the medium as too limited and primitive for his purposes: a third electronic piece, Atmosphères, was planned but eventually became a purely orchestral work (1961).

Ligeti has consistently declared himself opposed to the kind of pathos that so much earlier music, including Schoenberg's, had relied on. This helps to explain his ambivalent attitude towards German culture, and his preference for a writer like Kleist, whom he admires for 'the precision of his style, the way he describes dreadful, unbelievable things in a cool, precise manner'.[23] But coolness and precision are not to be confused with simplicity and clarity. At the heart of Ligeti's modernist aesthetic is the declaration that 'everything that is direct and unambiguous is alien to me. I love allusions, equivocal utterances, things that have many interpretations, uncertainties, background meanings.'[24] Even if, in practice, this leads to techniques which acknowledge and challenge, things that are,

[20] Ligeti in Conversation, 81.
[21] See Richard Steinitz, Musical Times, 137 (1996): 'Music, Maths and Chaos' (Mar.), 14–20, 'The Dynamics of Disorder' (May), 7–14, 'Weeping and Wailing' (Aug.), 17–22.
[22] See György Ligeti, 'Pierre Boulez: Decision and Automatism in Structure Ia', Die Reihe, 4 (1960), 36–62.
[23] Ligeti in Conversation, 57.   [24] Ibid. 102.

at least potentially, 'direct and unambiguous', rather than totally exclude them, the comment provides a useful yardstick with which to judge his achievements, and to evaluate the role of an attitude to the past that he himself characterizes as 'ambivalent . . . denying tradition by creating something new, and yet at the same time allowing tradition to shine through indirectly through allusions: that is essential for me'.[25]

Ligeti's early hostility to the inaudible complexities of serialism created that 'desire to search back for a fundamental simplicity in the musical idea itself'[26] that is evident in the slowly shifting, massive textural blocks of his early orchestral scores, *Apparitions* (1958–9) and *Atmosphères*. But he was no less convinced (in opposition to Cage) that 'a work of art is a finished and defined thing. It has nothing to do with everyday life. . . . It is something artificial.'[27] Hence his most explicitly surrealistic compositions, such as *Poème symphonique* for 100 metronomes (1962) and the pair of vocal works—*Aventures* and *Nouvelles aventures* (1961–5)—that treat their nonsense texts as the source for miniature dramas of constantly shifting emotional extremes, are at once intensely mannered and unusually clear-cut in their aesthetic effects.

Ligeti's concern for possible conjunctions between simplicity and artificiality is well illustrated by his early focus on textures which originate from a very specific and tightly controlled polyphony, or 'micro-polyphony'. At the stage in his development represented by the *Requiem* (1963–5) Ligeti used the contrast between precisely articulated rhythmic and harmonic elements, and those which were more diffuse and less explicitly defined in time and register, as the foundation of his structures. These factors are especially clear in *Clocks and Clouds* (1972–3), a work for female chorus and orchestra which alludes to an essay by the philosopher Karl Popper, and the music explores the binary opposition between the slowly shifting imprecision of cloud-like harmonic shapes and the mechanically exact rhythmic markings of time patterns. Persistently cloud-like textures had dominated earlier pieces, like the orchestral *Lontano* (1967). This begins in 4/4 time at crotchet 64, but a rigid sense of pulse is to be avoided, and one does not hear a regular succession of such beats; the polyphonic entries all take place within quintuplet, quadruple, or triplet subdivisions of the beat (Ex. 14.5).

Given that these entries generate dense cluster-chords which change their internal constitution almost imperceptibly, the pervasive cloudiness is manifest, but too predictable a uniformity is avoided by imaginative instrumentation and skilful handling of the underlying dynamic fluctuations. *Lontano* is very much a study in cloud formation, but textural contrast is not totally excluded, with occasional *simultaneous* attacks on sustained harmonies, as with the string

[25] Ibid. 105.
[26] Richard Steinitz, 'Connections with Alice', *Music and Musicians*, 22 (Dec. 1973), 42.
[27] 'Ligeti Talks to Adrian Jack', *Music and Musicians*, 22 (July 1974), 25.

Ex. 14.5. Ligeti, *Lontano*, beginning

chord at letter H, and the entry of most of the instruments on octave Ds at letter X. In neither case, however, do these assertions of uniformity lead to clear, regular accentuation; the clouds are never transformed into clocks.

Between the mid-1960s and mid-1970s Ligeti composed a series of substantial works which explore the kind of techniques and aesthetic attitudes outlined above, sometimes to intensely expressionistic effect, as in the String Quartet No. 2 (1968), sometimes with a more refined, evenly balanced dialogue between lyrical and dramatic qualities (for example, the Chamber Concerto for thirteen players, 1969–70). But around the mid-1970s Ligeti took the decision to commit himself to a large-scale traditional genre, opera: and at much the same time he became aware of musical developments, in composers like Steve Reich, Terry Riley, and Conlon Nancarrow, which were in one sense to turn him away from 'clouds' towards 'clocks', and productively to broaden the base of his engagement with musical traditions, old and new, folk and art.

Appropriately, perhaps, the opera *Le Grand Macabre* (1974–7), by far Ligeti's largest work to date, is both summation and anticipation. Its often disconcerting mixture of farce and menace recalls the musical atmosphere of the earlier works, while its tendency, especially in the final stages, to a more euphonious, but not tonal, harmony and clear-cut rhythmic patterns foreshadows the technical characteristics of much that was to come later. During work on the opera, Ligeti composed a three-movement piece for two pianos called *Monument–Selbstportrait–Bewegung* (1976), and the full title of the second movement is 'Selbstportrait mit Reich und Riley (und Chopin ist auch dabei)': 'Self-portrait with Reich and Riley, and Chopin is in there too'. The multiple allusiveness which this title proclaims fits well with Ligeti's comments about his enthusiasm for ambiguity, quoted above, and while the more relaxed moods that go with such allusions might suggest that the work marks a decisive shift from modernism to post-modernism in the composer's development, the change of atmosphere is better ascribed to a shift of emphasis within the modernist concern for the multiple and the confrontational.

In the major works which followed the opera—the Horn Trio (1982), the first book of *Études* for piano (1985), the Piano Concerto (1985–8), the second book of *Études* (1988–94), the Violin Concerto (1989–93), and the sonata for solo viola (1991–4)—a stylistic 'impurity', to use Ligeti's own term,[28] creates textural stratifications which aspire to the status of an organic, homogeneous whole yet simultaneously resist such wholeness. The main difference between Ligeti's compositions and his new-found art-music enthusiasms—not just the minimalism, but also the intensely playful constructivism of Nancarrow—is in the resulting atmosphere, where playfulness can veer into an overtly lamenting tone with the greatest of ease. Since *Le Grand Macabre* Ligeti's language has shown itself able to bring consonance and dissonance into the kind of new associations

[28] See Constantin Floros, *György Ligeti: Jenseits von Avantgarde und Postmoderne* (Vienna, 1996), 30.

that mark him as one of Bartók's truest heirs: and it has also replaced the earlier clocks/clouds dialectic with a search for what Richard Steinitz has termed a 'precarious balance between order and disorder, pattern and chaos'.[29] It is that sense of the persistently precarious which separates Ligeti from 'pure' minimalism and also from 'post-modernism'—at least as that term is generally understood.

Ligeti's reinvigorated modernism is tangible in his continued refusal to allow his music to settle down into unambiguously resolving, stable structures: 'whereas the micropolyphony at the heart of works like *Apparitions* involved an enmeshing of individual parts to produce one composite sonic mass' (a consequence of Ligeti's enthusiasm for Ockeghem, though the result is far less stable), the works of the 1980s and 1990s explore 'a hierarchy of self-contained structures operating more independently and heard simultaneously on several levels'.[30] In this music, 'dramatic juxtapositions and superimpositions, rigour and capriciousness' coexist 'in more or less equal measure'.[31] Hence the immediate attractiveness, as well as the enduring fascination, of such works as the *Études* for piano. The delicate balance of differences and similarities between the hands at the start of Study No. 5, 'Arc-en-ciel' (Ex. 14.6), suggests that the later Ligeti is rather more subtly modernistic than the earlier one. No other contemporary composer has surpassed his capacity to alternate on more or less equal terms between exuberance and lamentation, turbulence and coherence.

Luciano Berio (b. 1925)

The modernist commitment to music as something more multiple than singular informs the thinking of Berio no less profoundly than that of Ligeti. Moreover, Berio's observation that by 'musical thought . . . I mean above all the discovery of a coherent discourse that unfolds and develops simultaneously on different levels'[32] indicates recognition of that fascinating, fluctuating divide between classicism and modernism which many twentieth-century composers have been concerned to explore. As one of modern music's 'great rememberers'[33] Berio has not persuaded all observers that he has always managed to preserve an appropriate balance between spontaneity and control, imaginativeness and integration. As David Osmond-Smith has claimed, from *Epifanie* (1959–62) onwards, all of Berio's major works 'bear the stamp of . . . tension' between the 'disparate, and centrifugal', and the 'periodic compulsion to recreate some centre ground between them by activating a synthesis'.[34] This sense of tension

---

[29]   Steinitz, 'Music, Maths and Chaos', 15.
[30]   Steinitz, 'Dynamics of Disorder', 8.
[31]   Steinitz, 'Music, Maths and Chaos', 18.
[32]   Luciano Berio, *Two Interviews*, ed. and trans. David Osmond-Smith (London, 1985), 84.
[33]   Paul Griffiths, *Modern Music and After: Directions since 1945* (Oxford, 1995), 324.
[34]   David Osmond-Smith, *Berio* (Oxford, 1991), 27.

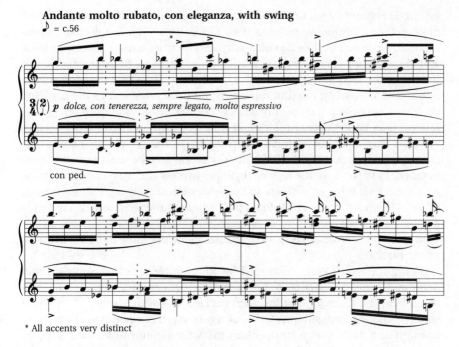

Andante molto rubato, con eleganza, with swing

* All accents very distinct

Ex. 14.6. Ligeti, *Étude No. 5*, 'Arc-en-ciel', beginning

may explain the evident exasperation of the composer's remark, in 1996, that 'classicism is nowadays like an empty box that can be filled with whatever we want'.[35] Yet it is surely an essential aspect of Berio's creative personality that such tensions are never wholly lost, and are frequently the source of his most individual and memorable achievements.

Though Berio's earliest work was tonal and romantic (like the song from 1948 included in *Recital I*, of 1972) he soon progressed, under the guidance of Dallapiccola, to an undogmatic exploration of twelve-note technique. Among his serial works are *Chamber Music* (1952), settings of James Joyce, a great and lasting influence; *Nones* (1954), an orchestral piece from a projected cantata on W. H. Auden's poem of that name; and *Serenata I* for flute and fourteen instruments (1957). In 1955 Berio was involved in setting up an electronic studio in Milan, the first stage of an extended commitment to electro-acoustic developments which led him to IRCAM (1974–80) and to his own research centre, Tempo Reale, in Florence (from 1987). Of particular significance during the Milan years was the pioneering combination of live performers and prerecorded sound in *Différences* (1958–9) for flute, clarinet, viola, cello, and harp. Here the complex yet subtle

---

[35] See H. Danuser (ed.), *Die klassizistische Moderne in der Musik des 20. Jahrhunderts* (Basle, 1997), 324.

interactions generate possibilities for purely musical drama that prompted some of Berio's most distinctive earlier scores. *Circles* (1960), the simplest and short-est, used small forces (female voice, harp, two percussionists), not electronics, and the verse of a single writer, e. e. cummings. There are five movements, and the text of the second reappears in the fourth, though making use of the music of the *first* movement; the fifth movement uses the same text as the first, and there are also clear points of contact between the music of both. Yet of greater interest than Berio's apparent flirtation with arch form in *Circles* is the balance between fixed and free elements, particularly in the sphere of rhythm. The central movement is both the freest in its notation and the most expressionistic in mood, but even here the regular rhythmic successions play a crucial part (as with the 4/4 bar on p. 30, where both the percussionists play in rhythmic unison, Ex. 14.7). The work was a vehicle for Cathy Berberian, and apart from using a wide range of vocal techniques the singer is required to play finger cymbals, claves, glass and wood chimes, to clap, to beat time, and to use three different locations on the platform.

During the 1960s, Berio continued his imaginative series of works for solo performers, called *Sequenze*, and their various elaborations, with instrumental ensembles, the *Chemins*. But his main concern was with a series of extended vocal, dramatic compositions, First, *Passaggio* (1963) has experimental attributes linking it with the theatrical 'happenings' that were a feature of the time. A speak-ing chorus is divided into five groups which are placed at different points in the auditorium and, whereas the single solo singer enacts 'the bare outline of a dramatic progression—a woman captured, interrogated, and finally freed', the choruses voice 'a wide, and often contradictory gamut of response in several different languages'. Listeners have to find their own path through 'the jungle' of these texts.[36]

Both *Laborintus II* (1965) and *Sinfonia* (1968–9) are concert works which continue the element of confrontation with generic conventions that distin-guishes *Passaggio*. From the textual point of view, *Laborintus II* is a notably oblique, discursive celebration of the 700th anniversary of Dante's birth, and although, as Osmond-Smith observes, 'with an instinctive sense of balance' Berio 'matched verbal ellipses and ambiguity with an increasingly direct musical idiom',[37] there is perhaps just too little music in this work to do full justice to the allusive, complex drama offered by the text. *Sinfonia* is very different, and it soon achieved the status of an exemplary modernist manifesto, its contemporary political references (for example to Martin Luther King) complemented by the third movement's confrontation between a text by Samuel Beckett and a symphonic movement by Mahler—a confrontation itself fragmented around a whole host of other musical references, a celebration of disconcerting diversity that creates a corresponding need to search for synthesis. Had Berio simply

---

[36] Osmond-Smith, *Berio*, 71.   [37] Ibid. 72.

fulfilled that need, then *Sinfonia* could have ended with a reversal of its earlier impulses to fracture and fragmentation. But the actual effect of the final movement is rather different. As Osmond-Smith characterizes it, the

search for similarities and common elements . . . now takes over as an autonomous principle. By means of it, Berio fuses together material from all the previous movements into a new and vitriolic synthesis. The gesture seems deeply indebted to the nineteenth-century cult of organic completion. In practice, it offers neither apotheosis nor resolution, but rather an explosion of raw energy.[38]

In this way, *Sinfonia's* essential modernism is reaffirmed rather than dissolved.

The consequences of that 'explosion of raw energy' have resonated through most of Berio's major works in the years since *Sinfonia*. The theatre-piece *Opera* (1969–70) is seminal in its 'progress from maximal diversity of resources in Acts I and II, to the richer musical concentration of Act III'.[39] *Coro* (1975–6) deals with the contrast between private, personal expressions of love and grief and the need for collective consciousness of political repression, the mosaic-like surface underpinned by symmetries which create a 'satisfying large-scale framework'.[40] In *Ritorno degli snovidenia* (1977), written for Rostropovich, the drama is more consistently private. The title, meaning 'the return of dreams', adumbrates a complex, enigmatic meditation on Russian folk materials, all-pervading yet never heard untransformed, reinforcing the music's resistance to the by now traditional modernist display of tension between the borrowed and the newly invented. As early as 1964 Berio had arranged a set of folksongs from various sources for mezzo and seven instruments, and in later years he has shown even greater interest in exploring dream-like confrontations with 'found', pre-existent musical objects: *Voci* (1984), for viola and ensemble, is based on (unheard) Sicilian folksongs, and shares *Ritorno's* aspirations to synthesis. By contrast, *Rendering* (1988) juxtaposes Berio's orchestrations of the surviving fragments for Schubert's 'tenth' symphony with his own material. This is a signally enigmatic undertaking, a reaffirmation of the simplest kind of modernist polarity. At once deferential and subversive, it is a celebration of incompatibility that leaves old and new worlds further apart than ever.

Between 1977 and 1984 Berio completed two large-scale operatic collaborations with Italo Calvino, *La vera storia* and *Un re in ascolto*, offering evidence of his concern to move closer to the conventions of traditional opera than was possible in his previous dramatic compositions. With the 'abandonment of the nervous rhythms of his earlier works for a broad, even tactus that will accommodate melodic gestures strongly rooted in the European lyrical tradition'[41] there is a more coherent, but no less subtle, treatment of dramatic themes. '*Un re in ascolto* offers a central focus, a protagonist to which everything can be related as part either of his outer or his inner world.'[42] But this movement

---

[38] David Osmond-Smith, *Playing on Words: A Guide to Luciano Berio's* Sinfonia (London, 1985), 74–5.
[39] Osmond-Smith, *Berio*, 97.   [40] Ibid. 83.   [41] Ibid. 106.   [42] Ibid. 117.

Ex. 14.7. Berio, *Circles*, end of Section 3

between inner and outer can still generate intriguing ambiguities that guard against any dilution of musical substance, and the prevailing harmonic density throws the lyric flow of the vocal lines into high relief. As a brief extract from 'Aria V' shows, the notes of the melodic line are doubled in various parts of the richly detailed accompaniment, yet this in no way weakens the communicative force of the music (Ex. 14.8).

Berio's music remains a tantalizing, elusive blend of density and directness,

Ex. 14.8. Berio, *Un re in ascolto*, from 'Aria V'

the kind of contrast that he himself might once have described in terms of Lévi-Strauss's metaphor of 'the raw and the cooked'.[43] The haunting rituals of *Ofanim* (1988) are followed by the understated eloquence of *Continuo* (1990), the most immediately obvious feature of which is a textural continuity which exists to be challenged in confrontations of varied densities which ensure an intricate kaleidoscope of rich colours. In the vivid dramatic enactments of *Chemins VI* (1996) for trumpet and ensemble, Berio's refined yet unpredictable musical imagination continues to provide substantial, purely musical delights. Most importantly of all, however, that 'alertness to the vulnerability of humanistic values'[44] which Osmond-Smith identified in the major vocal and dramatic compositions has given Berio's work a special, consistently individual resonance.

Pierre Boulez (b. 1925)

Born in the same year as Berio, Boulez can seem very different in his refusal to contemplate vulnerability in any shape or form. His relish for modernism's paradoxes has been proclaimed with typical panache: 'I believe that the fundamental unity of composing can only be found in the rupture, in the accident constantly absorbed by the law, at the same time as the constantly repeated destruction of the law by the accident',[45] and this celebration of the sheer aggressiveness of creativity is even more boldly displayed in the comment that 'a true work represents the annihilation of its own initial impulse; it surpasses and, at the same time, negates the original idea'.[46] Such attitudes reveal the resistance, especially to French conventions of good taste and musical decorum, of a composer who produced his first important works in his early twenties, and his first two piano sonatas, together with the *Sonatine* for flute and piano, all dating from the years 1945–8, mark one of the most assured débuts by any twentieth-century composer. The sheer speed with which Boulez digested and transformed existing techniques, not least Schoenbergian serialism, brought him, in less than a decade, to a confrontation with two of the three major post-war innovations, total serialism and electronics, and around 1953 he gradually began to explore the possibilities of the third, allowing performers a carefully controlled degree of choice in matters of rhythmic detail and structural sequence. Boulez was a friend of John Cage at the time of some of that composer's most radical initiatives, but it soon became clear to him that his own path would lead in a very different direction from that chosen by Cage.[47]

Over the decades Boulez's writings have provided an unfailingly provocative commentary on many aspects of musical life and work. While consistently

[43] Claude Lévi-Strauss, *Le Cru et le cuit* (Paris, 1964), is one of the source texts for Berio's *Sinfonia*.
[44] Osmond-Smith, *Berio*, 82.
[45] Pierre Boulez, *Jalons (pour une décennie)*, ed. J.-J. Nattiez (Paris, 1989), 290.
[46] Ibid. 33.
[47] See *The Boulez–Cage Correspondence*, ed. J.-J. Nattiez, trans. R. Samuels (Cambridge, 1993).

scathing about 'academicism' and lack of imagination in much earlier twentieth-century music, including most neo-classical and inter-war twelve-note compositions, he has come increasingly to appreciate the freer and more incisive features evident in earlier, expressionistic atonality (Webern's *Bagatelles*, Stravinsky's *Rite*) as well as in the understated flexibility of Debussy. Even so, the clearest appreciation of those compositional qualities which Boulez admires, and to which his own works might be assumed to aspire, can be found in his comments about Wagner. Boulez's appreciation of the *Ring* as an enterprise in which 'the hierarchy established by the traditional language gave place to mutual exchanges and to a fluidity in the emergence of musical entities',[48] and his celebration of *Parsifal* as a work in which 'for the first time we find an emphasis on uncertainty, indeterminacy, a definite rejection of finality and an unwillingness to stabilize musical events before they have exhausted their potential powers of evolution and renewal'[49] leads on to the declaration that Debussy 'is Wagner's true "heir"',[50] and of interest not for 'his vocabulary itself but its flexibility, a certain immediacy of invention, and precisely the local indiscipline in relation to the overall discipline'.[51] Flexibility, and the complexity that goes with the kind of ambiguities he admires in Berg, are what matter to Boulez.

What really interests me . . . is a work that contains a strong element of ambiguity and therefore permits a number of different meanings and solutions. The profound ambiguity may be found in a great classical work, though there it is limited by precise length and basic structural data. . . . On the other hand in today's music and today's means of expression it is possible to investigate this ambiguity, giving the work multiple meanings that the listener can discover for himself.[52]

Boulez's perceptions about the limitations of 'classicism' parallel his resistance to the stereotype of 'Frenchness'. Noting that 'the common hallmark of French art remains "good taste"—moderation and clarity', but that 'this general rule is confirmed by a series of important exceptions'[53] (including Berlioz), he often seeks to stress, with positively Xenakis-like vehemence, his own need to be confrontational: 'confrontation willed, provoked and accepted by the composer is the indispensable element that gives composition its fundamental *raison d'être*. We must never give in and simply follow the existing rules . . . but take action as direct as possible to transform those rules, which have often become nothing more nor less than the conventions of an established swindle.'[54] This is the Boulez who thrives on seeking out exaggerations and taking risks, who has 'the sort of temperament that tried to invent rules so as to have the pleasure of destroying them later; it is a dialectical evolution between freedom of invention

[48] Pierre Boulez, *Orientations*, ed. J.-J. Nattiez, trans. M. Cooper (London, 1986), 268.
[49] Ibid. 254.   [50] Ibid. 40.
[51] *Pierre Boulez: Conversations with Célestin Deliège* (London, 1976), 96.
[52] Boulez, *Orientations*, 462.   [53] Ibid. 408.   [54] Ibid. 478.

and the need for discipline in invention'.[55] The idea rings true: but so does the consequence that the conscious pursuit of such a dialectic has made the act of composition itself extremely difficult. It could even be the case that the powerful intellectual constraints with which Boulez has confronted his own spontaneous musicality have fuelled his creativity at the same time as helping to ensure that the products of that creativity are relatively few in number.

What might be termed a technique of systematic flexibility was present in Boulez's music from the beginning. As early as the Piano Sonata No. 1 (1946) there is an 'unacademic' kind of total chromaticism presenting successions of cells which gradually employ all the pitch-classes within a particular interval-span, avoiding the local shaping of traditional motivic structuring as efficiently as the overall forms avoid classical or romantic precedents.[56] Given the later direction of Boulez's music it is useful to stress the mobility of this evolutionary process, with regard both to the size of the individual cells and the order of the pitches within them, and it is not surprising that his experiments with a serial technique of maximal strictness and literalness, as in *Structures Ia* for two pianos (1952), should have been short-lived.

There was more potential in the early vocal works using texts by the surrealist poet René Char, *Le Visage nuptial* (original version 1946, revised 1989) and *Le Soleil des eaux* (1948, revised 1959 and 1968), works in which an arresting interaction between the kind of dramatic expressionism evident in the Piano Sonata No. 2 (1948) and a more understated, 'Gallic' lyricism is to be found. In Boulez's third composition using poems by Char, *Le Marteau sans maître* (1953–5) for mezzo-soprano and six players, the restricted forces employed bring the lyric element into greater prominence, although the often fragmented, volatile nature of the instrumental writing is like a distillation of the kind of suppressed expressionism found in Webern's pre-twelve-note miniatures.

The relationships between the nine movements of *Le Marteau* (a setting of three poems with instrumental commentaries) might suggest that a simple aleatory process is at work. The 'logical' scheme is as follows:

1a	Avant *L'Artisanat furieux* (instrumental)
1b	*L'Artisanat furieux* (vocal)
1c	Après *L'Artisanat furieux* (instrumental)
2a	*Bourreaux de solitude* (vocal)
2b	Commentaire I de *Bourreaux de solitude* (instrumental)
2c	Commentaire II de *Bourreaux de solitude* (instrumental)
2d	Commentaire III de *Bourreaux de solitude* (instrumental)
3a	*Bel édifice et les pressentiments* (vocal, 1st version)
3b	*Bel édifice et les pressentiments* (vocal, 2nd version)

---

[55] Boulez, *Conversations*, 64.
[56] See Gerald Bennett, 'The Early Works', in W. Glock (ed.), *Pierre Boulez: A Symposium* (London, 1986), 41–84.

But the actual scheme is 1a, 2b, 1b, 2c, 3a, 2a, 1c, 2d, 3b: Boulez comments that 'the cycles interpenetrate each other in such a way that the general form is itself a combination of three simpler structures',[57] and in this sense the design fore-shadows those later works whose schemes for alternative sectional succession observe certain requirements laid down by the composer. At the same time, however, Boulez's form-scheme underlines his preference for integration over separation, his concern to avoid the arbitrary randomness of collage. Nor does it totally exclude the 'classical' technique of cumulative repetition, or at least cross-reference: the work's final movement 'mingles elements taken from all three cycles, either textually (in the form of quotations) or *virtually*, as it were, by exploiting their potential developments. This last piece, therefore, represents an overlapping—both actual and potential—of the work's three cycles, thus forming the conjunction that concludes the work.'[58] If this is one productive way of shedding new light on an 'old' technique, another is Boulez's virtuoso trans-formation of traditional serial practice to generate the materials of a work in ways which, while not completely beyond the reach of determined analytical reconstruction, is more varied and sophisticated that anything found earlier in the century.[59]

After *Le Marteau* the basic principle of alternating, interwoven cycles remained important to Boulez, and evolved into a concept of structure as some-thing which itself can evolve, allowing a work to appear in different versions and to survive incomplete for long periods. The patron saint of this process is the poet Stéphane Mallarmé, whose presence is most palpable in the largest of the completed works, *Pli selon pli* (1957–65). Subtitled 'portrait de Mallarmé', this has five movements, of which the first and last, 'Don' and 'Tombeau', are principally orchestral, and related in structure. The three central movements, all called 'Improvisation', are anticipated in 'Don' (though this was written after them) and the degree of freedom for the performers increases until, in the third Improvisa-tion—all employ Mallarmé poems—the conductor is allowed to choose between various alternative segments.

In the way textures of great delicacy are framed by far more massive and turbulent material, *Pli selon pli* provides a model to which all of Boulez's later compositions relate in different ways. The incomplete Piano Sonata No. 3 (begun in 1956) has segments of volatile and reflective material whose order of perfor-mance is flexible within controls specified in the score (Ex. 14.9). *Domaines* (1970) takes the principle of mobility even more literally, since, in its final version for clarinet and six instrumental groups (1970) the soloist not only chooses the order in which the six passages of 'original' material and their 'mirrors' (modified retrogrades) will be heard, but plays each in the 'domain' of the appropriate instrumental group, moving about the platform as appropriate.

---

[57] Boulez, *Orientations*, 338.   [58] Ibid. 341.
[59] See Lev Koblyakov, *Pierre Boulez: A World of Harmony* (Chur, 1990).

Parenthèse

Ex. 14.9. Boulez, Piano Sonata No. 3, *Parenthèse*

Boulez has employed the interaction between a leading instrument and a supporting group in several compositions since 1970, and with sufficient consistency to suggest that he finds special satisfaction in exploring the ways in which a single, focal line can proliferate, generating its own distinct yet supportive materials. These intricate yet ultimately convergent textures give his music its characteristic refinement. It is not that the works in question lack intensity of expression, after the caricature model of Frenchness Boulez so despises, but that he is unfailingly alert to the dangers of stratified superimpositions that seem to reinforce crude varieties of separation rather than explore degrees of compatibility.

In *Rituel—in memoriam Maderna* (1974–5) for eight orchestral groups, mobility is ensured by the ways in which the music moves around the separately disposed groups of players on the platform, a process leading to ultimate convergence. Otherwise, apart from the ongoing elaborations of *Eclat/Multiples*, begun in 1965, his work has been dominated by his own typically self-critical and demanding involvement in electro-acoustics and computer synthesis at IRCAM, the institute for research into such technical possibilities at the Pompidou Centre in Paris. This sustained commitment to IRCAM coincided with a reduction in what had proved to be a phenomenally active and successful life as a conductor, but Boulez's tally of completed scores has not greatly increased. As well as the reworking of pieces which dated back to his earliest years (the orchestral versions of the *Notations* for piano), various other revisions, and a handful of shorter pieces, there are just two major works from the 1980s and early 1990s. In *Répons* (begun in 1981) for six soloists, ensemble, and electro-acoustic equipment, recurrent rhythmic patterns and even audibly focal pitches create an absorbingly immediate argument, and technology—a group of tuned percussion instruments, with piano and harp, have their sounds transformed by computer operations—intensifies the sense of drama and excitement, of response and reaction to response, that the music so vividly conveys. This broadening of expressive character, with no loss of textural intricacy and subtlety, is also evident in '. . . *explosante-fixe* . . .' (original material 1972, sextet version 1972–4, version for flutes, ensemble, and electronics begun in 1989).[60] The principal flute and its two satellites, 'fold upon fold', interact with ensemble and electronics in an extended, unbroken structure that moves memorably between turbulence and poetic reflection in Boulez's uniquely personal way, dominated by melodic material whose supple arabesques involve a greater degree of immediate, quasi-motivic repetition than the younger Boulez would have countenanced (Ex. 14.10). '. . . *explosante-fixe* . . .' serves to underline the continued validity, for Boulez, of the Mallarméan attitude, favouring a modernity of open-endedness and mobility, but rejecting the explicitly confrontational layerings of 'old' and 'new' that he dislikes in Berg's Violin Concerto and Stravinsky's *Agon*. The effect is less of an evenly balanced dialogue between explosiveness and fixity, rather of fixity exercising degrees of control over explosiveness, and leaving open the possibility of an equilibrium that can have an almost 'classical' refinement, even if the 'laws' that created it are negated and destroyed.

Hans Werner Henze (b. 1926)

Henze has spoken of his conscious concern to 'set up alternative worlds which . . . rattle . . . certainties'—the certainties in question being 'Schoenbergian serial technique and the Beethovenian idea of the sonata' which have long

[60] See Susan Bradshaw, 'The Instrumental and Vocal Music', in Glock (ed.) *Boulez Symposium* (London, 1986), 209–16.

Ex. 14.10. Boulez, '. . . *explosante fixe . . .*', material for each Transition section

provided 'the twin foundations of my musical thinking'.[61] In Henze's case, of course, these Germanic sources were always bound to provoke resistance as well as assent. Like most of the other composers discussed in this chapter, he grew up during the Second World War, and was deeply affected by his experiences. His development was therefore determined not only by hatred of fascism (reacting against his father's commitment to the Nazi cause) but also by his love-hate relationship with the Germanic music that came between Beethoven and

---

[61] Hans Werner Henze, *Language, Music and Artistic Invention*, trans. M. Whittall (Aldeburgh, 1996), 7.

Schoenberg. Admiration for Mahler and dislike of Wagner did much to determine the direction of Henze's engagement with opera. With his left-wing political sympathies he found it impossible to live in Germany, and in 1953 he settled
in Italy. Even so, his involvement with the Germanic cultural establishment was
not completely severed, and various kinds of interaction between the Italianate
and the Germanic, as well as between the radical and the conservative (in both
political and musical terms) serve to explain the character and content of his
major compositions since the mid-1950s.

Henze's early involvement with the post-war avant-garde was soon tempered
by his flair for music theatre, and from 1949, when his first opera, *Das
Wundertheater*, was produced, the type of vocal writing he wished to cultivate led him away from fractured angularity and strict serial technique. At this
stage the tension was between serialism and neo-classicism, Schoenberg and
Stravinsky: 'enslaved by one, enthralled by the other, I have tried ever since',
Henze declared in 1996, 'to sustain a double life, a contradiction, a dualism within
myself, and to draw the aesthetic consequences'.[62] The paradox here is that those
'consequences' should often seem to involve the attempt to resolve (or dissolve)
rather than to 'sustain' such dualisms. Although in its relish for clashing diversities a work like *Voices* (1973) seems to offer the very essence of a modernist
approach, Henze more often appears to be striving after reconciliations and
resolutions. For example, he has said of his opera *Der Prinz von Homburg* (1960)
that it is the 'tension between . . . two kinds of music'—expressionist-romantic
for dreams of love, serial for militarism—'which gives the opera its verve, its
specific character'.[63] In reality, however, these contrasting musical characteristics
have a stronger tendency to converge than to diverge, and in the works Henze
composed after his move to Italy, including *Homburg*'s operatic predecessor,
König Hirsch (1952–5, revised 1962) and its immediate successor, *Elegy for Young
Lovers* (1961), a distinct homogeneity of style emerged to match the often traditional character of the texture. In *Elegy* he achieved a new toughness and clarity
without sacrificing lyric beauty (Ex. 14.11), and yet the very approachability of the
music could appear to embody a rather passive cultural conformity of the kind
against which Henze, the would-be active Marxist, soon reacted.

The lightweight Symphony No. 5 (1962), written for Leonard Bernstein's New
York Philharmonic, was designed to produce a brilliant effect without seriously
challenging either performers or listeners. Yet in the same year, giving notice of
his intention to increase the ideological content of his work, Henze completed
the much more rewarding and substantial cantata, *Novae de Infinitio Laudes*, to
texts by Giordano Bruno, the Italian philosopher martyred by the Inquisition. Of
the two operas of the mid-1960s, *Der junge Lord* (1964) is a would-be sardonic
attempt to expose the social and moral defects of a small German town, while
The Bassarids (1966)—to a libretto by Auden and Kallman about the Bacchae—

---

[62] Henze, *Language, Music and Artistic Invention*, 7.   [63] Ibid. 8.

Ex. 14.11. Henze, *Elegy for Young Lovers*, from Act 1, Scene 10

is a more serious and complex examination of the forces making for social disruption.

The Bassarids, whose première at Salzburg was claimed by Henze as the decisive event in ensuring his disillusionment with the bourgeois glorification of expensive and exclusive theatrical display, is often discussed in terms of the extent to which it achieves precisely the kind of grand conjunction of diversities that the composer was shortly to reject as unsuitable for an actively political artist; its 'symphonic' form, its references to earlier tonal music, its mythologi-cal subject, all seem to proclaim the imperishability, the adaptability, of funda-mentally traditional aesthetic forms and concepts. Yet a Berg-like breadth of harmony, from simple triad to twelve-note cluster, offered Henze a repertoire of resources for widely different generic and stylistic allusions, and during the following decade he explored aspects of this potential diversity in forms more economical, flexible, and less tied to specific cultural traditions than grand oper-atic music drama. After *The Bassarids* Henze advanced into a world of more direct political statement and more hard-edged and varied musical expression, and it was here that his most enterprising accommodations with modernism, *Voices* in particular, are to be found. Henze has said that 'I found the term *musica impura* appropriate for music of the kind I practised in *Voices*',[64] and the music, like the texts, is extraordinarily diverse, moving between the world of 'high' and 'popular' art with the kind of clarity of focus and economy of means that is often missing in the compositions involving larger vocal and instrumental resources.

Since the later 1970s Henze has shown increasingly consistent signs of a concern to explore the possibilities of reconciliation—between his German roots and his Italian experiences, his Marxist sympathies and his inability to reject all bourgeois cultural values, and—most directly—between his renewed (Beethovenian, Schoenbergian) commitment to established large-scale musical genres (symphony, opera) and his desire to preserve his own personal identity within an essentially post-tonal world. His ability to provide convincing reinter-pretations of traditional genres is well demonstrated in the concerto for clarinet and thirteen players, *Le Miracle de la rose* (1981), and the seventh and eighth sym-phonies (1984, 1992–3). He has continued to work in various kinds of music theatre, including 'music drama' (*Das verratene Meer*, 1990),[65] and to compose large-scale, elaborately laid-out pieces that express personal grief (*Requiem*, 1990–2) and confront national guilt (Symphony No. 9, 1996–7). In music that is uninhibitedly emotional, elaborately interacting contrapuntal lines that echo traditional arpeggiations and chordal characteristics risk falling into diffuseness, alluding to functions which are no longer viable: this passage from *Requiem*'s 'Dies Irae' is typical (Ex. 14.12(i)). At the other extreme, the solo trumpet's blatant evocation (in the 'Rex tremendae') of the horrors of violence and warfare almost appears to relish the very thing it seeks to condemn (Ex. 14.12(ii)). In *Requiem* as a whole, nevertheless, the eloquent urgency of the writing is cumulatively con-vincing, and the listener's doubts about this or that technical detail are likely to be swept away by the emotional sincerity and dynamic energy of the musical narrative. *Requiem* confirms that the self-confessed Mahlerian impulse behind Henze's development over the years—the urge 'to find a wholly personal approach to music of the present and of the past, the trivial and the ritual music of all periods, on the basis of personal experiences and decisions'[66]—is a more

---

[64] Henze, *Language, Music and Artistic Invention*, 17.   [65] Ibid. 12.   [66] Ibid. 7.

(i)

Ex. 14.12. Henze, *Requiem*: (i) 'Dies Irae', from four bars before Fig. 17; (ii) 'Rex tremendae', from four bars before Fig. 2

fundamental factor than any essentially technical pursuit of confrontations and tensions. Henze is more concerned in the later works with transformations of earlier genres than with confronting them and setting up conflicts with them. The naturally rather diffuse character of his textural flow and formal organization (both clearly on display in *Requiem*) indicates an aspiration to organic proliferation rather than a continuation of the kind of heterogeneously assembled theatre pieces of the late 1960s and early 1970s (*El Cimarrón, Der langwierige Weg in die Wohnung der Natascha Ungeheuer*). In 1967, Henze could boldly claim

Ex. 14.12. (*cont.*)

(ii)

Ex. 14.12. (*cont.*)

that 'neither my music nor I know anything of tendencies towards synthesis'. Yet his simultaneous acknowledgement of tradition—'I have learned from Stravinsky and from the Viennese school what I had to learn, just as I have learned from much earlier masters, going back to Bach'[67]—indicates the deep-seated importance of long-standing aesthetic values for him, and helps to explain the ability of those traditional values to loom so large in the music of someone with such a relish for radical and modern thinking.

Karlheinz Stockhausen (b. 1928)

Henze's struggle to reinvent traditional genres while resisting abject surrender to the most fundamental conventions of style and structure that go with them is complemented by the evident ease with which Stockhausen leapt to the forefront of radical thought and practice around 1950, and has succeeded in remaining detached from most of what has become most orthodox in later twentieth-century music. Stockhausen's work is not thereby divorced from common concerns and principles, however, and his cycle of seven operas, *Licht*, begun in 1977 and scheduled for completion in 2002, embodies confrontation and transformation at every level. *Licht* is the ultimate expression of ways of thinking that are more philosophical than political, spiritual than aesthetic. From an early stage Stockhausen rejected all contemporary political ideologies. At the same time, he was sensitive to the possibilities of a completely new beginning for music: 'I was very much aware in 1951 that I was part of a new epoch; and that an epoch that had started hundreds of years ago, even 2,500 years ago with the way of thinking of the ancient Greeks, had finished with the last war.'[68] During the new Age of Aquarius, he came to believe that 'the work of art . . . represents . . . our transcendental consciousness', and it was the prime characteristic of that consciousness to give expression to 'a unique coherent model that forms part of the general order of the universe'.[69] Logically, therefore, 'the moral imperative of *Licht* . . . is of redeeming humanity from a condition of fragmented consciousness and restoring a primal intuition of the divine relatedness of all creation'.[70] In such a work the mundane technical attributes of modernism could be expected to become irrelevant: but, whether they did or not, they were certainly not so during the earlier phases of Stockhausen's musical career.

After a period of study which produced some quite conventional compositional exercises, Stockhausen attended Messiaen's classes in Paris in the early

---

[67] Hans Werner Henze, *Music and Politics. Collected Writings, 1953–81*, trans. P. Labanyi (London, 1982), 165.

[68] 'Spiritual Dimensions: Peter Heyworth talks to Karlheinz Stockhausen', *Music and Musicians*, 19 (May 1971), 36.

[69] Mya Tannenbaum, *Conversations with Stockhausen* (Oxford, 1987), 71.

[70] Robin Maconie, *The Works of Karlheinz Stockhausen*, 2nd edn. (Oxford, 1990), 294. See also Robin Macone, 'Stockhausen at 70', *Musical Times*, 139 (Summer 1998), 4–11.

1950s, and was soon launched on his pursuit of technical innovations: following contact with the composers of *musique concrète* 'I did the first, the very first composition with synthetic sound'.[71] This openness to new sound-sources, coupled with the rigorous examination and exploitation of existing sources, led to a remarkable sequence of works from the years 1951–6 in which he extended the serial principle, explored electronic music, and employed degrees of indeterminacy. In *Kreuzspiel* (1951), *Formel* (1951), *Kontra-Punkte* (1952–3), and *Gruppen* for three orchestras (1955–7), a serial method with its origins in the symmetries and all-embracing potentialities of Webern's twelve-note music flowered into an organizing principle of remarkable breadth and pervasiveness. Then in 1956, responding like Boulez and others to the ideas of Cage and the American experimentalists, Stockhausen completed Piano Piece XI, whose nineteen different segments can be played in any sequence the player chooses, according to certain simple guidelines as to tempo, dynamics, and mode of attack. In that same year he also finished *Gesang der Jünglinge*, in which a recording of a boy's singing voice and electronic sounds are brought together into a marvellously imaginative sonic tapestry.

Such a relish for diversity might seem to indicate a natural sympathy for modernist aesthetics, even at the expense of celebrating rather than redeeming that 'condition of fragmented consciousness'; and Stockhausen's development of what he termed 'Moment-form'—itself a natural progression from his earlier Group-form—offered the possibility of a radical alternative to traditionally fixed and goal-directed structural schemes. In essence, a work in Moment-form presents a number of musical entities, or Moments, each of which is 'individual and self-regulated, and able to sustain an independent existence. The musical events do not take a fixed course between a determined beginning and an inevitable ending, and the moments are not merely consequents of what precedes them and antecedents of what follows; rather the concentration on the NOW.'[72] This is the kind of fundamental rethinking of those 'old chains of cause and effect'[73] which may be Messiaen's greatest (if indirect) legacy to Stockhausen. Although a work in Moment-form need not be a celebration of disintegration, it implies a multivalent and mobile, rather than cumulative or goal-directed, response to the connectivity of a work's materials. In place of the progress through conflict and contrast to resolution, 'a composer is no longer in the position of beginning from a fixed point in time and moving forwards from it; rather he is moving in all directions within a materially circumscribed world'.[74]

Momente for soprano, four choral groups, and thirteen instrumentalists (1962–4, revised 1969) is Stockhausen's most vivid demonstration of the new

---

[71] *Music and Musicians* (May 1971), 36.

[72] Roger Smalley, '*Momente*: Material for the Listener and Composer', *Musical Times*, 115 (Jan. 1974), 25–6.

[73] Paul Griffiths, *Olivier Messiaen and the Music of Time* (London, 1985), 17.

[74] Smalley, '*Momente*', 26.

| – – – | $\frac{-}{-}$ | – | = = | $\frac{+}{-}$ | = = = = = = | $\begin{matrix}+\\+\\+\end{matrix}$ | Per
= = = = = | $\begin{matrix}+\\+\\-\end{matrix}$ | = = = = | + + + | $\begin{matrix}+\\+\\+\end{matrix}$ | + | $\begin{matrix}+\\+\end{matrix}$ | Per
+ + |

+ means higher or louder or longer or more segments
– means lower or softer or shorter or fewer segments
= means the same (similar) register, dynamics, duration, timbre and number of segments
PER means use regular periodicity

Ex. 14.13. Stockhausen, *Prozession*, extract from the piano part

formal principle.[75] But throughout the 1960s Stockhausen's restless imagination ensured a remarkable flexibility and variety in the nature of his compositions, which ranged from texts to stimulate improvisation (*Aus den Sieben Tagen*, 1968; *Für kommende Zeiten*, 1968–70), to explorations of other indeterminate notational methods, like the 'plus-minus' technique (*Plus-Minus*, 1963; *Prozession*, 1967, Ex. 14.13) and increasingly intense explorations of the interaction between live and electronically manipulated sound (*Kontakte*, 1959–60; *Mixtur*, 1964; *Mantra*, 1970).

Disillusionment with the idea of granting freedom to improvising musicians was one factor which led Stockhausen towards the grand controlling design of *Licht*, and it was from *Mantra* for two pianos and electronics—'my first composition based on a formula'[76]—that the idea of such a huge yet logically transformational scheme stemmed. *Licht*'s seven parts comprise *Donnerstag* (1978–80), *Samstag* (1981–4), *Montag* (1984–8), *Dienstag* (1988–91) and *Freitag* (1991–6), with *Mittwoch* projected for 1999 and *Sonntag* for 2002. Stockhausen's long-term ambition—'ultimately I want to integrate everything'[77]—is not in doubt, but at the same time, the sheer comprehensiveness of his 'metalanguage',[78] reaching out beyond music into gesture, movement, and requiring the central characters to be multiply represented by singers, players, and dancers, suggests a resistance to 'unity' in the simplest sense of the term. Nevertheless, the beauty of deriving everything in *Licht* from a short, elemental sonic formula is that there can be a flexible, spontaneous relationship between the formula itself as ultimate background and the myriad details of the seven separate operas.

Of its nature *Licht* absorbs within itself aspects of most if not all of the different phases of Stockhausen's earlier creative life, for example, his interest in the solo piano piece (*Samstag*, Scene 1), as well as with the kind of autobiographically based 'message of reconciliation'[79] that, in Maconie's view, is implicit in *Momente*, and the reaching out to the universe that is involved in large-scale conceptions like *Sternklang*, 1971 (a work to be performed out of doors) and *Sirius* (1975–7). But the comprehensiveness of Stockhausen's conception does not

---

[75] See Maconie, *Works of Stockhausen*, 127–37.
[76] See Tannenbaum, *Conversations*, 71.
[77] Jonathan Cott, *Stockhausen: Conversations with the Composer* (London, 1974), 225.
[78] Maconie, *Works of Stockhausen*, 291.   [79] Ibid. 263.

Ex. 14.14. Stockhausen, *Licht*, 'Donnerstags Abschied'

rule out a simple, ritualistic quality whose hypnotic effect is utterly unambiguous. For example, each of the five trumpet figures from the final section of *Donnerstags-Abschied* could hardly be simpler in themselves, yet their combination and context, played 'on high roof tops and balconies as the audience leaves the theatre' creates a magical effect (Ex. 14.14).

After the watershed of *Mantra*, Stockhausen's music is not merely melodic in its fundamental inspiration, but meditative, in a manner that remains bold and even forceful rather than withdrawn or delicately other-worldly (*Trans*, 1971; *Inori*, 1973–4). In this respect, tensions between the reflective and aggressive sides of the composer's personality are not so much integrated as interwoven to create the basis for the music's extraordinary expressive presence. What Maconie says of one early segment of *Licht—Der Jahreslauf* (1977)—might well prove to be true of the work as a seven-part whole: 'Stockhausen confronts and attempts an accommodation with the two sides of his nature as a composer, the one painstaking and methodical, relentlessly dedicated to working through a pre-ordained serial plan, the other a subversive propensity to break the spell, and go off on impulse in an entirely different direction.'[80] Yet if working in terms of elaborations of the cycle's basic formula truly enables the composer 'to reconcile freedom of manoeuvre with overall harmony of relationships',[81] it thereby suggests a positive dissolution of modernist procedures, modernist constraints, as

---

[80] Ibid. 266.   [81] Ibid. 270.

well as modernism's innate resistance to unambiguous portrayals of spiritual transcendence. Maconie declares that 'it is this underlying sense of continuity—melodic, structural, and procedural—which distinguishes *Licht* above all from the earlier *Momente*'.[82] He nevertheless also acknowledges that what is 'underlying' in this hugely ambitious attempt to reconstruct 'the essential perceptions of myth in an imagery and idiom intended to be both timeless and transcultural'[83] may help to create an actual impression of heterogeneity, of resistance to all-determining continuity. *Licht is* at once autobiographical, bound up with the composer's own experiences and family life, and grandly universal, other-worldly; moreover, 'for all its monumentality of scale, there is as much of the comic life and rhetoric of the European cabaret tradition, of Dada and surrealism, the magical and bizarre, in Stockhausen's conception as there is of the pomp and circumstance of church and operatic ritual'.[84] In this pervasive contrast between sacred and secular, therefore, an element of modernistic proliferation and stratification might be felt to survive, and even to prosper, reflecting the element of turbulence, the other side of the methodological coin which Maconie interprets solely in terms of fractal mathematics' ability to generate self-similar formulae. True though it surely is that 'from the time of *Mantra* through *Inori* and *Sirius* to *Licht*' Stockhausen 'has dedicated himself with increasing daring and subtlety to the invention of complex self-similar musical structures whose every dimension, from the whole to the smallest particle, is configured to the same formula',[85] the fact that he is not able to call on a musical language with tonality's perceptibly integrated, consistent, and all-embracing functionality must render the nature and influence of that 'self-similarity' more ambiguous than might at first be expected.

[82] Maconie, *Works of Stockhausen*, 287.　　[83] Ibid. 293.　　[84] Ibid.　　[85] Ibid., p. ix.

Contrasts between relative simplicity and relative complexity, between the exploitation of repetition and attempts to avoid it, have been part of twentieth-century music from the beginning. But it was only around 1960, in the United States, that an approach of such consistency, and techniques of such evident reductiveness, emerged that commentators sensed the need for a new label. Alongside the experimentalism of Cage and his followers, minimalist music seemed to offer an alternative to the twentieth century's persistent concern with preserving or extending earlier stylistic and generic traditions, and with devising complex, avant-garde alternatives to those traditions. Even if, from a late-century perspective, all it appears to have offered is 'the mystical rational-ism of serialism in a new guise'[1] that newness has proved sufficiently substan-tial and long-lasting to establish an immense gulf between it and the sounds and stylistic qualities of 'old' serialism. Minimalism cannot simply be equated with anti-modernism, however, and the paradoxes and ambiguities soon accumulate when the two phenomena are considered together. Such consideration suggests that the principal factor in this alternative music is not so much its 'minimal' content as its experimental attitude, confronting the need to win a place for its products within the existing institutional framework of concerts and recordings, and therefore to challenge mainstream modernism on its own ground.

Minimalist music itself might be thought modernist in its divided nature, split between the need to challenge traditional concepts of 'the work' and the no less patent need to conform to traditional methods of dissemination (concerts, recordings, published materials). Many minimalist composers have undoubt-edly found these twin needs a strength rather than a weakness. A leading feature of their music is the concern to experiment with the nature of musical experience itself, and to seek alternatives to the subtle, diversified complexities of modernism and modern classicism alike. The generative principle of such minimalism, as expressed by Steve Reich, is that 'I want to be able to hear the processes happening throughout the sounding music',[2] and the implication

---

[1] Ivan Hewett, 'Different Strains', *Musical Times*, 138 (Feb. 1997), 22. Detailed studies of minimalist music in its experimental context may be expected over the coming years. For the moment, there is an historically interesting account of origins and objectives in Michael Nyman, *Experimental Music: Cage and Beyond* (2nd ed., Cambridge, 1999). For a concise critical survey with useful documentary features, see K. Robert Schwarz, *Minimalists* (London, 1996).

[2] Cited in Schwarz, *Minimalists*, 11.

of this is that, far from being minuscule in length as well as minimal in content, such compositions project audible change, slowly, over extended periods of time. The music is concerned less with achieving a sublime stasis, more with clearly detectable transformation, with process, and in very simple and direct ways.

The paradox is profound. Highly complex twentieth-century music, from Schoenberg's *Five Orchestral Pieces*, Op. 16 to Ferneyhough's String Quartet No. 4, offers an emotional experience which can prove appealing, offensive, absorbing, baffling: the tension is between the elaboration of the content and the elemental nature of the experience. The sustained single intervals or slowly changing, small-scale patterns of the purer minimalist works allow time for the ear to dig deeper into the subtleties and complexities of the individual sonorities. Even a single interval, sustained through long periods of time by instrumentalists whose bowing or breathing inevitably varies the timbre and intensity of that interval, can acquire a rich multiplicity of overtones, harmonic spectra that draw the listener into a subtle, fascinating sound-world. Even though the ear cannot construct a traditional, evolutionary, goal-directed musical experience from these spectra, the aural response is not necessarily more positively passive than in the case of complex works. Minimalist music is more likely to induce a trance-like state in the listener than complex compositions, just as repeated hearings of minimalist works are far less likely to provide those gradual changes of perspective and comprehension that listeners can expect from repeated hearings of Boulez or Ferneyhough. Some minimalists acknowledge their enthusiasm for religious rituals—often non-Western— and aim at a mystical experience transcending mere aesthetics. Others see their essential experimentalism in political rather than religious terms. But in every case there is a strong message, and the need to promulgate that message may well justify the apparently irresistible tendency for composers to compromise the initial purity of their minimalism in order to invade—and attempt to transform—the bastions of those persistent, traditional forms and genres.

La Monte Young (b. 1935) and Terry Riley (b. 1935)

The paradoxes on which minimalism thrives are embodied in the work of its most seminal master, La Monte Young. A natural pioneer—Young was born in a log cabin in a remote part of Idaho, and his early 'musical' memories are of the wind and the humming of power lines—Young survived early exposure to the very different traditions of cultivated jazz and the post-Webernian avant-garde, seeking in an almost Partchian manner to explore musical essences in which nothing in the nature of sound itself would be taken for granted, and the tendency of the radical to involve the ritual would be explicit. With *Composition 1960 #7*, in which the perfect fifth B–F♯ is 'to be held for a long time', the ethos is that of a concentrated meditation in which players and listeners are one. What is aesthetically intolerable and technically crude by conventional standards offers itself as the basis of a new experience, untainted by tradition yet unashamedly manipulative in its very passivity.

Composition 1960 #7 represents only one aspect of Young's work: other *1960* pieces involve verbal instructions to perform surreal actions which need have no obvious musical consequences, and their closeness to Cage's experimental ventures has often been noted. Yet Young has distanced himself from Cageian 'multiplicity' by promoting what he termed 'the theatre of the singular event',[3] and his attitude represented what Terry Riley, an early associate, described as 'a Zen-like approach to the present; not waiting for the next thing to come along, but simply enjoying what's happening right then'.[4] Young's work has been dominated since 1964 by a single project, *The Well-Tuned Piano*, whose great length— it can last for up to six hours—and simple materials offer an imaginative representation of minimalism's basic tenets. At the same time, however, the music transcends standard minimalist characteristics in its harmonic subtlety and complexity (the result of a special tuning system), as well as its improvisatory flexibility and sense of organic unfolding, 'consisting of simple repeated chords or melodies' which imperceptibly shift over time. Indian music and religion are the decisive influences, and when Young talks of 'praying before each concert that I will be pure enough and strong enough to let this source of inspiration come through me'[5] he offers graphic evidence of his remoteness from the commercial musical world—a remoteness all the more striking in view of his early commitment to progressive jazz. Young is a deeply serious composer, whose potential to promote a constructive cross-over between serious and commercial musics has remained blocked by his preference for the margins of modern musical life.

For other pioneers the secular world of the 1960s was more attractive, and it was a Californian friend of Young's, Terry Riley, who initiated links between a new simplicity and the new technology, offering an enterprising alternative to manifestations of the 'old' complexity, which itself took on a new lease of life in the 1960s as serialism lost some of its post-war rigour. Riley's use of recorded echo effects in *Music for The Gift* (1963) revealed the expressive and structural potential of insistent, gradually changing repetitions of short musical segments: and it was this idea which Riley transferred to live instruments the following year in the ensemble piece *In C* (1964). Here 53 melodic fragments—which, as the selection shown in Ex. 15.1 indicates, vary considerably in their own individual degree

---

[3] Cited in Schwarz, *Minimalists*, 31.   [4] Ibid. 28.   [5] Ibid. 43.

Ex. 15.1. Riley, *In C*, selected materials

of minimalism—can be played in any order, each one repeated as often as the player likes before moving on to the next, and irrespective of how far the other players have got in their traversal of the same 53 segments. The resulting super-impositions are heard against the co-ordinating background of repeated Cs—an effect suggested at rehearsal by Steve Reich.

Riley, with his rock-music enthusiasms and cross-over appeal, achieved a considerable degree of commercial success in his early years. Like Young, he has shunned the consistent confrontations with more mainstream musical life that mark the work of Steve Reich and Philip Glass, while not resisting that seemingly inevitable tendency for minimalist music to turn towards enriching modes of transformation as it engaged with developments in technology. The layering 'to dizzying densities'[6] evident in *Rainbow in Curved Air* (1968) indicates the possibilities of processes of change and elaboration that would be followed with resourceful consistency by minimal music's two most prominent practitioners, Reich and Glass.

Steve Reich (b. 1936)

The early compositions of Steve Reich followed hard on the heels of *In C*, yet were quite different in content and effect, with a more determined, mechanistic feel to them that soon became identified with East Coast, as opposed to Riley's West Coast, predilections. From the beginning, however, Reich's rigorously explicit techniques were not incompatible with unambiguously engaged content: both *It's gonna rain* (1965) and *Come Out* (1966) possess dramatic and, in the latter case, political dimensions—using words spoken by a black victim of police brutality—that have returned with remarkable effectiveness in Reich's later, much longer texted works like *Different Trains* (1988) and *The Cave* (1993).

Reich developed his more assertive vein of minimalism from *Piano Phase* (1967), through *Four Organs* (1970), and on to *Drumming* (1971), an imposing and masterly demonstration of the new manner's musical strengths. *Drumming* adumbrates the essence of minimalism's later evolution both on account of its length (*c.* 90 minutes) and in its embrace of non-Western musical elements. The piece was inspired by the subtle phasing routines of African (Ewe) drumming, and it was under the pressure of the richness of these materials that Reich began to work with more diverse elements, to erode the initial austerity of his minimalist aesthetic in the interests of more substantial, absorbing, and, ultimately, heterodox musical statements.

Drumming was no less seminal for Reich in the combination it offered between large-scale rhythmic phasing and euphonious, modal pitch

---

[6] Cited in Schwarz, *Minimalists*, 47.

organization, something quite distinct from functional tonality but capable of creating a new vitality in relations between consonance and dissonance that are 'emancipated' while carrying little of the striving and tension this concept has in the work of its main proponent, Arnold Schoenberg. Nevertheless, during the 1970s and, to some degree, the 1980s, Reich's willingness to compose larger works for more substantial instrumental and orchestral forces prompted a more wide-ranging approach to harmony and tone colour alike. This phase reached a peak with *Music for Eighteen Musicians* (1974–6), continued with *Variations for Winds, Strings and Keyboards* (1979) and on to *The Four Sections* (1989), although by this time Reich was ready to turn his back on this relatively 'mainstream' phase of his work. While he has continued to compose abstract instrumental pieces, like *Nagoya Marimbas* (1994), it is the scores with evident 'extra-musical' content that have made the greatest impact, and which involve the reaffirmation of minimalism's essential simplicity and experimentalism—an originality not compromised by degrees of association, as in *City Life* (1994), with the century's greatest seeker after objective musical expression, Igor Stravinsky.

In *Different Trains*, for multi-tracked string quartet mixed in with speech and train sounds, music's capacity to act as a political and moral force is underlined, as Reich offers an autobiographical meditation on the very different aspects of Jewish experience in the war years. The basic material, derived from speech patterns which are incorporated into the texture, may indeed be 'minimal' (Ex. 15.2(i)) but the interaction between speech and music never degenerates into mechanical parroting. 'In the extraordinarily poignant music that accompanies Rachella's final reminiscence, Reich would seem to be suggesting that while America provided a new world in which to escape the external reminders of Nazi oppression, the internal wounds of the Holocaust are not so easily resolved.'[7] Rachella is a concentration camp survivor whose statement, 'there was one girl who had a beautiful voice, and they loved to listen, the Germans, and when she stopped singing they said "more, more", and they applauded', generates the overlapping counterpoints of the work's final section. The beginning of this is shown in Ex. 15.2(ii), with the musical shape of Rachella's actual words (see Ex. 15.2(i)*d*) forming the middle voice on the upper stave.

What Reich himself has described as 'both a documentary and a musical reality'[8] balances formal sophistication and straightforward musical thinking with winning conviction, and an 'intriguing ambiguity'[9] is carried over into the even more ambitious and richly textured processes of *The Cave*. Here, in a drama involving the precise and intricate interaction between speech (on video), song, and instrumental music around the politically charged topic of the Cave of the

[7] Christopher Fox, 'Steve Reich's *Different Trains*', *Tempo*, 172 (Mar. 1990), 4.
[8] Ibid. 7.   [9] Christopher Fox's phrase, ibid.

Ex. 15.2. Reich, *Different Trains*: (i) samples of basic materials *a* 1st movt., *b* 2nd movt., *c* 3rd movt., *d* 3rd movt., (ii) 3rd movt., bars 591–3

Patriarchs at Hebron, which is significant for Jews, Muslims, and Christians alike, the balance between a Nancarrow-like focus on almost mechanical technical precision and the uninhibited quality of the dramatic and emotional content give the piece an 'extraordinary ambivalence, at once cold and heated'.[10]

---

[10] Ivan Hewett, 'Reich/Korot: *The Cave*', *Musical Times*, 134 (1993), 601.

Statements of belief are filtered through impersonal mechanisms, which come across as both 'inexpressive' and 'startlingly vivid'.[11] So, although in Ivan Hewett's judgement *The Cave* ultimately 'refuses to play the modernist game of allusions, blurred edges, multiple viewpoints, layers of meaning—it is exactly what it appears to be', it is still 'a mysterious piece',[12] and that mystery stems at least in part from the ways in which it brings minimalist directness and modernist ambiguity into conjunction. Above all, *The Cave* reasserts minimalism's experimental stance, and, not surprisingly, Reich has spoken scathingly of the way in which Glass, Adams, and others have succumbed to the archaic lure of opera, rather than seeking out new forms of music theatre. Reich himself seems certain to avoid such dangerous contaminations.

Philip Glass (b. 1937)

In its earlier stages the career of Philip Glass appeared to move in harmonious parallel with that of Reich, yet Glass, with his very different background (which included a period of study with Nadia Boulanger in Paris), has proved to be significantly, even disconcertingly, different. Glass's Young-like interest in Indian culture has not obliged him to reject an equally strong engagement with Western popular music (Brian Eno, David Bowie), or to abandon subtlety in his pursuit of 'a broader public'.[13] Glass's early works, like *Music in Fifths* (1969) were hard-edged and engaging to an extent that even Reich found difficult to match, and this phase culminated in the large-scale *Music in Twelve Parts* (1971–4) which, like Reich's *Music for Eighteen Musicians*, involved the kind of structural and textural shifts and contrasts that challenged minimalism from within. Not surprisingly, perhaps, the greatest quality of a work that lasts some three and a half hours is the emergence of ambiguities, a sense of 'something that is at once perfect, mechanical, and yet unreachable and uncertain',[14] a steadily changing state in which the conjunction of 'sugary sonorities' and 'a sensibility of monastic asceticism . . . accounts for much of the weird fascination of the music. We become aware of an interesting disjunction between the abrupt nature of the local changes and the gradual nature of the global ones'—a process that in principle seems more classical than modernist, and fits well with the 'anti-expressive aesthetic of the music'.[15]

Music in Twelve Parts was indeed a *magnum opus*, and demonstrated that, as far as Glass was concerned, 'minimalism was over'.[16] In turning to music theatre and opera, he needed greater flexibility and a more traditional, romantic expressive style: yet this did not mean that the repetitive processes and simple

[11] Hewett, 'Reich/Korot: *The Cave*', 601.   [12] Ibid. 599.
[13] Cited in Schwarz, *Minimalists*, 168.
[14] Hewett, 'Different Strains', 20.   [15] Ibid. 21.
[16] Schwarz, *Minimalists*, 128.

modal materials of his minimalist phase would be totally rejected. Indeed, it is their persistence which helps to make some of his later compositions so problematic.

With its rejection of conventional linear narrative, Glass's first stage work, *Einstein on the Beach* (1976), confirmed that the radical ideals of minimalist aesthetics could serve to generate provocatively original transformations of traditional concepts of music drama. But with *Satyagraha* (1976), a study of Gandhi, 'Glass began a long, gradual march back toward convention' and a 'steady re-embrace' of 'much of the harmonic and melodic language he had previously shunned, until by the end of the decade his once austere minimalism would project an almost neo-Romantic expressive force. . . . [A]fter *Satyagraha*, there could be no doubting Glass's desire to court the mainstream.'[17] As for *Satyagraha* itself, this demonstrates the interesting consequences which arise when unvaried repetition and cumulative variation combine, with music that, while not developmental or evolutionary in the traditional sense, generates cumulative rather than static effects. The final act, which depicts the New Castle protest march of 1913 (a non-violent demonstration against racial discrimination), ends with an aria for Gandhi (tenor) to Sanskrit text, whose vocal line (Ex. 15.3(i)) consists of thirty statements of an ascending scale. These are grouped in five sections to which the orchestral accompaniment gradually adds extra layers: section 1 (Ex. 15.3(i)) has strings and organ only; section 2 (Ex. 15.3(ii)) adds woodwind and double bass; section 3 retains the arpeggiated texture of its predecessor but changes the bass line (Ex. 15.3(iii)); section 4 reverts to the original bass line and adds flute arpeggios (Ex. 15.3(iv)), while the final section (Ex. 15.3(v)) changes the position of the clarinet arpeggios and combines the two bass lines.

Further operatic stages on Glass's 'long march' include *Akhnaten* (1984) and *The Voyage* (1992), and although in these works it is possible to detect the features of a style that is almost romantic in its lyrical plangency, there has been less acclaim for Glass's attempts at a *rapprochement* with symphonic music. Schwarz says that the 'three-movement, forty-minute Symphony No. 2 (1994) is remarkably conventional, even banal, a virtual embrace of the conservative European tradition that Glass once shunned. . . . Neither *Music in Twelve Parts* nor *Einstein* could have arisen in an environment as stultifyingly predictable as this one.'[18]

John Adams (b. 1947)

John Adams has demonstrated that accommodations with tradition which do not generate stultifying predictability are possible from within a minimalist

---

[17] Ibid. 144.   [18] Ibid. 166.

Ex. 15.3. Glass, *Satyagraha*, Act 3, materials for Gandhi's final aria

predisposition. In his compositions the energy and rhythmic insistence of minimalism have been transformed, though not contradicted, by more complex
stratifications and developmental processes. While there is more than a hint of
modernist perspectives in the range of stylistic associations which Adams sets
up in some of his earlier compositions, it seems clear that his relish for the resulting instabilities was a passing phase on the way to a more integrated, even classical approach in his music of the 1990s.

Like Philip Glass, Adams is a devotee of rock music, and not-a-little sceptical
about what he has termed the 'stark and unforgiving'[19] character of contemporary serious music. Yet there is a considerable contrast between a work like
Grand Pianola Music (1981–2), an almost complacently commercial example
of undemanding concert music wearing minimalist costume, and the Chamber
Symphony (1992), which has altogether richer qualities—at least when viewed
from a standpoint that regards the concert-music tradition as worth preserving
and does not accept that contributions to it are sell-outs to a feeble sub-
neo-classical eclecticism. There is even a hint of expressionistic agitation in the
complex rhythmic instabilities of music which seems in part to be mocking
its own capacity to suggest the dangerous state of a machine ready to run amok
(Ex. 15.4). Yet Adams's range of expression is not confined to the bold and
the brash. Like Reich, he is attracted to politically correct subject-matter,
not only in moving vocal settings like *The Wound-Dresser* (1989) but also in a
pair of operas, *Nixon in China* (1987) and *The Death of Klinghoffer* (1991), which
are exemplary demonstrations of how real characters and events can be presented in imaginative and non-exploitative ways. For those who resist the
emphasis on ritual as opposed to realism in such works, the use of repetitive
pattern-making in the music will seem thin and weak: but others will judge this
a proper response to the conviction that, to make its full effect, contemporary
subject-matter is best treated, in the theatre, as mythic rather than as 'real'. It
remains to be seen whether Adams can continue his engagement with elements
of the modern 'mainstream' without risking the damaging dilutions evident in
Glass, or whether, like Reich, he prefers to reassert his own most personal radical
and even experimental attributes. Meanwhile, his works provoke strikingly different reactions, and what one commentator hears in terms of the stark qualities of a revived modernism as 'a dramatic commentary on irreconcilable
opposites' (*El Dorado*, 1992–3)[20] is dismissed by another as a 'hollowness ...
which borrows the signs and gestures of a radical intent to dress up something
terribly ordinary'.[21]

---

[19] Schwarz, *Minimalists*, 179.
[20] Robert Cowan, *Gramophone* (Apr. 1997), 48.
[21] Hewett, 'Different Strains', 23.

Ex. 15.4. Adams, Chamber Symphony, 3rd movt., from bar 143

Ex. 15.4. (*cont.*)

Ex. 15.4. (*cont.*)

The Sacred and the Simple

Just as it seems inevitable that a musical aesthetic designed to make an immediate and strong appeal to audiences should seek out subjects no less immediate within the world of politics and social life, so it makes sense that composers with strong religious convictions should consider whether or not those convictions can be validly expressed through a musical language suitable for contemplative rituals, uncontaminated by connection with the more turbulent and destructive aspects of twentieth-century culture. Through such considerations, of course, composers risk being deemed 'eccentric', yet this has not proved a deterrent.

Whereas earlier in the twentieth century eccentricity tended to imply flamboyant elaboration—in Ives, Grainger, Sorabji, for example—the sense of oddity in more recent times has associated itself with extreme paring-down. Hence the 1990s interest in the Soviet-born Galina Ustvolskaya (b. 1919), whose austerely titled trio of *Compositions* (1970–5) not only require unusual forces (for example, No. 1 is for piccolo, tuba, and piano) but reduce their musical material to the minimum required for music that is, the composer declares, 'infused with a religious spirit' and 'best suited to performance in church'.[22]

Ustvolskaya is a true original but, like Young and Riley, she remains on the margins of modern musical life. Henryck Górecki (b. 1933), Arvo Pärt (b. 1935), and John Tavener (b. 1944) are the most widely admired examples of composers whose strong religious feelings have led them away from an initial engagement with aspects of later twentieth-century expressionism and complexity, and all three have achieved a purity and directness of utterance that distinguishes them from others, like Einojuhani Rautavaara (b. 1928) or Giya Kancheli (b. 1935), whose aspirations to accessibility have promoted a more neo-romantic style, often in relation to less explicitly sacred subject-matter. Even so, attempts to consider Górecki, Pärt, and Tavener under the same technical and aesthetic criteria soon break down. Pärt has concentrated on the genres of sacred vocal music, where he has consistently applied the 'tintinnabuli' techniques that he began to develop around 1970. Unlike him, Górecki and Tavener have not avoided the major 'secular' genres—concerto, string quartet, opera—and, in Górecki's case at least, feelings of anxiety and even bitterness are shown to be compatible with his minimalist style. These feelings develop from that blend of 'inner sorrow and compassion'[23] governing the work that most fully embodies his creative personality, the Symphony No. 3 ('Symphony of sorrowful songs', 1976), and in the string quartet *Already it is Dusk* (1988) there are unarguably affecting juxtapositions of reflective and aggressive musics, each involving the presence of persistent dissonance (Ex. 15.5).

In technical respects it has been easy enough to detect in these composers a tendency to re-establish a kind of tonality, or modality, a music in which such traditional features as a controlling bass line and distinctions between consonance and dissonance can be clearly heard. Yet the nature of those distinctions should alert us to the fact that—even in the simplest of Pärt's choral settings, for example—the world is not that of traditionally functional tonal harmony. Though dissonance does not explode the musical fabric into atonal, expressionistic fragments, it is undoubtedly 'emancipated', more prominent and less subject to rules of resolution and containment than was formerly the case (and may still be in more overtly neo-romantic composition). For some listeners, therefore, the survival of such strongly articulated emblems of tension and instability enables them to respond to Pärt's music as something other than the raptly transcendent vehicle for the conveyance of supra-human, eternal values to which Pärt himself appears to aspire, and which is fully displayed in his large-scale *Passio Domini Nostri Jesu Christi Secundum Johannem* (1982).

In an eloquent, extended discussion which merits close attention, Paul Hillier has noted that, although Arvo Pärt's later music is not strictly speaking written

---

[22] See B. Morton and P. Collins (eds.), *Contemporary Composers* (London, 1992), 937.
[23] Adrian Thomas, *Górecki* (Oxford, 1997), 94.

Ex. 15.5. Górecki, *Already it is Dusk*, bars 116–29

Ex. 15.6. Pärt, *Passio*, from Fig. 62

for liturgical use, 'it none the less seems to have absorbed the same criteria, which direct composers of sacred music away from exclusively aesthetic or subjective goals, towards the continuation and preservation of a tradition'.[24] Hillier traces Pärt's reaction against a modernity which not only lacked 'the binding strength of tonality' but also tonality's 'focus on a still centre as a point of radiant permanence'.[25] Pärt regrets the severing of 'cultivated'[26] music from its vernacular roots, and appears to regard the loss of individual 'human' expression, with all the doubts and tensions appropriate to modern life, as a sacrifice worth making.

Hillier argues that Pärt's objective is 'a musical language in which originality and self-expression are not the point':[27] and yet his demonstration of the principles of tintinnabular composition, which in essence involves the contrapuntal shadowing of triadic pitches according to principles of adjacency which permit quite a strong degree of secundal dissonance, raises questions about the degree of personal expression in its most characteristic musical products. Hillier evidently believes that the non-functional nature of these dissonances reduces their 'tension-creating power',[28] perhaps in the way that Debussy's frequent use of chains of major seconds seems to indicate the possibility of a new norm of relative consonance rather than a reinforcement of what, under other rules, is undoubtedly dissonant (Ex. 15.6). The point is that the sheer starkness with which dissonances emerge in Pärt's textures can render their role as some kind of 'higher' consonance ambiguous, and helps to make possible the element of human feeling evident in his *Stabat Mater* (1985), as well as what Hillier himself describes as the 'dramatic conception' of the *Miserere* (1989).[29] It is the

---

[24] Paul Hillier, *Arvo Pärt* (Oxford, 1997), 5.   [25] Ibid. 35.   [26] Ibid. 65.
[27] Hillier, *Arvo Pärt*, 22.   [28] Ibid. 160.   [29] Ibid. 151.

unchanging—some would say the monotonous—nature of Pärt's musical world, rather than the basic nature of his musical language, that offers the strongest resistance to more mainstream twentieth-century modes of expression.

In a penetrating critique, David Clarke concludes that Pärt is a composer who attempts what the modernists have refused to attempt, and yet, because his techniques cannot simply be defined as 'pre-modern', he can be heard 'as giving voice on modernism's behalf to a song that it itself may not sing'.[30] Other commentators, such as the composer Gavin Bryars, are wholly convinced of the central significance of the Pärt initiative, declaring that 'there can be little doubt that the revelation of his music has been one of the most important factors in the development of a new sensibility in recent music'.[31] For Bryars, this 'new sensibility' involves a more straightforward response to the tortuous convolutions of modernism than is proposed by Clarke, regarding modernism itself as something to be overcome, and forgotten, rather than reinvigorated and reaffirmed. By contrast, Susan Bradshaw, in a commentary on *Passio*, argues that not only are the classic virtues of variety and goal-directedness reassimilated by Pärt, but the modernist qualities of tension and ambiguity are not entirely lost either. In these terms, the elements of a new (truly post-modern?) synthesis are already in place. *Passio* is music with 'an astonishing variety not only of texture but of melodic shape, range, emphasis and, above all, pacing of events within and around its hypnotically unchanging pulse', as well as a 'sense of evolutionary intensity—of controlled movement towards an eventual outcome'.[32] Such a response is either dangerously at odds with the composer's true concerns, or penetrates to an essential truth that offers compositions like Pärt's—and even Tavener's—as a particularly promising source for the music of the future.

To an even greater extent than Górecki, and in strong contrast to Pärt, John Tavener has not sought to suppress a well-nigh erotic luxuriance in certain works of devotional spirituality. *The Protecting Veil* (1987), for cello and strings, does not exclude darker inflections of its warm, major-triad-based harmony, but the straining fulfilment of its slow-moving melodic arcs can suggest a self-regarding religiosity rather than an urgent desire to lose oneself in the supra-human. No less questionable is Tavener's decision to apply extended meditativeness to the operatic medium (*Mary of Egypt*, 1992). *The Repentant Thief* (1990), for clarinet, percussion, and strings is a much finer achievement, a concert work on a sacred theme, but subtitled 'dance-lament', and with a rhythmic vigour and harmonic astringency that show its repetitive form and simple language to best effect: the basic materials shown in Ex. 15.7 are all heard against sustained A-based consonance. Here something akin to the unforced eloquence of Tavener's earlier, large-scale compositions like *In Alium* (1968), *Ultimos Ritos* (1972),

[30] David Clarke, 'Parting Glances', *Musical Times*, 134 (1993), 684.
[31] See Morton and Collins (eds.), *Contemporary Composers*, 729.
[32] Susan Bradshaw, 'Pärt: *Passio*', *Tempo*, 168 (Mar. 1989), 51.

(i) REFRAIN

sopra, con molto rubato e espressione

(ii) DANCE

(iii) LAMENT

Ex. 15.7. Tavener, *The Repentant Thief*, principal clarinet motives: (i) Refrain; (ii) Dance; (iii) Lament

Thérèse (1979), and *Akhmatova Requiem* (1979–80) is recaptured, and distilled into a new clarity.[33]

Andriessen and Others

Even if later composers begin to build consistently on technical foundations developed by Pärt, it is difficult to conceive that the character of his texts and subject-matter will receive equal devotion. Religious belief may have triumphantly survived the turmoils of the twentieth century, but so has secular humanism, and several important composers have already demonstrated the ability to tackle large themes from within the technical possibilities that minimalism offers. Adams's operas have already been mentioned, while in Europe the challenge confronting large-scale minimalist composition when it moves back into an uncertain secular world and returns to the centre of current

---

[33] See Malcolm Crowthers, 'An Interview with John Tavener', *Musical Times*, 135 (1994), 9–14.

musical concerns—repertory, promotion, and the rest—is well represented by the work of Louis Andriessen (b. 1939).

Though Andriessen has declared American music the principal influence on his own development, it was liberal-radical, Marxist-humanist political thinking (not dissimilar to that of Henze[34]) which determined the ideological content of his works, as well as their abrasive musical character. This harshness, quite distinct from the more controlled insistence of contemporary American minimalism, is first apparent in *De Staat* (1972–6), and reaches its fullest representation in the four-part theatre-piece *De Materie* (1984–8). *De Materie* is also notable for its variety, however, and in its closing stages the development of the composition's ideas about such topics as the relation between thought and feeling, rationality and personal emotion, requires a spoken narrative, in the persona of Marie Curie, to replace, not simply complement, the austere musical lament of the final movement's early stages. It is as if Andriessen is exasperated with the exhaustion of music's expressive authenticity and prefers, in the end, to let words speak for themselves—the ultimate 'minimal' technique.

The link between minimalist composition and 'ethical' subject-matter extends into the ideologically committed music of the Andriessen-pupil Steve Martland (b. 1959)—for example, the heavy-metal, 'dirty' minimalism of the orchestral composition *Babi Yar* (1983). More broadly, experimentalism and political radicalism have continued to make common cause, most spectacularly in the later work of Cornelius Cardew (1936–81), which embraces elements of nineteenth-century style, as does Frederic Rzewski (b. 1938) in his post-Lisztian piano variations on the revolutionary song *The People United Will Never be Defeated* (1975). Even without such highly charged extra-musical content, or such 'experimental' flexibility with regard to style, minimalist music can range from the Satie-esque reticence and brevity of Howard Skempton (b. 1947) to the quasi-disco exuberance of Michael Torke (b. 1961) or Graham Fitkin (b. 1963). Such composers are often accused of commercial opportunism, and none more frequently than Michael Nyman (b. 1944), whose cannibalization of seventeenth- and eighteenth-century idioms in scores for films by Peter Greenaway has aroused especial indignation. Yet Nyman cannot be plausibly accused of writing the same piece over and over again, or of avoiding more sensitive, serious topics. His opera after Oliver Sacks, *The Man who Mistook his Wife for a Hat* (1986), has 'lyrical vocal lines over restless, chuggy, repetitive phrases and doublings of tonal, primary-coloured chords within regularly repeated harmonic blocks'. All is not saccharine predictability, however. 'Unexpected metrical shifts and harmonic angularities suggest a curious conjunction between Stravinsky and rock and roll.'[35] It is often through such conjunctions that minimalism most efficiently

---

[34] See above, Ch. 14, pp. 312–20.

[35] See Annette Morreau, 'Michael Nyman', *The New Grove Dictionary of Opera*, ed. S. Sadie (London, 1992), iii. 638.

performs its primary function of offering an alternative to high-art seriousness and grandeur which is something more than either a mockery or a total rejection of everything that high art has continued to stand for, even during the twentieth century.

The volatile musical scene of the late twentieth century embraces contrasts and oppositions which are mobile rather than static, promoting interactions as much as preserving separations. Moreover, distinguishing between 'opposition' and 'interaction' is as much a matter of personal taste as of provable 'fact'. Aesthetic response to organized sound is never more fragile than when the compositions are relatively new, the styles relatively unfamiliar: and so a survey like the following, in this chapter and its successor, is consciously constrained and provisional, a personal response to certain landmarks selected from a terrain of immense diversity and complexity.

Bernd Alois Zimmermann (1918–1970)

Much of what is most memorable in music in the later twentieth century seems to reflect Schoenberg's perception that the appropriate response of truly modern artists to their situation must be expressionist—a 'cry of distress'.[1] The need for that 'cry' to be structured, given a permanent and satisfying design, is one reason why such art need not in itself be unrelievedly negative: the commitment to the act of making and communicating is itself positive, and the result, to the listener, may therefore be cathartic, promoting a spirit of stoic, or even exalted acceptance. Such considerations have helped to make Bernd Alois Zimmermann a composer of special relevance to the 1990s, in which his music has been rediscovered after a period of relative neglect. Zimmermann was a modernist, claiming that 'we live in harmony with a huge diversity of culture from the most varied periods [and] feel at home in this network of countless tangled threads'.[2] During his lifetime, and for a while thereafter, Zimmermann's bold representations of that 'network' had gained the reputation of being self-indulgent, overemphatic, and incoherent. Longer perspectives, or simply more competent performances, have helped to show that his unsparing exploitations of stylistic clashes, while even more lurid and expressionistic than Berg's, do not destroy coherence. In Zimmermann's opera *Die Soldaten* (1958–64), reliance on such formal models as rondo and toccata provides the kind of procedural consistency comparable to

[1] Cited in Willi Reich, *Schoenberg, a Critical Biography*, trans. L. Black (London, 1968), 56.
[2] Bernt Alois Zimmermann, cited by Paul Griffiths in *Die Soldaten*, English National Opera Programme, 1996.

that of *Wozzeck*, and it is because of that consistency that the opera makes such a powerful physical and dramatic impact, an effect echoed in other works: for example, the *Requiem for a Young Poet* (1967–9), whose textual and musical materials are even more diverse.

Zimmermann's obsessive aesthetic concerns were addressed through a wide variety of media, and his chamber compositions can be even more absorbing than the larger-scale works, presenting starkly characterized studies of difference and conflict in economical close-up. *Intercommunicazione* for cello and piano (1967) is such a work, a gripping, sustained exploration of very basic types of sonority, unremittingly dark in tone yet with a strange kind of richness emerging from the imagination with which its materials are explored and developed (see Ex. 16.1). In such a work the pursuit of truth as a personally authentic 'discourse' has priority over concerns with beauty, and in this respect Zimmermann is an important precursor of many of the composers considered below.

Symphonists

That 'spirit of stoic, or even exalted acceptance' aroused by certain works of Zimmermann's can, of course, be suggested far less ambiguously, and in music that comes closer in form, style, or just in atmosphere, to the classical tradition. The later works of Elliott Carter have already been associated with such an atmosphere,[3] and in terms of relatively radical, progressive stylistic attributes, demonstrating that music can be atonal without restricting itself emotionally to pessimism and lamentation. But there are others whose symphonic music invokes the spirit of modern classicism against a more traditional, if no less vital background than Carter's, and foremost among these are two disciples of Sibelius and Nielsen, the Dane Vagn Holmboe and the Englishman Robert Simpson.

Vagn Holmboe (1909–96) composed thirteen symphonies as well as numerous concertos and string quartets. This is music whose striding, regular rhythms and often euphonious harmony exemplify the vigour of a tradition that can evoke the well-nigh ethical fervour of Hindemith's *Mathis der Maler* (Holmboe's Symphony No. 8 of 1951 and No. 13 of 1994 are particularly good examples) at the same time as such specific Nordic models as Nielsen's Fifth or Sibelius's Seventh. Though Holmboe may employ chorale-like affirmations, the predominant spirit of his music is of hopeful questing rather than unalloyed confidence: there is a characteristically twentieth-century scepticism, as in the dying falls of the thirteenth and final symphony, alongside echoes of what is perceived as a less complex past. As is particularly evident in the Symphony No. 9 (final version 1969), darker moods can help to promote a cogent balance of diversities, and his

---

[3] See above, p. 262.

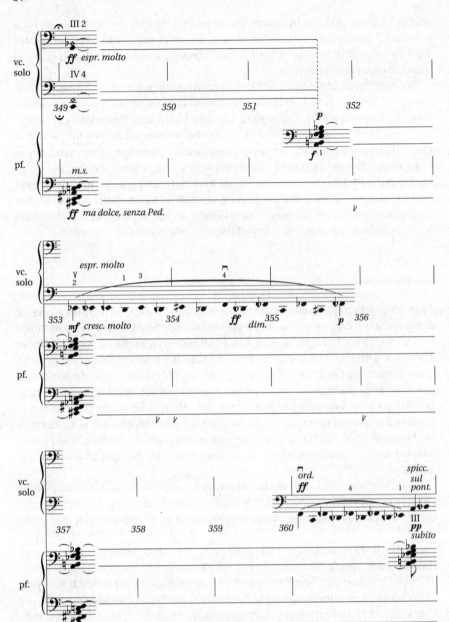

Ex. 16.1. Zimmermann, *Intercommunicazione*, from bar 349: each numbered bar should last between 1 and 2 seconds

Ex. 16.1. (*cont.*)

conclusions can be terse to a fault. Like other successfully 'conservative' modern composers, Holmboe shows that maintaining an absorbing discourse as a well-proportioned structure unfolds matters more than the immediate memorability of the basic material employed to generate that structure.

In a late-century musical climate dominated as much by the collecting instincts of CD buyers as the preferences of concertgoers—perhaps more—the series of symphonies has become a decisive emblem of significant achievement, with many practitioners from Malcolm Arnold (b. 1921) and Havergal Brian (1876–1972) to Alan Hovhaness (b. 1911) and Eduard Tubin (1905–82) attracting impassioned partisanship, even if their stars occasionally wane as rapidly as they have risen. Like Holmboe, however, Robert Simpson (1920–97) broke through to a more stable, sustained level of acceptance. With remarkable consistency, Simpson's eleven symphonies and fifteen string quartets represent the conjunction of a relatively conservative stance in respect of matters of technique and form (explicitly acknowledging the great tradition from Haydn and Beethoven through Bruckner and on to Sibelius and Nielsen, but bypassing the more diffuse tendencies which culminate in Mahler) and a progressive attitude to the language itself. This does not embrace 'atonality', still less serialism, but it finds new energy and purpose in the contrapuntal interactions of textures focused on an active bass line, and produces a sense of engagement with profound yet far from abstract or remote issues which is as appealing in its evident humanity as in its glimpses of the transcendent. None of Simpson's symphonies demonstrates these qualities more impressively than No. 5, a forty-minute single-movement design in which, as David Fanning has written, 'moods of terror, anger, anxious probing and fierce determination are right on the surface, and there is a feeling of terrific will-power being exerted to transmute these moods into a symphonic

Ex. 16.2. Simpson, Symphony No. 5 (1972), thematic materials

experience'.[4] As Ex. 16.2 shows, the material through which Simpson achieves these effects is forcefully shaped, with a compulsive rhythmic profile, and the composer exploits cumulative repetition (even side-drum figures reminiscent of Ravel's *Bolero*) without lapsing into the predictable, the four-square, or anything at all that threatens to weaken this hugely imposing and spontaneously arresting musical discourse. One cannot choose but hear.

[4] David Fanning, CD review in *Gramophone* (Feb. 1995), 58.

The French composer Henri Dutilleux (b. 1916) has created a strong impression in symphonic music stemming from very different traditions to those inspiring Holmboe and Simpson. Beginning his career in a post-war France where young composers tended to gravitate towards the radical tendencies of Messiaen and his pupils (Boulez, in particular), Dutilleux seemed doomed to inherit the mantles of urbane good humour from Poulenc and earnest symphonic busyness from Roussel. The early Piano Sonata (1945–6) and Symphony No. 1 (1950) are substantial, well-made, and far from lightweight, though lacking sufficient distinctiveness to win sustained enthusiasm for their particular traditionalisms. Gradually, however, Dutilleux's idiom acquired greater subtlety and variety through a penetrating assessment of more fundamental twentieth-century possibilities, as found in Debussy and Stravinsky, as well as, to a degree, in Berg. The strength and depth which Dutilleux eventually achieved is shown in the series of works composed after the mid-1960s: the Cello Concerto, 'Tout un monde lointain' (1968–70), *Ainsi la nuit* for string quartet (1976), the orchestral triptych *Timbre, espace, mouvement* (1978), and the Violin Concerto, 'L' Arbre des songes' (1985). Though far from undramatic, and with a strong poetic quality, most obviously reflected in the subtitles of the two concertos, Dutilleux affirms as much through understatement as through any alignment with the grander and more assertive processes of his 'Northern' contemporaries. The well-digested conjunction of Debussy and Stravinsky ensures a sense of mystery and ritual, and a refinement which has nothing in the least effete about it. Above all, there is the kind of expressive depth that is no less affecting for its avoidance of barnstorming rhetoric and for its reliance on a sophisticated appreciation of what can be achieved with well-tried but freshly imagined instrumental resources. The beginning of the second movement, 'Miroir d'espace', from *Ainsi la nuit*, is an excellent example of Dutilleux's distinctive blend of intensity and refinement (Ex. 16.3).

Toru Takemitsu (1930–1996)

The Japanese composer Toru Takemitsu was no less committed than Dutilleux to the exploration of textural refinements, in an idiom that, while stemming from Debussy, was also indebted to the highly perfumed dissonances and formal juxtapositions found in Messiaen. With Takemitsu we step aside from the symphonic in any shape or form. Concerned to create and sustain an atmosphere rather than to pursue an argument, this composer did not always avoid the inconsequential or the excessively protracted. Many of his compositions evoke dream-like states, and at his best Takemitsu attains an individual expressive depth, the sense that the music is reaching further into matters of human consciousness and feeling than words can ever do. Within the relatively simple boundaries of the piano pieces *Les Yeux clos* (1979, 1989) or the composition for

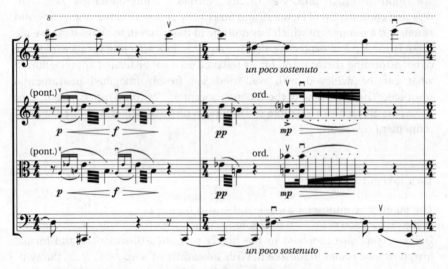

Ex. 16.3. Dutilleux, *Ainsi la nuit*, 2nd movt., opening: 'Miroir d'espace'

chamber orchestra *Rain Coming* (1982), Takemitsu creates an atmosphere which, while avoiding the challenging confrontations of more pugnacious rhetoric, possesses sufficient formal diversity and textural imagination to demonstrate that this kind of polished understatement can be as memorable, aesthetically, as

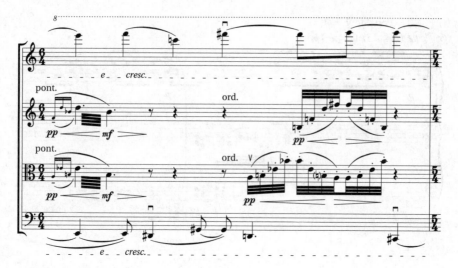

Ex. 16.3. (*cont.*)

many more conventionally dramatic forms of expression. The opening of *Les Yeux clos II*, with its stable, repeated fifth coloured and contextualized by more febrile yet no less delicate material (Ex. 16.4) delineates a world in which meditativeness itself seems to aspire to a kind of transcendence. This music nevertheless has little in common with the overt spirituality of a Pärt or a Tavener.

Valentin Silvestrov (b. 1937), Alfred Schnittke (1934–1998)

The assumption that, to be symphonic, music should embody a degree of active argument, may be used to suggest that an essentially meditative symphony—still more a minimalist one—is inherently implausible. After all, Bruckner's great meditations are enclosed by structures of enormous 'forensic' power and, without Allegros, the Adagios would lose their formal validity, as well as a good deal of their expressive substance. Attempts to break the mould are inevitably disconcerting, and critical response to the Symphony No. 5 (1980–2) by Valentin Silvestrov (b. 1937) has been divided. What makes this work particularly memorable is the understated dialectic of its engagement with the past. Though hardly ever assertive, it is far from a mere reflection of what the composer admires in the music of the romantic tradition. Its apparent nostalgia for a world of Mahlerian languor is uneasy rather than wholehearted, and while its constant repetitions suggest affinities with minimalism, the withdrawn, melancholic atmosphere could hardly be more different. Silvestrov seems to be suppressing the kind of 'late-Soviet' expressionism found particularly in Schnittke, not simply

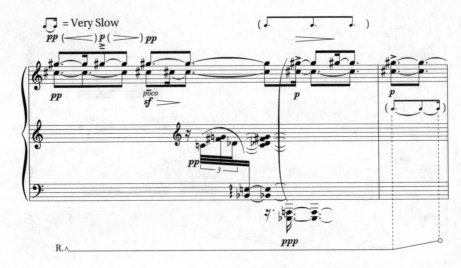

Ex. 16.4. Takemitsu, *Les Yeux clos II*, opening

bypassing it, still less refusing to acknowledge its existence. It is for such reasons that his Fifth Symphony haunts the mind, even when one would rather it did not.

By the mid-1990s, the Russian-born Alfred Schnittke had become one of the most frequently performed and recorded of all contemporary composers. His career—and not least his heroic battle against serious illness—could easily be portrayed as a metaphor for the triumphs and tragedies of developments in serious music as it grappled simultaneously with the social, political upheavals of the late twentieth century and also with the evident fact that its own identity was ineradicably bound up with perceptions about the persistent, ever more vitally influential musical past.

When a life is as eventful as Schnittke's there is an even stronger temptation than usual to link life and work—as Alexander Ivashkin unashamedly does in comments like the following:

he always felt the lack of a proper knowledge of classical music in his childhood. His later music is full of fresh, childlike, joyful Classical allusions, quotations, idioms—probably because he did not get enough of this in his early years. The shocking clashes of style in his music were clearly determined by the personal and social circumstances of his early childhood and youth, the time he spent in different cultures and 'styles', indeed in different worlds.[5]

Ivashkin's comments are valid as far as they go, but the other side of the Schnittke coin is that of consistency. In keeping with his considerable debt to Shostakovich and, through Shostakovich, to Mahler, Schnittke drank deeply from the well in which late romanticism turns towards expressionism, Mahler to Berg, music as sigh of sorrow to scream of pain. The impulsiveness of Schnittke's pursuit of the possibilities inherent in extreme expression led to some massive miscalculations, like the opera *Life with an Idiot* (1990–1). Even in a work as widely admired as the Viola Concerto (1985) repetitive insistence is pushed to the very verge of counterproductive formal stagnation, the genre threatened with abuse as much as with creative reinvigoration. But there was no point in expecting Schnittke to take the path of mediation. In his supremely provocative *Stille Nacht* for violin and piano (1978) the gradual smearing of Gruber's pretty little ditty is so shocking that it is difficult to remain unpersuaded of the composer's deeply serious intent. Nothing meant merely to provoke could be so nakedly disturbing, so unambiguously subversive (Ex. 16.5).

Just as Schnittke shunned mediation, so he escaped the confines of a single critical pigeonhole. In works like the *Choral Concerto* (1984–5) he showed signs of aspirations to serenity (without parody) that his long-standing willingness to employ consonant harmony had always made conceivable. In the end, however, the most memorable and authentic role for Schnittke was that of the master able to reanimate a traditional genre with a personal blend of allusion and self-projection. The Schnittkean expressionism of the String Trio (1985) is arguably the finest example of all, but the string quartets, concertos, and symphonies all contribute to the image of a major force whose ability to subject his own urge to stylistic and formal continuities to radical, even disruptive critique from within has produced some of the most important music of its time.

[5] Alexander Ivashkin, *Alfred Schnittke* (London, 1996), 52.

Ex. 16.5. Schnittke, *Stille Nacht*, opening

György Kurtág (b. 1926)

In his biography of Schnittke, Ivashkin makes much of the frustrations of the composer's stressful life in the Soviet Union. Schnittke was able to visit the West for the first time only in 1977, at the age of 43, and then, after he had missed many performances of his compositions because of restrictions, the year in which Gorbachev's *perestroika* really began to make a difference (1985) was also the year in which his health problems became acute. Despite these, Schnittke soon took up permanent residence outside Russia, joining the long line of twentieth-century composer-exiles.

Of these, none is more celebrated than Bartók, and few commentators have been slow to point up the analogy between Bartók's flight from his homeland, in 1939, and Ligeti's in 1956. While Ligeti's fame grew rapidly as he responded to his new environment, another Hungarian composer destined for comparable significance, György Kurtág, was virtually unheard of. Kurtág's development would no doubt have been very different if he had not spent some time studying in Paris in 1957, but he then returned to Hungary, and it was not until the later 1970s that his music began to make much impression in the West.

Many later twentieth-century composers have found particular inspiration in the expressionist miniatures of Schoenberg and Webern, but none has turned this inspiration to more profound effect than Kurtág. In part, the richness of his musical personality lies in the connections he has established between a range of contrasting associations—including the concentrated force of many Webern miniatures, the lyrical luminosity of the later serial compositions, and the integration between a national accent and an advanced compositional practice found in such works of Bartók as the violin sonatas and the third string quartet. It was a quartet that Kurtág declared to be his 'Op. 1' in 1959, and although lacking the extreme concentration and originality of his later compositions, this is already far from the kind of robust yet backward-looking neo-classicism that passed for contemporaneity in many Eastern-bloc composers during the 1950s and 1960s. Kurtág's ability to respond in an utterly personal manner to such aspects of Western avant-garde music as he was able to encounter is demonstrated with particular power in the sequence of vocal collections beginning with *The Sayings of Peter Bornemisza*, which occupied him during the middle 1960s. With an intensity unrivalled in the music of its time—only the more sustained expressionistic scores of Peter Maxwell Davies, like *Revelation and Fall* (1965), run it close—the extended sequence of miniatures comprising *Bornemisza* projects its contrasting yet predominantly black moods in music of extraordinary freedom and focus which, apart from anything else, puts the more textural kind of indeterminate composition of Lutosławski and Penderecki (b. 1933) firmly into the shade.

This sequence of works continues with *Messages of the Late Miss R. V. Troussova* (1976–80), *Scenes from a Novel* (1981–2), and *Fragments to Poems by Attila Joszef*

(1981) before reaching its fulfilment in the *Kafka Fragments* for soprano and violin of 1985–6. Consisting of thirty-nine, mainly tiny, movements, divided into three parts, this is by no means the most demanding of Kurtág's cycles to perform, but it encapsulates the spell-binding dramatic and lyric character of his work. These are intimately personal texts, and the music, varying in notation from strict to (relatively) free, responds with an uninhibited directness to the verbal imagery, in a way that is both explicitly illustrative and also alert to the psychological drama that the words reflect. No. 5 from Part 1 (Ex. 16.6) is representative in its sheer 'presence', and the way a very simple idea—the violin moves from G over C to D over G while the voice takes a different route between D/G and G/C—is composed out with material whose vividly expressive shapes are both supremely flexible and utterly unsentimental. In 'Berceuse', the text is 'Wrap your coat, lofty dream, around the child', and the music manages to combine a dream-like feeling of innocence and precarious security with a texture in which 'wrapping' is suggested by the entwining lines of voice and violin.

At this stage of Kurtág's career—the mid-1980s—it was the raw immediacy of his music, and the lacerating honesty with which its essentially humanistic values were affirmed, that were most apparent. More recently, as his works have begun to function even more directly as laments and memorials, his vehement expressionism has been monumentalized, ritualized, even though its world

Ex. 16.6. Kurtág, *Kafka Fragments*, Part 1 No. 5, 'Berceuse'

remains unremittingly secular, with none of Schnittke's Christianizing tendencies. Additional subtleties have accrued from the development of fellow feeling
with composers as different as Schumann (a shared love of cyphers and other
allusive techniques) and Luigi Nono (revered above all for his unflagging open-
mindedness and refusal to compromise). Kurtág has also added another modern
poet of lament to his collection of texts, and in his treatment of Beckett's *What
is the Word?* (1990–1) as an accompanied melodrama for an actress rediscovering
the ability to speak after an accident he reveals the serendipity of genius, matching means and ends with rare precision.

There are no less substantial musical rewards in *. . . quasi una fantasia . . .* for
piano and groups of instruments (1989) and the orchestral *Stele* (1994), which
brings into the fullest focus the power of Kurtág's later music to sustain and
intensify the expression of sorrow by way of simple repetitions which have the
cumulative effect of uplifting rather than depressing the sympathetic listener.
This is the more true since the ritual side of composition for Kurtág can involve
play as well as commemoration. The parodies and games of the ongoing *Játékok*
sequence for two pianists can employ the ferocious aggression of the earlier
vocal collections and then, in a flash, change direction and tone to something
utterly different but no less persuasive. Kurtág's earlier, hyper-modernist discontinuities may be less clearly in evidence in his later works, but the source of
its expressive force in authentically twentieth-century materials and procedures
is undiminished.

Luigi Nono (1924–1990)

In 1979 Kurtág composed some brief settings of Akhmatova and Dalos for unaccompanied chorus under the title *Omaggio a Luigi Nono*. This tribute, which
Nono reciprocated a few years later in *Omaggio a György Kurtág* for contralto,
flute, clarinet, bass tuba, and live electronics, introduces the name of a composer
widely revered by his fellow professionals but disconcerting even to many open-
minded contemporary-music enthusiasts, not least because of his lack of compromise in both his life and his work.

Taken as a whole, Nono's career pursued a consistently radical route. One commentator has seen him as following 'a Utopian path, actively seeking to engage
and change people'.[6] At first the utopian recipe involved radical politics (Nono
was active in the Italian Communist Party) and the kind of all-embracing serial
techniques that were anathema to Soviet—and other—Stalinists. The integration
of avant-garde procedures and humanist ideals in *Il Canto Sospeso* (1956) and
the opera *Intolleranza 1960* (1960–1) can be interpreted as embodying either
an exceptional ideological purity or—unintentionally—an ironic ambiguity.

---

[6] Michael Gorodecki, 'Luigi Nono: A History of Belief', *Musical Times*, 133 (1992), 17.

Intolleranza, in particular, appears to have been so closely rooted in the need to shake up complacent Venetian opera-goers in the early 1960s (a kind of Brechtian parable without the sarcasm) as to resist transplantation into other environments and later times when the issues demanded cooler and more sophisticated treatment. Whereas in *Il Canto Sospeso* the conjunction between the texts (the hopes of political prisoners of war) and the music (serialism aspiring to a new, post-Webernian level of lyric intensity) worked well, in the opera there seemed to be a serious mismatch between the subject-matter (intolerant treatment of immigrants), which is no more subtly presented than it might be on the front page of a tabloid newspaper, and the music, which aspires to embody all the qualities of high modern art, in the tradition of the angular yet impassionedly lyrical vocal style of Nono's father-in-law, Arnold Schoenberg.

Nono's pursuit of an active engagement between musical modernity and left-wing politics continued for many years, but it could well have been his overriding commitment to modernism itself as something needing to change with the times that eventually led his music into different regions. It was not that, after 1980, the political commitment disappeared: rather, as Michael Gorodecki suggests, 'Nono's political beliefs were now (simply) *private* beliefs. The wish to change his audience was through the sound itself.'[7] Whereas as late as the 'azione scenica' *Al gran sole carico d'amore* (1975)—an elaborate stage work—that 'sound' had been at times brash, at other times urgently eloquent, it now moved into a world where it seemed constantly on the verge of silence: utterances were fragmented, gnomically allusive, and various dramatic archetypes counted for more than contemporary political issues.

This process of fragmentation began in . . . *Sofferte onde serene* . . . (1975), for piano and tape, which avoids explicit political content (it reflects the close friendship between Nono and the pianist Pollini, at a time when both had suffered family bereavements) and signals a shift of emphasis away from large-scale concert or theatre works to music which owes much to the disciplines and possibilities of the electronic studio. The full force of Nono's change of direction became apparent in *Fragmente—Stille, an Diotima* (1980), an extended composition for string quartet (without electronics) which baffled some commentators in its reliance on extended silences and very quiet gestures, with only the occasional outburst to jolt the listener out of the meditative state induced by such apparent predictability.

In this work Nono completed the transition from large-scale, flamboyantly dramatic political engagement in music to a withdrawn, Beckett-like concern to grasp a few fugitive sounds, as if refusing to admit that the creative impulse had finally been defeated by a *Zeitgeist* dominated by greed and corruption. Yet it would be wrong to infer that Nono had turned from an art of hope to an anti-art of despair. There may be an unsparingly pessimistic quality to these late works,

---

[7] Gorodecki, 'Luigi Nono', 14.

but because they engage with certain archetypal poetic images they are able, almost against the odds, to move towards the kind of affirmation of the continued necessity for art which can find a place within even the most decadent and hopeless cultures. This may be the art that the late twentieth century deserves, in Nono's view, but it is an art that uses late twentieth-century resources, especially electronics, to suggest that fragmentation and discontinuity could themselves be made poetically expressive and aesthetically nourishing. Goredecki identifies in *Fragmente—Stille, an Diotima* a 'fundamental quality of fragility ... reflected in the elusive poetic quotations from Hölderlin sprinkled across the score for the players to intone silently to themselves', and to which the title alludes (Diotima being Hölderlin's ideal embodiment of love). 'At its root is an attitude filled with uncertainty, but also a boundless quest in the search for the unknown; musically speaking a faith and openness to all the possible discoveries of listening and imagination made along the path.'[8] And it was by means of this continued 'faith and openness' that Nono was able to sustain his utopian vision.

The major work of these later years was the opera *Prometeo* (1981–5). Though far from a conventional narrative treatment of the story of the mythic, romantic-heroic figure, this 'tragedy to be perceived through the hearing only'— there is no staging as such, the performers mingling with the audience, and little by way of comprehensible text—is the ultimate manifestation of Nono's exploratory modernism, a 'structure of discontinuity'. Yet it is as likely to succeed in 'changing' its audiences as any of the composer's more didactic earlier pieces, and most commentators on the work seem to accept that its impact is, ultimately, positive. In the end, it is the quiet refinement of the sound, the magical effects of what one reviewer has called this 'strange, beautiful ceremony', [9] that bring to *Prometeo* some of the positive attributes of the work of art. The message seems to be, 'Listen carefully, seriously, to the fugitive sounds of late-modernist music, and your perceptions of the world may change. Like Prometheus, you may even experience a new freedom.' The means could hardly be more different from those of *Intolleranza 1960*, but the message is not so different, and the question for the future to consider is whether *Prometeo* has a better chance of survival, of sustaining and achieving its ambitions, than does the more overtly Marxist piece. *Prometeo* makes 'extreme demands' of the listener, yet it offers 'a challenging redefinition of how music may encompass myth and drama':[10] in this way, it links itself with, and even celebrates, a great tradition that it might otherwise appear determined to subvert.

A sense of 'strange, beautiful ceremony' is no less evident in *Omaggio a György Kurtág* (1983–6), whose slow accumulations of quiet sonorities have their already potent air of distilled expressionism increased still further by the use of electronic

[8] Ibid. 16.   [9] Michael Oliver, *Gramophone* (Dec. 1995), 150.
[10] Ibid.

Ex. 16.7. Nono, *Omaggio a György Kurtág*, bars 42–9

transformation: the markings under bar 45 in Ex. 16.7 identify the point at which electronic sound emerges. As the performance notes in the score explain, 'Aria intonata' is a progression from breath noise ('soffio') to sung pitch: 'tibet' in the tuba part indicates 'a change in timbre obtained by continually varying . . . the shape of the oral cavity', a quality 'similar to Tibetan vocal technique'.

With their open embrace of modernist polarities— 'an amalgamation of melodic continuity and a fragmentation implying open-endedness'[11]—Nono's

---

[11] Jürg Stenzl, '*Prometeo*—a Listener's Guide', essay with recording on EMI Classics 5 55209 2 (1995), 58.

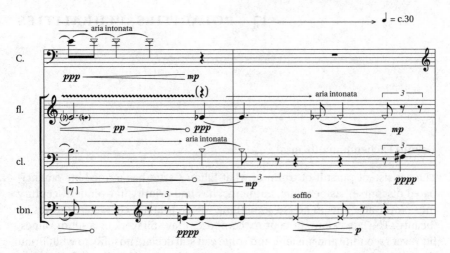

Ex. 16.7. (*cont.*)

late compositions reflect an essentially contemporary melancholia that plumbs
deeper levels of feeling than more classically balanced, playful music can hope
to do. It offers less consolation too, but in its concern with the strategies of power,
desire, and identity, it seems—as do many works of Kurtág, or the fine Hölder-
lin-based *Scardanelli* cycle (1975–91) by Heinz Holliger (b. 1939)—to affirm that
the true role of the artist is to act as the conscience of the present. By contrast,
more optimistic music offers a possible model for the future, while speaking
strongly to the present of the extent to which complexity can move away from
reflecting stress to hinting at exuberance and even at a kind of serenity. Some
additional perspectives on these very different possibilities are provided in
Chapter 17.

Helmut Lachenmann (b. 1935)

The consistent pursuit of truth, of what Elliott Carter has termed an 'emancipated discourse',[1] as personal, authentic, has had priority in twentieth-century music over attempts to create something whose primary characteristic was its 'beauty'. The late twentieth-century composer may still work by a set of values, however recondite and austere, and some can still declare hostility to what Brian Ferneyhough perceives as 'the present state of value-free pluralism'.[2] Composers may even reach the point of concerning themselves exclusively with 'rigidly constructed denial, with the exclusion of what appears to me as listening expectations pre-formed by society'. This radical declaration was made by Helmut Lachenmann and applies, he claims, to his compositions since *TemA* (1968) and *Air* (1968–9). It might seem to be the ultimate in negative anarchism, yet it was clearly framed from a position of extreme idealism:

if the act of composing is meant to go beyond the tautological use of pre-existent expressive forms and—as a creative act—to recall that human potential which grants man the dignity of a cognisant being, able to act on the basis of this cognition, then composition is by no means a 'putting together' but rather a 'taking apart' and more: a confrontation with the interconnections and necessities of the musical substance.[3]

The paradox, then, is that only by embracing denial is Lachenmann able to affirm in a way he considers right for the time and place in which he finds himself. A disciple of Nono, and believing that music must 'oppose itself to normative and sanitising pressures in society, as part of a wider political engagement',[4] he can easily appear threatening, like a commissar seeking to enforce change. Another composer who thinks along comparable lines, Richard Barrett (b. 1959), has acknowledged that Lachenmann's music 'usually presents a forbidding face to the world, thanks to his avoidance of any kind of formal continuity or cross-referencing'; yet (perhaps because of this alignment with modernist methodologies) it is music 'whose expressive impact can often be

---

[1] Elliott Carter, *Collected Essays and Lectures, 1937–1995*, ed. J. W. Bernard (Rochester, NY, 1997), 188.
[2] Brian Ferneyhough, *Collected Writings*, ed. J. Boros and R. Toop (Amsterdam, 1995), 27.
[3] Helmut Lachenmann, in B. Morton and P. Collins (ed.), *Contemporary Composers* (London, 1992), 526. See also Ian Pace, 'Positive or Negative: The Music of Helmut Lachenmann', *Musical Times*, 139 (Jan. and Feb. 1998), 9–17, 4–15.
[4] Ibid.

powerful'. Not only does Lachenmann convey 'a profoundly humanistic attitude to the responsibility of the composer', but 'what appears in theory to be denial is indeed transformed in practice into affirmation'.[5]

Playing the 'transformation' card here seems too easy an option, and the most many listeners will be prepared to accept is that Lachenmann's music enacts a confrontation between affirmation and denial, between power of expression, subtlety of form, and a spirit of austerity that seems to speak far more directly of contemporary (anti-Marxist) realities than of anything more visionary or compassionate. Lachenmann may have his vision of a 'different and, by implication, better world',[6] but his music's engagement is with the bad world of the present, and it is therefore most notable, in another sympathetic assessment, for its 'black humour, its visceral impact and destructive commentary on past models'.[7] This is nowhere more explicit than when Lachenmann turns away from his normally complex materials to the utter simplicity of a nursery rhyme, 'Hänschen klein', and makes thoroughly alarming child's play out of it (Ex. 17.1). Larger scale confrontations of 'past models' and traditional genres are offered in Lachenmann's second string quartet (1989), subtitled 'Dance of the Blessed Spirits', while his two-hour opera in twenty-three scenes, *Das Mädchen mit den Schwefelhölzern*, first performed in 1997, combines radical and traditional features, in that, while 'the work utilizes vocal and instrumental sonorities which do not conform with a bourgeois aesthetic', it welds those sonorities

into a coherent musical structure. Individual sections are frequently based on standard forms, and the work is 'symphonic' insofar as it creates an overriding impression of organic growth. Within the overall form, individual gestures are equally convincing, as is the dramatic and musical pacing of the work. In short, the music conveys a sense of authority that is Beethovenian in character, if not in substance, while the handling of the subject-matter includes a religious dimension that occasionally suggests echoes of Bach.[8]

It seems only right that a composer as fiercely idealistic as Lachenmann should be spoken of in terms of such 'classic' precedents, as the very foundations of radical modernism are confronted and transformed. By comparison, even the ideas of a composer as consistently committed to the labyrinthine montages of musical complexity as Brian Ferneyhough might seem to toy with compromise. Art inspired primarily by political rather than aesthetic impulses (or by the conviction that the subordination of the aesthetic to the political cannot be avoided) will inevitably be uncomfortable, if not completely unacceptable. In any case, the twentieth-century composers whose stylistic pilgrimages have been found especially inspiring as models for their successors have tended to be those whose development can be comprehended primarily if not exclusively

---

[5] Ibid. 527.   [6] Ian Pace, *Tempo*, 197 (July 1996), 52.
[7] Gavin Thomas, 'The Poetics of Extremity', *Musical Times*, 134 (1993), 196.
[8] John Warnaby, *Tempo*, 201 (July 1997), 38.

Ex. 17.1. Lachenmann, *Ein Kinderspiel*, No. 1, 'Hänschen klein', bars 1–8 and 23–end

in musical terms. In the 1990s, one of the most important of those models was Giacinto Scelsi.

Giacinto Scelsi (1905–1988)

Like other composers born in the early years of the century—Tippett, Carter, Messiaen, Lutosławski—Scelsi came to believe that the musical language of his first maturity required root-and-branch revision if it were not to lapse into sterility. The crisis, which for Scelsi involved a period of physical and mental breakdown, came in the late 1940s. Before that, as the String Quartet No. 1 (1944) reveals, his music was in many ways traditional in form and style, with a gently consonant ending expressing the vision of a possible future that Scelsi himself would soon reject. Not, for him, the more evolutionary approach of a Shostakovich, also born in the century's first decade, who managed to avoid stagnation by intensifying the early characteristics of his style, rather than by drastically transforming them.

Between the mid-1940s and mid-1950s Scelsi's music can be seen as transitional. The fluent, fantastical thematicism of the first quartet is still perceptible in the *Divertimento No. 3* and *Coelocanth* (both 1955), which threaten to grow diffuse yet prove to be triumphs of inventive musical shaping. But it is two works of the late 1950s, the String Trio (1958) and the *Four Pieces for Orchestra* (1959), which reveal the full extent of the change on which Scelsi had embarked.

In the trio, the free-wheeling, wide-ranging ideas and textures of the earlier works are replaced by the kind of microtonal meditation around single, sustained pitches that evokes exotic musics and non-Western rituals. In the brief orchestral pieces, there is a use of instrumental colours whose weightiness and occasional harshness serve an urgent expressiveness: and it is this expressiveness which ensures that, despite the potential for sinking into some kind of static minimalism (one can also detect this danger in the second and third quartets of 1961 and 1963), Scelsi was able to maintain, and intensify, a thrilling sense of drama. A short piece like *Ko-Lho* for flute and clarinet (1966) might initially suggest close conformity to the kind of concentrated monody pioneered by Varèse in *Density 21.5* and taken up by many composers after 1950. Like other such works, *Ko-Lho* exploits the inherent tension between a restricted pitch-field and flexibility of rhythm, and at the beginning its gradual opening-up of the space around the initial D and E has an appropriate feeling of inevitability and purpose (Ex. 17.2(i)). Later, however, as Ex. 17.2(ii) illustrates, the music flowers melodically, and motivically, making it clear that the overall shape of the piece involves more than the preservation of a single 'state'. Scelsi's concern to work 'within' sounds, using microtonal inflections, links him with that primitivistic aspect of post-war avant-garde composition that scorns traditional standards of aesthetic beauty, and yet the subtlety of acoustic effect that results helps to

Ex. 17.2. Scelsi, *Ko-Lho*: (i) beginning

restore a modernistic conjunction between primitive and complex that, in Scelsi's case, is the more accessible for the relatively small scale of the musical designs involved.

Scelsi developed a preference for titles which reflected his non-Western predilections: for example, *Anahit* (1965), the Egyptian name for Venus, and *Konx-Om-Pax* (1969), combining the old Assyrian, Sanskrit, and Latin words for peace. In *Anahit*, one of the composer's finest and most approachable scores,

Ex. 17.2. Scelsi, *Ko-Lho*: (ii) bars 27–34

there is play with allusions to consonant harmony which interacts with a non-Western concern with microtonal inflections. Such music shows why Scelsi is such an important influence on 'spectral' composers like Tristan Murail and Gérard Grisey.[9] But in most of his later works, instrumental no less than vocal, an impulse which seeks to evoke a sense of the transcendent is projected through music whose character stems from the attempted synthesis of diverse factors:

[9] See below, p. 385.

active and contemplative, Western and non-Western, minimal and expressionist, even tonal and atonal. Just as Scelsi's titles indicate a concern with mediation between sacred and secular, human and divine, so the music proceeds by
challenging as well as confirming its strongly directed motion between sustained
and elaborated pitch-centres. Scelsi can create moods which progress naturally
from the granitic and grandiose to the tender and refined. It may be that the very
greatest twentieth-century music (Carter, Tippett, and Messiaen come to mind)
is rather less single-minded, more positive about the challenges posed by confronting contrast and conflict. But there is nothing simple-minded about the way
in which Scelsi composed. His is a music of essences that communicates with
passionate persuasiveness.

Scelsi's interest in extending the expressive range of conventional instruments,
particularly evident in his work with the cellist Frances-Marie Uitti—*Trilogia*
(1957–61) and *Ko-Tha* (1978)—signifies another conjunction helping to define the
general scope and character of twentieth-century music: that is, a sense of ritual
than can veer between relatively solemn commemoration and more lighthearted
play. The spirit of delight does not entirely disappear in music composed since
1950, and within the expressive space separating the solemn and the lighthearted
there is the possibility of structural play between images of discontinuity (the
mosaic and the montage) and continuity (the 'flow' of spirals, the maze-like
textural web).

Franco Donatoni (b. 1927), Mauricio Kagel (b. 1931)

Two composers often associated with the spirit of play are Donatoni and Kagel.
Donatoni shares with Scelsi the fact that his musical development represents a
triumph over mental breakdown, and a protracted search for an acceptable creative identity. To what extent his early compositions, embodying as they did an
attempt to 'reconcile [Darmstadt-influenced] serialism with the ideas of John
Cage', were directly responsible for that breakdown is difficult to say, though one
informed commentator has no qualms about declaring that, in the years before
1975, Donatoni's 'experiencing of the contemporary serial world, together with
the infinity of possibilities of Cage, was to lead him down a dark spiralling tunnel
where identity, both musical and personal, would become lost'. The orchestral
Duo per Bruno (1974–5) was, accordingly, a work of 'profound negativity' despite
the fact that 'its rich, multilayered sound-world' suggested 'a possible . . . change
of musical thinking' which the composer was at first unable to recognize and
act on.[10]

Donatoni's creative rebirth—his new-found 'joy and euphoria'—was signalled
in *Spiri* (1978) for eight instruments, and from that time, by 'concentrating on the

---

[10]   Michael Gorodecki, 'Who's Pulling the Strings?', *Musical Times*, 124 (1993), 247–8.

flow of the horizontal, a new sense of "play" began to enter the music, the surface always vibrating, nervously and exuberantly twisting and turning through sprays of arabesque'. In *Spiri* and its successors, usually small-scale but immensely lively and attractively laid out, Donatoni 'accumulated a vast technique of microstructural control which would give rise to an overall freedom—a freedom derived directly from the kind of organic structural sense he has absorbed from Bartók [the fourth quartet was a particular favourite], but which had been for so long submerged'.[11] Such later works for chamber ensemble as *Tema* (1981), *Cadeau* (1985), and *Refrain* (1986) have a Stravinskian sharpness and vitality, and a stronger gestural profile than *Spiri* itself, helped by the feeling that it does no harm to challenge that 'organic structural sense' with the vivid momentariness of distinctive episodes. In *Refrain*, scored for the rarefied ensemble of piccolo, bass clarinet, viola, double bass, mandolin, guitar, harp, and marimba, jazzy rhythms in the double bass initiate a form in which block chords (the refrain: see Ex. 17.3) and more diverse textures interact in ways that evoke not only Stravinsky but also such later devotees of mosaic-orientated design as Birtwistle. Reliance on decorative pattern-marking is as immediately attractive as it is in the more solidly organized rhythmic world of Steve Reich or John Adams, and the prevailing, if hard-won, lightness of touch is all the more effective for the vibrant compactness of the structure.

Like Donatoni, Kagel has been much sought after as a teacher, and another quality linking the two (despite obvious and enormous differences of style and scope) is an evident scepticism in face of the more pretentious aspirations of composers the solemnity of whose self-esteem is matched only by the self-protective impenetrability of their work. Kagel appears to have suffered none of the crises of identity and motivation that affected Donatoni. Relishing the role of the outsider, as an Argentinian long resident in Germany, he has nevertheless proved adaptable enough to temper the more extravagantly surreal manifestations of his earlier years (culminating in the encyclopaedic *Staatstheater* of 1971), perhaps recognizing that a more sober kind of irony, in which understatement stands in for wildly demonstrative anarchism, might prove to have a good deal more staying power, and a greater capacity to change the perceptions of those who encounter it. If this is so, then Kagel's tricentennial tribute, the *Sankt-Bach-Passion* (1985), could be the most important of his large-scale works.

Any composer who espouses the Dadaist gospel and rejoices in the 'subversion of received (and recognizable) musico-generic devices'[12] in works requiring elaborate and extended presentation always, and in Kagel's case doubtless willingly, runs the risk of producing a density and complexity difficult to distinguish from that obtained when all the compositional elements are strictly ordered and firmly fixed. Where the difference lies tends to be in an unambiguously

[11] Ibid.
[12] Ian Pace, 'Music of the Absurd? Thoughts on Recent Kagel', *Tempo*, 200 (Apr. 1997), 30.

Ex. 17.3. Donatoni, *Refrain*, bars 28–30

subversive spirit, a style which rejects lyrical solemnity as forthrightly as it caricatures the ritualistic pretensions of the conventional concert or operatic performance. It can indeed appear that *Staatstheater*, for example, is all too obviously concerned to caricature and deconstruct the conventions of operatic production and performance, and that something so unambiguous and single-minded, when built on a substantial scale, is likely to lack the sophistication and subtlety of the genre it so vigorously seeks to undermine. Here, again, the more understated relation between Kagel's *Sankt-Bach-Passion* and its very specific yet noble baroque model is more satisfying in its own terms as a commentary intended to have strong contemporary resonance than is the more blatantly parodistic *Staatstheater*.

Many elements of the *Passion* are intended to allude to the components of an actual work by Bach, whereas *Staatstheater* is a blanket response to the whole idea of opera rather than to any specific representation of the genre. The most convincing defence of *Staatstheater* is therefore that which sees its principal strength in the degree of difference between it and its model. By avoiding (unlike most other 'anti-operas') any hint of actual characterization and staging in relation to a dramatic subject, *Staatstheater* makes it impossible for the audience to maintain the normal separation between itself and the performers. It is by this token closer to a Cageian happening than to a work of art in the normal sense, whereas the *Sankt-Bach-Passion*, if less subversive of art as such, achieves a more powerfully surreal impact from having moved back inside the genre it seeks to deconstruct. Above all, Kagel takes care throughout to keep his distance from Bach's actual music. There is no direct quotation or parody of Bach's own work, and the manner Kagel adopts veers between the kind of earnest sobriety of a style not too remote from Hindemith or Hanns Eisler to more openly expressionistic gestures. There is a basic constructivism (again the spirit of Cage is evoked), involving the use of materials deriving from Bach's name, and the results of this are particularly clear in one of the tenor solos (No. 13: Ex. 17.4). The vocal line uses first the BACH motif, then a transposition (C♯, C, E♭, D), before extending another version of the motif (B, C, B♭, A) downwards by three semitones. The accompaniment also uses lines in which adjacent semitones and tones are prominent, and the character of the whole is not too remote from an extended B♭ tonality. Here the text is soberly recounting Bach's appointments in Weimar and Arnstadt. Elsewhere there is more than a hint of wry humour, gently mocking the virtual deification of Bach by twentieth-century musicians. Yet even the presence of lines like 'Ein' feste Burg is uns'rer Bach' does not detract from the respectful, even reverential tone with which the story of Bach's life is told. As a demonstration of the ability to celebrate a great tradition while unaggressively distancing oneself from it, Kagel's work has considerable appeal. For some commentators,[13] his later work tries too hard to be liked, and is compared to its

---

[13] Pace, 'Music of the Absurd?', 30.

Ex. 17.4. Kagel, *Sankt-Bach-Passion*, from No. 13

detriment with the high-principled lack of compromise found in Lachenmann
or Dieter Schnebel (b. 1930). Kagel's music has remained remarkably distinctive,
nevertheless, and his ability to balance humour and solemnity makes him one
of the most valuable and refreshing presences on the late twentieth-century
musical scene.

den Or - ga - nis - ten-dienst   an der   neu-en Kir-che   in   Arn - stadt.

Ex. 17.4. (cont.)

Peter Maxwell Davies (b. 1934)

To turn from Kagel's celebration of the life and work of an actual composer to Peter Maxwell Davies's, in his opera *Taverner* (completed in 1970), is to return to a world defined by the literalness of its skilfully managed confrontations between past and present. No less crucial to Maxwell Davies's success, and also to the questioning of the quality of his achievement that has become increasingly insistent since the 1970s, is the confrontation between an uninhibitedly expressionistic rhetoric and a meditative lyricism that seems, at its most characteristic, to be striving for an unattainable stability and serenity. From the very beginning of his career, Maxwell Davies found himself responding to diverse sources: manipulations of chant, and deployment of modality, in medieval and renaissance music; the motivic, tonal drama of the classic and romantic symphony, with its increasing tendency, in Tchaikovsky and Mahler, to confront structural hierarchies with less stable symmetries; and the polarized yet interactive routines pertaining to atonal and twelve-note manipulations on the one hand and to neo-classical pastiche and parody on the other. In such works as *Antechrist* (1967), *Eight Songs for a Mad King* (1969), and the opera *Resurrection* (completed 1987), Maxwell Davies acknowledged a substantial debt to Mahler and Berg, explicitly grappling with his sources, and creating disturbing dramas from the conflict between the evocative simplicity of survivals from the past and the complications of modern psychological perspectives. More consistently, however, at least in the extended series of symphonies and concertos that has dominated his output since the later 1970s, he has sought to establish a style which is consistent in manner, and in which tensions between old and new are worked out below the surface, in aspects of the music's formal and harmonic organization which can seem aurally opaque.

The music of all periods involves technical features which the composer may manipulate but which are not easily audible—the highest levels of hierarchic tonal structures, for example. But if what is apparent on the surface is heard as clear and coherent, thinking listeners tend not to complain that important matters are being concealed from their perception. While such a work as Maxwell Davies's large-scale Symphony No. 6 (1996), which culminates in a moving lament inscribed retrospectively to the memory of the Orkney poet George Mackay Brown, has had a powerful impact on audiences, some commentators remain troubled by what they interpret as the diffuseness of moment-to-moment motions and progressions in structures that span between thirty and sixty minutes. As I have described it elsewhere,[14] the gap between what is perceptible as fixed, structurally predominant, and what is free, weaving a path between recurrences of those more stable elements, may often seem to be too wide for a satisfactory balance to be achieved, and Davies's greatest successes have occurred when he has continued to exploit contrast and conflict, as between 'found' materials and his own style in, for example, the *Strathclyde Concerto No. 5* for violin, viola, and strings (1991). Ex. 17.5, from the beginning of the second movement, shows Davies's juxtaposition of a compressed statement of themes from Haydn's overture *L'isola disabitata* (a work which he had decided to refer to in the concerto) and serially constructed material of his own. In examples like this, the expression is in the tension, the form in the instability. Maxwell Davies is most successful, most immediately accessible, when he openly exploits the differences between old and new, borrowed and newly composed musics, turning aside from his immensely ambitious attempt to preserve the symphonic heritage by synthesizing its most basic elements with the very different aesthetic concerns and technical possibilities of the present.

Harrison Birtwistle (b. 1934)

Comparisons between the compositions of Peter Maxwell Davies and Harrison Birtwistle often seek to identify the ways in which differences of style reflect different attitudes to tradition. It is not that Birtwistle is indifferent to the past—he is not an 'experimentalist', like Cage or Feldman—but the elements from earlier times to which he alludes are fundamental cultural artefacts like mythic plots and dramatic rituals, and the evocation of specific generic models—like fugue in *Pulse Shadows. Meditations on Paul Celan* (1991–6)—is exceptional. When it comes to underlying musical materials, Birtwistle can be just as concerned as Maxwell Davies with aspects of centricity and symmetry; but he responds in an utterly individual way to the challenge of turning the arbitrary into the personal, as when he works with randomly generated strings of pitches—material with no history, and therefore quite unlike the chant-derived serial matrices of which Maxwell Davies is so fond. Though the result is the reverse of inexpressive, it can

---

[14] Arnold Whittall, 'Britten, Maxwell Davies and the Sense of Place', *Tempo*, 204 (Apr. 1998), 5–11.

Ex. 17.5. Maxwell Davies, *Strathclyde Concerto No. 5*, 2nd movt., beginning

display a granitic objectivity which is far removed from Davies's urgent and involved discourses.

After a few early miniatures, Birtwistle's output has been dominated by large-scale orchestral and vocal works whose modernist form-schemes, often mosaic-like, underpin a musical atmosphere in which irresistible evocations of melancholia, and of the human struggle to survive against the weight of dark, implacable forces, gain momentum through assertions of rhythmic energy and harmonic density as consistent as they are coherent. Like Maxwell Davies, Birtwistle has evolved a modernism that takes particular strength from the enduring cultural values of its models, those deriving from Greek drama as much as the boldly sculpted forms of Stravinsky, Messiaen, or Varèse.[15] While Birtwistle's rejection of generic titles like symphony and concerto is an obvious indication of his ability to distance himself from the past, it is still as relevant to describe a large-scale orchestral composition like *Earth Dances* (1985–6) as 'symphonic' as it is to accept that *Gawain* (1989–91) and *The Second Mrs Kong* (1994) belong to the operatic tradition, renewing it without strenuously attempting to resist it. The ending of *Earth Dances*, shown in summary in Ex. 17.6, indicates the conclusion of a process pursued with proper symphonic breadth and seriousness, albeit with a no-less-proper modernist emphasis on layered superimpositions and juxtapositions. Reiterations of a D which has been the work's principal, if intermittent centre of gravity, are ultimately displaced by the elementary strategy of stepping down to C—an effect which, heard in context, is both disconcerting and satisfying. It is not a rejection of closure as cadential completion—an assertion that it is enough for an authentically twentieth-century composition simply to stop—rather a demonstration that, in a modernist context, the 'sense of an ending' can involve something other than the confirmation of a pre-established goal.[16]

Considered together, as they so often are, Maxwell Davies and Birtwistle offer two neatly contrasted angles on modernism, two very different ways of sustaining and exploring fundamental discontinuities and polarities. That both may also be felt to aspire towards a more stable kind of modern classicism does not undermine the feeling that their music is most convincing and most successful at breaching the listener's emotional defences when, as in Birtwistle's *Melencolia I* (1976) or Maxwell Davies's *Worldes blis* (1969) and Symphony No. 6, it takes melancholy moods and projects them through a cogent argument and a complex yet stable form. The melancholy is not thereby transformed into something else, but it stands for the human acceptance of contemporary reality, a reality in which important works of art can find an honoured place.

---

[15] See Michael Hall, *Harrison Birtwistle* (London, 1984), and Arnold Whittall, 'Modernist Aesthetics, Modernist Music: Some Analytical Perspectives', in J. M. Baker *et al.* (eds.), *Music Theory in Concept and Practice* (Rochester, NY, 1997), 157–80.

[16] See Arnold Whittall, 'Comparatively Complex: Birtwistle, Maxwell Davies and Modernist Analysis', *Music Analysis*, 13 (1994), 139–59.

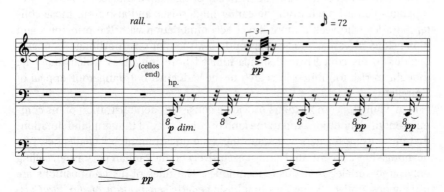

Ex. 17.6. Birtwistle, *Earth Dances*, ending (selected lines only)

Brian Ferneyhough (b. 1944)

While many, if not most, younger British composers tend to prefer less strenuous modes of expression than those of Maxwell Davies or Birtwistle, and also less monolithic, drawn-out formal designs, there remains a group for whom the pair represent the failure of the grand progressive impulse, and a sad decline into relative conformity and conventionality. The possible elements for such a critique are prominent in the compositions, and writings, of Brian Ferneyhough, where the desire to achieve 'systematic unification (or at least the peaceful coexistence) of extremes of constructional or informal modes of composition' is proclaimed.[17] Ferneyhough has been withering about 'the present state of value-free pluralism' (something he tends to associate with collage-like forms) and 'the current [1982] defeatist denunciation of "progress"'.[18] Yet he has also been positive about the determining roles that ambiguity and multiplicity must play in a viable contemporary style. His ideal therefore is not an integration purging the music of all active contrast, but a kind of montage, by means of which 'both *consistency* and *fracture* can be made to seem interestingly complementary rather than simply staring resentfully at each other over an unbridgeable void'.[19] With comments, in 1992, on his tendency 'to focus on the interruptive nature of the fragment as constituting one of the main distinctions between the Modern and subsequent periods',[20] Ferneyhough aligned himself with the kind of conscious continuation of the earlier, romantic genre of the fragment, which he sees as a persistent twentieth-century force, not least in the later work of Nono. Ferneyhough's aesthetic principles are indeed close to those that identify a mainstream modernism, rooted in the early nineteenth century and reaching its full expression in the early twentieth. It is the extreme intricacy of his actual musical language that separates Ferneyhough from the earlier modernists, and also from those contemporaries who seek a more direct accommodation with the principles and dimensions of earlier music. Appropriately, therefore, Ferneyhough is unambiguous in his concern to distance himself from initiatives which might be thought to risk too much in search of the seductive but dangerous appeal of simplicity.

Ferneyhough's compositions provide a consistent demonstration of his commitment to elaboration, and to the kind of complexity of thought (and notation) that presents performers with daunting, even unsurmountable challenges. Ferneyhough has concentrated almost exclusively on the human performer, calling only rarely on electro-acoustic techniques. The titles of his compositions are usually descriptive, sometimes in a basic generic sense—*Intermedio alla Ciaccona* (1986), *Trittico per Gertrude Stein* (1989)—often in a more allusive yet concrete poetic vein. Central to his output before 1990 is the sequence of seven compositions, *Carceri d'invenzione* (1981–6)—'dungeons of invention'—invoking

---

[17] Ferneyhough, *Collected Writings*, 131.
[18] Ibid. 27.   [19] Ibid. 438.   [20] Ibid. 484.

the etchings of Piranesi. These intricate yet uninhibitedly expressive pieces explore images of constraint and resistance to constraint in a range of textures extending from solo piccolo and solo violin to bass flute with prerecorded tape, a quintet of flute, oboe, harpsichord, cello, and soprano, and three differently constituted chamber orchestras, one with solo flute.

Ferneyhough does not work with traditional kinds of consistency. Even when restricting himself to a single line of relatively narrow registral space, as in the first section of *Carceri d'invenzione*, *Superscriptio* for piccolo (1981), the constantly evolving line is more splintered than centred, and even though for most of the time it is not literally fragmented by the insistent use of rests between sounds, its feeling of ebb and flow does not coexist with any sense of gravity, of focus on a governing feature, whether a single pitch or a recurring motive.

The result is nevertheless a music of consistent character—unremittingly unstable, exuberant, unpredictable—and increasing familiarity with it makes it possible for the listener to sense degrees of dialogue between relatively stable and less stable features. With *On Stellar Magnitudes* for mezzo-soprano and five instruments (1994), Ferneyhough's own notes stress the music's 'mercurial character', in which

changes of mood and texture should be instantaneous, with no perceptible transition. Part of the drama of the work depends on the unstable and mutable relationship gradually established between the vocal materials and the initially more 'objective' instrumental discourse. Fundamental ambiguity and momentary, seemingly arbitrary interaction are thus of the essence, and should on no account be glossed over in the interests of a superficially more seamless dramatic flow.[21]

Ferneyhough's resistance to traditional concepts of line, evident in these comments, is perfectly appropriate, given the nature of his music: and yet the dramatic character to which he also alludes implies that certain types of contrast are essential, and these can take the form of relatively stable elements which may be subordinate and transitional, yet offer the ear a marker—even a kind of background by means of which to gauge the 'mercurial character' of the whole. For example, in the later stages of *On Stellar Magnitudes* (Ex. 17.7) flute, clarinet, violin, and cello play typically unstable patterns in rhythmic unison, while the more continuous, if no less highly volatile, flow in the piano involves many repeated notes, and the soprano, too, begins each of her short phrases in the same way. This is, of course, one extreme of Ferneyhough's dialectic, and what for more conventional composers would be a norm is for him an exception. But the fact that such an effect is present at all is an indication that an element of traditional rhetoric is not utterly alien to a composer whose sense of fantasy and sheer aural imagination have always been greater than any concern with austere system-building and respect for rules.

[21] Brian Ferneyhough, Performance Notes with *On Stellar Magnitudes* (Edition Peters No. 7420; London, 1995).

Ex. 17.7. Ferneyhough, *On Stellar Magnitudes*, bars 137–41

Stability of the kind shown in Ex. 17.7 is rarely glimpsed in Ferneyhough, and his music is less about the consistent deployment of challenges to such stability than about occasional, and probably illusory, glimpses of meaningful constraints within a world of fiercely volatile flux. Such strategies keep Ferneyhough, and other composers who maintain complexity as a central aesthetic principle, at a

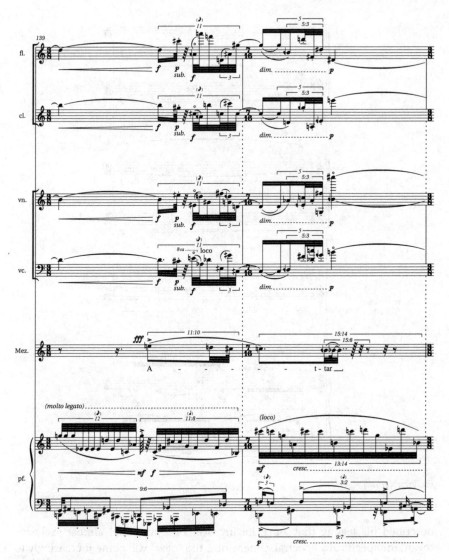

Ex. 17.7. (*cont.*)

safe distance from the kind of more 'mainstream' music that retains the desire
to control and shape a directed musical line, or to propose as a fundamental
factor a concept of stability—such as the harmonic series—which the music will
then challenge, and enrich, but not destroy. In an interview from 1991, expressing an understandable frustration with 'dualistic simplifications', Ferneyhough

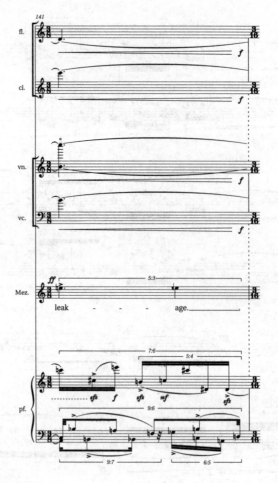

Ex. 17.7. (*cont.*)

described his feeling that 'once having overcome its initial almost exclusive regard for specifically spectral dimensions, the "new" will come increasingly to resemble the "old" by seeking richer textural and formal contexts, themselves resulting in a more obviously complex and structurally ambiguous practice'.[22] This seems a perfectly plausible diagnosis, since the so-called 'spectral' composers were making an increasingly rich and appealing contribution to the contemporary scene from the mid-1970s onwards. Among their number Tristan Murail and Magnus Lindberg stand out.

[22] Ferneyhough, *Collected Writings*, 423.

Tristan Murail (b. 1947), Magnus Lindberg (b. 1958)

Tristan Murail composed his first mature works 'around recurring harmonic spectra (e.g. the natural overtone series) whose simple consonances provide easily recognisable "beacons" ',[23] and which represent that basic dissatisfaction with the fractured syntax and more mechanistic priorities of the kind of serialism tested to destruction by the Boulez generation. Murail's initial concern, which came to fruition in his big orchestral score *Gondwana* (1980), was with 'the twin notions of process and total continuity' as 'an unbroken flow of perpetually imitating texture and timbre'.[24] Nevertheless, in what seems a natural evolution towards a more diverse and, in one sense at least, conventional kind of compositional technique, 'his more recent music has delved into the areas of discontinuity, abridged process, and contradicted expectation'. In *Désintégrations* (1982–3—significant title!) 'the raw material is derived from instrumental spectra analysed by computer', but the structure 'consists of eleven highly contrasted sections'. In *Vues aériennes* for piano, violin, cello, and horn (1988) there is the 'multiple recomposition of a single process'[25] which is satisfyingly flexible in form and instantly engaging in musical thought. In the score Murail describes the central section of the work in Messiaen-like terms as illustrating 'lumière du midi (lumière brillante, point-de-vue frontal, pas de distorsion)', and it embodies the material which the rest of the work explores from different angles: Murail makes the comparison with Monet's Rouen cathedral series. As the brief extract from 'lumière du midi' shows (Ex. 17.8), the music's profile is given force and clarity by the rhythmic coordination between horn and piano on the one hand, violin and cello on the other. Much use is made of quarter tones, and the prominence of the horn line (elsewhere it is muted and otherwise kept at a distance) reinforces that feeling of closely knit dramatic activity which gives Murail's music its distinctive presence.

The integration of harmony and timbre which spectral techniques promote makes it possible to transform traditional kinds of harmonic thinking without losing touch with the feeling for hierarchy on which the communicativeness of tonality has always depended. The music of Murail and Lindberg (among others) may in consequence have a more immediate appeal than that of more complex composers, yet such music is far from superficial or slight, not least because inherent ambiguities remain so prominent a part of its character.

With Magnus Lindberg the 'immense energy' so characteristic of his music is 'frequently generated by the conflict between primitivism and extreme sophistication',[26] an explosive combination well displayed in the ensemble composition *Kraft* (1983–5). To say that 'an underlying theme in *Kraft* is the creation of

[23] Julian Anderson, 'In Harmony: The Music of Tristan Murail', *Musical Times*, 134 (1993), 321.
[24] Ibid.   [25] Ibid. 323.
[26] John Warnaby, 'The Music of Magnus Lindberg', *Tempo*, 181 (June 1992), 25.

Ex. 17.8. Murail, *Vues aériennes*, Section 3B, beginning

some kind of order from chaos'[27] might seem to offer a recipe for anodyne conformity, yet it is the presence of bold, multi-faceted musical thought that brings
such a strong and personal sense of purpose to Lindberg's work. This is even

---

[27] Warnaby, 'The Music of Magnus Lindberg', 26.

Ex. 17.9. Lindberg, *Arena II*, bars 398–406 and final cadence

more prominent in the orchestral piece *Kinetics* (1989), which 'stresses the importance of continuity' and 'opens up new possibilities, particularly in the harmonic domain'.[28] Lindberg has continued to explore these factors in works like *Joy* (1991), the Clarinet Quintet (1992), and *Engine* (1996), reinforcing the harmonic rewards of a spectralist approach, not least its ability to connect with the twentieth century's ongoing absorption in octatonicism. With textural continuity there can even come a feeling of lyric apotheosis, and while collapse into predictable pattern-making is not always avoided, such episodes are usually offset by a satisfyingly broad melodic flow.

The final section of *Arena II* (1996) for chamber orchestra demonstrates the strengths of this style. As Ex. 17.9 shows, the initial G/D♭ polarity between melody and bass yields to the prospect of a diatonic (D♭/A♭) resolution in bar 401. This is a passing moment of relative stability, however, and despite the D♭/A♭ in the outer parts a G♯ persists in an inner voice. The lines then diverge and, at the final

---

[28] Ibid. 28.

cadence, shown in abstract form in the Example, the bass motion of G to D♭ (C♯) supports a twelve-note sonority made up of D♭ major, E♭ minor, G major, and A minor triads. Lindberg ensures satisfying closure through rhythm and texture, as well as through the suggestion that the harmonic argument has reached a point of maximum clarity: what is resolved and completed is an argument about the nature of a cadence appropriate to the music's harmonic character and circumstances.

An End-of-Century Mainstream?

Many of the most interesting composers active at the turn of the millennium work with comparable interactions between flow and fracture, the sense of a goal and the feeling of floating in goalless, if not utterly featureless, musical space. Such music comes closest to occupying a late-century mainstream, and one thoughtful historian, Michael Hall, chose to approach the evident preference for an element of compromise in late-century British music with the argument that many composers born since 1945 'wanted their music to sound avant-garde, yet they were not prepared to jettison tradition. Above all, they were not willing to abandon the presence of line, though for them "line" meant nothing so obvious as a melodic line, but a thread that ran unobtrusively through the piece.'[29] The music of Colin Matthews (b. 1946), Oliver Knussen (b. 1952), John Woolrich (b. 1954), Simon Holt (b. 1958), George Benjamin (b. 1960), and Thomas Adès (b. 1971) supports Hall's diagnosis. For example, Matthews's *Broken Symmetry* (1990–2) takes up the model carved out by Birtwistle in his 'mechanical pastorals', in which that 'unobtrusive' thread is challenged but not ultimately destroyed by the upheavals and juxtapositions evident on the musical surface. The vitality and diversity of the contemporary British mainstream can be hinted at by a simple roll call: Knussen's Horn Concerto (1994–5), Woolrich's *Lending Wings* (1989), Holt's *Sparrow Night* (1989), Benjamin's *Three Inventions* (1994–5), Adès's *Asyla* (1997), and also by the demonstrable unfairness of excluding others, such as Julian Anderson (b. 1967), Robin Holloway (b. 1943), Judith Weir (b. 1954), who have a no-less urgent claim to be included in such a list. Moreover, such fuzzy categorizations will always run the risk of appearing to downgrade the no-less-substantial achievements of composers who work more determinedly in the border regions linking mainstream and avant-garde. In the British context the outstanding example is James Dillon (b. 1950), whose *Nine Rivers* sequence, begun in 1982 and completed in 1996, is imaginative and potent enough—not least in the way it balances turbulent complexity with impetuous lyricism—to merit book-length study on its own.

The nature of what can be termed 'mainstream' is nothing if not flexible, as

---

[29] Michael Hall, *Leaving Home: A Conducted Tour of Twentieth-Century Music* (London, 1996), 214–15.

attempts to place composers from countries other than Britain in this class will show. A single example must suffice. The German Wolfgang Rihm (b. 1952) is exactly the kind of prolific, eclectic musician who attracts the scorn of purists from both the complex and minimalist (or experimentalist) extremes of the musical spectrum. 'For Rihm', Paul Griffiths declares, 'system is anathema',[30] and yet tradition is inescapable. On the basis of a background embracing Mahler, Berg, Zimmermann, Stockhausen, and Nono, and an abiding belief in 'breakage and freedom',[31] Rihm is never able to escape from those confrontations between his own perceptions and his awareness of what others have achieved. There is nothing more traditional than to search for the new, and in *Gesungene Zeit. Music for violin and orchestra* (1991–2) the paradoxes of apparent continuity—only a part of a larger fragment, Rihm claims[32]—and of driving towards silence as the best way of making music's sounding presence felt are boldly on display (Ex. 17.10). As an ending, this is as persuasive in its own meticulously evanescent fashion as is Lindberg's confidently asserted conclusion to the incisive confrontations of *Arena II*.

The Musicologist Speaks . . .

Michael Hall ended his 'conducted tour of twentieth-century music' with the claim that 'this century has produced more variety, more choice for the listener than any in the past'. At the same time 'most composers have refused to pamper their listeners', and 'those prepared to meet the challenges of the new music have found themselves taken into worlds that are exciting and rewarding'.[33]

Another erudite and encyclopaedic commentator, Paul Griffiths, has also focused on variety, observing that 'it was in the early 1960s . . . that the idea of a single way forward became untenable', and that after 'a relatively barren period . . . what happened in the mid-1980s was quite extraordinary'. Griffiths links the achievements of Birtwistle, Berio, Messiaen, Kurtág, and others with a turn 'from dogma to openness, from the institutional to the personal, from the mechanical to the natural, from invented histories to discovered ones'.[34] The implication is that music moved in parallel to life at a time when one dogma at least—Soviet Marxism—came to a surprisingly sudden end.

Robert P. Morgan has drawn less sanguine conclusions from a similar argument.

To the extent that music can be said to express the general spirit of an age it cannot be expected to mirror a consensus that does not exist elsewhere. At least until there is a

[30] Paul Griffiths, *Modern Music and After: Directions since 1945* (Oxford, 1995), 259.
[31] Ibid. 258.
[32] Notes with recording on DG 437 093 2 (1992).
[33] Hall, *Leaving Home*, 266.
[34] Griffiths, *Modern Music*, 328–9.

Ex. 17.10. Rihm, *Gesungene Zeit*, ending

profound shift in contemporary consciousness, it seems likely that music will retain its present pluralistic and uncentered quality. For music to change, the world will have to change.[35]

Morgan clearly regrets the absence of a 'system of shared beliefs and values and a community of artistic concerns'.[36] But such a thing has surely never been conceivable under modern conditions. For evidence that, even within musicology, a 'system of shared beliefs' is conspicuous by its absence I need only cite the comment concerning popular music by Rose Rosengard Subotnik that 'its pluralism has been more encompassing, and its relativism more positive, than their counterparts in art music'.[37] Roger Scruton does not go this far, but in his attempt to discriminate between the good and the bad in contemporary popular styles,[38] he reflects Subotnik's unease with assumptions about the status of the so-called serious composer at the end of a century in which serious music has failed to combine progressiveness in the technical sense with ever-widening popular appeal and comprehension. For Subotnik and Scruton, the view of Elliott Carter concerning the superiority of twentieth-century art music, quoted on page 6 of this book, is evidently to be challenged—as, in consequence, is one of the premises behind the present text.

In 1993, Harvard University Press published David Lewin's *Musical Form and Transformation: 4 Analytic Essays*, a study, over some 160 pages, of four short twentieth-century compositions from the perspective of Lewin's ideas about the nature and significance of 'transformational networks'. Lewin emphasizes that these networks 'are only metaphorical pictures of certain things that happen over the pieces as wholes, pictures that make manifest certain characteristic (recurrent) transformational motifs'.[39] Reflecting a process of increasing comprehension, these networks are the product of activity close to the musical surface rather than of hierarchies generated from a deep structure, and to this extent Lewin might be felt to have some sympathy with Fred Lerdahl, who claims that 'listeners to atonal music do not have at their disposal a consistent, psychologically relevant set of principles by which to organize pitches at the musical surface. As a result, they grab on to what they can: relative salience becomes structurally important, and within that framework the best linear connections are made.'[40]

Not the least of the virtues of the impact of Schenkerian analysis in the later twentieth century has been to encourage acceptance of the possibility that post-tonal music is precisely that. To expect a comparable 'syntax', a comparable

[35] Robert P. Morgan, *Twentieth-Century Music* (New York, 1991), 489.
[36] Ibid.
[37] Rose Rosengard Subotnik, *Developing Variations* (Minneapolis, 1991), 289.
[38] Roger Scruton, *The Aesthetics of Music* (Oxford, 1997).
[39] David Lewin, *Musical Form and Transformation* (New Haven, 1993), p. xiii.
[40] Fred Lerdahl, 'Atonal Prolongational Structures', *Contemporary Music Review*, 4 (1989), 84.

sense of hierarchy, between Webern and Boulez on the one hand, and Bach and Beethoven on the other, is pointless. Listeners will 'organize' post-tonal music as they may, and some composers have undoubtedly sought to force listeners to confront the issue of difference from the past by resisting consistency, repetition, explicit thematic identity, and variation. In music dominated by fractured rhythms and textures it is difficult to perceive anything as more salient than anything else. Yet, as Lewin and Lerdahl demonstrate, it is not impossible: in the absence of contrast between repetition and non-repetition, there may still be degrees of co-ordination within the texture: points of simultaneous attack contrasting with the absence of such points (see Ex. 17.7 above). To this extent, a feeling of dialogue between degrees of convergence and divergence, stability and instability, can still be sensed and an experience is still to be had, even if the syntax of the text remains inscrutable. There may still be a salient *atmosphere*, of magic or menace, often suggesting a peculiarly modern form of the sublime or 'sentimental' apprehension of nature: either that or, in the absence of any anecdotal rhetoric, the composition may be a celebration of form itself as sublime. Ultra-fragmented musical texts reject tradition in an even more fundamental sense when they no longer evoke the traditional *topoi* or figures on which expression in Western music has depended for so long, and still depends in Ligeti and many others. It is also possible to explore the opposition, the dialogue, between such topical presences and their absence, as in Maxwell Davies (see Ex. 17.5 above), and in this way pessimists and optimists alike might come to welcome the survival of varieties of modernism that shun the 'value-free pluralism' that Ferneyhough derides and approach that 'peaceful coexistence of extremes' of which he is more tolerant.

At the end of the twentieth century, serious art music is still modern, still plural, its classicizing potential still strong, its radical inheritance continually reasserted and continually questioned, while its need to relate to aspects of the wider world, like ethnic identity and technological advance, remains undiminished. It is possible to imagine an extreme reaction against such twentieth-century concerns in the years immediately ahead, with the twenty-first century striving to learn from the twentieth by rejecting it, lock, stock, and barrel, in order to secure the total and final demise of anything that might be thought of as avant-garde. But the twenty-first century might only be able to do that if it rejects everything pre-twentieth-century as well—Bach and Beethoven as well as Berg, Mozart as well as Mahler and Maxwell Davies. Will it happen? It will be for twenty-first-century commentators to tell that tale.

Acknowledgements

Ex. 2.1. Puccini, *La fanciulla del West.* Copyright G. Ricordi & Co. (London) Ltd. Used by permission.

Ex. 2.2. Elgar, Symphony No. 2. Reproduced by permission of Novello & Co., Ltd., 8/9 Frith Street, London W1V 5TZ.

Ex. 2.6. Sibelius, Symphony No. 4. © Breitkopf & Härtel, Wiesbaden.

Ex. 2.7. Strauss, *Elektra.* Reproduced by kind permission of Boosey & Hawkes Music Publishers Limited, and Schott Musik.

Ex. 2.8. Ives, *Concord Sonata.* Copyright © 1947 (Renewed) by Associated Music Publishers, Inc. (BMI). International copyright secured. All rights reserved. Reproduced by permission.

Ex. 2.10. Stravinsky, *Petrushka.* Reproduced by kind permission of Boosey & Hawkes Music Publishers Limited.

Ex. 2.11(i), (ii). Schoenberg, *Das Buch der hängenden Gärten.* Copyright Universal Edition Ltd. Reproduced by permission.

Ex. 2.11(iii). Schoenberg, *Three Piano Pieces*, Op. 11. Copyright Universal Edition Ltd. Reproduced by permission.

Exx. 2.12, 13. Webern, *Five Movements for String Quartet.* Copyright Universal Edition Ltd. Reproduced by permission.

Exx. 3.1, 2. Nielsen, Symphony No. 5. Reproduced by permission of Chester Music Ltd. on behalf of Edition Wilhelm Hansen, 8/9 Frith Street, London W1V 5TZ.

Ex. 3.3. Sibelius, Symphony No. 6. Reproduced by permission of Chester Music Ltd. on behalf of Edition Wilhelm Hansen, 8/9 Frith Street, London W1V 5TZ.

Ex. 3.4. Sibelius, Symphony No. 7. Reproduced by permission of Chester Music Ltd. on behalf of Edition Wilhelm Hansen, 8/9 Frith Street, London W1V 5TZ.

Exx. 3.5, 6. Vaughan Williams, Symphony No. 6. Copyright Oxford University Press.

Exx. 4.1, 2. Strauss, *Capriccio.* Reproduced by kind permission of Boosey & Hawkes Music Publishers Ltd., and Schott Musik.

Ex. 4.3. Weill, *Aufstieg und Fall der Stadt Mahagonny.* Copyright Universal Edition Ltd. Reproduced by permission.

Exx. 4.4, 5. Janáček, *Káťa Kabanová.* Copyright Universal Edition Ltd. Reproduced by permission.

Ex. 4.6. Prokofiev, *War and Peace.* Reproduced by kind permission of Boosey & Hawkes Music Publishers Ltd.

Ex. 4.7. Britten, *Peter Grimes.* Reproduced by kind permission of Boosey & Hawkes Music Publishers Ltd.

Ex. 4.8. Britten, *Death in Venice.* Copyright Faber Music.

Exx. 5.1–6. Bartók, String Quartet No. 3. Reproduced by kind permission of Boosey & Hawkes Music Publishers Ltd.

Exx. 5.7, 8. Bartók, String Quartet No. 6. Reproduced by kind permission of Boosey & Hawkes Music Publishers Ltd.

Ex. 6.1. Stravinsky, *Pulcinella.* Reproduced by kind permission of Boosey & Hawkes Music Publishers Ltd.

Ex. 6.2. Stravinsky, *Symphonies of Wind Instruments.* Reproduced by kind permission of Boosey & Hawkes Music Publishers Ltd.

Ex. 6.3. Stravinsky, *Oedipus Rex.* Reproduced by kind permission of Boosey & Hawkes Music Publishers Ltd.

Exx. 6.4–6. Stravinsky, Symphony in C. Copyright Schott & Co. Ltd. Reproduced by permission.

Ex. 6.7. Stravinsky, *The Rake's Progress.* Reproduced by kind permission of Boosey & Hawkes Music Publishers Ltd.

Ex. 7.1. Hindemith, String Quartet No. 1. Copyright Schott & Co. Ltd. Reproduced by permission.

Exx. 7.2, 3. Hindemith, String Quartet No. 3. Copyright Schott & Co. Ltd. Reproduced by permission.

Exx. 7.4, 5. Prokofiev, Symphony No. 5. Reproduced by kind permission of Boosey & Hawkes Music Publishers Ltd.

Exx. 7.6, 7. Prokofiev, Symphony No. 6. Reproduced by kind permission of Boosey & Hawkes Music Publishers Ltd.

Ex. 7.8. Shostakovich, String Quartet No. 13. Reproduced by kind permission of Boosey & Hawkes Music Publishers Ltd.

Ex. 7.9. Shostakovich, Symphony No. 10. Reproduced by kind permission of Boosey & Hawkes Music Publishers Ltd.

Ex. 8.1. Schoenberg, Suite for Piano. Copyright Universal Edition Ltd. Reproduced by permission.

Ex. 8.2. Schoenberg, Variations for Orchestra. Copyright Universal Edition Ltd. Reproduced by permission.

Ex. 8.3 Schoenberg, *Von heute auf morgen.* Copyright Universal Edition Ltd. Reproduced by permission.

Exx. 8.4, 5. Schoenberg, String Quartet No. 4. Copyright © 1939 (Renewed) by G. Schirmer, Inc. (ASCAP). International copyright secured. All rights reserved. Reprinted by permission.

Ex. 8.6. Schoenberg, String Trio. Copyright Boelke-Bomart Inc. Reprinted by permission.

Ex. 9.1. Berg, Chamber Concerto. Copyright Universal Edition Ltd. Reproduced by permission.

Exx. 9.2, 3. Berg, *Lyric Suite.* Copyright Universal Edition Ltd. Reproduced by permission.

Ex. 9.4. Berg, *Lulu.* Copyright Universal Edition Ltd. Reproduced by permission.

Ex. 9.5. Berg, Violin Concerto. Copyright Universal Edition Ltd. Reproduced by permission.

Ex. 10.1. Webern, Three Songs Op. 25. Copyright Universal Edition Ltd. Reproduced by permission.

Ex. 10.2. Webern, Piano Variations Op. 27. Copyright Universal Edition Ltd. Reproduced by permission.

Exx. 10.3–7. Webern, String Quartet Op. 28. Copyright Universal Edition Ltd. Reproduced by permission.

Ex. 10.8. Webern, Cantata No. 2, Op. 31. Copyright Universal Edition Ltd. Reproduced by permission.

Ex. 11.1. Stravinsky, *Abraham and Isaac*. Reproduced by kind permission of Boosey & Hawkes Music Publishers Ltd.

Ex. 11.2. Stravinsky, *Requiem Canticles*. Reproduced by kind permission of Boosey & Hawkes Music Publishers Ltd.

Ex. 11.3. Gerhard, Symphony No. 4. Copyright Oxford University Press.

Ex. 11.4. Dallapiccola, *Sex carmina Alcaei*. Copyright Schott & Co. Ltd. Reproduced by permission.

Ex. 11.5. Babbitt, *Composition for Twelve Instruments*. Reprinted by permission of Associated Music Publishers, Inc.

Ex. 11.6. Babbitt, *Canonical Form*. Edition Peters No. 66979 © 1984 by C. F. Peters Corporation, New York. Reproduced on behalf of the publishers by the kind permission of Peters Edition Limited, London.

Ex. 12.1. Tippett, *Concerto for Double String Orchestra*. Copyright Schott & Co. Ltd. Reproduced by permission.

Ex. 12.2. Tippett, *King Priam*. Copyright Schott & Co. Ltd. Reproduced by permission.

Ex. 12.3. Messiaen, *Quatuor pour la fin du temps*. Reproduced by permission of Editions Alphonse Leduc, Paris/United Music Publishers.

Ex. 12.4. Carter, Sonata for cello and piano. Reprinted by permission of Associated Music Publishers, Inc. (BMI).

Ex. 12.5. Tippett. *The Knot Garden*. Copyright Schott & Co. Ltd. Reproduced by permission.

Exx. 12.6, 7. Messiaen, *Méditations*. Reproduced by permission of Editions Alphonse Leduc, Paris/United Music Publishers Ltd.

Ex. 12.8. Carter, String Quartet No. 2. Copyright © 1961 (Renewed) by Associated Music Publishers, Inc. (BMI). International copyright secured. All rights reserved. Reprinted by permission.

Ex. 12.9. Carter, *Of Challenge and of Love*. Reproduced by kind permission of Boosey & Hawkes Music Publishers Ltd.

Ex. 12.10. Messiaen, *Saint François d'Assise*. Reproduced by permission of Éditions Alphonse Leduc, Paris/United Music Publishers Ltd.

Ex. 12.11. Tippett, *Byzantium*. Copyright Schott & Co. Ltd. Reproduced by permission.

Ex. 13.1. Varèse, *Intégrales*. Copyright G. Ricordi & Co. (London) Ltd., used by permission.

Ex. 13.2. Varèse, *Ecuatorial*. Copyright G. Ricordi & Co. (London) Ltd., used by permission.

Ex. 13.3. Varèse, *Déserts*. Copyright G. Ricordi & Co. (London) Ltd., used by permission.

Ex. 13.4. Cage, *45' for a Speaker*. Copyright Calder & Boyars Ltd. and (in USA) Wesleyan University Press.

Ex. 13.5. Cage, *Cheap Imitation*. Edition Peters no. 66754. © 1977 by Henmar Press Inc., New York. Reproduced on behalf of the publishers by kind permission of Peters Edition Limited, London.

Ex. 13.6. Nancarrow, Study No. 11. Copyright Schott & Co., Ltd. Transcription by Kyle Gann, reproduced by permission.

Ex. 13.7. Feldman, *palais de mari*. Copyright Universal Edition Ltd. Reproduced by permission.

Ex. 14.1. Lutosławski, *Preludes and Fugue*. Reproduced by permission of Chester Music Ltd., 8/9 Frith Street, London W1V 5TZ.

Ex. 14.2. Lutosławski, Symphony No. 4. Reproduced by permission of Chester Music Ltd., 8/9 Frith Street, London W1V 5TZ.

Ex. 14.3. Xenakis, *ST/4* (i). Reproduced by kind permission of Boosey & Hawkes Music Publishers Ltd.

Ex. 14.4. Xenakis, *N'Shima*. Reproduced by permission of Éditions Salabert, Paris/United Music Publishers Ltd.

Ex. 14.5. Ligeti, *Lontano*. Copyright Schott & Co. Ltd. Reproduced by permission.

Ex. 14.6. Ligeti, *Étude No. 5*, 'Arc-en-ciel'. Copyright Schott & Co. Ltd. Reproduced by permission.

Ex. 14.7. Berio, *Circles*. Copyright Universal Edition Ltd. Reproduced by permission.

Ex. 14.8. Berio, *Un re in ascolto*. Copyright Universal Edition Ltd. Reproduced by permission.

Ex. 14.9. Boulez, Piano Sonata No. 3. Copyright Universal Edition Ltd. Reproduced by permission.

Ex. 14.10. Boulez, '. . . *explosante fixe* . . .' Copyright Universal Edition Ltd. Reproduced by permission.

Ex. 14.11. Henze, *Elegy for Young Lovers*. Copyright Schott & Co. Ltd. Reproduced by permission.

Ex. 14.12. Henze, *Requiem*. Copyright Schott & Co. Ltd. Reproduced by permission.

Ex. 14.13. Stockhausen, *Prozession*. Copyright Universal Edition Ltd. Reproduced by permission.

Ex. 14.14. Stockhausen, *Licht*, 'Donnerstags Abschied'. Reproduced by kind permission of Stockhausen Verlag.

Ex. 15.1. Riley, *In C*, selected materials. Copyright, Terry Riley.

Ex. 15.2. Reich, *Different Trains*. Reproduced by kind permission of Boosey & Hawkes Music Publishers Ltd.

Ex. 15.3. Glass, *Satyagraha*, Act 3. © Dunvagen Music Publishers, Inc.

Ex. 15.4. Adams, Chamber Symphony. Reproduced by kind permission of Boosey & Hawkes Music Publishers Ltd.

Ex. 15.5. Górecki, *Already it is Dusk*. Reproduced by kind permission of Boosey & Hawkes Music Publishers Ltd./Polskie Wydawnictwo Muzyczne.

Ex. 15.6. Pärt, *Passio*. Copyright Universal Edition Ltd. Reproduced by permission.

Ex. 15.7. Tavener, *The Repentant Thief*. Reproduced by permission of Chester Music Ltd., 8/9 Frith Street, London W1V 5TZ.

Ex. 16.1. Zimmermann, *Intercommunicazione*. Copyright Schott & Co. Ltd. Reproduced by permission.

Ex. 16.2. Simpson, Symphony No. 5. Copyright Alfred Lengnick & Co., a division of Complete Music Ltd.

Ex. 16.3. Dutilleux, *Ainsi la nuit*. Reproduced by permission of Editions Heugel et cie., Paris/United Music Publishers Ltd.

Ex. 16.4. Takemitsu, *Les Yeux clos II*. Copyright Schott & Co., Ltd. Reproduced by permission.

Ex. 16.5. Schnittke, *Stille Nacht*. Reproduced by kind permission of Boosey & Hawkes Music Publishers Ltd.

Ex. 16.6. Kurtág, *Kafka fragments*. Reproduced by kind permission of Boosey & Hawkes Music Publishers Ltd./Editio Musica Budapest (Copyright 1992).

Ex. 16.7. Nono, *Omaggio a György Kurtág*. Copyright G. Ricordi & Co. (London) Ltd., used by permission.

Ex. 17.1. Lachenmann, *Ein Kinderspiel*. © Breitkopf & Härtel, Wiesbaden.

Ex. 17.2. Scelsi, *Ko-Lho*. Reproduced by permission of Editions Salabert, Paris/United Music Publishers Ltd.

Ex. 17.3. Donatoni, *Refrain*. Copyright G. Ricordi & Co. (London) Ltd., used by permission.

Ex. 17.4. Kagel, *Sankt-Bach-Passion*. Edition Peters no. 8600. © 1994 by Henry Litolff's Verlag, Frankfurt. Reproduced on behalf of the publishers by kind permission of Peters Edition Limited, London.

Ex. 17.5. Maxwell Davies, *Strathclyde Concerto No. 5*. Reproduced by kind permission of Boosey & Hawkes Music Publishers Ltd.

Ex. 17.6. Birtwistle, *Earth Dances*. Copyright Universal Edition Ltd. Reproduced by permission.

Ex. 17.7. Ferneyhough, *On Stellar Magnitudes*, bars 137–41. Edition Peters No. 7420. © 1995 by Hinrichsen Edition, Peters Edition Limited, London. Reproduced by kind permission of the publishers.

Ex. 17.8. Murail, *Vues aériennes*. Reproduced by permission of Editions Salabert, Paris/United Music Publishers Ltd.

Ex. 17.9. Lindberg, *Arena II*. Reproduced by permission of Chester Music Limited, 8/9 Frith Street, London W1V 5TZ.

Ex. 17.10. Rihm, *Gesungene Zeit*. Copyright Universal Edition Ltd. Reproduced by permission.

Bibliography

Abbate, Carolyn, *Unsung Voices: Opera and Musical Narrative in the Nineteenth Century* (Princeton, 1991).

Adorno, T. W., *Mahler: A Musical Physiognomy*, trans. E. Jephcott (Chicago, 1992).

—— *Quasi una fantasia: Essays on Modern Music*, trans. R. Livingstone (London, 1992).

Agawu, Kofi, 'Stravinsky's *Mass* and Stravinsky Analysis', *Music Theory Spectrum*, 11 (1989), 139–63.

Anderson, Julian, 'In Harmony: The Music of Tristan Murail', *Musical Times*, 134 (1993), 321.

Antokoletz, Elliott, *The Music of Béla Bartók. A Study of Tonality and Progression in Twentieth-Century Music* (Berkeley and Los Angeles, 1984).

Ashbrook, William, and Harold Powers, *Puccini's* Turandot, *the End of a Great Tradition* (Princeton, 1991).

Ayrey, Craig, and Mark Everist (eds.), *Analytical Strategies and Musical Interpretation* (Cambridge, 1996).

Babbitt, Milton, 'Some Aspects of Twelve-Tone Composition', *Score*, 12 (1955), 53–61.

—— 'Three Essays on Schoenberg' and 'Remarks on the Recent Stravinsky', in B. Boretz and E. T. Cone (eds.), *Perspectives on Schoenberg and Stravinsky* (Princeton, 1968), 47–60, 165–85.

—— 'On *Relata I*', in R. S. Hines (ed.), *The Orchestral Composer's Point of View* (Norman, Okla., 1970), 11–38.

—— 'Stravinsky's Verticals and Schoenberg's Diagonals: A Twist of Fate', in E. Haimo and P. Johnson (eds.), *Stravinsky Retrospectives* (Lincoln, Nebr., 1987), 15–35.

Bailey, Kathryn, *The Twelve-Note Music of Anton Webern* (Cambridge, 1991).

—— (ed.), *Webern Studies* (Cambridge, 1996).

—— 'Symmetry as Nemesis: Webern and the First Movement of the Concerto, Opus 24', *Journal of Music Theory*, 40 (1996), 245–310.

—— *The Life of Webern* (Cambridge, 1998).

Baker, James M., *The Music of Alexander Scriabin* (New Haven, 1986).

—— David W. Beach, and Jonathan W. Bernard (eds.), *Music Theory in Concept and Practice* (Rochester, NY, 1997).

Beaumont, Antony, *Busoni the Composer* (London, 1985).

Behr, Shulamith, David Fanning, and Douglas Jarman (eds.), *Expressionism Reassessed* (Manchester, 1993).

Benjamin, George, 'Last Dance', *Musical Times*, 135 (1994), 432–5.

Bennett, Gerald, 'Boulez: The Early Works', in W. Glock (ed.), *Pierre Boulez: A Symposium* (London, 1986), 41–84.

Berg, Alban, and Arnold Schoenberg, *The Berg–Schoenberg Correspondence: Selected Letters*, ed. Juliane Brand, Christopher Hailey, and Donald Harris (London, 1987).

Berio, Luciano, *Two Interviews*, ed. and trans. D. Osmond-Smith (London, 1985).

Bernard, Jonathan W., 'A Response to Nattiez', *Music Analysis*, 5 (1986), 207–31.
—— *The Music of Edgard Varèse* (New Haven, 1987).
Bernstein, David W., review of Pritchett 1993, in *Music Theory Spectrum*, 18 (1996), 265–73.
Bois, Mario, *Iannis Xenakis: The Man and his Music* (London, 1967).
Boretz, Benjamin, 'Babbitt', in John Vinton (ed.), *Dictionary of Twentieth-Century Music* (London, 1974).
—— and Edward T. Cone (eds.), *Perspectives on Schoenberg and Stravinsky* (Princeton, 1968).
—— and —— (eds.), *Perspectives on American Composers* (Princeton, 1971).
Botstein, Leon, 'The Enigmas of Richard Strauss: A Revisionist View', in B. Gilliam (ed.), *Richard Strauss and his World* (Princeton, 1992), 3–32.
Boulez, Pierre, *Conversations with Célestin Deliège* (London, 1976).
—— *Orientations*, ed. J.-J. Nattiez, trans. M. Cooper (London, 1986).
—— *Jalons (pour une décennie)* (Paris, 1989).
—— *Stocktakings from an Apprenticeship*, trans. S. Walsh (Oxford, 1991).
—— and John Cage, *The Boulez–Cage Correspondence*, ed. J.-J. Nattiez, trans. R. Samuels (Cambridge, 1993).
Bradshaw, Susan, 'Boulez: The Instrumental and Vocal Music', in W. Glock (ed.), *Pierre Boulez: A Symposium* (London, 1986), 209–16.
—— 'Pärt: *Passio*', *Tempo*, 168 (Mar. 1989), 51.
Brand, Juliane, and Christopher Hailey (eds.), *Constructive Dissonance: Arnold Schoenberg and the Transformations of Twentieth-Century Culture* (Berkeley and Los Angeles, 1997).
Breton, André, *Manifestes du Surréalisme* (Paris, 1962).
Brett, Philip (ed.), *Benjamin Britten: Peter Grimes* (Cambridge, 1983).
Brindle, R. Smith, 'Italy', in F. W. Sternfeld (ed.), *Music in the Modern Age* (London, 1973), 283–307.
Bryars, Gavin, 'Arvo Pärt', in B. Morton and P. Collins (eds.), *Contemporary Composers* (London, 1992), 728–9.
Burkholder, J. Peter (ed.), *Charles Ives and his World* (Princeton, 1996).
Butchers, Christopher, 'The Random Arts: Xenakis, Mathematics and Music', *Tempo*, 85 (Summer 1968), 2–5.
Butler, Christopher, *Early Modernism: Literature, Music and Painting in Europe, 1900–1916* (Oxford, 1994).
Cage, John, *Silence* (Cambridge, Mass., 1967).
—— *A Year from Monday* (London, 1968).
Carley, Lionel, *Delius: A Life in Letters*, 2 vols. (London, 1983 and 1988).
Carpenter, Humphrey, *Benjamin Britten: A Biography* (London, 1992).
Carter, Chandler, 'Stravinsky's "Special Sense": The Rhetorical Use of Tonality in *The Rake's Progress*', *Music Theory Spectrum*, 19 (1997), 55–80.
Carter, Elliott, *Elliott Carter: Collected Essays and Lectures, 1937–1995*, ed. Jonathan W. Bernard (Rochester, NY, 1997).
Chew, Geoffrey, 'Pastoral and Neoclassicism: A Reinterpretation of Auden's and Stravinsky's *Rake's Progress*', *Cambridge Opera Journal*, 5 (1993), 239–63.
Christensen, Thomas, review in *Music Theory Spectrum*, 15 (1993), 94–111.
Clarke, David, 'Parting Glances', *Musical Times*, 134 (1993), 680–4.
Cohn, Richard, 'Bartók's Octatonic Strategies: A Motivic Approach', *Journal of the American Musicological Society*, 44 (1991), 262–300.

Cone, Edward T., 'Stravinsky: The Progress of a Method', *Perspectives of New Music*, 1 (1962), 18–26.

—— 'The Uses of Convention: Stravinsky and his Models', in P. H. Lang (ed.), *Stravinsky: A New Appraisal of his Work* (New York, 1963), 21–33.

Cooper, David, *Bartók: Concerto for Orchestra* (Cambridge, 1996).

Cooper, Martin (ed.), *New Oxford History of Music*, x. *The Modern Age (1890–1960)* (London, 1974).

Cott, Jonathan, *Stockhausen: Conversations with the Composer* (London, 1974).

Cowan, Robert, review in *Gramophone* (Apr. 1997), 48.

Cowell, Henry, *New Music Resources*, ed. D. Nicholls (Cambridge, 1996).

Craft, Robert, *Stravinsky: Chronicle of a Friendship, 1948–1971*, rev. edn. (Nashville and London, 1994).

Crichton, Ronald, 'Pénélope' (Fauré), in *The New Grove Dictionary of Opera*, ed. S. Sadie (London, 1992), iii. 943–4.

Crowthers, Malcolm, 'An Interview with John Tavener', *Musical Times*, 135 (1994), 9–14.

Dahlhaus, Carl, *Nineteenth-Century Music*, trans. J. B. Robinson (Berkeley and Los Angeles, 1989).

Dalen, Brenda, 'Freundschaft, Liebe und Welt': The Secret Programme of the Chamber Concerto', in D. Jarman (ed.), *The Berg Companion* (London, 1989), 142–50.

Dallapiccola, Luigi, 'Meeting with Webern: Pages from a Diary', *Tempo*, 99 (1972), 2–7.

Danuser, Hermann (ed.), *Die klassizistische Moderne in der Musik der 20. Jahrhunderts* (Basle, 1997).

DeLio, Thomas (ed.), *The Music of Morton Feldman* (Westport, Conn., 1996).

Dembski, Stephen, and Joseph N. Straus (eds.), *Milton Babbitt: Words about Music* (Madison, 1987).

Drew, David, 'Brecht versus Opera', *Score*, 23 (1958), 7–10.

—— 'Topicality and the Universal: The Strange Case of Weill's *Die Bürgschaft*', *Music and Letters*, 39 (1958), 242–55.

—— 'Modern French Music', in H. Hartog (ed.), *European Music in the Twentieth Century* (Harmondsworth, 1961), 252–310.

—— *Kurt Weill: A Handbook* (London, 1987).

Dubiel, Joseph, 'The Animation of Lists', part 3 of 'Three Essays on Milton Babbitt', *Perspectives of New Music*, 30 (1992), 82–131.

Edwards, Allen, *Flawed Words and Stubborn Sounds: A Conversation with Elliott Carter* (New York, 1971).

Evans, Peter, 'Music of the European Mainstream: 1940–1960', in M. Cooper (ed.), *The Modern Age, 1890–1960* (London, 1974), 387–502.

Evans, Peter, *The Music of Benjamin Britten*, rev. edn. (Oxford, 1996).

Fanning, David, *The Breath of the Symphonist: Shostakovich's 10th* (London, 1988).

—— (ed.) *Shostakovich Studies* (Cambridge, 1995).

—— review in *Gramophone* (Feb. 1995), 58.

—— *Nielsen: Symphony No. 5* (Cambridge, 1997).

Feldman, Morton, *Essays*, ed. Walter Zimmerman (Kerpen, 1985).

Ferneyhough, Brian, *Collected Writings*, ed. J. Boros and R. Toop (Amsterdam, 1995).

—— *On Stellar Magnitudes* (Performance Notes; London, 1995).

Floros, Constantin, *György Ligeti: Jenseits von Avantgarde und Postmoderne* (Vienna, 1996).

Ford, Andrew, *Composer to Composer: Conversations about Contemporary Music* (London, 1993).

Fox, Christopher, 'Steve Reich's *Different Trains*', *Tempo*, 172 (Mar. 1990), 2–8.

Franklin, Peter, ' ". . . his fractures are the script of truth."—Adorno's Mahler', in S. Hefling (ed.), *Mahler Studies* (Cambridge, 1997), 271–94.

—— *The Life of Mahler* (Cambridge, 1997).

Frogley, Alain, 'Vaughan Williams and Thomas Hardy', *Music and Letters*, 68 (1987), 42–59.

—— (ed.), *Vaughan Williams Studies* (Cambridge, 1996).

Gann, Kyle, *The Music of Conlon Nancarrow* (Cambridge, 1995).

Gerhard, Roberto, 'Tonality in Twelve-Tone Music', *Score*, 6 (1952), 23–5.

—— 'Developments in Twelve-Tone Technique', *Score*, 17 (1956), 61–72.

Geuss, Raymond, 'Berg and Adorno', in *The Cambridge Companion to Berg*, ed. A. Pople (Cambridge, 1997), 38–50.

Gilliam, Bryan (ed.), *Richard Strauss: New Perspectives on the Composer and his Work* (Durham, NC, 1992).

—— (ed.), *Richard Strauss and his World* (Princeton, 1992).

Glock, William (ed.), *Pierre Boulez: A Symposium* (London, 1986).

Goehr, Alexander, *Finding the Key: Selected Writings*, ed. D. Puffett (London, 1998).

Gorodecki, Michael, 'Luigi Nono: A History of Belief', *Musical Times*, 133 (1992), 10–17.

—— 'Who's Pulling the Strings?', *Musical Times*, 134 (1993), 246–51.

Griffiths, Paul (ed.), *Igor Stravinsky:* The Rake's Progress (Cambridge, 1982).

—— *Olivier Messiaen and the Music of Time* (London, 1985).

——*Modern Music and After: Directions since 1945* (Oxford, 1995).

Hahl-Koch, Jelena, *Arnold Schoenberg and Wassily Kandinsky: Letters, Pictures and Documents*, trans. J. Crawford (London, 1984).

Hailey, Christopher, *Franz Schreker (1878–1934): A Cultural Biography* (Cambridge, 1993).

Haimo, Ethan, *Schoenberg's Serial Odyssey: The Evolution of his Twelve-Tone Method, 1914–28* (Oxford, 1990).

—— 'Atonality, Analysis, and the Intentional Fallacy', *Music Theory Spectrum*, 18 (1996), 167–99.

—— and Paul Johnson (eds.), *Stravinsky Retrospectives* (Lincoln, Nebr., 1987).

Hall, Michael, *Harrison Birtwistle* (London, 1984).

—— *Leaving Home: A Conducted Tour of Twentieth-Century Music* (London, 1996).

Hall, Patricia, *A View of Berg's* Lulu *through the Autograph Sources* (Berkeley and Los Angeles, 1996).

Hatch, Christopher, and David W. Bernstein (eds.), *Music Theory and the Exploration of the Past* (Chicago, 1993).

Headlam, Dave, *The Music of Alban Berg* (New Haven, 1996).

Hefling, Stephen (ed.), *Mahler Studies* (Cambridge, 1997).

Henze, Hans Werner, *Music and Politics: Collected Writings, 1953–81*, trans. P. Labanyi (London, 1982).

—— *Language, Music and Artistic Invention*, trans. M. Whittall (Aldeburgh, 1996).

Hepokoski, James, 'Fiery-Pulsed Libertine or Domestic Hero? Strauss's *Don Juan* Reinvestigated', in B. Gilliam (ed.), *Richard Strauss: New Perspectives on the Composer and his Work* (Durham, NC, 1992), 135–75.

—— *Sibelius: Symphony No. 5* (Cambridge, 1993).

Hewett, Ivan, 'Reich/Korot: *The Cave*', *Musical Times*, 134 (1993), 599–601.

——'Different Strains', *Musical Times*, 138 (Feb. 1997), 20–3.

Heyworth, Peter, 'Spiritual Dimensions: Peter Heyworth Talks to Karlheinz Stockhausen', *Music and Musicians*, 19 (May 1971), 32–9.

Hillier, Paul, *Arvo Pärt* (Oxford, 1997).

Hindemith, Paul, *The Craft of Musical Composition*, i, trans. A. Mendel (New York, 1945).

Hines, R. S. (ed.), *The Orchestral Composer's Point of View* (Norman, Okla., 1970).

Hinton, Stephen, *Kurt Weill: The Threepenny Opera* (Cambridge, 1990).

——'Weill', *The New Grove Dictionary of Opera*, ed. S. Sadie (London, 1992), iv. 1124–9.

Honegger, Arthur, *I am a Composer*, trans. W. O. Clough and A. A. Willman (London, 1966).

Howell, Tim, 'Sibelius Studies and Notions of Expertise', *Music Analysis*, 14 (1995), 315–40.

Hyde, Martha M., *Schoenberg's Twelve-Tone Harmony: The Suite Op. 29 and the Compositional Sketches* (Ann Arbor, 1982).

——'Neoclassic and Anachronistic Impulses in Twentieth-Century Music', *Music Theory Spectrum*, 18 (1996), 200–35.

Ivashkin, Alexander, *Alfred Schnittke* (London, 1996).

Ives, Charles, *Essays before a Sonata and Other Writings* (London, 1969).

Jack, Adrian, 'Ligeti Talks to Adrian Jack', *Music and Musicians*, 22 (July 1974), 24–30.

Jackson, Timothy L., review of Milstein 1992, *The Journal of Musicological Research*, 15 (1995), 285–311.

Janáček, Leoš, *Intimate Letters: Leoš Janáček to Kamila Stósslová*, ed. and trans. J. Tyrrell (London, 1994).

——*Janáček's Works: A Catalogue of the Music and Writings of Leoš Janáček*, ed. N. Simeone et al. (Oxford, 1997).

Jarman, Douglas, *Alban Berg: Wozzeck* (Cambridge, 1989).

——(ed.), *The Berg Companion* (London, 1989).

——*Alban Berg: Lulu* (Cambridge, 1991).

——'Secret Programmes', in A. Pople (ed.), *The Cambridge Companion to Berg* (Cambridge, 1997), 167–79.

John, Nicholas (ed.), *Jenůfa/Kát'a Kabanová* (ENO Opera Guide No. 33; London, 1985).

Johnson, Julian, 'The Status of the Subject in Mahler's Ninth Symphony', *19th Century Music*, 18 (1994), 108–20.

Johnson, Robert Sherlaw, *Messiaen* (London, 1975).

Keller, Hans, 'Schoenberg's Comic Opera', *Score*, 23 (1958), 27–36.

Kemp, Ian, 'Hindemith', *The New Grove*, ed. S. Sadie (London, 1980), viii. 573–87.

——*Tippett: The Composer and his Music*, rev. edn. (Oxford, 1987).

Kennedy, Michael, *The Works of Ralph Vaughan Williams* (Oxford, 1971).

Kielian-Gilbert, Marianne, 'Stravinsky's Contrasts: Contradiction and Discontinuity in his Neoclassic Music', *The Journal of Musicology*, 9 (1991), 448–80.

Koblyakov, Lev, *Pierre Boulez: A World of Harmony* (Chur, 1990).

Kostalanetz, Richard (ed.), *John Cage* (London, 1971).

Kowalke, Kim (ed.), *A New Orpheus: Essays on Kurt Weill* (New Haven, 1986).

Kramer, Lawrence, *Classical Music and Postmodern Knowledge* (Berkeley and Los Angeles, 1995).

Krellmann, Hanspeter, 'Orff', *The New Grove*, ed. S. Sadie (London, 1980), xiii. 707–10.

Lachenmann, Helmut, statement in B. Morton and P. Collins (eds.), *Contemporary Composers* (London, 1992), 526.

Laki, Peter (ed.), *Bartók and his World* (Princeton, 1995).

Lambert, Philip, *The Music of Charles Ives* (New Haven, 1997).

Lang, Paul Henry (ed.), *Problems of Modern Music* (New York, 1962).

—— *Stravinsky: A New Appraisal of his Work* (New York, 1963).

Layton, Robert, 'Martinu and the Czech Tradition', in R. Simpson (ed.), *The Symphony* (Harmondsworth, 1967), ii. 218–29.

Lendvai, Ernö, *Béla Bartók: An Analysis of his Music* (London, 1971).

—— *The Workshop of Bartók and Kodály* (Budapest, 1983).

Lerdahl, Fred., 'Atonal Prolongational Structures', *Contemporary Music Review*, 4: S. McAdams and I. Deliège (eds.), *Music and the Cognitive Sciences* (1989), 65–87.

Lesure François, and Richard Langham Smith (eds.), *Debussy on Music* (London, 1977).

Levi, Erik, 'Orff', in *The New Grove Dictionary of Opera*, ed. S. Sadie (London, 1992), iii. 750–2.

Lewin, David, *Musical Form and Transformation: Four Analytic Essays* (Cambridge, Mass., 1993).

Ligeti, György, 'Pierre Boulez: Decision and Automatism in *Structure 1a*', *Die Reihe*, 4 (1960), 36–62.

—— *Ligeti in Conversation* (London, 1983).

Lochhead, Judy, 'Lulu's Feminine Performance', in A. Pople (ed.), *The Cambridge Companion to Berg* (Cambridge, 1997), 227–44.

Maconie, Robin, *The Works of Karlheinz Stockhausen*, 2nd edn. (Oxford, 1990).

—— 'Stockhausen at 70', *Musical Times*, 139 (Summer 1998), 4–11.

Mead, Andrew, *An Introduction to the Music of Milton Babbitt* (Princeton, 1994).

Mellers, Wilfrid, 'Stravinsky's Oedipus as 20th-Century Hero', in P. H. Lang (ed.), *Stravinsky: A New Appraisal of his Work* (New York, 1963), 34–46.

—— *Poulenc* (Oxford, 1993).

Messiaen, Olivier, *Technique of My Musical Language*, trans. J. Satterfield (London, 1957).

—— *Music and Color: Conversations with Claude Samuel*, trans. E. T. Glasgow (Portland, Oreg., 1994).

Meyer, Felix, and Anne C. Shreffler, 'Webern's Revisions: Some Analytical Implications', *Music Analysis*, 12 (1993), 355–79.

Milstein, Silvina, *Arnold Schoenberg: Notes, Sets, Forms* (Cambridge, 1992).

Minturn, Neil, *The Music of Sergei Prokofiev* (New Haven, 1997).

Mitchell, Donald (ed.), *Benjamin Britten: Death in Venice* (Cambridge, 1987).

Moldenhauer, Hans, and Rosaleen Moldenhauer, *Anton von Webern: A Chronicle of his Life and Work* (London, 1978).

Moore, Jerrold Northrop, *Edward Elgar: A Creative Life* (Oxford, 1984).

Morgan, Robert P., *Twentieth-Century Music* (New York, 1991).

—— *Modern Times (Man and Music*, viii; London, 1993).

Morreau, Annette, 'Michael Nyman', in *The New Grove Dictionary of Opera*, ed. S. Sadie (London, 1992), iii. 637–8.

Morton, Brian, and Pauline Collins (eds.), *Contemporary Composers* (London, 1992).

Murtomäki, Veijo, *Symphonic Unity: The Development of Formal Thinking in the Symphonies of Sibelius* (Helsinki, 1993).

Nattiez, Jean-Jacques, 'Varèse's *Density 21.5*: A Study in Semiological Analysis', trans. A. Barry, *Music Analysis*, 1 (1982), 243–340.

Nectoux, Jean-Michel, *Gabriel Fauré: A Musical Life*, trans. R. Nichols (Cambridge, 1991).

Neighbour, Oliver, 'The Place of the Eighth among Vaughan Williams's Symphonies', in
   Alain Frogley (ed.), *Vaughan Williams Studies* (Cambridge, 1996), 213–33.
Nelson, Mark, 'Folk Music and the "Free and Equal Treatment of the Twelve Tones": Aspects
   of Béla Bartók's Synthetic Methods', *College Music Symposium*, 27 (1987), 59–115.
Nestyev, Israel, *Prokofiev* (London, 1960).
Neumeyer, David, *The Music of Paul Hindemith* (New Haven, 1986).
Nichols, Roger, 'Debussy', in *The New Grove*, ed. S. Sadie (London, 1980), v. 292–314.
—— *The Life of Debussy* (Cambridge, 1998).
—— and Richard Langham Smith (eds.), *Debussy: Pelléas et Mélisande* (Cambridge, 1989).
Nicholls, David, *American Experimental Music, 1890–1940* (Cambridge, 1990).
Nordwall, Owe (ed.), *Lutosławski* (Stockholm, 1968).
Nyman, Michael, *Experimental Music: Cage and Beyond* (2nd ed., Cambridge, 1999).
Oliver, Michael, review in *Gramophone* (Dec. 1995), 150.
Orledge, Robert, *Satie the Composer* (Cambridge, 1990).
Osmond-Smith, David, *Playing on Words: A Guide to Luciano Berio's Sinfonia* (London,
   1985).
—— *Berio* (Oxford, 1991).
Ottaway, Hugh, *Vaughan Williams Symphonies* (London, 1972).
Ouellette, Fernand, *Edgard Varèse: A Musical Biography*, trans. D. Coltman (London, 1973).
Pace, Ian, 'Recent Lachenmann Discs', review in *Tempo*, 197 (July 1996), 51–4.
—— 'Music of the Absurd? Thoughts on Recent Kagel', *Tempo*, 200 (Apr. 1997), 29–34.
—— 'Positive or Negative: The Music of Helmut Lachenmann', *Musical Times*, 139 (Jan./Feb.
   1998), 9–17, 4–15.
Paddison, Max, *Adorno's Aesthetics of Music* (Cambridge, 1993).
Parks, Richard S., *The Music of Claude Debussy* (New Haven, 1989).
Partch, Harry, *Genesis of a Music*, 2nd edn. (New York, 1974).
Perle, George, 'Berg's Master Array of the Interval Cycles', *Musical Quarterly*, 63 (1977), 1–30.
—— 'The Secret Programme of the *Lyric Suite*', *Musical Times*, 118 (1977), 629–32, 709–13,
   809–13.
—— *The Operas of Alban Berg*, 2 vols. (Berkeley and Los Angeles, 1980 and 1985).
Phipps, Graham, 'Tonality in Webern's Cantata I', *Music Analysis*, 3 (1984), 125–58.
—— 'Harmony as a Determinant of Structure in Webern's Variations for Orchestra', in C.
   Hatch and D. W. Bernstein (eds.), *Music Theory and the Exploration of the Past* (Chicago,
   1993), 473–504.
Pople, Anthony, *Berg: Violin Concerto* (Cambridge, 1991).
—— 'Misleading Voices: Contrasts and Continuities in Stravinsky Studies', in C. Ayrey and
   M. Everist (eds.), *Analytical Strategies and Musical Interpretation* (Cambridge, 1996),
   271–87.
—— 'In the Orbit of *Lulu*: The Late Works', in A. Pople (ed.), *The Cambridge Companion to
   Berg* (Cambridge, 1997), 204–26.
—— (ed.), *The Cambridge Companion to Berg* (Cambridge, 1997).
Pritchett, James, *The Music of John Cage* (Cambridge, 1993).
Prokofiev, Sergei, *Soviet Diary and Other Writings*, ed. and trans. O. Prokofiev and C. Palmer
   (London, 1991).
Rae, Charles Bodman, *The Music of Lutosławski* (3rd ed., London, 1999).
Rauchhaupt, Ursula (ed.), *Schoenberg, Berg and Webern: The String Quartets: A Documen-
   tary Study* (Hamburg, 1971).

Reich, Willi, *Schoenberg, a Critical Biography*, trans. L. Black (London, 1971).

Retallack, Joan (ed.), *Musicage: John Cage in Conversation with Joan Retallack* (Hanover, NH, 1996).

Ringer, Alexander L., *Arnold Schoenberg: The Composer as Jew* (Oxford, 1990).

Rogers, Lynne, 'Stravinsky's Break with Contrapuntal Tradition: A Sketch Study', *The Journal of Musicology*, 13 (1995), 476–507.

Salter, Lionel, 'Mompou', in *The New Grove*, ed. S. Sadie (London, 1980), xii. 476.

Samson, Jim, *The Music of Szymanowski* (London, 1980).

—— *Music in Transition: A Study of Tonal Expansion and Atonality, 1900–1920* (Oxford, 1993; 1st publ. London, 1977).

Samuels, Robert, *Mahler's Sixth Symphony: A Study in Musical Semiotics* (Cambridge, 1995).

Scher, Steven Paul (ed.), *Music and Text: Critical Inquiries* (Cambridge, 1992).

Schiff, David, *The Music of Elliott Carter* (London, 1998).

—— 'Carter's New Classicism', *College Music Symposium*, 29 (1989), 115–22.

Schoenberg, Arnold, *Arnold Schoenberg Letters*, ed. Erwin Stein, trans. E. Wilkins and E. Kaiser (London, 1964).

—— *Structural Functions of Harmony*, ed. L. Stein (London, 1969).

—— *Style and Idea*, ed. L. Stein (London, 1975).

Schroeder, David, 'Not Proven', *Musical Times*, 137 (1996), 21–3.

Schwarz, K. Robert, *Minimalists* (London, 1996).

Scruton, Roger, *The Aesthetics of Music* (Oxford, 1997).

Sessions, Roger, *Roger Sessions on Music: Collected Essays* (Princeton, 1979).

Shreffler, Anne C., ' "Mein Weg geht jetzt vorüber": The Vocal Origins of Webern's Twelve-Tone Composition', *Journal of the American Musicological Society*, 47 (1994), 275–339.

Simpson, Robert, *Sibelius and Nielsen, a Centenary Essay* (London, 1965).

—— (ed.), *The Symphony*, 2 vols. (Harmondsworth, 1967).

Skowron, Z. (ed.), *Lutosławski Studies* (Oxford, forthcoming).

Smalley, Roger, '*Momente*: Material for the Listener and Composer', *Musical Times*, 115 (1974), 23–8.

Somfai, László, *Béla Bartók: Composition, Concepts, and Autograph Sources* (Berkeley and Los Angeles, 1996).

Steinitz, Richard, 'Connections with Alice', *Music and Musicians*, 22 (Dec. 1973), 42–7.

—— *Musical Times*, 137 (1996): 'Music, Maths and Chaos' (Mar.), 14–20; 'The Dynamics of Disorder' (May), 7–14; 'Weeping and Wailing' (Aug.), 17–22.

Stenzl, Jürg, '*Prometeo*—a listener's guide', essay with recording on EMI Classics, 1995.

Stevens, Halsey, *The Life and Music of Béla Bartók*, 3rd edn., ed. M. Gillies (Oxford, 1993).

Stokes, Adrian, *The Image in Form: Selected Writings* (Harmondsworth, 1972).

Stravinsky, Igor, *Poetics of Music*, trans. A. Knodel and I. Dahl (New York, 1947).

—— *Autobiography* (New York, 1962).

—— 'The Composer's View', in Paul Griffiths (ed.), *Igor Stravinsky: The Rake's Progress* (Cambridge, 1982), 2–4.

—— and Robert Craft, *Conversations with Igor Stravinsky* (London, 1959).

—— and —— *Expositions and Developments* (London, 1962).

—— and —— *Themes and Conclusions* (London, 1972).

—— and —— *Dialogues* (London, 1982).

Stucky, Steven, *Lutosławski and his Music* (Cambridge, 1981).

Subotnik, Rose Rosengard, *Developing Variations: Style and Ideology in Western Music* (Minneapolis, 1991).

Tannenbaum, Mya, *Conversations with Stockhausen* (Oxford, 1987).

Taruskin, Richard, *The New Grove Dictionary of Opera*, ed. S. Sadie (London, 1992): Prokofiev, 'The Fiery Angel', ii. 189–90: 'Semyon Kotko', iv. 312–13: 'The Story of a Real Man', iv. 556–7: 'War and Peace', iv. 1100–5.

—— 'Back to Whom? Neoclassicism as Ideology', *19th Century Music*, 16 (1993), 286–302.

—— 'Revising Revision', *Journal of the American Musicological Society*, 46 (1993), 114–38.

—— 'Public Lies and Unspeakable Truth: Interpreting Shostakovich's Fifth Symphony', in D. Fanning (ed.), *Shostakovich Studies* (Cambridge, 1995), 17–56.

—— *Stravinsky and the Russian Traditions: A Biography of the Works through* Mavra, 2 vols. (Berkeley and Los Angeles, 1996).

Thomas, Adrian, *Górecki* (Oxford, 1997).

Thomas, Gavin, 'The Poetics of Extremity', *Musical Times*, 134 (1993), 193–6.

Tippett, Michael, *Tippett on Music*, ed. M. Bowen (Oxford, 1995).

Toller, Owen, *Pfitzner's* Palestrina: *The 'Musical Legend' and its Background* (London, 1997).

Tresize, Simon, *Debussy: La Mer* (Cambridge, 1994).

Tyrrell, John, 'Janáček', in *The New Grove Dictionary of Opera*, ed. S. Sadie (London, 1992), ii. 872–80.

—— *Janáček's Operas: A Documentary Account* (London, 1992).

van den Toorn, Pieter, *The Music of Igor Stravinsky* (New Haven, 1983).

Varèse, Edgard, 'The Liberation of Sound', in B. Boretz and E. T. Cone (eds.), *Perspectives on American Composers* (Princeton, 1971).

Varèse, Louise, *Varèse: A Looking-Glass Diary* (London, 1975).

Varga, Bálint András, *Conversations with Iannis Xenakis* (London, 1996).

Vinton, John (ed.), *Dictionary of Twentieth-Century Music* (London, 1974).

Vlad, Roman, *Stravinsky*, 3rd edn. (Oxford, 1978).

Volkov, Solomon (ed.), *Testimony: The Memoirs of Dmitri Shostakovich* (London, 1979).

Wai-Ling, Cheong, 'Scriabin's Octatonic Sonata', *Journal of the Royal Musical Association*, 121 (1996), 206–28.

Walsh, Stephen, *The Music of Stravinsky* (London, 1988).

—— *Stravinsky:* Oedipus Rex (Cambridge, 1993).

Warnaby, John, 'The Music of Magnus Lindberg', *Tempo*, 181 (June 1992), 25–30.

—— Lachenmann review, *Tempo*, 201 (July 1997), 37–8.

Waterhouse, John C. G., 'Respighi', in *The New Grove*, ed. S. Sadie (London, 1980), xv. 757–9.

Watkins, Glenn, *Pyramids at the Louvre: Music, Culture, and Collage from Stravinsky to the Postmodernists* (Cambridge, Mass., 1994).

Webern, Anton, *The Path to the New Music*, ed. W. Reich, trans. L. Black (Bryn Mawr, 1963).

—— *Letters to Hildegard Jone and Josef Humplik*, ed. J. Polnauer, trans. C. Cardew (Bryn Mawr, 1967).

—— *Sketches (1926–45), Facsimile Reproductions from the Composer's Autograph Sketchbooks in the Moldenhauer Archive* (New York, 1968).

Wen-Chung, Chou, 'Varèse: A Sketch of the Man and his Music', *Musical Quarterly*, 52 (1966), 151–70.

White, Eric Walter, *Stravinsky: The Composer and his Works*, 2nd rev. edn. (London, 1979).

White, Hayden, 'Commentary: Form, Reference, and Ideology in Musical Discourse', in S. P. Scher (ed.), *Music and Text: Critical Inquiries* (Cambridge, 1992), 288–319.

Whittall, Arnold, '*Byzantium*: Tippett, Yeats, and the Limitations of Affinity', *Music and Letters*, 74 (1993), 383–98.

—— 'Comparatively Complex: Birtwistle, Maxwell Davies and Modernist Analysis', *Music Analysis*, 13 (1994), 139–59.

—— ' "Symphony in D major": Models and Mutations', in A. Frogley (ed.), *Vaughan Williams Studies* (Cambridge, 1996).

—— 'Berg and the Twentieth Century', in *The Cambridge Companion to Berg*, ed. A. Pople (Cambridge, 1997), 247–58.

—— 'Modernist Aesthetics, Modernist Music: Some Analytical Perspectives', in J. Baker, D. Beach, and J. Bernard (eds.), *Music Theory in Concept and Practice* (Rochester, NY, 1997).

—— 'Summer's Long Shadows', *Musical Times*, 138 (Apr. 1997), 14–22.

—— 'Between Polarity and Synthesis: The Modernist Paradigm in Lutosławski's Concertos for Cello and Piano', in Z. Skowron (ed.), *Lutosławski Studies* (Oxford, forthcoming).

Williamson, John, *The Music of Hans Pfitzner* (Oxford, 1992).

—— 'Dissonance and Middleground Prolongations in Mahler's Later Music', in S. Hefling (ed.), *Mahler Studies* (Cambridge, 1997), 248–70.

Wilson, Elizabeth, *Shostakovich: A Life Remembered* (London, 1994).

Wilson, Paul, *The Music of Béla Bartók* (New Haven, 1992).

Wörner, Karl, *Stockhausen, Life and Work*, trans. G. W. Hopkins (London, 1973).

Wright, Simon, *Villa-Lobos* (Oxford, 1992).

Xenakis, Iannis, *Formalized Music* (Bloomington, Ind., 1971).

York, Wes, 'For John Cage', in Thomas DeLio (ed.), *The Music of Morton Feldman* (Westport, Conn., 1996).

Index